THE NEW TESTAMENT

A NEW TRANSLATION

VOLUME ONE

The Gospels and the Acts
of the Apostles

THE NEW TESTAMENT

A NEW TRANSLATION

VOLUME TWO
The Letters and the Revelation

By WILLIAM BARCLAY

COLLINS
LONDON—NEW YORK

Library of Congress Catalog Card No: 68-54594

Foreword

THIS second volume of the translation of the New Testament contains the New Testament Letters and the Revelation, and thus completes the task.

When the translator moves from the Gospels to the Letters, he moves to a new world in translation. It is the difference between translating a narrative and translating an argument. Obviously the argument is far harder to translate. Equally obviously it is an even more obligatory task to try to translate the argument. There are few people who cannot understand the narrative of the Gospels in the Authorized Version; there are equally few who can understand the arguments of the Letters in the Authorized Version.

I have arranged the Letters of Paul in the order in which I think they were written. The only other change in order I have made is that I have placed Jude beside Second Peter, because the two Letters are very closely connected.

In the translation of the Letters there are three things which I have done.

Paul particularly tends to write in very long sentences. For instance, in the Greek there is no full stop between Ephesians 1.3 and Ephesians 1.14. I have regularly broken up the long sentences into shorter units. On the other hand, there are times when Paul writes very elliptically, almost as if he was giving us sermon notes rather than the finished article. In these cases I have expanded the translation to try to make the meaning clear. Further, in the New Testament there occur passages in which the point depends on certain Jewish or Greek pictures or customs. I have on occasion incorporated and integrated the explanation into the text for the sake of clarity and for the sake of the person who has to read without a commentary.

I have added a glossary of words of special interest. The glossary does not make any attempt to be complete, and what has been included and omitted has been largely a matter of personal choice. I have also added a section in which the expansions I have made in the text are explained.

As in the case of the first volume, the Greek text that I have used is the 1966 text of the United Bible Societies Greek New Testament.

It is my hope and prayer that this translation may do something to make the message of the New Testament clearer and more compelling for those who read it today. A translation will go out-of-date; that message is for all time.

The University of Glasgow,

July, 1969

WILLIAM BARCLAY

Contents

Foreword   5

General Introduction to the Letters of Paul   7

Introduction to Galatians   9
GALATIANS   11

Introduction to 1 and 2 Thessalonians   21
1 THESSALONIANS   23
2 THESSALONIANS   29

Introduction to 1 and 2 Corinthians   33
1 CORINTHIANS   36
2 CORINTHIANS   66

Introduction to Romans   84
ROMANS   87

Introduction to Ephesians   116
EPHESIANS   118

Introduction to Colossians   127
COLOSSIANS   129

Introduction to Philemon   136
PHILEMON   137

Introduction to Philippians   139
PHILIPPIANS   140

Spirit and Matter—A Note on the Background of Thought
in New Testament Times   148

Introduction to 1 and 2 Timothy and Titus   151
1 TIMOTHY   153
2 TIMOTHY   161
TITUS   167

Introduction to Hebrews   171
HEBREWS   173

CONTENTS

Introduction to James   195
JAMES   197

Introduction to 1 Peter   204
1 PETER   206

Introduction to 2 Peter   215
2 PETER   217

Introduction to Jude   222
JUDE   223

Introduction to 1 John   226
1 JOHN   227

Introduction to 2 John   234
2 JOHN   235

Introduction to 3 John   236
3 JOHN   238

Introduction to Revelation   240
REVELATION   243

New Testament Words   277
  Notes on Passages   340

General Introduction to the Letters of Paul

IT is unfortunate that the Letters of Paul were ever called epistles, for the word epistle tends to remove them out of the ordinary run of things into a special theological and literary category. They are in the real sense of the term letters.

Greek letters were written to a pattern and a formula, and Paul's letters exactly observe the pattern which every Greek letter followed. Here is a letter written by a newly-enlisted soldier called Apion to his father Epimachus. Its date is some time in the second century A.D.

'Apion to Epimachus his father and lord heartiest greetings. First of all I pray that you are in good health and continually prosper and fare well with my sister and her daughter and my brother. I thank the Lord Serapis [his god] that, when I was in danger at sea, he saved me. As soon as I entered Misenum I received my travelling money from Caesar, three gold pieces. And I am well. I beg you therefore, my dear father, write me a few lines, first regarding your health, secondly regarding that of my brother and sister, thirdly that I may kiss your hand, because you have brought me up well, and on this account I hope to be quickly promoted, if the gods will. Give many greetings to Capito, and to my brother, and sister, and to Serenilla, and my friends. I send you a little portrait of myself at the hands of Euctemon. My military name is Antonius Maximus. I pray for your good health.'

The pattern of the letter is first, the address, second, a prayer and a thanksgiving, third, the general contents, fourth, the closing greetings. This is exactly the pattern of Paul's letters. Paul's letters are real letters.

Further, Paul's letters are not treatises. He did not sit down at a desk in undisturbed study and contemplation. They are all written in the dust and heat of the day. They are all written to meet some situation which was threatening the churches he loved so well. They are not timeless theological essays; they are written to meet some particular occasion. This is what sometimes makes them very difficult. Reading them can be like listening to one side of a telephone conversation. We have often to deduce what the situation was from the letters themselves. Paul wrote for the day to day needs of the church. True, he brought the eternal truths to these situations, but he would have been astonished, if he had known that his letters would still be being read and studied far down the twentieth century.

Still further, Paul did not hand-write his letters, apart sometimes from some very few sentences and the authenticating signature at the end. He dictated them. We even know the name of one of his secretaries, for Tertius slipped in his own name and greetings in the Letter to the Romans (Romans 16.22). We must not therefore think of Paul sitting at his desk carefully polishing each sentence, until the style was faultless and the grammar perfect. We must think of him striding up and down his room, seeing in his mind's eye the people to whom he was writing, and pouring out a flood of often impassioned and excited words to the secretary who strove to take it all down. The letters of Paul are not literary products; they come from the arena of life. They have not the cool detachment of the theologian in his study; they throb with the passionate concern of the pastor for his people.

I have arranged Paul's letters in the order in which I think they were written, in order that the development of his thought may be seen.

Introduction to the Letter to the Galatians

THE Letter to the Galatians is a short letter, but there is no letter which has more of the very essence of Paul in it, and it may well have been the first letter that Paul wrote to his people.

From the beginning to the end of his life Paul had his enemies, and in the Letter to the Galatians he is defending himself from them. So this letter has been said to be like 'a sword flashing in a great swordsman's hand'. In this letter two things are under attack.

i. Paul's apostleship was under attack. Paul was not one of the original Twelve; he had begun life as a savage persecutor, out to obliterate Jesus and his church, and therefore Paul was vulnerable to attack. Further, the qualification for apostleship was that a man must have been a member of the original followers of Jesus and must have been a witness of the resurrection (Acts 1.21,22), and once again Paul was open to attack.

Paul never denied his past (1.13,14), but what he did claim was that his apostleship was nothing less than a special appointment from Jesus Christ and from God the Father (1.1;1.11,12).

ii. This gave him a gospel which was particularly and peculiarly his. But it was not a gospel which was different from that of the church. It was known to and fully approved by the leaders of the church (2.2). But Paul's gospel had one characteristic. It was intended by God, and accepted by the church, as being specially for the Gentiles (1.16; 2.7-9). It was this gospel which was under attack.

It was under attack by a certain kind of Jewish Christian. There were Jews who genuinely believed that, since the Jews were the chosen people, and since Jesus was God's greatest gift to men, a man must become a Jew before he could become a Christian, and that therefore he must first become circumcised, and then he must obey the Jewish law, with all its regulations about food, and about Sabbath observance, and about separation from the Gentiles (3.1-6).

To Paul the trouble about this was that the implication was that a man could, so to speak, earn the favour of God by doing certain things to his body, and obeying certain rules and regulations. To Paul the only way to get right with God was faith, which meant throwing oneself unconditionally on the free mercy of God, as Abraham had done so many centuries before (3.10-22). As Paul saw it, all that a man could do was to take what God offered, in faith in the love of Jesus

9

Christ. So there was always this clash between faith and works, and this is what Galatians is all about.

iii. But what about the law? Was it not holy, given on Mount Sinai, the law of God? The law still had its uses, as Paul saw it. It defines sin, and thereby makes a man conscious of sin—but it cannot cure sin. It is like the slave who took the schoolboy to the door of the school, but had to leave him there. The law showed a man his sin, and by so doing, drove a man to the mercy of God in faith, because no one can keep the law. The law showed a man that any attempt to save himself must end in defeat. He must in faith accept the offer of God that Jesus brought to men (3.19-29).

iv. The Christian therefore has complete freedom from the law. Does this mean that the Christian can do what he likes? No, because this Christian freedom is conditioned by the Christian's sense of responsibility to others and his love for Jesus. He is free—but he is never free to injure his brother, or to grieve God. He is free to live the life the Spirit gives him, and to be released from his own lower nature (5.1-26).

v. So the letter comes to its close with practical injunctions and a final appeal from Paul.

This is the letter which tells all men that the only way to be right with God is to take what God offers in penitence and in love. Then into life will come the liberty which is, not licence, but true freedom to serve men and to love God.

The Letter to the
GALATIANS

Chapter 1

THIS is a letter from Paul, and from all the brothers who are with him, to the congregations in Galatia. I write to you as an apostle, and my apostleship comes from no human source and was conferred on me by no human agent. It was conferred on me through the direct action of Jesus Christ and of God the Father, who raised him from the dead. ₃Grace to you and every blessing from God our Father and from the Lord Jesus Christ, ₄who gave himself for our sins. His purpose was to rescue us from this present evil world, for this was the will of our God and Father. ₅Glory be to him for ever and ever. Amen.

₆I am surprised that you are so quickly deserting the God who called you by the grace of Christ and transferring your loyalty to a different gospel—₇not that it is another gospel, for there is no such thing. It is nothing other than an attempt by certain people to upset you and to pervert the gospel of Christ. ₈But even if we or an angel from heaven should preach a gospel to you which is at variance with the gospel we have already preached to you, let God's curse be on him. ₉As I have already said, and as I repeat now, if anyone is preaching to you a gospel which is at variance with the gospel you have already received, let God's curse be on him.

₁₀When I talk as bluntly as I am talking now, is it men's approval I am out to win, or is it God's? Do I sound as if I was trying to ingratiate myself with men? If I were still trying to ingratiate myself with men, I would not be the servant of Christ.

₁₁I tell you, brothers, the gospel which I preach is no human affair. ₁₂I owe my knowledge to no man's instruction and to no man's teaching. No! It came to me by direct revelation from Jesus Christ.

₁₃You have heard of my former career when the religion of the Jews was my religion. You are well aware that there were no bounds to my persecution of God's church, and that I tried to blast it out of existence. ₁₄In my fanatical enthusiasm for my ancestral traditions, I outstripped most of my contemporaries and my compatriots in my progress in the Jewish way of life and belief. 15But God had a purpose for me even before I was born. He called me by his grace, 16and he chose to reveal his Son to me, and through me to others. His purpose was that I might tell the good news about him to the Gentile world. When he called me, I did not seek the advice of any human being, 17nor did I go up to Jerusalem to visit those who were apostles before I was. No! The first thing I did was to go off to Arabia. Then I came back again to Damascus.

18Then three years later I went up to Jerusalem to make the acquaintance of Cephas, and I stayed with him for a fortnight. 19The only other apostle I saw was James the Lord's brother. 20Before God what I am writing to you is absolutely true. 21Then I went to the districts of Syria and Cilicia. 22To the Christian congregations in Judaea I was personally unknown. 23All that they had heard was a report that their former persecutor was now preaching the faith which he had once tried to blast out of existence. 24And what had happened to me provided them with a reason for praising God.

Chapter 2

FOURTEEN years elapsed before my next visit to Jerusalem. On that occasion I went up with Barnabas, and I took Titus too along with me. 2This visit was the result of direct divine guidance. I had a private meeting with the most respected leaders of the church, at which I referred to them the gospel which I am in the habit of preaching among the Gentiles. I took this step because I wanted to be sure that my efforts in the past and in the present had not been, and would not be, all to no purpose. 3Not even Titus, who was with me, Greek though he is, was compelled to be circumcised. 4The question of his circumcision was indeed raised by certain spurious Christians who had been insinuated into the discussion in an underhand way. They had wormed their way in, with the purpose of spying out a way to launch an attack on the Christian freedom which we possess, for it was their intention to reduce us to spiritual slavery. 5Not for a moment did we yield to their attempts to subject us to the law. My one aim was to preserve the integrity of the gospel for you. 6The leading figures in the church—what they were makes not the slightest difference to me; status symbols mean nothing to God—the leading lights, I say, had no new suggestions to put forward. 7On the contrary, they recognized that I had been entrusted with the gospel for the un-circumcised Gentiles, just as Peter had been entrusted with the gospel for the circumcised Jews. ₈For he whose power was operative in and for Peter to make him an apostle to the circumcised Jews was equally operative in and for me to make me an apostle to the Gentiles. ₉So then, James and Cephas and John, whom all regard as pillars of the church, recognized the special grace which had been given to me. They pledged themselves to accept me and Barnabas as partners in a partnership in which our sphere should be the Gentiles and theirs the Jews. ₁₀The only thing they did ask us to do was to remember the poor, which was the very thing that I had already every intention of doing.

₁₁When Cephas came to Antioch, I opposed him to his face, for he stood self-condemned. ₁₂He had been in the habit of sharing meals with the Gentiles until a group of men from James arrived. When they arrived, he began to withdraw, and finally tried completely to separate himself from fellowship with the Gentiles, because he was scared of the party who insisted on the observance of the Jewish law. ₁₃The rest of the Jewish Christians became involved in this two-faced conduct, to such an extent that even Barnabas was swept away in this situation in which the conduct of these people was a complete denial of their alleged Christian beliefs. ₁₄When I saw that they were leaving the straight road of the true gospel, I said to Cephas in front of them all: 'You were born and bred a Jew, and you are prepared to mix with the Gentiles and to abandon the Jewish way of life. How then can you try to compel the Gentiles to live by the Jewish law?'

₁₅We are Jews by birth; we are not Gentile sinners—as a Jew would call them. ₁₆But we very well know that no man can get into a right relationship with God by means of doing the things that any law pre-scribes. The only way to get into a right relationship with God is through faith in Christ Jesus. So we took the decision to become be-lievers in Christ Jesus, in order to get into a right relationship with God through faith in Christ, and not through doing what any law prescribes, because no one can get into a right relationship with God by trying to do what any law prescribes.

₁₇If in our aim to get into a right relationship with God through Christ it becomes obvious that we too are sinners, does this mean that Christ is the promoter of sin? God forbid! ₁₈The way in which I would really prove myself a sinner would be by rebuilding that whole edifice of legalism which I have already pulled down. ₁₉My very at-tempt to obey the law compelled me in the end to live a life in which the law has for me become a dead letter. Only thus could I live to God. I have been crucified with Christ. 20My own life is dead; it is Christ who lives in me. True, my physical life goes on, but its mainspring is faith in the Son of God who loved me and gave himself for me. 21I am not going to treat the grace of God as if it did not exist. For, if it is possible to get into a right relationship with God by means of any law, then Christ might as well not have died.

Chapter 3

MY Galatian friends, the trouble with you is that you will not use your common-sense! Who has put a spell on you? The story of Jesus on his cross was told to you so vividly that it seemed to be happening before your very eyes. 2Will you answer me one question? Did you receive the Spirit as a consequence of observing the law, or simply because you heard the offer and accepted the way of faith? 3How can you be so senseless? You began in the Spirit. Are you going to end up by trying to win salvation by doing something to your body? 4Are you simply going to write off all the great facts of your Christian experience? Surely it cannot all go for nothing! 5Does he who gives you the Spirit so generously, and who works miracles among you, do so because you observe the law, or because you heard the offer and accepted the way of faith? 6You have exactly the same experience as Abraham. Abraham took God at his word, and that act of faith was accepted as putting him into a right relationship with God.

7So then, you are bound to see that it is the people who rely entirely on faith who are the sons of Abraham. 8Scripture foresaw that it would be by faith that God would bring the Gentiles into a right relationship with himself, and recounts how the good news was announced to Abraham long ago: 'All nations shall be blessed in you.' 9So then, all who rely on faith are blessed along with Abraham the man of faith. 10All those who rely on obedience to the prescriptions of the law are under a curse, for scripture says: 'Anyone who does not consistently do everything that is written in the book of the law is accursed.' 11It is clear that no one can get into a right relationship with God by obedience to any kind of legal system, because, 'It is the man who is right with God through faith who will find life.' 12It is not by faith that the law operates. What the law actually says is that those who keep its prescriptions shall find life by means of them. 13But

Christ ransomed us from the curse of the law by taking the curse upon himself for our sakes, for scripture says: 'Everyone who is hanged from a tree is accursed.' 14This happened that the blessing which was given to Abraham might go out to the Gentiles in Christ Jesus, so that through faith we might receive the Spirit as he promised.

15Brothers, I take an analogy from ordinary everyday life. Even in the case of an ordinary business contract, no one cancels it and no one adds clauses to it once it has been finally ratified. 16Now the promises were made to Abraham and to his *issue*. When God made the promise, he did not say, 'and to your *issues*,' as if he was speaking about many. He said 'and to your *issue*,' in the singular, as if he was speaking about one definite person, and that one person is Christ. 17What I mean is this—the law, which came into existence four hundred and thirty years later, cannot cancel an agreement already made by God, and so render the promise inoperative. 18For, if the right to inherit the promise depends on any kind of law, then it no longer depends on a promise; but in point of fact it was through a promise that that right was graciously given to Abraham by God. 19What then is the function of the law? The law was introduced into the situation to define what wrong-doing is. But it was only intended to last until Abraham's 'issue,' to whom the promise had been made should come. The law was transmitted through angels and in the person of a mediator. 20This is to say that the validity of the law depends on two parties, one to give it and one to keep it, and on a mediator to bring it from the one to the other. But a promise depends on only one person, the person who makes it, and when there is only one person involved there is no necessity for a mediator. And in this case God is the one person, and on him alone the promise depends.

21Is this then to say that the law and the promises are in opposition to each other? God forbid! If there was any such thing as a law which is able to give men life, then it really would have been possible to get into a right relationship with God by relying on such a law. 22But, as scripture says, no one ever kept any such law, and therefore the whole universe is imprisoned in the power of sin. The situation was designed so that the promise which depends on faith in Jesus Christ might come true for those who have such faith.

23Before the coming of the era of faith we were the law's prisoners, locked up in its power until the coming of the way of faith which was destined to be revealed. 24The law was therefore the servant who brought us to the door of the school of Christ, so that in Christ's school we might be made right with God through faith. 25Once faith had come, we did not need any such servant any more.

26This is true because you are all sons of God through faith because of your connection with Christ Jesus. 27For all those who have become one with Christ through baptism are, as it were, clothed with the life of Christ. 28Because your connection with Christ makes you one with each other, in your society there can be no Jew or Greek, no slave or free man, no male and female. 29If you are Christ's, then you are descendants of Abraham, with the right to possess all that God promised him.

Chapter 4

WHAT I mean is this—so long as the heir is a minor, he is to all intents and purposes no different from a slave, although he is the owner of the whole estate. 2Even although he is the owner he is under the control of guardians of his person and trustees of his property, until the date his father fixed arrives. 3It is the same with us. When we were spiritually minors we were no different from slaves, under the control of that elementary knowledge of God which was all the world could attain. 4But when the necessary period had been completed, God sent his Son, born as any child is born, brought up under the Jewish law, 5to ransom those whom the law held in its power, for it was his purpose that the time of slavery should end and the time of sonship begin. 6That you are sons is proved by the fact that God sent the Spirit of his Son into our hearts, crying: 'Father! Dear Father!' 7The result is that you are no longer in the position of a slave; you are in the position of a son. And, if you are in the position of a son, God has made you an heir.

8There was a very different time, when you did not know God, and when you had consented to become slaves to gods who are not really gods at all. 9But as things now are you have come to know God—or, to put it more correctly, you are known by God. How then can you turn back to the weak and poverty-stricken rudiments of religion that once were all you knew? How can you want to relapse into that servitude all over again? 10You scrupulously observe days and months and special occasions and years. 11You worry me, for I cannot help being afraid that all the toil I spent on you has gone for nothing.

12I appeal to you, brothers, to put yourselves in my place, as indeed

I put myself in yours. I have no complaints against you. 13You know that the first of my two visits to you was due to the fact that I was ill, and it was that illness which gave me the chance to bring the good news to you. 14That physical illness might well have been a temptation to you to despise me, and to recoil in disgust from me. But, so far from that, you received me as if I were an angel of God, and as you would have received Christ Jesus himself. 15You were so happy to have me! What has happened? I declare that, if it had been possible, you would have plucked out your eyes and given them to me. 16Do you regard me as your enemy because I tell you the truth? 17These people pay a great deal of attention to you, but not with any honourable motive. What they really want is to separate you from me, and to make you pay a great deal of attention to them. 18It is an excellent thing to have people taking an interest in you, so long as their motives are honourable, and I would gladly see you enjoying that interest and attention always and not only when I am actually with you. 19You are already my dear children, but now I have to endure the birth-pangs all over again, until the nature of Christ is brought to birth within you. 20I wish I was with you just now. I wish I did not need to talk to you like this. But I must, because I am at my wit's end to know what to do about you.

21You want to submit yourselves to the law. Tell me, then, will you not listen to what the law says? 22Scripture tells us that Abraham had two sons. One was the slave-girl's son, and the other was the free woman's son. 23The slave-girl's son was born by natural human processes; the free woman's son was born as a result of the promise of God. 24These things form an allegory. These two women stand for two covenants. The one, that is, Hagar, represents the covenant which had its beginning on Mount Sinai, and which bears children destined for slavery. 25Hagar stands for Mount Sinai in Arabia, and she corresponds to the present Jerusalem, for she and her children are slaves. 26But the heavenly Jerusalem is the free woman, and it is she who is our mother, 27for scripture says:

'Rejoice, you barren one, who bore no child,
    break out into a shout of joy,
    you who have never known the pangs of childbirth.
For the children of the woman who was left all alone
    shall be more than those of the woman who has a husband.'

28You, brothers, are children of God's promise, as Isaac was. 29In the old days long ago the child born in the purely human way persecuted the child born as a result of the action of the Spirit—and the same still happens today. 30But what does scripture say? 'Drive out the slave-girl and her son, for the slave-girl's son will not be allowed to share the inheritance with the free woman's son.' 31You can see from all this, brothers, that we are not the children of any slave-girl; we are the children of the free woman.

Chapter 5

CHRIST set us free, and means us to stay free. Take your stand on that, and never again submit to any yoke of slavery.

2I, Paul, tell you that, if you get yourselves circumcised, Christ will be no good to you. 3Once again I solemnly state to every man who gets himself circumcised that he is under obligation to carry out every item of the law. 4If you try to get into a right relationship with God through any legal system, you have by that very act severed your connection with Christ. You have removed yourselves from the sphere of grace. 5It is by the help of the Spirit that we eagerly await the hoped-for right relationship with God which comes from faith. 6Once a man becomes a Christian, whether or not he is circumcised is meaningless. What matters is faith working in love.

7You were making excellent progress. Who stopped you obeying the truth? 8Whatever arguments were used to persuade you certainly did not come from the God who calls you. 9Once even the slightest infection gets into a society, it spreads until the whole society becomes infected. 10The fact that you and I are united in the Lord makes me completely confident that you will agree with me. But the person who is upsetting you will have to pay the penalty—and it does not matter who he is. 11As for me, brothers, if I still proclaim the necessity of circumcision, why am I still being persecuted? If indeed I was still proclaiming circumcision as a necessity, then those who believe in circumcision would no longer find the cross offensive. 12I wish the people who are disturbing you would castrate themselves, let alone circumcise themselves!

13Brothers, you were called to be free. But one thing you must guard against. You must not use your freedom as an opportunity to give full play to the demands of your lower nature. No! You must use it lovingly to serve one another. 14For the whole law is summed up in one sentence: 'You must love your neighbour as yourself.' 15But, if you go on biting and savaging one another like wild animals, you must be careful that you do not end up by destroying one another.

16What I mean is this—make the Spirit the rule of your life, and then you will never be out to satisfy the desires of your lower nature. 17For the desires of our lower nature run counter to the desires of the Spirit, and the desires of the Spirit run counter to the desires of our lower nature. These two are permanently opposed to one another, and the result is that the very things you want to do are the very things you cannot do. 18But, if you are led by the Spirit, you are not under the domination of law. 19Anyone can see the kind of things for which the lower part of our nature is responsible, things like fornication, impurity, blatant immorality; 20idolatry and sorcery; enmity, strife and jealousy; outbursts of explosive temper, selfish ambition, divisions, the party spirit, 21envy; drunkenness, revelling, and the like. 21I told you before, and I tell you again, people who practise things like these will never enter into possession of the Kingdom of God. 22But the harvest which the Spirit produces is love, joy, peace; patience, kindness, goodness; fidelity, 23the strength of gentleness, self-control. No law forbids things like that. 24Those who belong to Christ Jesus have once and for all crucified their lower nature with its passions and desires. 25If the Spirit is the ruling principle of our lives, we must march in step with the Spirit. 26We must have no desire for empty prestige, no provoking of one another, no jealousy of one another.

Chapter 6

BROTHERS, if anyone is detected in some wrong act, you who are spiritual must correct him. You must do so gently, and you must, each of you, look to yourself, in case you too are tempted. 2Help each other to carry your burdens, for, if you do, you will fulfil Christ's law. 3If anyone has a good opinion of himself, when in fact he has nothing to be pleased about, he is deluding himself. 4It is his own work that a man must test, and then any sense of achievement that he has will be the result of judging himself by himself, and not of comparing himself with someone else. 5For everyone has to shoulder his own personal pack. 6If anyone is under instruction in the Christian message, he should share with his teacher all the good things he has. 7Make no mistake—you can't make a fool of God! A man will reap whatever he sows. 8If a man sows in the field of his own lower nature, from that lower nature he will reap a life that is doomed to decay. But if he sows in the field of the Spirit, the harvest will be eternal life. ₉We must never get tired of doing the fine thing, for, when the right time comes, we will reap the harvest of it, if we never relax our efforts. ₁₀So then, whenever we get the chance, we must do good to everyone, and especially to those who are members of the family of the faith.

₁₁See in what big letters I am writing to you in my own handwriting! ₁₂It is these people who wish to make an impressive outward display of their religion who are trying to compel you to get yourselves circumcised. In point of fact, they really want to escape persecution for the cross of Christ. ₁₃These advocates of circumcision don't themselves make any great success of their law-keeping. They want you to be circumcised to enable them to boast that they have persuaded you to accept as essential an outward mark on your body. ₁₄God forbid that I should boast about anything except about the cross of our Lord Jesus Christ, that cross by which the world has been crucified to me and I to the world! ₁₅Whether a man is circumcised or not circumcised is of no importance. What matters is the creating of the man all over again. ₁₆Mercy and every blessing on all those who will make this the rule of their life and conduct, and on God's Israel.

₁₇In future let no man go on making things difficult for me, for the scars I bear on my body brand me as the slave of Christ.

₁₈Brothers, the grace of our Lord Jesus Christ be with your spirit. Amen.

Introduction to the First and Second Letters to the Thessalonians

THE background to the Letters to the Thessalonian church is to be found in the story of Paul's work at Thessalonica in Acts 17.1-9.

Behind that story there is a situation of the first importance for the early Christian missionaries. As we learn from the story in Acts, Paul's stay in Thessalonica extended over no more than three weeks, and it ended in a situation in which he had to be smuggled out by night. As we learn from the letters themselves, the whole situation had left the new converts a legacy of serious trouble, in which life had become very dangerous (1.1.6; 1.2.9-16; 2.1.5).

The question which faced Paul was this. Was it possible in three weeks' work to lay the foundations of a Christian community, which would stand fast when things were difficult? If so, the evangelization of Europe in a life-time was a practical proposition. Or, was missionary work to be a long, slow process, in which the missionaries had to settle in a place for months or even years before a church could really be said to be founded? Thessalonica presented a test case.

It is no wonder that Paul was worried. In his worry he sent Timothy to find out how things were going (1.2.17-19; 1.3.1-6). It was when Timothy and Silas caught up with him again in Corinth (Acts 18.5) that Paul wrote his letters. In the letters three things appear.

i. Paul had no need to worry. The Thessalonians were standing fast (1.1.3-10; 1.3.6-10). It was clear that even a short campaign, even if it ended in the flight of the missionary, could be permanently effective.

ii. But there were other things. Paul had to meet criticism of himself. He was criticized as being concerned with what he could get out of his converts in power and in money. So he hotly denies that he had used flattery, that he had sought prestige, that he had been dictatorial (1.2.1-8). Above all, he hotly denies that he had ever made anything out of his converts, and points out that he had toiled night and day at his trade, so as not to be a burden to anyone (1.2.9-12; 2.3.7).

iii. A serious theological problem had arisen, and this problem is at the very heart of the Thessalonian correspondence.

An essential part of the Christian message was the return of Jesus Christ, the Second Coming. At that time the church, including Paul, expected the Second Coming at any moment. They expected it today, tomorrow, certainly within their own lifetime. In Thessalonica this produced two problems.

a) The Thessalonians were disturbed about what was to happen to those who died before the Second Coming arrived. Would they miss the glory? Paul assures them that those who died in Christ would lose nothing (1.4.13-18).

b) An even more serious problem came from the fact that many of the Thessalonians had stopped work, and were doing nothing but stand about talking in excited groups, waiting for the Second Coming. Ordinary everyday life had collapsed in this hysterical expectation. Paul tells them that there will be signs before the Second Coming emerges, and above all a last conflict with the forces of evil (2.1.3—2.2.16). He urges them not to stand idle and gossiping, but to get on with the day's work and to live life as it comes (2.3.6-13). His attitude is that, when Jesus Christ comes, a man cannot be found doing anything better than an honest day's work.

The Thessalonian letters show the practical problems of the early missionary and the theological problems which a not fully grasped faith must bring.

The First Letter to the
THESSALONIANS

Chapter 1

THIS is a letter from Paul and Silvanus and Timothy to the congregation of the Thessalonians who belong to God the Father and to the Lord Jesus Christ. Grace to you and every blessing.

2We always thank God for you all, when we mention you in our prayers. 3We continually remember in the presence of our God and Father the activity of your faith, and the toil of your love, and the constancy of your hope in our Lord Jesus Christ. 4You are brothers to us and dear to God. We know that God has chosen you, because our gospel came to you not simply as a message in words; it came with the dynamic power of the Holy Spirit, and carrying complete conviction. 5Equally, you know what we were like when we were with you, and that it was for your sake that we were what we were. 6As for you, you took us and the Lord as your example, for the coming of the Christian message brought you at one and the same time serious trouble and the joy which the Holy Spirit gives. 7The result was that you became an example to all in Macedonia and Achaea who accept the Christian faith. 8It is not only in Macedonia and Achaea that the message of the Lord has sounded out from you. The story of your loyalty to God has so spread all over that there is no need for us to say anything about it. 9Everywhere people are talking about you, and telling the story of the welcome you gave us, and of how you turned to God, and left your idols to become the servants of the real and living God, 10and to await the coming of his Son from heaven, that Son whom God brought back to life when he had died, Jesus who rescues us from the wrath which is coming on the world.

Chapter 2

Y OU yourselves know, brothers, that our visit to you was not wasted time. 2As you know, we came to you after experiencing insult and injury at Philippi. But God made us able freely and fearlessly to tell you the good news of God—and not without a struggle. 3Our appeal to you is not the result of some delusion; there is no element of sensuality in it; it is not designed to deceive. 4No! God tested us and thought us fit to be entrusted with the good news. That is the way in which we speak, not as if we were trying to win human approval. God tests men's hearts, and it is at his approval that we aim. 5We did not come with flattering talk, as you are well aware, nor, God is our witness, did we ever use our message as a disguise for exploiting you. 6We never tried to acquire a human reputation either in your eyes or in the eyes of anyone else. 7We could quite well have made heavy demands as the envoys of Christ. So far from that, when we were living among you, we were as gentle as a nurse cherishing her children. 8We cared for you so much that it was our desire to share with you, not only the good news of God, but even our very lives, because you were so dear to us. 9You remember, brothers, how, when we proclaimed the good news of God to you, we laboured and toiled, how we worked night and day, to avoid being a burden to any of you. 10You can give evidence, and so can God, how devoutly and justly and blamelessly we behaved to you who are believers. 11As you know, we treated you as a father treats his children. 12To each one of you individually we made our appeal and our plea, calling on you out of our own experience of Christ, to live lives worthy of the God who is calling you into his glorious Kingdom.

13There is another reason why we continually thank God. We thank him because, when you received the message of God, which you heard from us, you accepted it not as a human message, but, as indeed it is, as a message from God—and that message is at work in you who believe. 14You followed the example, brothers, of the Christian congregations in Judaea, because you too underwent the same suffering at the hands of your fellow-countrymen as they did at the hands of the Jews. 15For the Jews killed both the Lord Jesus and the prophets, and persecuted us. They defy God; they are the enemies of the human race; 16for they try to stop us bringing to the Gentiles that message by which the Gentiles can be saved. By this they put the finishing touch to their record of sin. But God's wrath has finally caught up with them.

17When, brothers, you and I were lost to each other for a short time, you were for us out of sight, but not out of mind. And so we longed all the more eagerly to see you face to face. 18We therefore wished to come to you—more than once I, Paul, planned this—but Satan blocked our road. 19What hope or joy or achievement can we lay claim to when we stand before our Lord Jesus when he comes— what except you? 20For it is you who are our glory and our joy.

Chapter 3

So then, when we could not stand it any longer, we decided that there was nothing for it but for us to be left behind in Athens alone, 2while we sent Timothy, our colleague and God's fellow-worker in spreading the good news of Christ, to encourage you to stand fast for your faith, 3and to urge that no one should be shaken by these troubles. You yourselves well know that, when we become Christians, we are bound to be involved in trouble. 4When we were with you, we warned you that we would be in trouble, and, as you know, it has turned out to be so. 5That is why, when I could stand it no longer, I sent to find out how your faith was surviving, for I was worried in case the tempter had tempted you, and all our hard work had gone for nothing.

6Timothy has just come back from you to us, and has brought us good news about your faith and love. He tells us that you always think kindly of us, and that you are longing to see us, just as much as we are longing to see you. 7So then, in all our distress and trouble the story of your faith has set our mind at rest about you. 8It makes life worth living for us, if you remain unshakably true to your Lord. 9How can we adequately thank God for you, and for all the joy you have brought us before our God? 10Night and day we keep pouring out our prayers to be allowed to see you again and to repair any deficiencies in your faith.

11It is our prayer that our God and Father himself and our Lord Jesus may open up the way for us to visit you. 12It is our prayer that the Lord may make your love for each other and for all men to grow until it overflows, just as ours does for you. 13It is our prayer that he may strengthen your hearts, until you can stand in blameless holiness before our God and Father, when our Lord Jesus comes with all those who are dedicated to him.

Chapter 4

IT remains to say, brothers, that there is something which I want to ask you to do and to urge upon you as a Christian fellowship. You have received instructions from us on how you must behave to please God, and indeed you do so behave. I want you to intensify your efforts more and more. ₂You know what orders the Lord Jesus gave us to give to you. ₃It is God's will that you should walk the road to holiness and that you should have nothing to do with fornication. ₄It is his will that each of you should know how to be master of his own body, to keep it in the road to holiness and to use it honourably. ₅You must not allow your body to be at the mercy of the passions and desires, as the heathen who are ignorant of God do. ₆No one must try to overreach his fellowman in business, or try to exploit him, because, as we have already very definitely told you, the Lord exacts the penalty for all such actions.* ₇For God did not call us to live a life soiled with impurity; he called us to walk the road to holiness. ₈Therefore, to disregard these instructions is to disregard not man but God, who gives his Holy Spirit to us.

₉About the love which should be characteristic of the Christian fellowship, there is no necessity that I should write to you, for you yourselves have been taught by God to love one another. ₁₀And indeed you do keep this rule of love to all your fellow-Christians all over Macedonia. But, brothers, we urge you to intensify your efforts. ₁₁We urge you to have no other ambition than to live quietly, and to mind your own business, and to do an honest day's work, as we instructed you to do. ₁₂Then the people outside the church will admire your life and conduct, and you will be able to live in independence.

₁₃I do not want you, brothers, to get wrong ideas about those who sleep death's sleep, because I do not want you to grieve like those who are not Christians and who have nothing to hope for. ₁₄We believe that Jesus died and rose again. We therefore also believe that in the

---

*An alternative translation of verses 4-6 is: ₄*Each of you must know how to possess a wife in a holy and honourable way,* ₅*not with lustful passion, like the heathen who do not know God.* ₆*In this matter no one must overreach his fellowman, or invade his rights, for, as we have already very definitely told you, the Lord exacts the penalty for all such actions.*

same way God will bring with Jesus those who died in the Christian faith.

15What we are going to say to you, you must regard as a message from the Lord. We who are still alive, and who will survive until the Lord comes, will not take precedence over those who have already fallen asleep in death. 16The Lord himself will come down from heaven, with a shout of command, with the archangel's voice, when God's trumpet-call sounds. Then Christians who died believing in Christ will rise first. 17Then, after that, we who are still left alive will be caught up with them into the clouds, to meet the Lord in the air. And so we shall be always with the Lord. 18So then, this is the message with which you can comfort and encourage each other.

Chapter 5

THERE is no necessity, brothers, for me to write to you about the periods and dates of these events, 2for you yourselves well know that the day of the Lord is to come as a thief comes during the night. 3When people are talking of how peaceful and secure life is, then destruction will be on them, as suddenly as the labour pains come to a pregnant woman—and there will be no escape for them. 4But you, brothers, are not in the dark. The great day cannot catch up on you like a thief, 5for you are all sons of the light and sons of the day. We do not belong to the night or to the dark. 6So then, we must not sleep as the rest of the world does. We must be sleeplessly and soberly on the watch. 7Sleepers sleep at night; those who get drunk are drunk at night. 8But we who belong to the day must be sober. We must put on faith and love as a breastplate, and the hope of salvation as a helmet, 9for God has not destined us to be the victims of the divine wrath; he has destined us to win salvation through our Lord Jesus Christ, 10who died for us. He died for us so that, awake or asleep, we should live in his presence and his company. 11So then we must encourage each other, and we must always make life stronger and better for each other—as indeed you do.

12We ask you, brothers, to give full recognition to those who work so hard in your society, for they are your leaders in the Christian fellowship, and they are there to give you good advice. 13Hold them in the highest respect and affection because of the work they do. Nothing must ever be allowed to interrupt your personal relationships with each other. 14We appeal to you, brothers, to warn those who will not accept discipline, to encourage the nervous and timid, to help the weak, to have patience with everyone. 15You must see to it that no one tries to repay injury with injury. You must always aim at doing nothing but kindness to each other and to all.

16You must be happy all the time. 17You must never stop praying. 18You must find something to be grateful to God for in everything, for this is the way in which God wishes you who are Christians to live. 19You must not try to put a stop to the activity of the Spirit. 20You must not contemptuously dismiss the work and words of the prophets. 21You must test everything and retain what is good. 22You must have nothing to do with any kind of evil.

23It is my prayer that the God of peace may completely consecrate you. I pray that you may be kept sound in spirit, soul and body, for then you will be blameless, when our Lord Jesus Christ comes. 24You can rely on him who called you to do this for you.

25Brothers, pray for us too. 26Greet all the brothers with the kiss of peace. 27In the name of the Lord I charge you to have this letter read to the whole congregation.

28The grace of our Lord Jesus Christ be with you.

The Second Letter to the
THESSALONIANS

Chapter 1

THIS is a letter from Paul and Silvanus and Timothy to the congregation of the Thessalonians, who belong to God our Father and to the Lord Jesus Christ. ₂Grace to you and every blessing from God the Father and from the Lord Jesus Christ.

₃For us, brothers, it is nothing less than a duty always to thank God for you. That we should do so is fitting, because your faith goes from strength to strength, and your love for each other, of each for all and all for each, grows ever greater. ₄So much so is this the case that we cannot help telling God's other congregations how proud we are of you because of your fortitude and your unswerving loyalty amidst all the persecutions and the troubles you are going through. ₅It all goes to prove the justice of God's judgment, for it is designed to enable you to show that you deserve to be citizens of the Kingdom of God for which you are suffering. ₆For God in his justice is bound to square the account by sending trouble to those who trouble you, ₇and by sending relief to you who are now going through troubles, and to us too, when the Lord Jesus bursts from heaven on to the stage of history with his mighty angels ₈and in flaming fire, to execute divine vengeance on those who refuse to recognize God, and on those who refuse to obey the gospel of our Lord Jesus. ₉Men like that will pay the penalty of eternal destruction and banishment from the presence of God and his mighty glory. ₁₀This is what will happen on that great day when he comes to be welcomed with glory by his own dedicated people, and with awe and wonder by all who put their faith in him, and by you too, for you accepted the truth which out of our own experience we declared to you. ₁₁Our constant prayer for you is that our God will find you worthy of the invitation he sent to you, and that he may turn all your good intentions into actions, and powerfully help you to live the life that faith demands. ₁₂Then the name of the Lord Jesus will be glorified because of you, and you because of him, in the grace of our God and of the Lord Jesus Christ.

Chapter 2

WE want to speak to you, brothers, about the coming of our Lord Jesus Christ and about the way in which we are to be gathered to him. 2We want to ask you not to be suddenly thrown off your balance, and not to get into a state of panic because of some message which claims to be inspired, or some statement or some letter purporting to come from us, and alleging that the day of the Lord has already come. 3You must allow no one to deceive you in any way. That day cannot come until the Great Rebellion has taken place, until there appears upon the scene the man who is the incarnation of lawlessness, the man with God's doom on him, 4the universal enemy, the one who in his pride exalts himself against every divinity acknowledged by men and every object of man's worship, the one who in the end invades God's temple and takes his seat there, with the claim that he is God. 5You cannot have forgotten that I told you all this when I was still with you. 6You know about the restraining power which at present holds things in check, so that the Wicked One will not burst upon the world until his own proper time. 7For the power of lawlessness is secretly at work even now, but it will remain secret only until the restraining power is removed from the scene. 8Then the Lawless One will openly emerge, and the Lord Jesus will blast him out of existence with the breath of his mouth and with the blinding brilliance of his coming. 9It is the power of Satan which will be operative in the coming of the Lawless One. He will come equipped with all kinds of power and will produce miracles and wonders calculated to deceive. 10With all sin's power to mislead, he will come to those who are doomed to perish because they shut their minds to the love of truth which could have saved them. 11So God sends them a power which deludes them into believing what is a lie, 12and the end will be the judgment of all who refused to believe the truth and who deliberately chose sin.

13Brothers, you are dear to God, and we can do no other than always thank God for you, because God chose you as the first to be saved by the Spirit's consecrating power and by your acceptance of the truth. 14It was for that that he called you through the good news which we brought to you, because he wanted you to have as your own the glory of our Lord Jesus Christ. 15So then, brothers, stand fast, and keep a tight grip of the traditions you were taught by us, whether by word of mouth or by our letter. 16It is my prayer that our Lord Jesus Christ himself and God our Father, who loved us and gave us through his grace encouragement for time and eternity and a good hope, 17may give comfort and courage to your hearts, and make them strong always to do and to speak all that is good.

Chapter 3

IT only remains, brothers, to ask you to pray for us. Pray that the word of the Lord may make the same splendid progress as it did with you. 2Pray that we may be rescued from perverse and wicked men, for it is not all who have faith. 3You can rely on the Lord to strengthen you and protect you from the Evil One. 4The Lord gives us confidence in you, and we are sure that you are keeping, and will keep, our instructions. 5It is our prayer that the Lord may direct your hearts to remember the way in which God has loved you and all that Christ triumphantly went through for you.

6It is our order to you, brothers, in the name of the Lord Jesus Christ, to withdraw yourselves from any brother who is living a work-shy and indisciplined life and whose conduct does not agree with the tradition you received from us. 7You yourselves are well aware how you ought to take us as your pattern and example. For we did not live in an indisciplined idleness when we were with you. 8We never accepted our maintenance from anyone for nothing. So far from that, we sweated and toiled, we worked night and day, to avoid being a burden to any of you. 9It was not that we did not have the right to maintenance; it was to provide you with ourselves as a pattern and example to copy. 10For even when we were staying with you we used to insist to you that no man who was not willing to work should be allowed to eat. 11News has reached us that in your society there are some who are living workshy and indisciplined lives, idle in their own affairs, and interfering in everyone else's. 12Our instructions and our plea to such in the name of the Lord Jesus Christ are that they should go on quietly with their own business, and so earn their own living. 13As for you, brothers, never get tired of living the good life. 14If anyone pays no attention to what we have said in this letter, mark him well. Refuse to associate with him in the hope that that will make him ashamed of himself. ₁₅I do not say that you must treat him as an enemy; you must warn him as a brother.

₁₆I pray that the Lord of peace himself may give you every blessing at all times and in every way. The Lord be with you all.

₁₇In my own handwriting—every good wish from Paul. This is the sign which authenticates every letter. This is my autograph. ₁₈The grace of our Lord Jesus Christ be with you all.

Introduction to the First and Second Letters to the Corinthians

THE story of Paul's work in Corinth is told in Acts 18.1-17. Corinth was one of the places where Paul stayed longest, for we are told that he worked in Corinth for eighteen months. There are no letters which give us so vivid a picture of life in the early church, for, as it has been said, these letters take the roof off the church, and let us see what was going on inside.

It will help to have in our minds a scheme of the course of Paul's correspondence with Corinth.

i. It began with a letter which is prior to our first Corinthian letter. This letter is referred to in 1.5.9. It was a letter which told the Corinthians to have nothing to do with the immorality of the heathen world. It was not until A.D.90 that Paul's letters were collected, and by that time it may well have been that the editors did not quite know how to arrange them. It may be that this previous letter became embedded in 2 Corinthians, and it is perhaps contained in 2 Corinthians 6.14-7.1. The sense suits, and, if that section is removed, it makes good sense to pass from 6.13 to 7.2.

ii. Certain information came to Paul from Corinth, and in the meantime he had sent Timothy to Corinth to mend matters (1.4.17). The information came from members of Chloe's household, who had come to Ephesus from which Paul wrote (1.1.14); from a letter which the Corinthians had sent Paul, and which is answered in 1.7.1-1.15.58; and from Stephanas, Fortunatus and Achaicus, the bearers of the Corinthians' letter (1.16.7).

iii. Paul answered this in our first letter.

iv. The letter was ineffective and Paul paid a quick visit to Corinth. The evidence of this visit is in 2.12.14, and 2.13.1,2, where he speaks of a third visit, and, if there was to be a third, there must have been a second. This visit was also a failure and a heartbreak to Paul (2.1.23; 2.2.1).

v. Since the visit was ineffective, he wrote again, this time a very stern letter, which he came near to regretting having sent (2.2.4; 2.2.9; 2.7.8). It may be that this painful letter is in 2 Corinthians 10-13, which is one of the most heartbroken letters that Paul ever wrote. It is likely that it ought to come before 2 Corinthians 1-9, and that it was misplaced when the letters were edited. He also sent Titus to Corinth to try to settle things.

vi. Paul then left Ephesus to journey to Corinth by way of Macedonia. He was desperately worried, but in Macedonia he met Titus, who brought news that the trouble was over. And then Paul wrote the letter we have in 2 Corinthians 1-9, in which there is the calm after the storm.

As we have seen, in the first letter Paul dealt with the news which Chloe's people had brought him, and with the letter which the Corinthians had sent him. The problems were as follows.

i. First, there are the problems of which Chloe's people informed Paul.

a) The Corinthian church is torn and divided by sects and parties (1.1.10-1.4.21).

b) There has been a shocking case of immorality involving a son and his stepmother.

c) Members of the congregation do not hesitate to go to law with each other, for the Greeks were always a litigious people (1.6.1-11).

d) There is flagrant and blatant sexual immorality even among so-called Christian people (1.6.12-20).

ii. The subjects on which the Corinthians asked Paul's advice were many and varied.

a) There were questions about marriage (1.7.1-40). Paul's answers to these questions, answers in which he clearly prefers the unmarried state, are governed by the fact that he expected the Second Coming at any moment, and therefore wished people to have no earthly ties at all. He believed himself and all men to be living in a very temporary situation.

b) There were questions about meat which had been offered to idols (1.8.1–1.11.1). In those days nearly all social occasions were held in heathen temples. Only a token part of the sacrifice was burned on the altar, and part of the rest was given to the worshipper, who made a feast of it and invited his friends. If a Christian refused to attend such parties, he cut himself off from nearly all social occasions.

c) There were questions about worship in church.

1. There was the question about women who tried to worship with their heads uncovered (1.11.2-16). In those days for a woman to go bare-headed was the sign that she was a loose woman, and was an invitation to immorality.

2. There were questions about the Lord's Supper. In those days the Lord's Supper included the Love Feast, but what should have been a

noble expression of Christian fellowship had become an occasion for the stressing of social distinctions and the formation of cliques (1.11.17-34).

3. There was the problem of spiritual gifts. The phenomenon of speaking with tongues, and the way in which people coveted it, were bidding fair to reduce the church services to chaos (1.12-1.14).

iii. Finally, there were questions about the resurrection of the body. By the resurrection of the body Paul meant rather the survival of a man's total personality as an individual than the resurrection of the physical body (1.15.1-58).

In the second letter, as we have seen, we should very likely read chapters 10 to 13 first. In them Paul is forced to meet the accusations of his opponents, and, much against his will, to state his own claims. Finally, chapters 1 to 9 show us the relief after the anxiety.

The Corinthians letters show us another thing which to Paul was very important. The Jerusalem church was the mother church, but it was a very poor church. Paul had therefore organized a collection for the Jerusalem church from the younger churches. He speaks of it in both letters (1.16.1-11; 2.8.1-9.15). To Paul this collection was a way of marking the unity of the church, by showing that each church felt a Christian responsibility for the others. To give is to demonstrate oneness.

In the Corinthian correspondence we see better than anywhere else in the New Testament the practical problems of the early church.

The First Letter to the
CORINTHIANS

Chapter 1

THIS is a letter from Paul, called by God's will to be an apostle of Jesus Christ, and from Sosthenes, our colleague, 2to God's congregation at Corinth, those whose union with Christ has consecrated their lives to God, those whom God has called to be his own, and to everyone everywhere who calls on the name of our Lord Jesus Christ, their Lord and ours. 3Grace to you and every blessing from God our Father and from the Lord Jesus Christ.

4I always thank my God for you. I thank him for his grace which was given to you in Christ Jesus. 5For through your union with him your lives have been enriched in everything, with the result that you are equipped with every kind of knowledge and with complete ability to communicate it. 6You are in fact the proof that what Christ promised has happened. 7The result is that there is no spiritual gift which you do not possess, while you eagerly await the time when our Lord Jesus Christ will again burst upon the stage of history. 8It is he who will so strengthen you to the very end that on the day when our Lord Jesus comes no one will be able to level any charge against you. 9You can rely on God by whom you were called to share the life of his Son, Jesus Christ, our Lord.

10I urge you, brothers, by the name of our Lord Jesus Christ, to live in harmony with one another, and not to allow divisions to exist between you. You must be united and unanimous in your general attitude to life and in each particular decision. 11I say this because, brothers, a report has reached me through Chloe's people. They tell me that there are quarrels in your society. 12I refer to the fact that each one of you has his slogan: 'I belong to Paul'; 'I belong to Apollos'; 'I belong to Cephas'; 'I belong to Christ.' 13Has Christ been torn into pieces? Was it Paul who was crucified for you? Was it in Paul's name that you were baptized? 14I am thankful that the only people among you I did baptize were Crispus and Gaius. 15That at least stops any of you claiming that you were baptized in my name. 16I did baptize Stephanas' family too. Beyond that, I cannot think of anyone whom I baptized. 17For Christ did not send me to baptize, but to bring the good news, nor did I use the artifices of rhetoric, for I did not want the simple fact of the cross of Christ to be emptied of its power by human cleverness.

18The story of the cross makes nonsense to those who are on the way to ruin, but to us who are on the way to salvation it is the power of God. 19For scripture says:

> 'I will destroy the wisdom of the wise,
> I will bring to nothing the cleverness of the clever.'

20Where is the sage? Where is the expert in the law? Where is the clever debater whose questions never looked beyond the horizons of this world? Has God not turned this world's wisdom into folly? 21In God's wisdom the world through its wisdom never succeeded in getting to know God. God therefore decided to save those who believe by the folly of the message we preach. 22And folly they believe it to be, for the Jews ask for miraculous demonstrations of the power of God in action, and the Greeks look for wisdom, 23but we preach Christ, and Christ on his cross, a message which to the Jews is actually a barrier to belief, and which to the Gentiles is nonsense. 24But to those whom God has called, both Jews and Greeks, he is Christ the power of God and the wisdom of God. 25For the folly of God is wiser than the wisdom of men, and the weakness of God is stronger than the strength of men.

26Brothers, you see God's way of calling you. There are few among you who are wise as the world counts wisdom; there are few who are influential; there are few of aristocratic birth. 27But God has chosen the things the world counts foolish to shame the wise; God has chosen the things the world counts weak to shame the strong. 28God has chosen the things which the world counts quite undistinguished in birth, and which it despises, things which the world regards as mere nothings, to destroy things as they are. 29And he did this to ensure that no human being should have any cause for pride in the presence of God. 30It is his doing that you have entered into fellowship with Jesus Christ. God has made him our wisdom, our goodness, our way to holiness, our liberation. 31And he did this to ensure that what scripture says might come true: 'If any man is proud, he must be proud of what the Lord has done for him.'

Chapter 2

WHEN I came to see you, brothers, I did not come proclaiming God's secret with any special kind of rhetorical or philosophical brilliance. ₂I had in fact made up my mind that in my preaching to you I would forget everything except Jesus Christ, and him upon his cross. ₃I was very conscious of my own inadequacy; I was apprehensive and very nervous, when I came to you. ₄My message and my preaching were not delivered in professionally persuasive language. But they were characterized by the undeniable presence of the Spirit and of power. ₅This was my deliberately chosen method, because I wanted your faith to depend, not on man's cleverness, but on God's power.

₆There is a wisdom which we do teach to mature Christians, but it is not this world's wisdom, nor is it the wisdom of this world's rulers, for they are already passing from the scene. ₇What we do teach is the secret wisdom of God, which only God's own people can understand, a wisdom which until now has remained concealed, but which long ago before time began God framed and destined for our glory. ₈None of this world's rulers knew it. If they had known it, they would not have crucified the Lord of glory. ₉No! It is the wisdom of which scripture says:

'God has prepared for those who love him
what no eye has ever seen, and no ear has ever heard,
and what no human mind has ever even thought of.'

₁₀It is through the Spirit that God has given us the revelation of his truth, for the Spirit searches out everything, even the deep things of God. ₁₁What human being knows a man's mind, except the man's own inmost spirit? Just so, no one knows God's mind except God's Spirit. ₁₂It is not the spirit of the world that we have received, but the Spirit whose source and origin is God, to enable us to understand the gifts which God in his grace has given to us. ₁₃When we interpret spiritual truths to people who have the Spirit, we speak about these gifts in language which was not taught us by human wisdom, but which was taught us by the Spirit. ₁₄A man who does not possess the Spirit refuses to accept the truths which the Spirit of God gives him. Such a man regards them as nonsense. He cannot understand them because a man needs the Spirit rightly to evaluate them. ₁₅The man who has the Spirit can rightly evaluate everything, and he himself is subject to no man's judgment. 16To quote scripture:

'Can anyone know the mind of the Lord?
Can anyone instruct him?'

And we do have the mind of Christ.

Chapter 3

BROTHERS, it was quite impossible for me to speak to you as I would speak to people who have the Spirit; I had to speak to you as to people whose horizons were limited to this world, as to those who had never got beyond the stage of infancy in their Christian faith. 2In my teaching I gave you milk to drink. I could not give you solid food; you were not able to digest it, and you are not able to do so even yet, 3for you are still worldly people. While envy and quarrelling flourish among you, you cannot but admit that you are still worldly people, and that your conduct is based on purely human motives. 4When one of you says: 'I belong to Paul', and another: 'I belong to Apollos', are you not behaving like men untouched by Christ? 5What after all is Apollos? What is Paul? We are both servants of God through whom you entered the Christian faith; and each of us carried out the task God gave him to do. 6I planted the seed; Apollos watered it; but it was God who made the plant grow. 7It is not the man who plants the seed, or the man who waters it, who is really important; the really important person is God who makes it grow. 8There is no difference between the man who plants the seed and the man who waters it. Each of them will receive his own reward for his own work. 9We work together and we work for God. You are God's garden; you are God's building.

10In the privilege and the task which God gave me, like a wise master-builder, I laid the foundation. Someone else is erecting the building upon it. Each man must be careful how he erects his building. 11No one can lay any other foundation than the one which has been laid, for that foundation is Jesus Christ. 12Whatever superstructure a man raises on that foundation—be it of gold, or silver, or precious stones, or wood, or hay, or stubble—13each man's work will be shown up in its true character. The day of judgment will clearly show what it is, for that day will break upon the world's sight with fire, and the fire will test the character of each man's work. 14If the work which a man has built on that foundation survives the test, he will receive a reward. 15But if a man's work perishes in the flames, he will lose it, but he himself will be saved, but like a man rescued from a fire. 16Are you not aware that you are God's temple, and that the Holy Spirit has his home in you? 17If anyone destroys God's temple, God will destroy him, for the temple of God is holy—and you are that temple.

18Do not allow anyone to mislead you. If any of you thinks he is wise, as this world reckons wisdom, he must become a fool in order to become really wise. 19For this world's wisdom is nonsense as God sees it. For scripture says:

'He traps the wise in their own cleverness.

20And again: .

'The Lord knows that the arguments of the sages are futile.

21You talk about 'belonging' to people. You must never make your connection with any man a cause for pride. 22It is not a case of you belonging to some human person. For everything belongs to you— Paul and Apollos and Cephas, the world and life and death, the present and the future—23and you belong to Christ, and Christ belongs to God.

Chapter 4

YOU must think of us as Christ's servants and as stewards of the secrets of God. 2Now the first quality that anyone looks for in a steward is reliability. 3To be called upon to undergo your judgment, or the judgment of any human court, matters very little to me. For that matter, I do not even judge myself. 4My conscience is clear, but that does not necessarily mean that I am acquitted. My judge is the Lord. 5You must therefore stop this habit of passing premature judgments. You must wait until the Lord's coming, for he will light up the things which are hidden in darkness, and will lay bare the motives of the heart. And then each man will receive from God such praise as he deserves.

6Brothers, although these things do not really apply to us at all, I have for your sakes applied them to myself and Apollos by way of example, because I want you by taking us as an example to learn the principle that to go beyond what scripture says is forbidden, and so to stop your self-important practice of singing the praises of one leader and blackguarding another. 7Who sees anything specially outstanding in you? What do you possess that you did not receive? If you received it as a gift, why pride yourself as if it had not been a gift but an achievement? 8No doubt you have arrived at a stage when you have not an unsatisfied longing left! No doubt you have arrived at a stage when you are spiritual millionaires! No doubt you have entered into your kingdom and left us far behind! I wish that you had entered into your kingdom, and that we could share it with you! 9For I think that God has brought us apostles on to the scene like the little company of captives who bring up the rear of a victorious general's pageant of triumph and who are doomed to die in the arena. We have become a public spectacle to the world, both to angels and to men. 10We are fools for Christ's sake; you are wise with Christian wisdom. We are weak; you are strong. Yours is the glory; ours, the disgrace. 11To this hour we live in hunger and in thirst; we are ill-clad; we are beaten up; we are homeless vagrants. 12We sweat it out, working with our hands. We meet insult with blessing; persecution, with endurance; slander, with appeal. 13To this day we are regarded as no better than the scum of the earth and the off-scourings of humanity.

14I am not writing like this to shame you. I am doing it to warn you, for I regard you as my dear children. 15You may have thousands of guardians in your Christian life; you have only one father. For it was I who through the gospel became your father in the Christian faith. 16I therefore appeal to you to take me as your pattern and example. 17It is for this very reason that I am sending Timothy to you. He is my dear child and faithful in the Lord's service. He will remind you of the way I live as a Christian, and which I everywhere teach in every congregation. 18There are some who are inflated with defiant self-conceit, not really believing that I intend to come to visit you. 19But I will come, and, if the Lord wills, I will come soon, and then I will discover, not how these inflated characters can talk, but what they can do. 20For the Kingdom of God does not consist of talk but of power. 21Make your own choice! Do you want me to come to you with a rod of discipline, or lovingly and in the spirit of gentleness?

Chapter 5

I HAVE actually received a report that there is a case of sexual immorality among you, and a case so shocking that it is not practised even by pagans, for a man is living with his step-mother, as man and wife. ₂In face of this are you still inflated with self-conceit? Should this not rather have been a matter for tears of sorrowful shame? A man who perpetrated a deed like that should have been totally expelled from your fellowship. ₃Although I am absent from you in body, I am present in spirit, and, as if I were present, in the name of the Lord Jesus I have already come to a decision about the man who has done this terrible thing. ₄When you have met, and when I am present with you in spirit, acting in the power of our Lord Jesus ₅you must banish such a man from the fellowship of God's people, and consign him to Satan. This you must do so that this salutary and painful discipline may mortify this man's fleshly desires, so that on the day of the Lord his spirit may be saved. ₆Your proud pretensions have an ugly look about them. Are you not well aware that an evil influence can from the smallest beginnings spread like an infection through a whole community? ₇Get rid of the last remnants of the tainted life that once you lived, so that not a suggestion of evil infection may be left. That is the way you ought to be in any event, for the last evil taint ought to have been eradicated from your life, just as before the Passover sacrifice the last particle of leaven is removed from every house. For Christ is for us the Passover lamb, sacrificed for our deliverance. ₈Let us then live life as if it was a continual festival, with not a taint of evil or wickedness left, but in the purity of sincerity and truth.

₉I wrote to you in my letter not to associate with immoral people. ₁₀I obviously did not mean the people out in the world who are immoral or sinfully greedy, and thieves or idolaters. If you had to avoid them, you would have to retire from the world altogether. ₁₁What I did write was that you must refuse to associate with anyone who claims the name of fellow-Christian, if he is living an immoral life, if he is sinfully greedy, if he is an idolater, if he uses abusive language, if he is a drunkard or a thief. With such a man you must not even share a meal. ₁₂What business of mine is it to exercise judgment on the man outside the church? But it is obviously your business to exercise judgment on people inside it. ₁₃God will exercise judgment on people outside the church. Remove the evil man from your fellowship.

Chapter 6

IF any of you has a dispute with another member of the church, can he really bring himself to take his case to the pagan law-courts, and not to God's people? ₂Is it possible that you are not aware that it is God's people who are going to judge the world? And, if the world is to be judged by you, are you really incompetent to exercise judgment in the most trivial matters? ₃Are you not aware that we are to judge angels? How much more then mundane matters of everyday life? ₄If you do embark upon law-suits about such mundane matters, how can you submit them for decision to men who have no kind of respect within the Christian community? ₅Shame on you! Are you asking me to believe that in your own society there is not a single wise man, able to give a decision between one Christian and another? ₆Must Christian go to law with Christian, and that before people who are not Christians? ₇In point of fact, to have such law-suits with each other at all is to fail to maintain the standard of the Christian life. Why do you not rather submit to be injured? Why do you not rather submit to being swindled? ₈So far from that, it is you who do the injuring and the swindling—and it is your fellow-Christians who are your victims. ₉Bad men will never enter the promised possession of the Kingdom of God. Make no mistake! Fornicators, idolaters, adulterers, homosexuals, perverts, ₁₀thieves, those whose desires are never satisfied, drunkards, those who use abusive language, robbers, will never enter into the promised possession of the Kingdom of God—and you know it! ₁₁And that is what some of you were like, but you have been washed clean in baptism; you have started out on the road to holiness; through the name of the Lord Jesus Christ, and through the Spirit of our God you have entered into a new relationship with God.

₁₂'There is nothing which I may not do,' you say. I quite agree, but it is not everything whose results make it worth doing. 'There is nothing which I may not do,' you say. I quite agree, but there is nothing by which I will allow myself to be dominated. ₁₃'Food is for the stomach,' you say, 'and the stomach for food.' True, but the day will come when God will destroy both the stomach and the food. The body was never meant for fornication; it was meant for the Lord, and the Lord for the body. 14God raised the Lord from the dead, and he will raise us also by his power. 15Are you not aware that your bodies are parts of Christ? And am I then going to take the limbs which rightly belong to Christ and make them the limbs which belong to a prostitute? God forbid! 16You must be well aware that, if a man joins himself to a prostitute, he becomes physically one with her. For as scripture says: 'These two shall become one person.' 17But, if a man joins himself to the Lord, he becomes spiritually one with him. 18Have nothing to do with fornication. Every other sin which a man may commit is outside his body, but the fornicator sins against his own body. 19Are you not aware that your body is the temple of the Holy Spirit, who dwells within us, and whom we have received from God, and that you therefore do not belong to yourselves? 20He bought you for himself—and it did not cost him nothing. Therefore honour God with your body.

Chapter 7

WITH reference to the contents of your letter, and in particular in regard to the point you make that it is an excellent thing for a man to have nothing to do with women, my verdict is this. 2In order to avoid illicit sexual relationships, each man must have his own wife, and each woman her own husband. 3A husband must discharge to his wife the sexual duty which he owes her, and so must a wife to her husband. 4The wife is not in sole control of her own body; the husband has his rights. Equally, the husband is not in sole control of his own body; the wife has her rights. 5You must not wrongly withhold from each other that to which each of you has a right, unless it is by mutual consent, for a limited period, and for the purpose of concentrating upon prayer. Thereafter you must resume your normal relationship with each other again. This is necessary to prevent Satan from tempting you, because self-control is very difficult for you. 6I am stating this as a concession, not laying it down as a command. 7My own personal wish is that all men should be like myself. But each man has his own special gift from God, one of one kind, and another of another.

8My advice to those who are not married and to widows is that it is an excellent thing, if they remain as I myself have remained. 9But, if they find self-control impossible, then they must marry, for it is better to marry than to live a life continually inflamed with unsatisfied sexual desire. 10To those who are married my orders are—and they are not mine but the Lord's—that the wife must not separate from her husband. 11If she does so separate, she must remain unmarried or be reconciled to her husband. And a husband must not divorce his wife. 12To the rest there is no definite word of the Lord that I can quote, but my own advice is this. If a Christian has a pagan wife, and if she is willing to live with him, he must not divorce her; 13and if a Christian wife has a pagan husband, and if he is willing to live with her, she must not divorce her husband. 14The pagan husband is brought into the circle of God's people through his wife, and the pagan wife is brought into the circle of God's people through her Christian husband. If that principle were not so your children would be pagan, but in point of fact they are within the circle of God's people. 15If the pagan partner wishes to separate, he or she must do so. The Christian brother or sister is at liberty to take his or her own decision in such matters. God meant marriage to be a perfect human relationship between two people. 16Remember that as a wife, for all you know, you may very well be the means of saving your husband. Remember that as a husband, for all you know, you may very well be the means of saving your wife.

17The one thing to remember is that each man must go on living the life God gave him to live, and living in the circumstances in which he was when God called him. These are in fact the principles that I lay down in all the congregations. 18Was any man called already circumcised? Then he must not try to obliterate the mark of circumcision. Has any man been called uncircumcised? Then he must not have himself circumcised. 19Both circumcision and uncircumcision are quite irrelevant. What matters is obedience to God's commands. 20Each man must remain in the same circumstances in which his call to be a Christian came to him. 21Were you a slave when you were called? Don't let that worry you. All the same, if you can obtain your freedom, you are better to make use of the opportunity than to refuse it. 22The man who was called to be a Christian as a slave is the Lord's free man; and equally, the man who was called to be a Christian as a free man is Christ's slave. 23You have been bought at a price. Do not become the slaves of men. 24Brothers, it is the duty of each man in the sight of God to remain in the condition in which he was when God's call came to him.

25In regard to those who have accepted a voluntary virginity, I cannot cite any definite commandment of the Lord; but I give my own opinion, and I give it as one who is to be trusted, because I have received God's mercy. 26In view of the present threatening situation in my opinion this is an excellent thing, I mean that it is an excellent thing that a man should stay as he is. 27Are you bound to a wife? Then do not seek any loosening of the marriage bond. Has your marriage been dissolved? Then do not seek a wife. 28But, if you do marry, you have committed no sin; and, if a virgin marries, she has committed no sin. But people who do so will encounter all the everyday problems that such a physical relationship brings. And I would want to spare you that. 29But this, brothers, I do say—there is not much time left now, and, since that is so, from now on those who have a wife must live as if they had no such ties. 30Both those who mourn and those who rejoice must live from now on as if mourning and rejoicing were quite irrelevant. If people buy, they must do so on the understanding that they have no secure possession of anything. 31Those who are involved in the world's business must live as if they were not immersed in it, for this world in its present changing form will not last much longer. 32I want you to be free from distracting worries. An unmarried man's one thought is for the Lord's business. His one aim is to please the Lord. 33But, once a man has married, his one thought is for this world's business. His one aim is to please his wife. 34The result is that he lives a divided life. The one thought of an unmarried woman and of a virgin is for the Lord's business. Her one aim is to be dedicated to God in body and in spirit. But, once a woman has married, her one thought is for this world's business. Her one aim is to please her husband. 35It is for your good I am telling you this. I have no desire to put a leash on your liberty. All I am urging on you is that you should live a lovely life in undistracted concentration on the Lord.

The situation referred to in verses 36-38 is uncertain. In general, the advice of these verses is given to a man in regard to 'his virgin,' and the propriety of marriage for her. There are three possibilities.

(a) The advice may be to a father, who is uncertain whether it is his Christian duty to keep his unmarried daughter in a state of perpetual virginity, or to allow her to marry.

(b) The advice may be to a man in regard to the girl to whom he is engaged to be married, and who is uncertain whether his Christian faith makes marriage undesirable and perpetual virginity the truly Christian state.

(c) It is just possible that the reference is to a practice which certainly existed in the church later. Whether it existed in the time of Paul is not certain. In this practice a man and a woman decided to live together, but to have no sexual relationships at all. This was obviously a relationship which put a severe strain on both. And the question may be whether, when such a relationship is in danger of becoming intolerable, marriage is allowed.

In view of the three possible references there are three possible translations, and we give all three translations of verse 36.

(a) *Advice to a father*

36If a father thinks that he is acting unfairly towards his unmarried daughter, if she has passed the years of youth and has arrived at maturity, then he ought to let matters take their course. Let her do as she likes. There is no sin in that. Let them (i.e. the girl and her lover) marry.

(b) *Advice to someone engaged to be married*

36If a man thinks that he is acting unfairly to the girl to whom he is engaged to be married in deciding not to marry, if passions are strong, then he ought to let matters take their course. Let him (or her) do as he (or she) wishes. There is no sin in that. Let them marry.

(c) *Advice to those who have undertaken to live together with no sexual relationships*

36If a man thinks that he is acting unfairly towards the girl with whom he has decided to live but not to have any sexual relationships, if passions are strong, then he ought to let matters take their course. There is no sin in that. Let them marry.

37But, if a man's mind is firmly made up, from choice and not from compulsion, and if he is in full control of his own will, and has come to a final decision and has made up his mind that the girl must remain a virgin, he will do well. 38This is to say that, if a man gives his virgin daughter in marriage (or, marries his fiancée, or, marries the girl he had decided to live with and to remain unmarried), he does well; but if he does not, he will do still better.

39For a woman, her marriage cannot be dissolved during the lifetime of her husband. But, if her husband dies, she is at liberty to be married to anyone she wishes, only it must be a Christian marriage. 40But in my opinion she is happier if she remains as she is—and I think that I too have God's Spirit.

Chapter 8

This chapter deals with the problem of eating meat which had formed part of a sacrifice to a heathen idol, a subject to which Paul returns in 10.25-32. In this matter the Christian was faced with three problems which in the first century were very real.

(a) A sacrifice was seldom burned entire. A token part was burned, and then part of the meat became the perquisite of the priest, and part was given to the worshipper. The worshipper usually gave a meal with his share of the meat to his friends in the precincts of the heathen temple. Most social occasions were so held An invitation to dine usually read like this: 'I invite you to dine with me at the table of the Lord Serapis.' or of some other god. The question was whether or not a Christian could attend such a meal. The verdict is that he could not attend, because he could not sit at the table of Christ and the table of demons, with whom the heathen gods were identified. This meant that the Christian was to a large extent cut off from social life.

(b) The priests received far more meat than they could use. They sold it to the shops, whence it was sold to the public. Paul's verdict is that the Christian can buy in the shops and ask no questions.

(c) Sometimes the worshipper took the meat home with him and used it for a meal in his own house. In this case Paul's verdict is that the Christian may eat what is put before him, and ask no questions. But, if someone with a sensitive conscience warns him that the meat was meat offered to an idol, then he must not eat, more for the protection of the other person's conscience than for his own sake.

However remote the whole question is from modern life, it clearly presented a social problem of the first importance for the Christians of New Testament times.

A ND now with regard to the points you raise about meat that has formed part of a sacrifice to an idol, we are well aware that, as you say, 'We all have knowledge.' Your kind of 'knowledge' inflates a man with self-conceit; love builds him up in character. 2If a man fancies that he has attained to some degree of knowledge, he has not yet reached the stage when he has any knowledge at all in the real sense of the term. 3But if anyone loves God, he is recognized by God as his.

4Well then, with regard to the matter of eating meat which has formed part of a sacrifice offered to an idol, we know very well, that, as you say, 'An idol stands for something which has no real existence in the order of the universe,' and that, 'There is only one God.' 5For, even if there are so-called gods in heaven or on earth—and indeed there are plenty of 'gods' and plenty of 'lords'—6as far as we are concerned

There is one God, the Father,
    from whom everything comes,
    and to whom we go;
and one Lord Jesus Christ,
    through whom all things came into being,
    and through whom we live.

7But it is not everyone who possesses this knowledge. There are some people who up to now have been accustomed to idol-worship, and, when they eat a piece of meat which was part of a sacrifice made to an idol, they still cannot escape the feeling that this meat is the property of a false god. Their conscience is over-sensitive, and, since they cannot help feeling they are doing the wrong thing, their conscience is violated. ₈Food will not affect our standing with God. We are not minus something, if we do not eat; and we are not plus something, if we do eat. ₉But you must be careful that this liberty of yours does not turn out to be the very thing which becomes a barrier in the way of those who are weak in the faith. ₁₀It is in the heathen temples that people hold their social occasions, and the meat for the meal is their share of the meat that was offered to the idol. Well then, if someone whose conscience is weak and over-sensitive sees you with your superior knowledge sitting as a guest at a party in the shrine of a heathen idol, will he not be encouraged by your action to eat meat which has formed part of a sacrifice offered to an idol? ₁₁The result will then be that the man with the sensitive conscience is encouraged to violate his conscience, and so your superior knowledge becomes his ruin—and he is your fellow-Christian for whom Christ died. ₁₂By thus sinning against your fellow-Christians, and by thus striking a blow at their conscience in all its sensitiveness, you are sinning against Christ. ₁₃That is why if anything I eat makes it easier for my brother to go wrong, I will never eat meat again, for I refuse to do anything which will make it easier for my brother to go wrong.

Chapter 9

Do I not possess the liberty of a Christian? Have I not the rights of an apostle? Have I not seen Jesus the Lord? Did the Lord not give me you as my handiwork? ₂I may not be an apostle in the eyes of others; in yours at least I certainly must be. The fact that you are Christians is the seal which guarantees that I genuinely am an apostle.

₃To those who want to put me on trial this is my defence. ₄Have we no right to food and drink at the expense of the Christian community? ₅Have we no right to take a Christian wife with us on our travels, as the other apostles do, including the Lord's brothers and Cephas? ₆Or, are Barnabas and I the only apostles who are not exempt from having to work for a living? ₇Who ever serves as a soldier at his own expense? Who ever plants a vineyard without eating the grapes? Who ever tends a flock without getting any of its milk? ₈It is not only human authority that I have for speaking like this. Does the law not say the same? 9For there is a regulation in Moses' law: 'You must not muzzle the ox, when it is threshing the grain.' (That is, the ox must be free to eat what it is threshing.) Is it about oxen that God is concerned? 10Or, is it not quite clearly with us in mind that he says this? Quite certainly it was written with us in mind, for the ploughman is bound to plough and the thresher to thresh in the expectation of receiving a share of the produce. 11We sowed the seeds which brought you a harvest of spiritual blessings. Is it too much for us to expect in return to reap some material help from you? 12If others have the right to make this claim on you, surely we have still more?

But we have never made use of this right. So far from that, we put up with anything, rather than risk doing anything that would hamper the progress of the gospel. 13Are you not aware that those who perform the sacred ritual of the Temple use the Temple offerings as food, and that those who serve at the altar share with the altar in the sacrifices which are placed on it? 14In the same way, the Lord gave instructions that those who preach the gospel should get their living from the gospel. 15As for myself, I have never claimed any of these rights, nor am I writing now to see that I get them. I would rather die first! No one is going to turn the one claim in which I take a pride into an empty boast! 16If I preach the gospel, I have nothing to be proud of. I can't help myself. For me it would be heartbreak not to preach the gospel. 17If I do this because I choose to do it, I would expect to get paid for it. But if I do it because I can do no other, it is a task from God with which I have been entrusted. 18What pay do I get then? I get the satisfaction of telling the good news without it costing anyone a penny, and of thus refusing to exercise the rights the gospel gives me.

19I am a free man, and no man's slave; yet I have made myself every man's slave in order to win more men for Christ. 20When I was working among the Jews, I lived like a Jew, in order to win the Jews. When I was working among those who accept the law, I lived like a man who accepts the law—although I myself do not accept it—in order to win those who accept the law. 21When I was working among Gentiles, to whom the Jewish law means nothing, I lived like a man who has no use for the law—although I am far from disregarding the law of God, and very much subject to the law of Christ—in order to win those who do not accept the law. 22To those who are weak in the faith and over-sensitive in conscience, I have made myself like them, in order to win them. I made myself all things to all men, in order to save some of them by every possible means. ₂₃Everything I do is done for the sake of the gospel, so that I may be a partner in its blessings.

₂₄You are well aware that on the race-track all the runners run the race, but only one receives the prize. Just so, you must run to win. ₂₅No athlete ever relaxes his self-discipline. They discipline themselves to win a crown that must fade; we do so to win a crown that cannot fade. ₂₆I do not run without a goal clear before me. I do not box like a man engaged in shadow-boxing. ₂₇I batter my body; I make it realize that I· am the master, for I do not want to preach to others, and then to find that I myself have failed to stand the test.

Chapter 10

BROTHERS, you must never forget that our ancestors all journeyed under the pillar of cloud, and all passed safely through the Red Sea. ₂In the cloud and in the sea they were all baptized as followers of Moses. ₃They all ate the same supernatural food, ₄and they all drank the same supernatural drink, for they drank from the supernatural rock which accompanied them on their journey—and that rock was Christ. ₅Nevertheless most of them incurred the displeasure of God, and the desert was strewn with their dead bodies. ₆These events are intended as symbolic warnings to us not to set our hearts on evil things, as they did. ₇Nor must you become idolaters, as some of them did. As scripture says: 'The people sat down to eat and drink and rose up to indulge in their heathen sport.' ₈Nor must we commit fornication as some of them did, in consequence of which twenty-three thousand died in a day. ₉Nor must we try to see how far we can go with God and get away with it, as they did, and in consequence were destroyed by serpents. ₁₀Nor must you grumble against God, as some of them did, and in consequence were killed by the Angel of Death. ₁₁What happened to them is intended as a symbolic warning to us. These events were recorded as advice to us, for we are living in the age to which all the ages have been leading up. ₁₂One warning emerges from all this—anyone who thinks that he is standing securely must be careful in case he collapses. ₁₃You have been involved in no trials except those which are part of the human situation. You can rely on God not to allow you to be tested beyond what you are able to cope with. No! When trial comes he will send you along with it the way out of it, to enable you to bear it.

14Therefore, my dear friends, have nothing to do with idolatry. 15I assume that I am speaking to sensible people. Decide for yourselves whether what I say is reasonable or not. 16You would agree that the cup of blessing for which we give thanks is a means of sharing in the blood of Christ. You would agree that the bread which we break is a means of sharing in the body of Christ. 17Because there is one loaf, and because we all receive a share of the one loaf, although we are many, we are one body. 18Look at actual Jewish practice and belief. The worshippers receive their share of the meat of the sacrifice and eat it; the altar receives its share. Does that not make altar and worshippers partners? 19What is my argument? That a thing offered to an idol has any real existence? Or that an idol itself has any real existence? 20No, but I am arguing that the sacrifices of the pagans are offered to demons and not to God, and I do not want you to become partners with the demons. 21You cannot drink the cup of the Lord and the cup of demons. You cannot share the Lord's table and the demons' table. 22Or, do we want to make God jealous? Are we stronger than he is?

23I quite agree with you that we are free to do anything—but that is not to say that everything is to our good. It is perfectly true that we are free to do anything—but it is not everything that strengthens life and character for ourselves and for others. 24No one must concentrate solely on his own good; he must be equally interested in the other man's good. 25Eat anything that is sold in the meat-market, and never mind asking questions to satisfy your conscience, 26for the earth and everything in it belongs to the Lord. 27If a non-Christian invites you to a meal and you decide to go, eat everything that is put before you, and never mind asking questions to satisfy your conscience. 28But, if anyone present says to you in warning: 'This meat was part of a sacrifice offered to an idol,' then don't eat it. Don't eat it for the sake of the man who warned you and for the sake of his conscience. 29I am not talking about your conscience. (Your conscience is clear.) It is the other man's conscience I am talking about. (His conscience is oversensitive.) 'But,' you say, 'why should my liberty have to submit to the judgment of another man's conscience? 30If I partake and thank God, why am I bitterly attacked for eating food for which I said grace?' 31Your eating, your drinking, your every action must be to the glory of God. 32You must live in such a way that you give no offence either to Jews or to Greeks or to the church of God. 33I try not to get up against anyone in anything, for it is not my own good that I am out for, but the good of all. The one thing I want is for them to be saved. 11.1And you must try to copy me, as I try to copy Christ.

Chapter 11

The practical background of verses 2-16 of this chapter is the fact that in the Middle East in the time of Paul a woman who went about unveiled in public would be regarded as a loose woman. On the other hand a woman's veil was her protection and her authority. Without her veil she was open to any man's approach; with her veil she was unmolested. The trouble was that in Corinth women in their new Christian emancipation were liable to act in a way which would shock the public and bring discredit on the Christian community.

YOU say that I am never out of your memory, and that you never lose your grip on the instruction I handed on to you. This is greatly to your credit. 3I want you to understand that Christ is the head of every man, that man is the head of woman, and that God is the head of Christ. 4If in public worship any man prays or preaches with his head covered, he dishonours his head. 5But if any woman prays or preaches with her head uncovered, she dishonours her head. It is exactly the same as if her head was shaved. 6For if a woman is going to abandon wearing a veil, she might as well go the whole way and have her hair cut short. If it is disgraceful for a woman to have her hair cut short or to shave her head, then she ought to continue to wear a veil. 7A man ought not to cover his head, for he is the image and glory of God, but woman is the glory of man. 8For man was not made from woman, but woman from man. 9And further, man was not created for the sake of woman, but woman for the sake of man. 10So then, for the sake of the angels a woman ought to wear on her head the veil which gives her her own authority. 11But it must be remembered that from the Christian point of view man is essential to woman, and woman is essential to man. 12Originally woman was made from man; and now man comes into being through woman. And everything comes into existence from God. 13Exercise your own judgment. Can you honestly say that it is fitting for a woman to engage in public prayer to God unveiled? 14Does not nature itself teach us that for a man long hair is a disgrace, 15but for a woman long hair is her glory? This is so because she has been given her hair as a covering. 16If anyone thinks that he would like to go on arguing about this, let it suffice to say that we have no such custom as the participa-

53

tion of unveiled women in public worship, nor have the congregations of God.

In the first days of the church the Sacrament of the Lord's Supper was closely connected with a congregational meal known as the *Agapē*, or Love Feast. This was a real meal, and should have been a valuable way of expressing the fellowship of all classes and conditions of men within the unity of the church. But in Corinth the congregation at the *Agapē* had broken up into cliques and sections and groups, and that which was meant to symbolise unity had become the cause of disunity.

17One piece of instruction I must give you about a matter which is not to your credit. The fact is that your meetings as a congregation do more harm than good. 18In the first place, I am informed that, when you meet as a congregation, you are split into mutually exclusive groups, and I am prepared to believe that to some extent this is so. 19I suppose that there are bound to be differences in your society, if for no other reason than to make it clear which of you are of sterling faith. 20When you meet together it is impossible for you to eat the Lord's Supper, 21for each of you is in far too big a hurry to eat his own meal, and the result is that some go hungry while others are drunk. 22Have you no homes of your own where you can eat and drink? Or, do you think so little of the church of God that you think nothing of publicly humiliating members who are poor? What am I to say to you? Am I to commend you for conduct like this? I certainly do not!

23The tradition which I have handed on to you goes right back to the Lord. That tradition tells that on the night on which he was being delivered into the hands of his enemies, the Lord Jesus took a loaf, 24and, when he had thanked God, he broke it into pieces and said: 'This means my body which is for you. You must continue to do this to make you remember me.' 25In the same way, after the meal, he took the cup too, and said: 'This cup stands for the new relationship with God made possible at the cost of my death. You must continue to do this, as often as you drink it, to make you remember me.' 26For every time you eat this loaf and drink the cup you are publicly proclaiming the Lord's death, until he comes again.

27The consequence is that anyone who eats the bread or drinks the cup of the Lord in a way that contradicts all that the Lord meant it to be will be guilty of a crime against the body and blood of the Lord. 28A man must examine himself before he eats his share of the bread and drinks his share of the cup, 29for a man's eating and drinking become a judgment on himself, if in eating and drinking he does not realize that the church is the body of Christ, and therefore a unity with no divisions. ₃₀This is the reason why many of you are ill and weak, and why a considerable number of you have died. ₃₁If we would examine ourselves, we would not be undergoing the judgment of God. ₃₂But, when we do undergo judgment, we are being disciplined by the Lord to save us from being involved in the final condemnation of the world. ₃₃So then, brothers, when you meet for a common meal wait for one another. ₃₄If anyone is hungry, he must eat at home. This will prevent your meeting together from becoming the means whereby you incur judgment. I will settle the other matters when I come.

Chapter 12

WITH regard to the points you raise about the gifts which the Spirit gives, I want you to realize what the position really is. ₂You know that when you were pagans you were ever and again swept away to the worship of dumb idols, under the influence now of one leader and now of another. ₃I therefore want you to understand that no one speaking under the influence of the Spirit of God can say: 'A curse on Jesus!' And no one except under the influence of the Holy Spirit can say: 'Jesus is Lord.'

₄There are different kinds of spiritual gifts, but they are the gifts of the same Spirit. ₅There are different spheres of service, but the service is of the same Lord. ₆There are different kinds of effects, but it is the same God who produces them in every case and in every person. ₇The visible effect which the Spirit produces in each of us is designed for the common good. ₈To one man there is given through the Spirit power to express intellectual wisdom in words; to another by the same Spirit there is given power to communicate knowledge in words. ₉By one and the same Spirit faith is given to one man, and the gift of healing to another; ₁₀the power to work miracles to another; the gift of prophecy to another; the ability to discern whether or not spirits are from God to another; the gifts of different kinds of ecstatic speech to another; the ability to interpret such speech to another. ₁₁It is one and the same Spirit who produces all these different effects, and who, as he wishes, distributes them to each individual person.

₁₂The body is a single unity, although it has many parts, and all the parts of the body, many as they are, are one united body. It is exactly so with Christ. ₁₃Whether we are Jews or Greeks, whether we are

slaves or free men, through the action of the one Spirit our baptism
has united us into one body. We are all saturated with the one Spirit.
14The body does not consist of one part, but of many. 15If the foot
should say: 'Because I am not a hand, I am not part of the body,' that
does not make it any the less part of the body. 16If the ear should say:
'Because I am not an eye, I am not part of the body,' that does not
make it any the less part of the body. 17If the whole body was an eye,
what would happen to the sense of hearing? 18If the whole body was
an ear, what would happen to the sense of smell? But in point of fact
God has appointed each part in the body as he wished. 19If all the parts
of the body were one part, where would the body be? 20But in point
of fact there are many parts, but there is one body. 21The eye cannot
say to the hand: 'I don't need you.' Nor, to take another example, can
the hand say to the feet: 'I don't need you.' 22So far from that, the
parts of the body which seem to be weaker are in fact more essential.
23We attach greater honour to those parts of the body which we
regard as dishonourable. The unlovely parts of our body are surrounded with a greater modesty, 24of which the lovely parts have no
need. But God has blended the body together, and has given more
honour to the parts which lack honour. 25His design was that there
might be no division in the body, but that the parts of the body
should be equally concerned for each other's welfare. 26So, if one
part of the body suffers, all the parts suffer in sympathy with it; and,
if one part is honoured, all the parts share its joy.

27You are the body of Christ, and each of you is a part of it. 28In the
church God has appointed, first, apostles; second, prophets; third,
teachers; then, those who have the power to work miracles; then,
those who possess gifts of healing or of helping others; those who have
the ability to administer the affairs of the church, and those who have
the gift of various kinds of ecstatic speech. 29Obviously everyone is
not an apostle. Obviously everyone is not a prophet or a teacher.
Obviously everyone does not have the power of working miracles 30or
special gifts of healing. Obviously everyone cannot speak in ecstatic
speech or interpret such speech. 31Set your hearts on possessing the
greater gifts. And now I am going to show you the way which is by
far the best.

Chapter 13

EVEN if I could speak the languages of men and of angels,
if I am without love,
I am no better than a clanging gong
or a clashing cymbal.
2Even if I have the gift of prophecy,
even if I understand all the secrets
which only the initiates know;
even if I am wise with all knowledge;
even if I have faith so complete
that it can move mountains,
if I am without love,
there is no value in my life.
3Even if I dole out everything I possess,
even if I welcome a martyr's death in the flames,
if I am without love,
it is all no good to me.

4Love is patient with people; love is kind.
There is no envy in love;
there are no proud claims;
there is no conceit.
5Love never does the graceless thing;
never insists on its rights,
never irritably loses its temper;
never nurses its wrath to keep it warm.
6Love finds nothing to be glad about
when someone goes wrong,
but is glad when truth is glad.
7Love can stand any kind of treatment;
love's first instinct is to believe in people;
love never regards anyone or anything as hopeless;
nothing can happen that can break love's spirit.
8Love lasts for ever.
Whatever prophecies there may be,
they will some day be ended;
whatever utterances of ecstasy there may be,
they will some day be silenced;

whatever knowledge there may be,
it will some day pass away.
₉We have but fragments of knowledge
and glimpses of prophetic insight;
₁₀but when the complete will come,
the fragmentary will be ended.
₁₁When I was a child,
I had a child's speech;
I had a child's mind;
I had a child's thoughts.
But, when I became a man,
I put away childish things.
₁₂Now we see bewildering shadows in a mirror,
but then we shall see face to face;
now I know a fragment of the truth,
but then I will know as completely as I am known
₁₃The truth is that these three things last for ever—
faith, hope, love—
and the greatest of them is love.

Chapter 14

Throughout this chapter there runs a contrast between speaking with tongues, or speaking in a tongue, and prophesying. Speaking in a tongue does not mean speaking in a foreign language. There was, and still is, a phenomenon in which a man poured out a torrent of sounds in an ecstasy and in no known language without any conscious effort on his part, and as if some spiritual power was speaking in him and through him. And there were also those who had the gift of interpreting this ecstatic and otherwise unintelligible flow of sounds. This gift was greatly admired and much coveted in the church at Corinth. On the other hand, there was prophecy. Prophecy does not here mean foretelling the future; it means powerfully proclaiming the message of God. Unlike the ecstatic speaking in tongues prophecy was completely intelligible, and in this chapter is very nearly the equivalent of preaching.

SPARE no effort to possess love, and set your heart on the gifts the Spirit gives, and especially on the ability to proclaim the message of God with prophetic power. ₂When a man is speaking in ecstatic language, he is speaking not to man but to God, for no one understands what he is talking about. He is no doubt under the influence of the Spirit, but he speaks in a way that no ordinary person can understand. ₃But when a man proclaims the message of God, he speaks in such a way that his words build up the spiritual life of his hearers, and bring them courage and comfort. ₄When a man is speaking in ecstatic language, he is no doubt building up his own spiritual life; but the man who proclaims God's message builds up the spiritual life of the whole congregation. ₅I would be happy if you all spoke in ecstatic language; but I would be still happier if you all proclaimed God's message. The man who clearly proclaims the message of God is greater than the man who speaks in ecstatic language, unless such a speaker explains what it all means, for only then will the spiritual life of the whole congregation be built up.

₆If, brothers, I do come to you and speak to you in ecstatic language, what good will I do you, unless by my words I unveil the truth to you, or bring you new knowledge, or proclaim the message of God to you, or give you instruction? ₇Even in the case of inanimate musical instruments, for example a flute or a harp, unless they preserve the correct interval between the notes, how can anyone recognize the tune that is being played on the flute or the harp? ₈If no one can tell what call the bugle is sounding, how can anyone prepare for battle? ₉Just so, if you in your ecstatic language do not produce any intelligible and meaningful speech, how can anyone understand what you are saying? Your words will go whistling down the wind. ₁₀I do not know how many different languages there are in the world. No race is without its language. ₁₁But, if I do not understand the meaning of the language, I will be speaking gibberish to the speaker, and he will be speaking gibberish to me. ₁₂It is exactly the same with you. In your eagerness for spiritual gifts, you must set your heart on excelling in building up the spiritual life of the congregation. ₁₃That is why a man who speaks in ecstatic language must pray to be able to interpret what he says. ₁₄If I pray in ecstatic language, it is my spirit which prays. My mind is producing nothing at all. ₁₅What about it then? My prayers must be inspired, but my prayers must be the product of my own mind as well; my hymns must be inspired, but my hymns must be the product of my own mind as well. ₁₆If you pour out your ecstatic praises to God, how can the ordinary man who is there say Amen to your thanksgiving, since he has no idea what you are talking about? ₁₇No doubt your thanksgiving is a thing of beauty, but the spiritual life of the other man is not built up by it. ₁₈I thank God that I have the gift of ecstatic language more than any of you has. ₁₉But, for all that, in the congregation I would rather speak five intelligible words, to instruct others as well as myself, than ten thousand words in ecstatic language which no one can understand.

20Brothers, don't be childish. True, in evil you must be as innocent as babes, but you must be adult in your thinking. 21It stands written in the law:

'By men of strange tongues,
    and by the lips of strangers,
I will speak to this people,
    and even then they will not listen to me,
says the Lord.'

22'Strange tongues' are, therefore, designed to convince, not those who believe, but those who do not believe. The clear proclamation of the truth is designed to help, not the unbeliever, but the believer. 23If there is a meeting of the whole congregation, at which everyone speaks in ecstatic language, if ordinary people or non-Christians come in, they are bound to think that you are crazy. 24But if everyone is clearly proclaiming God's message, and a non-Christian or an ordinary person comes in, the whole service challenges and convicts his conscience. 25The secrets of his heart are laid bare, and the result will be that he will fling himself down and worship God. 'Truly,' he will say, 'God is among you.'

26How then, brothers, are we to sum all this up? When you meet together, each of you has something which he wishes to contribute to the gathering, a hymn, a piece of instruction, something that has been specially revealed to him, an ecstatic utterance, an interpretation of such an utterance. Everything must be done with the intention of building up the spiritual life of the congregation. 27If there is to be any speaking in ecstatic language, no more than two, or at the most three, must speak. They must speak in turn, and one person must interpret. 28If there is no interpreter available, then the man who wishes to speak in ecstatic language must not address the congregation at all. He must speak to himself and to God. 29Two or three may deliver their message from God with prophetic power. The others must exercise their judgment on what is said. 30If another person sitting in the congregation receives a special message from God, the first speaker must stop speaking. 31You can all give your message from God one at a time, and then everyone will be instructed and everyone will be encouraged. 32Those who want to deliver a prophetic message can, and must, control their inspiration, 33for God is not the God of disorder but of peace.

Following the custom of all the congregations of God's people, 34the women must remain silent at the meetings of the congregation.

They are not permitted to speak. They must remain in the subordinate position which the Jewish law assigns to them. ₃₅If they wish to find out about anything, they must put their questions to their own husbands at home, for it is quite improper for a woman to speak at a meeting of the congregation. ₃₆Did the word of God originate from you? Or, are you the only people to whom it came?

₃₇If anyone claims prophetic or special inspiration, he must realize that what I write is a commandment of the Lord. ₃₈If he refuses to recognize this, he is himself not to be recognized. ₃₉So, my brothers, set your heart on being able to proclaim God's message clearly. Do not try to stop those who speak in ecstatic language. ₄₀But everything must be done properly and in order.

Chapter 15

B ROTHERS, I want to remind you of the gospel which I preached to you, and which you received, the gospel on which you have taken your stand, ₂and by which you are being saved, if you keep a tight grip of it, in the form in which I preached it to you, unless your decision to believe was all for nothing. ₃As a first essential, I handed on to you the account of the facts that I myself had received. That account told that Christ died for our sins, as the scriptures said he must; ₄that he was buried, that he was raised to life again on the third day, as the scriptures said he would be; ₅that he appeared to Cephas and then to the Twelve; ₆that he then appeared to more than five hundred Christian brothers at one and the same time, of whom the majority survive to the present day, though some of them have died. ₇Next, he appeared to James, then to all the apostles. ₈Last of all, he appeared to me too, and my birth into the family of Christ was as violent and unexpected as an abortion. ₉For I am the least of the apostles. I am not fit to be called an apostle at all, because I persecuted God's church. ₁₀It is by the grace of God that I am what I am. Nor did that grace come to me to no effect. So far from that, I have toiled harder than all the rest of them put together, although it was not I who did the work but the grace of God which is my constant companion. ₁₁So then, whether I or they were the preachers, this is the substance of our preaching, and this is the faith which you accepted.

₁₂If then the substance of the Christian message is that Christ has been raised from the dead, how can some of you say that there is no resurrection of the dead? 13If there is no resurrection of the dead, then neither has Christ been raised. 14But, if Christ has not been raised, both the Christian message we preached to you and your faith are emptied of all meaning. 15If this is so, a further consequence is that we have clearly been making false statements about God, because we affirmed about God that he raised Christ, when in fact, if it is true that the dead are not raised, he did not do so. 16For, if the dead are not raised, neither has Christ been raised. 17And, if Christ has not been raised, then your faith is all a delusion; you are still at the mercy of your sins. 18Then further, we are bound to conclude, those who have died holding the Christian faith are dead and gone for ever. 19If our Christian hope does not reach beyond this life, then of all men we are most to be pitied.

20But in point of fact Christ has been raised from the dead. Just as the first-fruits are the guarantee that all the rest of the harvest will follow, so his resurrection guarantees that those who have died will rise again. 21For since it was through a man that death came into the world, it is also through a man that resurrection of the dead came. 22In Adam all die, and, just so, in Christ all will be brought to life. 23But each in his own order. First of the whole harvest is Christ; then at his coming those who belong to Christ. 24Then the end will come, and, after Christ has destroyed every rule and authority and power in the spirit-world, he will hand over the Kingdom to God the Father. 25He must reign until God has reduced all his enemies to complete subjection. 26Death will be the last enemy to be destroyed. 27Scripture says: 'God has completely subjected all things to him.' But, when scripture says that 'all' things have been subjected to him, it is quite clear that that does not include God himself, who subjected all things to him. 28When all things have been subjected to him, then the Son too will himself be subjected to him who subjected all things to him, for the final purpose is that God should be all in all.

29Again, what will happen to those who get themselves baptized on behalf of the dead? If the dead are not raised to life at all, what is the point of their being baptized for them? 30And as for us—why are we in hourly peril of our life? 31Brothers, by the pride I have in our joint fellowship in Jesus Christ our Lord, I swear I take my life in my hands every day. 32If I had to fight with men like wild beasts at Ephesus, what was the point of it for me?

'Let us eat and drink,
  for tomorrow we shall die'

is a sound policy, if the dead are not raised. 33Make no mistake—'bad companions corrupt good morals.' 34Return to your sober senses, and stop your sinning. There are some of you who are utterly ignorant of God. I say it to shame you.

35But someone will ask: 'How are the dead to be raised to life? What kind of body will they have?' 36Only a fool would ask a question like that! When you sow a seed, it does not come to life unless it dies. 37And, when you sow a seed, what you sow is not the body which it is going to become, but a naked seed, maybe of corn or of some other grain. 38God gives it the body he has chosen for it, and to each seed he gives its own body. 39All flesh is not the same flesh. Men have one kind of flesh, and animals another, and birds another, and fishes another. 40There are heavenly bodies and there are earthly bodies. The heavenly bodies have one kind of splendour and the earthly bodies another. 41The sun has one kind of splendour, the moon another kind of splendour, the stars another kind of splendour. One star differs from another in splendour.

42It is so with the resurrection of the dead. What is buried in the earth, like a seed, in decay is raised imperishable. 43What is buried in dishonour is raised in glory. What is buried in weakness is raised in power. 44It is a physical body that is buried in the ground like the seed; it is a spiritual body that is raised. If there is a physical body, there is bound also to be a spiritual body. 45Thus scripture says: 'The first man Adam became a life-having person.' The last Adam became a life-giving spirit. 46But it was not the spiritual which came first; it was first the physical, then the spiritual. 47The first man was made of the dust of the earth; the second Man is from heaven. 48What the man made of dust was, all men made of dust are. What the Man from heaven is, all the heavenly are. 49We have worn the likeness of the man of dust; so we shall wear the likeness of the heavenly Man.

50Brothers, what I mean is this. Flesh and blood can never possess the Kingdom of God, nor can that which is subject to decay possess immortality. 51Look! I will tell you the secret that God has revealed. We shall not all die, but we shall all be changed, 52in a split second, in the time it takes to blink an eye, when the last trumpet sounds. For the trumpet shall sound, the dead shall be raised never to die again, and we shall be changed. 53This nature, which is subject to decay, must be clothed with the life that can never decay. This nature, which is subject to death, must be clothed with the life that can never die. 54When this nature which is subject to decay is clothed with the life which can never decay, and when this nature which is subject to death is clothed with the life which can never die, then the saying of scripture will come true:

> 55'Death is swallowed up, and victory is complete!
> Where, O death, is your victory?
> Where, O death, is your sting?'

56It is sin which gives death its sting, and it is the law which gives sin its power. 57But thanks be to God who gives us the victory through our Lord Jesus Christ. 58Therefore my dear brothers, stand firm and immovable. Work always for the Lord to the limit and beyond it in the certain knowledge that the Lord will never allow all your toil to go for nothing.

Chapter 16

ABOUT the collection for God's people—you must follow the same instructions as I gave to the congregations in Galatia. 2On the first day of the week, each of you must personally lay aside and save up a sum in proportion to his earnings. And then, when I come, you will not have to start organizing collections. 3When I arrive, I will give letters of introduction to those whom you approve for the task, and I will send them to Jerusalem to be the bearers of your gift. 4If it should seem worthwhile for me to go myself, they will make the journey with me.

5I will come to you after I have completed my journey through Macedonia—for I am on my way through Macedonia just now—6and it is possible that I may stay with you, or even spend the winter with you, so that you may help me on my way, wherever I may be going. 7I do not want to pay you a visit just now in the passing, for I hope to stay with you for some time, if the Lord permits it. 8It is my intention to stay on in Ephesus until the Day of Pentecost, 9for ample opportunity for effective work lies before me here, although there is strong opposition.

10If Timothy comes, see that you make him feel at home among you, for he is doing the Lord's work as I am. 11No one must look down on him. Send him on his way to join me with good-will, for I and the brothers are expecting him.

12As for our brother Apollos, I strongly urged him to visit you with the other brothers, but at the moment he was quite determined not to come, although he will come, when an opportunity arises.

13Always be on the alert. Stand firm in the faith. Play the man. Be strong. 14Your every action must be dictated by love.

15You know, brothers, that the household of Stephanas were the first converts in Achaea, and you know that they have organized themselves for the service of God's people. 16Well then, I urge you to accept the leadership of such men and of all who work and toil with them. 17I am glad that Stephanas and Fortunatus and Achaicus have arrived, because their presence has compensated for your absence. 18For they have set my mind at rest—and yours too. Such men deserve to have their services recognized.

19The congregations of Asia send you their good wishes. Aquila and Priscilla, with the congregation which meets in their house, send you warmest Christian greetings. 20All the brothers send you their good wishes. Greet one another with the kiss of peace.

21I Paul write this greeting in my own handwriting.

22If anyone does not love the Lord, a curse be on him! Marana tha. Our Lord, come!

23The grace of the Lord Jesus be with you. 24My love to you all in Christ Jesus.

The Second Letter to the
CORINTHIANS

Chapter 1

THIS is a letter from Paul, an apostle of Christ Jesus because God willed it so, and from Timothy our colleague, to God's congregation at Corinth, together with all God's people all over Achaea. 2Grace to you and every blessing from God our Father and from the Lord Jesus Christ.

3Let us give thanks to the God and Father of our Lord Jesus Christ. He is the merciful Father, the God from whom all courage and comfort come. 4It is he who encourages us in all our troubles, and he does so to give us the power to encourage others who are in every kind of trouble with that same encouragement which we ourselves have received from him. 5We have been involved in an overflowing tide of the sufferings of Christ; but equally through Christ the overflowing tide of his encouragement has been our support. 6If we are in trouble, it is meant for your encouragement and your salvation. If we are given courage and comfort, it is for your encouragement, encouragement which becomes more real and effective when you bear with gallantry the same sufferings as we too have experienced. 7And our hope for you is well founded, because we know that, if you have to share in the sufferings, you will share in the encouragement too.

8We want you to know, brothers, about the trouble in which we were involved in Asia. It fell upon us with such excessive and intolerable weight that we despaired even of survival. 9So serious was the situation that in our heart of hearts we believed that we had been sentenced to death. But it all happened to make us put our trust, not in ourselves, but in the God who raises the dead. 10It was he who rescued us from such threats of death, and it is he who will rescue us. In him we have set our hope, and he will go on rescuing us. 11All the time you too must be helping us by praying for us; and then the thanksgivings of many will rise to God for us, as they thank God for the gracious gift he gave us, as a result of many prayers.

12There is one thing in which we do take pride—the witness of our conscience that out in the world, and especially in our relationships with you, we have behaved with that simplicity and sincerity which are the gifts of God. It was not worldly wisdom but divine grace that always shaped our conduct. 13There is nothing in the letters we write to you but what you can read and understand—no hidden meanings. 14So far you do understand, but only partly. It is my hope that your understanding will become complete. Then you will come to recognize that on the day of the Lord Jesus your pride is in us, and ours in you.

15It was because I was so confident that you and I understand each other that I first planned to visit you. My plan was to give you a double favour. 16My plan was to travel to Macedonia by way of you, and to visit you again on my way back from Macedonia, and to be despatched by you on my way to Judaea. 17This was my original plan. Can you really believe that I light-heartedly and irresponsibly failed to keep it? Do you really believe that when I make plans I make them like a man with no moral standards at all, so that I can vacillate between yes and no to suit my own convenience? 18As surely as God keeps his word, I did not speak to you in terms of a vacillating and ambiguous yes and no. 19Jesus Christ the Son of God, who was preached among you through us—I mean through Silvanus and Timothy and myself—did not sway between yes and no. So far from that, with him the divine Yes happened. 20In him all God's promises find their yes. That is why when to the glory of God we say 'Amen' we say it through him—'through Jesus Christ our Lord.' 21It is God who assures us of the fact that we along with you belong to Christ; it is God who set us apart for our task; 22it is God who marked us as his own; it is God who gave us the Holy Spirit in our hearts as the foretaste and guarantee of all that is to come.

23I call upon God to witness to the truth of what I am going to say. I stake my life on it. It was because I did not want to hurt you that I did not come again to Corinth. 24It is not that we want to domineer over you in regard to what you are to believe, for you stand firm in the faith. But we are partners with you in your quest for joy.

Chapter 2

A BOUT this I made up my mind—I was determined not to pay you another distressing visit. ₂For, if I distress you, who is there left to cheer me, except the very persons I distressed? ₃This is the very reason why I wrote to you. I wrote because I did not want to come and be distressed by the very people who should have made me happy, for I was quite sure that, if I was happy, you would all be happy too. ₄I wrote that letter to you with a deeply troubled mind and a very sore heart. I wrote it in tears, and my object in writing to you was, not to distress you, but to tell you of my overflowing love for you.

₅If a certain person has been the cause of distress, it was not I whom he has distressed. He has at least—I don't want to overstress the matter —to some extent distressed all of you. ₆This punishment inflicted by the majority of the congregation is sufficient for a man like that. ₇You should therefore rather forgive him and encourage him. You do not want the man to be utterly overwhelmed by excess of grief. ₈I urge you therefore to affirm your love for him. ₉The reason why I wrote that letter was to test you, to see if you were prepared to give me your unquestioning obedience. ₁₀If you forgive a man for anything he has done, so do I. What I have forgiven—if there was anything for me to forgive—I have forgiven for your sake in the presence of Christ. ₁₁For we must not allow Satan to get the better of us. We know his schemes all too well.

₁₂When I went to Troas to tell the good news of Christ, I found that the Lord had provided ample opportunity for me to do so. ₁₃I was worried because my colleague Titus was nowhere to be found. So, instead of waiting there, I said good-bye to them, and left for Macedonia.

₁₄Thanks be to God, for he always gives us a place as sharers in the victory procession of Christ, and, just as at such an earthly triumph, the perfume of incense fills the streets, so God through us has displayed in every place the fragrance of the knowledge of himself. ₁₅You might call us in our work for God the means whereby the fragrance of Christ comes to those who are on the way to salvation and to those who are on the road to ruin. ₁₆For those who are on the way to ruin it is a deadly and poisonous stench; for those who are on their way to salvation it is a living and life-giving perfume. And who is fit for this task? ₁₇We are not like so many who make a commercial racket of preaching God's word. No! When we preach God's message, we do so in transparent sincerity, as sent by God and in the presence of God, and as servants of Christ.

Chapter 3

ARE we beginning to flourish our credentials all over again? Is it possible that we, like some people, need letters of introduction to you or from you? ₂You are our letter, written on our hearts, open to everyone to know and to read. ₃Clearly, you are a letter, written by Christ, and delivered by us. This letter is written, not in ink, but with the Spirit of the living God, written not on stone tablets but on human hearts.

₄We can make such a claim because of our confidence in God through Christ. ₅Not that we are in our own resources adequate for our task, nor would we claim that in ourselves we have achieved anything. Far from it! Any adequacy we have has its source in God, ₆for it is he who has made us capable of being servants of a new kind of relationship with himself, a relationship which is not dependent on any written code of laws, but on the Spirit. For the written law brings death, but the Spirit gives life.

₇If the dispensation of the law, which brings death, and which was carved in letters of stone, came into existence in a blaze of splendour, such splendour that the people of Israel could not look for any length of time at Moses' face because of its brightness, although it was a brightness which was only a transient and fading splendour, ₈how much greater must be the splendour of the dispensation of the Spirit? ₉If the dispensation which ends in man's condemnation by God had its splendour, how much more overflowing must be the splendour which puts a man into a right relationship with God? ₁₀Indeed, what was at one time clothed in splendour is now divested of its splendour, because of the new and surpassing splendour which has emerged. ₁₁For, if that which was transient and fading had its splendour, how much greater must be the splendour of that which lasts for ever?

₁₂With a hope like this, we have always spoken frankly and freely. ₁₃We have not been like Moses, who put a veil over his face to keep the people of Israel from watching the fading splendour, until it finally disappeared. ₁₄Their minds became impenetrably insensitive. To this very day their eyes are covered by the same veil, when they hear the lesson from the old covenant being read in the synagogue. That veil is still not taken away, because it is only when a man becomes a Christian that the veil is destroyed. 15But to this very day, when the writings of Moses are read in the synagogue, the veil still covers their hearts. 16But scripture tells us of Moses that, whenever he went in to speak with the Lord, he took off the veil, and so, whenever a man turns to the Lord, the veil is taken away. 17By the Lord he means the Spirit, and where the Spirit of the Lord is there is liberty, 18and, because there is no veil on our faces, the faces of us all reflect the glory of the Lord. We are thus being transformed into his very likeness, always moving on to greater and greater glory—and this is the work of the Lord, who is the Spirit.

Chapter 4

SINCE, in God's mercy to us, we have been given this piece of service to do, we never get discouraged. 2So far from that, we have renounced those practices which are so shameful that they have to be kept hidden; we do not live like clever rogues, nor have we the trick of twisting the word of God to suit ourselves. No! Our way of trying to commend ourselves to every man's conscience in the sight of God is to bring the truth into the full light of day, 3and, if the good news is being hidden, it is hidden only to those who are on the way to ruin. 4In their case the god of this world has blinded the minds of those who refuse to believe, with the result that they cannot see the light that has dawned on them, the light of the good news of the glory of Christ, who is exactly like God. 5It is not ourselves that we preach. We preach Jesus Christ as Lord, and ourselves as your servants for Jesus' sake. 6It is the God who said: 'Light will shine out of darkness,' who has made his light shine in our hearts to illumine them with the knowledge of the glory of God, seen in the face of Jesus Christ.

7We have this treasure, but we ourselves in whom the treasure is contained are no better than pots of clay. It has to be so, to make it clear that the supreme power belongs to God, and does not have its source in us. 8We are under pressure on every side, but never without a way out. We are at our wit's end, but never at our hope's end. 9We are pursued by men, but never abandoned by God. We are knocked down, but never knocked out. 10We always carry about in our bodies the death that Jesus died, so that in our mortal bodies his life too may be displayed. 11For us life means the continual danger of death for

Jesus' sake, for thus men will be enabled to see the life that Jesus gives in our body, subject though it is to death. 12So death is at work in us, but life is at work in you. 13Scripture says: 'I believed, and therefore I spoke.' We have the same spirit of faith and we too believe, and therefore we too speak. 14For we know that the God who raised the Lord Jesus will raise us too with Jesus, and will bring us into his presence along with you. 15Everything is for your sakes, and the purpose of it all is that grace, as it reaches more and more people, should beget an ever-increasing flood-tide of gratitude to the glory of God.

16That is why we never lose heart. So far from that, even if the physical part of us inevitably deteriorates, spiritually we are renewed every day. 17We have our troubles, but they are transitory and unimportant, and all the time they are producing for us a superlative and eternal glory, which will far outweigh all the troubles. 18And, all through it, it is not the things which are seen but the things which are unseen on which our gaze is fixed, for the things which are seen last only for their brief moment, but the things which are unseen last for ever.

Chapter 5

OUR present earthly body is like a tent in which a man lives temporarily when he is on a journey from one place to another. But we know that, if this temporary home is demolished, we have a house which God will give us, a house not built by any human hands, made to last in heaven for ever. 2In this present body we do indeed sigh deeply for what we have not got, for we long with all our hearts to have the house of our heavenly frame put on us over the top of this one, 3for, if we are so clothed, we will not be found naked. 4We who are in the temporary tent of this body sigh deeply, indeed we do. We feel oppressed, not because we want to strip ourselves of it, but because we want our new frame put on over the top of it, because then our mortality will be engulfed in the ocean of life. 5It is God who has fashioned us for this very purpose, and who has given us the Spirit as the pledge and the first instalment of the life into which we shall one day enter.

6So then we are always in good heart. We know that, so long as this body is our home, we are exiles from the Lord. 7It is by faith that we have to live, not by what we can actually see. 8We are in good heart. We would much prefer to leave our home in this body, and to make

71

our home with the Lord. ₉It is therefore our one ambition to please him, whether we have to stay in this world or whether we have to leave it. ₁₀For all of us must appear before the judgment seat of Christ, and then each of us will receive what is due to him for his actions in this body, whether his conduct was good or bad.

₁₁We know what the fear of God is, and it is in light of that knowledge that we try to persuade men. Our own life lies completely open to God, and, I hope, lies equally open to the verdict of your own conscience. ₁₂We are not trying to give ourselves a testimonial all over again, but we are trying to give you a chance to show your pride in us, because we want you to have an answer to those whose pride is in outward prestige and not in inner character. ₁₃If we seem to have taken leave of our senses, it is for God's sake. If we are sane and sensible, it is for your sake. ₁₄For us there is no escape from the love of Christ, for we have reached the certainty that one died for all men. And, if one died for all, we cannot escape the conclusion that all were dead. ₁₅So he died for us, and therefore all through life men must no longer live for themselves, but must live for him who for them died and was raised to life again.

₁₆The consequence of all this is that from now on we evaluate no man on purely human standards. There was a time when we evaluated Christ by human standards; we no longer do so. ₁₇When a man becomes a Christian, a new act of creation happens to him. His old life is gone for ever; a new life has come into being. ₁₈And the whole process is due to the action of God, who through Christ turned our enmity to himself into friendship, and who gave us the task of helping others to accept that friendship. ₁₉The fact is that God was acting in Christ to turn the world's enmity to himself into friendship, that he was not holding men's sins against them, and that he placed upon us the privilege of taking to men who are hostile to him this offer of his friendship. ₂₀We are therefore Christ's ambassadors. It is as if God was making his appeal to you through us. As the representatives of Christ we appeal to you to accept the offer of friendship that God is making to you. ₂₁For our sakes God identified Christ, who was entirely innocent of sin, with human sin, in order that we through him might be identified with the goodness of God.

Chapter 6

WE are God's collaborators. You have received the grace of God. We therefore urge you not to let it all go for nothing. 2God says:

'In the hour of my favour I heard you,
and in the day of deliverance I came to your help.'

Now the hour of God's favour has come; now the day of deliverance is here. 3We put no obstacle in any man's way, for we do not want our ministry to be open to criticism and blame. 4So far from that, we try to commend ourselves in every circumstance of life as the servants of God. We have met troubles, hardships, desperate situations with unfailing fortitude. 5We have endured the lash, imprisonment, the violence of the mob. We have toiled so hard that we have gone without sleep and food. 6Our life has been marked by purity, by wisdom, by patience, by kindness, by the possession of the Holy Spirit, by love which is utterly sincere. 7Our message has been characterized by the truth and the power of God. Goodness has been our armour both to commend and to defend the faith. 8We have known honour, and we have known disgrace. We have been slandered, and we have been praised. We have been called impostors, and we have spoken the truth. 9No one knows us, and everyone knows us. We have been dying for a long time, and we are still, as you can see, very much alive. We have been through the training-school of suffering, and still survive. 10We have known our sorrows, yet joy is ever with us. To look at us, you would think we are destitute, but we have brought God's wealth to many. On the face of it we have nothing, yet we possess everything.

11I have been very frank with you, my Corinthian friends. My heart is wide open to you. 12On our side there is no restraint at all. If there is restraint, it is in your hearts. 13I use a child's phrase—Let's have a fair exchange! Open your heart the same as I have opened mine.

14Stop trying to run in double harness with unbelievers. Can there be any partnership between right and wrong? Can there be any fellowship between light and darkness? 15What agreement can there be between Christ and Beliar? How can a believer share with an unbeliever? 16How can God's temple ever come to any possible agreement with idols? And we are the temple of the living God. As God has said:

73

'I will make my home amongst them,
and I will move about amongst them,
and I will be their God,
and they will be my people.'

17So then he goes on to say:

'You must come out and leave them.
You must separate yourselves from them, the Lord says.
You must have nothing to do with what is unclean,
and then I will accept you.
18And I will be a father to you,
and you will be sons and daughters to me,
says the Lord, the Almighty.'

Chapter 7

SINCE, then, my dear friends, we are in possession of promises like these, let us purify ourselves from anything that would defile us in body or in spirit, and let us aim at a completely consecrated life lived in the fear of God.

2Make room for us in your hearts. We have wronged no one; we have corrupted no one; we have taken advantage of no one. 3I am not saying this with any thought of condemning you. I have told you already that you are so dear to us that we wish nothing better than to face death and to share life with you. 4I am very frank with you; I am very proud of you. We may be involved in all kinds of trouble, but in spite of that my courage and comfort are complete, and my cup of joy is overflowing.

5Even after we arrived in Macedonia life was as exhausting as ever. We were surrounded by troubles. Outwardly, we were involved in battles; inwardly, we were the prey of fears. 6But God, who brings comfort and courage to the discouraged, cheered us by the arrival of Titus. 7It was not only his arrival which cheered us; it was also the encouraging treatment he received when he was with you, for he told us how much you long to see us, how sorry you are for the past, and how enthusiastically you support me. And all this made me happier yet. 8If I did distress you with that letter, I am not sorry. Even if at the time I was sorry about it—for I see that the letter did distress you, even if it was only for a time—9I am glad now, not glad that you were distressed, but glad that your distress led to a change of mind in you. Your distress was all part of the purpose of God, and was meant to ensure that you should not be the losers by anything we did. 10For distress, accepted as God means it to be accepted, produces a change of mind which leads to salvation, and which brings no regret to follow. But distress, regarded from the world's point of view, brings death. 11Just look at what this distress, sent in God's purpose and accepted in God's way, did for you! Look how eager it made you to show that you are innocent! Look how vexed you were with the whole situation! Look what fear it awoke, what longing to see me, what enthusiasm to defend me, what eagerness that justice should be done! You have proved yourselves to be completely guiltless in the whole affair. 12So then, if I did write that letter to you, it was not for the sake of the wrong-doer, nor was it for the sake of the person wronged. It was to demonstrate to you yourselves in the sight of God your own devotion to me. 13That is why we have been so comforted and encouraged.

But we have more to be thankful for than our personal encouragement.We were more than delighted to hear how happy you all made Titus by the way in which you made it possible for him to rest and relax in your company. 14I am specially gratified by this, because I did sing your praises to him, and I was not disappointed. Everything we have said to you is true, and just so the proud claims we made about you to Titus have been proved true too. 15And he thinks of you all the more affectionately, when he remembers how willing you all were to accept his instructions, and how you welcomed him with fear and trembling. 16It makes me happy to feel with what complete confidence I can depend on you.

Chapter 8

BROTHERS, we want you to know how the grace of God has been given to the congregations in Macedonia. 2Even when they were in the middle of an ordeal of severe trouble, their overflowing joy and their desperate poverty somehow combined to result in an equally overflowing wealth of generosity. 3They gave what they were able to give, I assure you, yes, and more than they were able to give. Absolutely spontaneously, they insistently pled with us for the privilege of sharing in the effort to help God's people in Jerusalem. 3Their generosity far exceeded our hopes. First, they gave themselves to the Lord, and then, because it was God's will, they gave themselves to us.

6It was Titus who was in charge of the first moves in the organisation of this gift. So we have invited him to visit you, and to see that it is brought to its conclusion. 7You are outstanding in every sphere, in faith, in speech, in knowledge, in all kinds of enthusiasm, in your love for us. I want you to be equally outstanding in the giving of this gift.

8When I speak like this, I am not issuing orders. I am using the story of the eagerness of others to test the genuineness of your love. 9You know the gracious generosity of our Lord Jesus Christ. You know that, although he was rich, he chose to become poor for your sakes, to make you rich through his poverty. 10I offer you my own personal opinion about this matter. You were not only the first to do this. As far back as last year, you were the first to want to do it. 11And now, in my opinion, the time has come, when the best thing that you can do for your own sakes is to finish the job, so that your eagerness to plan it may be equalled by your determination to complete it as generously as your resources allow. 12If the will to give is there, God will accept whatever gift a man's resources make it possible for him to give; he does not demand a gift which is beyond a man's resources to give. 13I am not asking you to give in such a way as to bring relief to others and distress to yourselves. What I am asking is that you should share and share alike. 14At the present moment your more than enough should be used to help their less than enough, so that some day their more than enough may be used to help your less than enough. In that way it will be a case of share and share alike. 15As scripture said about the manna:

> 'The man who gathered much
>   did not have too much,
> and the man who gathered little
>   did not have too little.'

16Thank God that he made Titus as enthusiastically eager to help on your behalf as I am myself. 17He welcomed our request to go to you. In fact, he went so eagerly that there was no need to ask him to go. 18We are sending with him that Christian brother whose praise all the congregations sing because of his services to the gospel. 19Not only is he universally praised; on this occasion he has also been elected by the congregations to accompany us on our journey with this gift which we are organizing for the Lord's glory and to show our eagerness to help. 20We are taking every precaution to ensure that no one can find anything to censure in our administration of this generous gift. 21It is our aim to act in such a way that both God and men will recognize that our actions are honourable. ₂₂So with them we are sending our Christian brother. We have had varied and frequent opportunities to test his enthusiasm to be of service, and on this present occasion he is all the more eager to help because of the great confidence he has in you. ₂₃As for Titus, he is my partner and my collaborator in helping you. As for the other brothers, they are envoys of the congregations and a credit to Christ. ₂₄Give them proof of your love, and proof that the proud claims I made about you are true. Such proof will through them reach the congregations.

Chapter 9

IT is superfluous for me to write to you about your aid for God's people in Jerusalem. ₂I know how eager you are to help. In fact, I am always boasting about it to the Macedonians. 'Achaia,' I told them, 'has had everything ready since last year.' The story of your enthusiasm has stimulated and challenged most of them. ₃I am sending the brothers to you because I do not want the proud claims we made for you in this matter to turn out to be quite unjustified, and I want to make sure that you are ready, as I said you were, ₄for I do not want the Macedonians to arrive with me and to find you quite unprepared. It would be acutely embarrassing for us—not to mention you—for us to be so sure of you and for that to happen. ₅I therefore thought it necessary to urge these brothers to go on ahead to you, and to get ready in advance the gift you promised to give. I want everything to be ready in good time, so that it will really look like a gift you wanted to give and not like an extortion that has been forced out of you.

₆Remember this—meagre sowing means meagre reaping; generous sowing means generous reaping. ₇Each person must make up his own mind what he is going to give. He must not give as if giving hurt him, or as if the money was being forced out of him. God loves a man who enjoys giving. ₈God can give you more than enough of every good gift, enough for you to have plenty for yourselves always and in any circumstances, and to have enough left over to contribute to every good cause. ₉As scripture says:

> 'He gave generously to the poor;
> his kindness lasts for ever.'

₁₀God, who gives seed to sow and bread to eat, will give you an abundant supply of seed, and he will make it grow into a plentiful harvest, which will be the result of your charity to others. ⅠⅠHe will always make you rich enough to be generous to every claim on you, and your generosity will make many people thank God when we have distributed it to those who need it; ⅠⅡfor this piece of Christian service, which you have accepted as your duty, not only supplies the needs of God's people, it also overflows in a tide of thanksgiving to God. ⅠⅢThis service, which you are rendering, will be proof to those who receive it that you really are pledged to obedience when you publicly declare your faith in the gospel of Christ. They will also see how generously you share what you have with them and with all. And, when they see this, they will praise God for it. ⅠⅣBecause God gave you a superabundance of his grace, their warmest affection will go out to you, and they will be praying for you. ⅠⅤThank God for his gift, which has no price, and which is beyond words to tell of.

Chapter 10

I PAUL am making a personal appeal to you, and I make it by the gentleness and the kindness of Christ. You say that when I am actually with you, I have nothing to say for myself, but that, when I am away from you, I can put on a brave show. ₂Please do not make it necessary for me to come and act with that same bravery, for I am perfectly certain that I can count on myself to act with boldness against some who declare that, as they see it, our conduct is governed by worldly rather than by Christian motives. ₃True, we live in the world, but the battles we fight are not worldly battles. ₄The weapons we use in our campaign are not the weapons the world uses. They are filled with divine power to demolish strongholds. We demolish false arguments, ₅and every towering obstacle, erected to prevent men from knowing God. We capture every thought, and compel it to become obedient to Christ. ₆Once you have rendered complete obedience to us, we are ready to punish any act of disobedience.

₇Look at the obvious facts of the situation. If anyone is sure that he belongs to Christ, he had better take another look at himself, because we belong to Christ just as much as he does. ₈The Lord gave me my authority to enable me to build up your spiritual life, not to demolish it. And suppose I have been making apparently excessive claims for it, my claims will in fact be completely vindicated. ₉I do not want you to get the idea that I am the kind of person who would try to scare you by means of my letters. ₁₀Some of you, I know, do allege: 'His letters are weighty and powerful, but he has no kind of presence when you meet him, and as a speaker he is beneath contempt.' 11Anyone who talks like that would do well to take into his calculations the fact that what we are in word in our letters in our absence we are in action in our presence.

12Of course, we would not venture to include ourselves among those who have such a high opinion of themselves, or to compare ourselves with them. They measure themselves by themselves; they are a mutual admiration society—a senseless proceeding. 13But we do not make claims that go beyond all proper limits. Our claims are limited to the sphere which God allotted to us—and that sphere includes you. 14For we are not exceeding our permitted boundary, as we would be if our limit did not extend to you, for indeed we were the first to reach you with the good news of Christ. 15We make no claims at all in regard to the work that others have done in spheres which are beyond our limits. Our hope is that, as your faith increases, we may have a still greater and greater place among you, but always a place within our limits. 16Then we will be able to bring the good news to regions beyond you, without making any claims about work done in some one else's sphere. 17As scripture says: 'If a man is going to take pride in anything, let him take pride in what God has done.' 18It is not the man who recommends himself who is approved; it is the man whom God recommends.

Chapter 11

I WISH that you would bear with me in a little folly. Please do! 1I am jealous for you with God's jealousy, for it was I who arranged your engagement to Christ as a chaste virgin bride to her one husband. 3But I am afraid that your minds may be corrupted, and that you may be seduced from your single-hearted devotion to Christ, just as the serpent with his clever lies seduced Eve. 4For, if someone comes and preaches another Jesus to you, different from the Jesus we have preached, or if you receive a different Spirit from the Spirit you received, or a different gospel from the gospel you were given, you have no difficulty in tolerating it. 5I do not believe that I am in any way inferior to these super-apostles. 6I may be inexpert in speech, but I am not in knowledge; and this is something that always and in all circumstances we have made perfectly clear.

7I accepted a low place to enable you to have a high one, for I preached the good news to you, and I did not take one penny piece for doing so. Was this where I went wrong? 8I robbed other congregations by taking pay from them to enable me to serve you. 9When I was staying with you, and when I was hard up, I bothered none of you for help. The brothers who came from Macedonia supplied me with all I needed. It was my principle, and it always will be, never to be a burden to you. 10As surely as the truth of Christ is in me, I will allow nothing anywhere in Achaea to despoil me of my pride in being able to make this claim. 11Why? Because I do not love you? God knows I do love you!

12I will go on doing as I am doing, because I want to deny every opportunity to those who are looking for an opportunity to make it seem that the work on which they pride themselves is the same as ours. 13Such men are not real apostles; they are not honest workmen; they disguise themselves as apostles of Christ. 14And no wonder, for Satan himself can disguise himself as an angel of light. 15It is therefore easy enough for his servants to disguise themselves as servants of goodness. But in the end they will get what their conduct deserves.

16I repeat, I do not want anyone to think me a fool. But even if you do think I am, accept me as a fool. Give me a chance to do just a little talking about the claims I am proud of. 17This isn't a Christian way to talk. All right! In this business of talking about the things I am proud of, I am talking like a fool. 18There is a lot of talking about human prestige going on; I am going to do some talking too. 19You are wise men; you find no difficulty in suffering fools gladly. 20You are quite prepared to put up with it, if someone treats you like slaves, if some one makes a meal of you, if someone preys on you, if some one gives himself airs, if someone slaps you across the face. 21If it comes to behaviour like that—to my shame!—you can charge me with being too much of a weakling to act like that. But, if anyone dares to make proud claims—this is fools' talk—I can be just as daring. 22Are they Hebrews? So am I. Are they Israelites? So am I. Are they descendants of Abraham? So am I. 23Are they servants of Christ? This is madman's talk—I am a better servant than they are. I have worked far harder. I have been in prison far oftener. I have been scourged far more severely. I have often been in peril of my life. 24Five times I received the forty less one lashes from the Jews. 25I have been beaten with rods three times. I have been stoned once. I have been shipwrecked three times. I have been twenty-four hours in the water. 26I have been frequently on the road. I have been in dangers from rivers, in dangers from brigands, in dangers from my fellow-countrymen, in dangers from the Gentiles, in dangers in cities, in dangers in the lonely places, in dangers at sea, in dangers from Christians who were no Christians. ₂₇I have worked and I have toiled. I have often gone without sleep. I have been hungry and thirsty. I have often had to go without food. I have known cold and exposure. ₂₈Apart altogether from the things I pass over, there is the daily pressure on me which my concern for all the congregations brings. ₂₉Who is weak without me sharing his weakness? Who is led astray without my burning concern?

₃₀If I must make my claims, I will base them on the things which show my weakness. ₃₁The God and Father of our Lord Jesus, he who is blessed for ever, knows that I am telling the truth. ₃₂In Damascus the governor under King Aretas ringed the city of the Damascenes with guards to ensure my arrest, ₃₃but I was lowered in a basket through an opening in the wall, and thus escaped his clutches.

Chapter 12

I MUST keep on talking about myself and about my claims—not that it does any good. I come now to visions and revelations given by the Lord. ₂I knew a man who was a Christian, and fourteen years ago—I have no idea whether it was a physical experience or a vision, God knows—he was snatched up to the third heaven. ₃I know that this man—I have no idea whether it was a physical experience or a vision, God knows—₄was snatched up into paradise, and that there he heard things which cannot be reduced to speech, and which no human being has any right to utter. ₅For a man like that I will make claims; for myself I will make no claims, except about the things which show my weakness. ₆If I do wish to make claims, they will not be the claims of a fool, for what I say will be the truth. But I spare you this, because I do not want anyone to have a higher opinion of me than he can form on the basis of what he sees me do and hears me say. ₇To prevent me therefore from being too uplifted by the superlative nature of the visions I experienced, I was given a physical condition which brought me pain like a stake twisting in my body. It was Satan's messenger, sent to batter me, to keep me from being too uplifted. ₈Three times I pled with God about this, and asked him to take it away. ₉'My grace is all you need,' he said to me. 'It is in weakness that my power becomes most powerful.' I shall therefore find my highest joy and my greatest pride in my weakness, for then the power of Christ will settle on me. 10So then, I have no objection to weaknesses, to insults, to hardships, to persecutions, to desperate situations for Christ's sake, for it is when I am weak that I am strong.

11I am behaving like a fool—it is you who forced me to. It ought to have been you who were vouching for my claims. I am in no way inferior to your super-apostles, even if I am a mere nobody. 12The things which are the characteristic hall-marks of any apostle happened among you. You saw me live a life in which again and again I passed the breaking-point and did not break, a life marked by demonstrations of the power of God in action, by wonders and by miracles. 13In what way were you made to feel inferior to the rest of the congregations, apart from the fact that I myself never bothered you for help? Forgive me for wronging you like that! 14I am ready to come to visit you for the third time. I will not be a nuisance to you. It is not your money I want; it is you. Children should not be saving up to help their parents; it is parents who should be saving up to help their children. 15As for you, I will most gladly spend all I have, and be myself completely spent for you. If I love you too much, will that make you love me less? 16We can take it as agreed that I was not a burden to you. But there is another charge—constitutionally I am supposed to be an unscrupulous rascal, and I am supposed to have trapped you by trickery. 17Did I take advantage of you through any of the people I sent to you? 18I asked Titus to visit you, and I sent our colleague along with him. ·Are you going to say that Titus took advantage of you? Did he and I not act under the guidance of the same Spirit? Did we not follow exactly the same course of action?

19Are you under the impression all along that it is to you we have been making our defence? It is before God, and as Christians, that we speak. My dear friends, everything we have said, we have said for the upbuilding of your spiritual life. 20I am afraid that, when I come, I may find you different from what I would like you to be, and that you may find me different from what you would like me to be. I am afraid that I may find in your society quarrelling and jealousy, explosive tempers and unbridled personal ambitions, slanderous talk and malicious gossip, swelling pride and general disorder. 21I am afraid that, if I come again, God may humiliate me in front of you, and that I may have to shed tears over many who sinned in the past, and who have not repented of their impurity, their sexual immorality, and the blatant licentiousness of their lives.

Chapter 13

I AM coming to visit you for the third time. Scripture says: 'Every fact must be established by the evidence of two or three witnesses.' ₂I have a warning to give to all those who sinned in the past, and to everyone else. I warned you before, on my second visit to you, and now in my absence I warn you again, if I come to you again, I will show no mercy. ₃You are looking for proof that Christ speaks through me—and you will get it. In his dealings with you he is no weakling; so far from that, he demonstrates his power among you. ₄True, it was in weakness that he died on the cross; but it is the power of God which gives him continuing life. True, we are one with him, and therefore we share his weakness, but, when we have to deal with you, the source of our life, as it is with his life, is the power of God.

₅It is yourselves you must examine, to see if you really are living in the Christian faith. It is yourselves you must test. You must be well aware that Christ Jesus is within you—unless you have failed the test altogether. ₆I hope that you will realize that we have been tested and have not failed the test. ₇It is our prayer to God that we may have to do nothing to hurt you. It is not that we want it demonstrated that we can meet the test. The one thing we want is that you should do the right thing, even if it should look as if we had failed the test. ₈For we cannot act against the truth; we can only act for it. ₉We are quite happy to be weak, provided you are strong. Our one prayer is for the complete correction of your lives. ₁₀My one reason for writing this letter to you before I come to visit you is to make sure that, when I do arrive, I will not have to deal with you severely with the authority which the Lord gave me, an authority to be used always to build up and never to pull down.

₁₁And now, brothers, good-bye! Try to correct your lives. Don't reject my appeals to you. Agree with one another. Live at peace with one another, and the God of love and peace will be with you. ₁₂Greet one another with the kiss of peace. All God's people send you their good wishes.

₁₃The grace of the Lord Jesus Christ, the love of God, the fellowship the Holy Spirit gives be with you all.

Introduction to the Letter to the Romans

THE Letter to the Romans was written from Corinth in A.D.57. It tells us itself of its occasion. One of the schemes which lay closest to Paul's heart was the collection given by the younger churches for the mother church at Jerusalem (1 Corinthians 16.1-4; 2 Corinthians 8 and 9). Here was a way really to mark the unity of the church, and really to demonstrate the concern for each other of each of its parts. When Paul wrote Romans the collection had been made. He was on the point of conveying it to Jerusalem, and he was conscious of the dangers that awaited him there, dangers which were in fact to lead to his arrest and his imprisonment. But Paul was thinking ahead. After he had been to Jerusalem, he planned to go to Spain. He had never been in Rome, and he had neither founded nor visited the church there. But his purpose was to visit the Roman church on his way to Spain (Romans 15.24-33). So, to prepare them for the visit which he hoped to pay, he wrote this letter.

Of all Paul's letters the Letter to the Romans comes nearest to being a treatise. It has been described by the adjective 'testamentary'. This is Paul's testament, the essence of his faith.

He begins by demonstrating that neither the Jewish nor the Gentile world had been able to get into a right relationship with God (chapters 1 and 2). The failure is total and universal (3.10-18).

True, the Jews possessed the law, but even the law was powerless to help. It in fact fomented sin, for it often happens that to forbid a thing is the surest way to awaken the desire for it (chapter 7).

What then is the way to a right relationship with God? It is the way of faith. That is the way that Abraham took. Circumcision and the law had nothing to do with it, because God blessed Abraham, and Abraham became the friend of God, before he was circumcised and long before the law ever came into the world.

The essence of the right relationship with God is not the hopeless task of keeping the law; it is justification by faith. In this great phrase Paul is using the word justification in a special sense. To justify a person ordinarily means to find reasons why a person was right to act as he did. But God justifies the ungodly (4.5), and it cannot mean that God finds reasons to prove that the sinner is right to be a sinner. In Greek the word for to *justify* is *dikaioun*. Greek verbs which end in *-oun* do not mean to make a person something. They mean to treat, reckon, account a person as something. And when Paul speaks about God justifying the sinner, he means that God treats the sinner as if he had been a good man. God treats the rebel as if he had been a loving son. And it is justification *by faith*, because it is only when we have absolute faith in what Jesus tells us about God that we can think about God like that at all.

Man as man is a sinner, for Paul holds to the fact of original sin (chapter 5). By that Paul does not mean a taint or a tendency to sin. He means that, because of the oneness, the solidarity, of the human race all men literally sinned in Adam. In chapter 5 he sets out his logical argument for this in five steps.

i. Adam sinned by breaking a definite commandment of God.

ii. The consequence was that death entered the world, for death is the consequence of sin.

iii. Between Adam and Moses there was no law, for the law was not yet given. There could therefore be no transgression of a law which did not exist.

iv. In spite of that men continued to die.

v. Why? Because, such is the solidarity of the human race, that all men had literally sinned in Adam, and therefore died (5.12).

The only thing that can reverse this process is the coming of Jesus Christ into the world, for, by becoming one with him, as we were once one with Adam, we can become alive (5.17-19).

But the question arises, if God treats the bad man as if he had been good, does this give us a licence to sin? Far from it! In baptism we become one with Jesus Christ, and then the old life of sin is left behind, and a new life is begun. Baptism is like dying to sin and rising to righteousness with Jesus Christ (chapter 6). And this new life is for ever supported by the Spirit helping us (chapter 8).

In chapters 9-11 Paul deals with the problem of the Jews. Why did they, God's chosen people, reject God's Son, when he came? That too, Paul finds, is all part of the purpose of God. The Jews rejected Christ in order that the gospel might go out to the Gentiles. But the day will come when the Gentiles will bring the Jews back in again, and Jew and Gentile will both be gathered in.

With Paul theology and ethics always go hand in hand, and chapters 12-15 are chapters of ethical guidance and advice. The letter ends with a note of introduction for Phoebe, and a list of greetings to Paul's friends.

Here in this letter we are faced with Paul's greatest principle—salvation by faith alone. As it has been put: 'All is of grace, and grace is for all.'

The Letter to the
ROMANS

Chapter 1

THIS is a letter from Paul ⁊to all those in Rome whom God loves, and who have been called by him to be his people. Grace to you and every blessing from God our Father and from the Lord Jesus Christ.

₁I write to you, because I have been called by God to be an apostle, and because I have been specially commissioned to bring men the good news of God. ₂It was this good news that God promised long ago through his prophets in the sacred scriptures. ₃The good news is about his Son, who in his human lineage was a direct descendant of David, ₄and who, because of the supreme holiness of his character, was by the resurrection designated beyond all question the Son of God. It is Jesus Christ our Lord I mean, ₅and it is through him that I have received the privilege of an apostleship, the task of which it is for his sake to lead all men of all nations into that submission to him which is the product of faith. ₆You too are included among those to whom my apostleship extends, for to you too the invitation of Jesus Christ has come.

₈I want to begin by saying that I thank my God through Jesus Christ for you all, because the report of your loyalty to Christ is being broadcast all over the world. ₉God himself can tell you, the God whom I serve with every fibre of my being in my work for the good news of his Son, that I unceasingly remember you in my prayers. ₁₀I constantly pray that at long last it may be God's will that a way should open up for me to visit you. ₁₁For I long to see you, because I want to share with you some of the gifts the Spirit gives, so that the foundations of your faith may be strengthened, ₁₂or rather, that you and I may both be cheered and encouraged, when we meet, I by your faith and you by mine. ₁₃I want you to know, brothers, that I have often had it in my mind to come to visit you, although up to now something has always happened to stop me, because I have harvested men for God all over the Gentile world, and I would like to do so among you too. ₁₄I owe a duty to Greeks and to non-Greeks, to the intellectuals and to the simple folk. ₁₅That is why I am so eager to tell the good news to you in Rome too.

₁₆I am quite sure that the good news will never let me down, for it is the saving power of God to everyone who accepts it, first to the Jews, then to the Greeks. ₁₇In it God's way of setting men right with himself is revealed as beginning and ending in faith, just as it stands written: 'It is the man who is right with God through faith who will find life.'

₁₈No one can fail to see that the wrath of God from heaven is directed against all the impious wickedness of men who are wickedly obstructing the progress of the truth. ₁₉What man can know about God is clear for them to see, for God made it clear to them. ₂₀Ever since the world was created, the invisible nature of God, his eternal power and deity, are clear for the mind to see through the things which God has made. Men are therefore left without defence, ₂₁because, although it was open to them to know God, they gave him neither praise nor gratitude. They allowed themselves to become involved in futile speculations which did nothing but darken their foolish minds. ₂₂Their alleged wisdom was in fact folly. ₂₃They substituted images, made in the shapes of mortal men, and of birds and beasts and reptiles, for the glory of the immortal God.

₂₄God therefore allowed them to go their own way, until, driven by the desires of their hearts, they ended up in a moral degeneration in which they were partners in dishonouring their own bodies. ₂₅This they did because they were men who substituted their untruth for God's truth. They have given their reverence and their worship to that which is created instead of to the Creator—praise be to him for ever and ever! Amen. ₂₆God therefore allowed them to go their own way, until they ended up as victims of their own dishonourable passions. Their women substituted unnatural intercourse with each other for natural intercourse with men. ₂₇In the same way, men abandoned natural intercourse with women, and were inflamed with passion for each other. Men perpetrated shameless things with men, and brought on themselves the inevitable consequences which such misguided conduct was bound to bring. ₂₈They deliberately refused to recognize God. God allowed them to go their own way, until they reached a stage when they were mentally and morally vitiated, and did things which no man ought to do. ₂₉They are filled with every kind of wickedness and evil, with the desire for that which no man has any right to desire, with viciousness. Their lives are permeated with envy, murder, quarrelling, underhand plotting, malignity. 30They became whispering scandal-mongers, slanderers, God-forsaken and God-defying, arrogant, braggarts, ingenious in the discovery of novelties in vice, disobedient to parents. 31They are without conscience, without honour, without family affection, without pity. 32Although they were well aware that in the judgment of God those who are guilty of such conduct deserve to die, they not only practise it themselves, but they also applaud others who practise it.

Up to this point Paul has been addressing the Gentile world. Now he turns to address the Jews.

Chapter 2

So then, my friend, if you, whoever you are, presume to pass judgment on other people, you have left yourself with no defence, for in the very act of judging some one else, you condemn yourself, for you yourself do exactly the same things as you condemn in others. 2You say that you are well aware that God's judgment rightly falls on people who do the kind of things that I have just been talking about. 3So then, you, my friend, condemn people who do things like that, and yet you yourself are in the habit of doing exactly the same things. Is it your idea that you yourself will escape God's judgment? 4Or, are you contemptuously trading on the wealth of God's kindness and forbearance and patience? Are you not aware that the kindness of God is meant to lead you to repentance?

5In the stubbornness and impenitence of your hearts you are storing up wrath for yourself on the day of wrath, the day when God's just judgment will burst upon the world. 6For God will settle accounts with every man on the basis of what each man has done. 7To those who in inflexible devotion to goodness seek for glory and honour and immortality, he will give eternal life. 8For those who in selfish ambition are disobedient to the right and obedient to the wrong, there will be anger and wrath. 9There will be trouble and anguish for the soul of every man whose conduct is evil, for the Jew first and for the Greek too. 10There will be praise and honour and every blessing for everyone whose conduct is good, for the Jew first and for the Greek too. 11For God has no favourites.

12If a man does not know the law, and sins, he will perish, although it will not be on the basis of the law that he is judged. If a man does know the law, and yet sins, it is on the basis of the law that he will be judged. 13If a man does no more than hear what the law says, that does not make him innocent in God's sight; but if a man does what the law commands, he will be innocent. 14When the heathen who do not possess any law do by natural instinct what the law demands, although they possess no law, they are their own law. 15, 16They show that the requirements of the law are written on their hearts. On the day when God judges the secrets of men through Jesus Christ, as my gospel says he will, their conscience will agree with the verdict, and their own inmost thoughts will accuse them, or even sometimes excuse them.

17You bear the name of 'Jew'; you have a law on which to lean; you pride yourself on your relation to God; 18you know his will; your instruction in the law gives you the ability to distinguish between competing moral choices; 19you are confident that you are qualified to be a leader of the blind, a light to those who are in darkness. 20You claim to be able to provide discipline for the foolish and instruction for the child. You believe that in the law you possess the embodiment of knowledge and truth. 21Well then, in view of all this, if you claim the right to teach others, what about teaching yourself?

You preach against stealing—do you yourself steal? 22You forbid adultery—do you yourself commit adultery? You abhor idols—do you yourself rob temples? 23You pride yourself that you have a law—do you yourself dishonour God by breaking the law? 24As scripture says: 'The name of God is insulted in heathen society because of your conduct.'

25Circumcision is only of value, when your whole conduct is based on the law; but, if you habitually break the law, your circumcision might as well be uncircumcision. 26If a man who is not circumcised obeys the just requirements of the law, surely he can be regarded as being as good as circumcised? 27The man who is physically uncircumcised, but who perfectly keeps the law, will judge you, if you habitually break the law, in spite of your written code of laws and your circumcision.

28The real Jew is not the man who is a Jew in visible externals, nor is external bodily circumcision the real circumcision. 29The real Jew is the man who is a Jew in his inner being, and the real circumcision is a thing of the heart. It is a spiritual thing, not conformity to any set of rules and regulations. When a man is really like that, he will receive the praise, not of men, but of God.

Chapter 3

WHAT then has a Jew got that no one else has got? Or, what is the use of circumcision? ₂Much in every way! First and foremost, there is the fact that the Jews were entrusted with the sacred words of God. ₃What then if some of them were unfaithful? Is their infidelity going to destroy God's fidelity? ₄God forbid! Even if every man was proved to be a liar, God must still be true. As scripture says of him: 'You must be proved right when you speak; you must triumph when you are on trial.'

₅You might plead that in point of fact our wickedness provides an opportunity for the proof of God's justice. What are we to deduce from that? Are you going to go on to argue that it was therefore unjust of God to launch the divine wrath upon us? This is the way in which the human mind might argue. ₆God forbid! On that argument, how could God judge the world at all? ₇Your argument is: 'If the effect of my falsehood is to enable God's truth to bring him more and more glory, why then am I still condemned as a sinner? Why should we not do evil in order that it may issue in good?' ₈This is in fact the very argument that some people slanderously allege that I use. An argument like that bears its condemnation on its face.

₉What then? Do we Jews enjoy any advantages? By no means! We have already charged all men, Jews and Gentiles alike, with being under the domination of sin. ₁₀It stands written:

'There is none who is righteous, not even one,
  ₁₁there is none who understands,
    there is none who seeks for God.
  ₁₂All have swerved aside, and all have gone bad;
    there is no one who practises goodness,
    not one single one.
  ₁₃Their throat is an open tomb,
    they use their tongues for treachery,
    the venom of asps is on their lips.
    ₁₄Their mouth is full of cursing and bitterness;
    ₁₅their feet are swift to shed blood.
  ₁₆The way they have chosen can bring them nothing
    but ruin and wretchedness.
  ₁₇They know nothing of the way which brings blessedness,
    ₁₈they never think of reverence for God.'

19We know that everything the law says, it says to those who are within the sphere of the law. This is designed to produce a situation in which no man is left with any defence, and in which the whole world has become subject to God's judgment. 20And this is brought about by the fact that no one can ever get into a right relationship with God through doing the things which any legal system prescribes. All that any legal system can do is to make men aware of what sin is.

21But a new situation has arisen. The world has been shown a way of being put into a right relationship with God apart from any kind of law. It is nevertheless a way which is already attested by the law and the prophets. 22It is a way of being put into a right relationship with himself which God has provided. That right relationship is reached through faith in Jesus Christ, and it is offered to all who have faith. There is no distinction. 23All have sinned; all have lost the divine glory which they were meant to have. 24And all can enter into a right relationship with God as a free gift, by means of his grace, through the act of deliverance which happened in Jesus Christ. 25It was God's purpose that Jesus Christ should be the one through whose sacrificial death sin can be forgiven through faith. Such a sacrifice was necessary to demonstrate God's justice, because in his forbearance he had not exacted from the men of past generations the penalty which their sins deserved. 26And it was necessary in order to demonstrate his justice at this present time, by showing that, although he is just, he nevertheless puts the man who has faith in Jesus into a right relationship with him.

27What then becomes of pride in our achievements? It is excluded. On what principle is it excluded? Is it on the principle that our achievement in keeping the law brings merit? No, it is excluded because the only thing that matters is faith. 28It is our argument that a man is put into a right relationship with God by faith, and that the performance of the things which any law demands has nothing to do with it. 29Is God the God of the Jews only? Is he not the God of the Gentiles too? Indeed, he is the God of the Gentiles too. 30He must be, if it is true that God is one. And since he is one, he will bring those who are circumcised into a right relationship with himself by means of faith, and he will bring those who are not circumcised into the same relationship through faith. 31Does this then mean that we are using faith to abolish the law? God forbid! We are placing the law on a firmer foundation.

Chapter 4

FROM the point of view of physical descent Abraham is our fore-father. What are we to say that his special discovery was? ₂We can say that, if Abraham was put into a right relationship with God through his own achievement, he has legitimate grounds for pride. But in point of fact, in regard to his relationship with God he has nothing on which to pride himself. ₃What does scripture say? 'Abraham took God at his word, and that act of faith was accepted as putting him into a right relationship with God.' ₄If a man produces some piece of work, his pay is credited to him, not as a gift given to him, but as a debt owed to him. ₅But, if a man does not claim to have produced anything, but simply puts his faith in the God who brings godless men into a right relationship with himself, then his faith is accepted as putting him into a right relationship with God. ₆You get exactly this situation in David's saying about the congratulation of the man whom God accepts apart altogether from anything that he has done:

₇'O the bliss of those who have broken the law
    and have been forgiven,
    whose sin has been put out of sight.
₈ O the bliss of the man whose sin is not debited against him
    by the Lord.'

₉Does this description of bliss apply only to those who are circumcised, or also to those who are uncircumcised? Let me repeat what I said: 'Abraham's act of faith was accepted as putting him into a right relationship with God.' ₁₀How was it so accepted? Was it while he was circumcised, or while he was uncircumcised? It was in fact not while he was circumcised, but while he was uncircumcised. ₁₁He received the badge of circumcision as the hall-mark of that right relationship with God, which was the result of his faith, before he was circumcised. This happened in order that he might be the father of all who have faith while they are uncircumcised, so that this faith may be credited to them as righteousness. ₁₂And it happened in order that he might also be the father of those who are not only circumcised, but who also take that same way of faith as our father Abraham did, while he was still uncircumcised.

₁₃The promise to Abraham and to his descendants was that Abraham should enter into possession of the world. It was not through any kind of law that this promise came to him; it came through that right relationship with God, which is the result of faith. 14For, if it was through any kind of law that they entered into this possession, then faith is emptied of all its meaning, and the promise is cancelled. 15Law and wrath are bound to go hand in hand. But where no law exists, there can be no such thing as a breach of the law. 16This is why the whole matter is based on faith. It was so based that it might all move in the realm of grace. This had to be so, in order to confirm the promise that was made to every one of Abraham's descendants. This promise was not made only to those who base their life on the Jewish law; it was also made to those who base their life on that same faith as Abraham had. For Abraham is the father of all of us. 17As scripture says of him: 'I have appointed you as father of many nations.' This promise was made in the presence of God, the God in whom Abraham had put his faith, the God who makes the dead live, the God whose summons goes out to things which do not yet exist, as if they already did exist. 18When there were no grounds for hope, Abraham took his stand on hope, and by an act of faith he did believe that he would become the father of many nations, as God had said—'So many will your descendants be.' 19His faith did not waver, although he was well aware that his body was as good as dead—for he was about a hundred years old—and that the life was gone from Sarah's womb. 20He never allowed lack of faith to make him question God's promise. So far from that, his faith was so strengthened that he praised God 21in the unshakable conviction that God is able, not only to make promises, but also to make his promises come true. 22That is why it was credited to him as righteousness. 23The fact that it was so credited is recorded, not only for Abraham's sake, 24but for our sake also, because it is also going to be credited to those who believe in him who raised from the dead our Lord Jesus, 25who was delivered to death that our sins might be forgiven, and raised to life that we might enter into a right relationship with God.

Chapter 5

IT is through faith that we have been put into a right relationship with God. We therefore are at peace with him because of what our Lord Jesus Christ has done for us. 2Through him we possess the entrance into that grace in which we stand, and our pride is in the glorious hope that God has given us. ₃More than that—we take a pride in our troubles, for we know that trouble produces fortitude, ₄and fortitude produces a character which has stood the test, and character produces hope, ₅and this hope never lets us down, for God's love has been poured into our hearts through the Holy Spirit who has been given to us. ₆For, while we were still in all our weakness, in God's good time Christ died for godless men. ₇It is very unlikely that anyone would be willing to die for a just man; it is just barely possible that some one might even dare to die for a good man. ₈But God proves how much he loves us by the fact that Christ died for us while we were still sinners. ₉Already, here and now, we have been put into a right relationship with God through the death of Jesus. Since that is so, we can be even more confident that through him we will be saved from the wrath to come. ₁₀It was the death of his Son which restored us to friendship with God, even when we were hostile to him. And, if that is so, now that we are God's friends, how much surer we can be that we will be saved by his continuing life! ₁₁And this is not merely a future hope. Here and now we can take a legitimate and joyful pride in our relationship with God, made possible through the work of our Lord Jesus Christ, for by him we have been made friends with God.

₁₂It was through one man that sin gained an entry into the world, and through sin came death. And so death spread to all men, because all had sinned. ₁₃Before there was law in the world, there was sin, but so long as there is no law, sin is not debited to anyone's account. ₁₄Now, although that is so, from the time of Adam until the time of Moses death exercised its sway over even those who had not actually sinned in the way in which Adam broke the command he had received.

In Adam the one who was to come was foreshadowed. ₁₅But there is no comparison between Adam's sin and God's free gift. By one man's sin the whole of mankind was involved in death. But the grace of God and the free gift, which came through the grace of the one man Jesus Christ, came in a far greater flood-tide of power to all mankind. ₁₆There is no comparison between the effect of God's free gift and the effect of that one man's sin. The verdict which followed the one sin was a verdict of condemnation; but the gift of grace which followed so many sins leads to a verdict of acquittal. ₁₇It is true that because of one man's sin death held sway because of that one man; but it is still truer that those who receive the far more effective power of grace with the free gift of a right relationship with God will reign in life because of what the one man Jesus Christ has done. ₁₈So then, the conclusion is that just as one man's act of sin resulted in condemnation for all men, so one man's act of righteousness resulted in life-giving acquittal for all men. ₁₉For, just as by one man's sin the rest of mankind were constituted sinners, so by one man's obedience the rest of mankind can be constituted righteous. ₂₀Into this situation there entered the whole legal system, with the inevitable result that breaches of the law increased. But the increase in sin was more than counter-balanced by the far greater increase in grace, ₂₁so that, to counteract sin's deadly reign, grace might hold sway in that right relationship with God, which leads to eternal life, and which was made possible through the work of Jesus Christ our Lord.

Chapter 6

WHAT inference are we to draw from all this? Are we—the suggestion is yours—to keep on sinning so that there may be more and more grace? ₂God forbid! We are men who have died to sin. How can we go on living in it? ₃You must be well aware that all of us who have been baptized into union with Christ have by that baptism been united with him in his death. ₄Through this baptism, which united us with him in his death, we were buried with him, so that, just as Christ was raised from the dead by the glory of the Father, we too should live a completely new kind of life. ₅If we have been so united with him that we died a death like his, we shall also be so united with him that we shall experience a resurrection life like his. ₆For we are well aware that the person we were in our pre-Christian days has been crucified with him, so that our sin-dominated personalities might be destroyed and we might be released from our slavery to sin. ₇Once a man is dead he cannot be prosecuted for his sin. ₈If we shared Christ's death, we believe that we shall share his risen life too. ₉We know that the resurrected Christ is never again to die; he is removed for ever from the sway of death. ₁₀For in the death he died he died once and for all to sin; in the life he lives he lives continuously to God. ₁₁So you must regard yourselves too as dead to sin, and in your Christian life you must regard yourselves as living continuously to God.

₁₂So then, there must be an end to the reign of sin in your mortal body. Sin must no longer command your obedience to the body's desires. ₁₃You must no longer place the various parts of your body at the service of sin, to be used as weapons in the hand of wickedness. You must take your decision to place yourselves at the service of God,

96

as those who were dead and are alive, and you must offer every part of your body to God, to be used as weapons in the hand of all that is right. ₁₄For sin will no longer hold sway over your life, for you are no longer under law; you are under grace.

₁₅What then? Are we to use the fact that we are not under law but under grace as a reason for sinning? God forbid! ₁₆It must be obvious to you that, if you place yourselves at anyone's service as his obedient slaves, you are the slaves of the person to whom you give your obedience. So you may choose to be the slaves of sin, and thereby end in death, or, you may choose to dedicate yourselves to obedience, and thereby end in a right relationship with God. ₁₇You were once slaves of sin, but, thank God, you chose to give whole-hearted obedience to the pattern of teaching to which you have been committed. ₁₈You have been emancipated from sin, and you have become slaves of goodness. ₁₉I am using human language, because it is all that weak human nature can grasp. For just as you yielded your bodies and all their parts to the servitude of impurity and to a lawlessness which issued in ever more lawlessness, so you must now yield them to goodness and walk the way to holiness. ₂₀When you were the slaves of sin, goodness exercised no control over you. ₂₁What good did it do you then? It left you nothing but a legacy of shame. For these things cannot end in anything but death. ₂₂But now there is a new situation. You are emancipated from sin and enslaved to God. And the result is that you are on the way to holiness, and the end of that road is eternal life. ₂₃For death is the wage that sin pays, but God's free gift is eternal life, lived in union with Christ Jesus our Lord.

Chapter 7

YOU must be well aware, brothers, for I am speaking to those who are familiar with a legal system, that the law has authority over a man only during his life-time. ₂A married woman is legally bound to her husband during his life-time. But, on the death of her husband, so far as she is concerned, the marriage law ceases to exist. ₃So then, if during the life-time of her husband she lives with another man, she is branded as an adulteress. But, on the death of her husband, she is no longer bound by the marriage law, and consequently she is not an adulteress if she marries another man. ₄Just so, my brothers, as far as the law is concerned you too are dead, because you have become part of the crucified body of Christ. This was to end your marriage to the law, and to allow you to be married to someone else, I mean to him who was raised from the dead. This was meant to make our lives fruitful for God. ₅So long as we were dominated by our lower nature, our sinful passions were active in our bodies, because the law incited them to work, thereby making our lives fruitful for death. ₆But a new situation has arisen. Our relationship to the law is completely obliterated. The law once held us in its grip, but now, as far as the law is concerned, we are dead. And the result is that we serve God in the new life of the Spirit, and not in the old life of the letter of the law.

₇What conclusion are we to draw from all this? Are we to conclude that the law and sin are one and the same thing? God forbid! All the same, this is true—I would not have known what sin is unless through the action of the law. What I mean is, I would not have known what it is to covet unless the law had said: 'You must not covet.' ₈It was through the commandment that sin found a bridgehead in me, and thus wakened in me all kinds of wrong desires. For where there is no law, the life goes out of sin. ₉I once enjoyed life in a state in which I knew nothing about the law. Then the commandment came into my life and sin sprang to life, ₁₀and life became death for me. So far as I was concerned that very commandment which was meant to bring life brought death. ₁₁For it was through the commandment that sin gained a bridgehead in me, and seduced me, and through it for me turned life into death. ₁₂So the law in itself is holy, and the commandment in itself is holy, just and good.

₁₃Did then that which was good turn life into death for me? God forbid! It was sin that turned life into death for me, and it did so by using to produce death that which in itself is good. This happened that the true characteristic of sin should be exposed, and that through its perverted use of the commandment sin should be shown to be superlatively sinful. ₁₄We know that the law is spiritual, but I am made of flesh and blood. I have been sold into sin's slavery. ₁₅My own actions are a mystery to me. What I do is not what I want to do but what I hate doing. ₁₆The fact that I do not want to do what I do proves that I agree that the law is good. ₁₇The fact is that it is not I who do it; it is the sin which has its home in me. ₁₈I am well aware that, as far as my lower nature goes, nothing good has its home in me. For the ability to wish to do the fine thing I possess; the power to do it I do not possess. ₁₉It is not the good that I want to do that I actually do; it is the evil that I do not want to do that I keep on doing. ₂₀If I do what I do not want to do, it is no longer I who do it. It is the sin which has its home in me which does it. ₂₁I find it to be a principle of life that, even when I want to do the right thing, the one thing that I can do is the wrong thing. ₂₂In my inner self I delight in the law of God, ₂₃but I am aware of a different law, operating in the physical parts of my body, and waging a constant campaign against the law which my reason accepts, and reducing me to captivity to that sinful principle which operates in my physical body. ₂₄I am a wretched creature. Who will rescue me from this body which turns life into death? ₂₅God alone can through Jesus Christ our Lord! Thanks be to him! So then, I am in a situation in which with the spiritual part of my nature I serve God's law, and with the lower part of my nature I serve sin's law.

Chapter 8

WE can therefore say that there is now no condemnation for those whose life is one with the life of Christ. ₂For, when through union with Christ Jesus I came under the law of the life-giving Spirit, I was emancipated from the law of death-bringing sin. ₃For what the law was unable to do—that is to say, to effect this emancipation from sin—because human nature rendered it impotent and ineffective, God did. He did it by sending his own Son with a human nature like our sinful nature. He sent him to deal with sin, and to deal with it as a human person. ₄He thus left sin without a case, and, because he won the victory over sin, the legitimate demand of the law is satisfied in us too, in us whose lives too are no longer directed by our lower nature, but by the Spirit. ₅Those who have allowed their lower nature to become the rule of their lives have an attitude to life which is dominated by their lower nature; those who have taken the Spirit as the rule of their lives have an attitude to life which is dominated by the Spirit. ₆To have a mind dominated by our lower human nature is to turn life into death; to have a mind dominated by the Spirit is to have real life and every blessing. ₇For the mind that is dominated by our lower human nature is hostile to God, for it neither does, nor ever can, submit to God's law. ₈It is impossible for those who are ruled by their lower human nature to please God. ₉But you are not ruled by your lower human nature; you are ruled by the Spirit, if it is true that the Spirit of God has really made his home in you. No one who does not possess the Spirit belongs to Christ. ₁₀But, if Christ is in you, the physical part of you may be doomed to death because of sin, but the spiritual part of you is destined for life because

of the right relationship with God into which you have entered. 11If
the Spirit of God, who raised Jesus from the dead, has his home in
you, God, who raised Christ from the dead, will give life even to your
bodies, subject to death though they are, through the power of his
Spirit, who comes and makes his home within you.

12So then, brothers, our duty is not to the lower part of our human
nature, nor are we bound to live as it dictates. 13For, if you live as the
lower part of your human nature dictates, you are on the way to
death. But, if by the help of the Spirit you put to death the life your
animal instincts make you want to live, you will really live. 14Only
those who are led by God's Spirit are God's sons. 15This Spirit you
have received does not leave you in the old relationship to God of
terrified slavery. No! This Spirit you have received makes you a son
in the family of God, and through this Spirit we can cry to God:
'Father, dear Father!' 16This same Spirit joins with our spirit in the
assurance that we really are children of God. 17If we are children of
God, then we are heirs to all the promises of God. Yes, fellow-heirs
with Christ, if our aim in life is to share his glory by sharing his
suffering.

18In my reckoning, whatever we are called upon to suffer in this
present time cannot compare with the glory which is going to burst
upon us. 19For the whole created universe eagerly and expectantly
awaits the day when God will show the world who his sons are. 20For
the whole created universe was involved in a process of meaningless
frustration, not of its own choice, but by the decree of God who did so
subject it. But the situation was never hopeless, 21because even the
created universe itself will be liberated from its servitude to death's
decay, and will come to enjoy the glorious liberty of the children of
God. 22For we know that up to now the whole created universe
groans in all its parts, like a woman in the birthpangs. 23This is not
only true of the created universe. We too, even although we have
received in the Spirit a foretaste of what the new life will be like, groan
inwardly, as we wait longingly for God to complete his adoption of us,
so that we will be emancipated from sin, both body and soul. 24It is
for this hope that we have been saved. But, if what we hope for is
already there to be seen, it is not hope at all. For why should anyone
go on hoping and waiting for what is already there for him to see?
25But, if we keep on hoping for what we cannot see, then eager hope
and patient waiting are combined.

26Even so, the Spirit helps us in our weakness. We do not know what
to pray for, if we are to pray as we ought, but the Spirit himself inter-

cedes for us, when the only prayers that we can offer are inarticulate cries. 27He who penetrates into the inmost depths of the human heart knows what the Spirit means, for it is by God's will that the Spirit pleads for God's people. 28We know that through the work of the Spirit all the different events of life are being made to work for good, for those who keep on loving God, those whom his purpose has called. 29For long ago, before they ever came into being, God both knew them and marked them out to become like the pattern of his Son, for it is his purpose that his Son should be the first and eldest of a great family. 30Not only did God mark out his own; he also called them. This call was an invitation to enter into a right relationship with himself, and for them this right relationship is the way to glory.

31What then are we to conclude in view of all this? If God is for us, who is against us? 32If God did not spare his only Son, but gave him up for the sake of us all, can we not be sure that with him there is nothing that he will not freely give us? 33Who can bring any charge against God's chosen ones? Not God, for it is God who acquits us. 34Who can condemn? We have as our intercessor Christ who died. Rather, I ought to say, Christ who was raised from the dead, and who is now at God's right hand. 35Who can part us from Christ's love for us? Shall trouble or distress or persecution or famine, nakedness or danger or the sword? 36As scripture says:

'All the day long we face death for your sake;
we are regarded as sheep to be slaughtered.'

37But he who loved us has enabled us, not only to overcome these things, but to emerge triumphant over them. 38I am quite sure that nothing in death or in life, no angel and no superhuman being, nothing in the world as it is and nothing in the world as it will be, 39no power of the heights and no power of the depths, nor anything else in all the created universe will be able to part us from the love which God has shown us in Christ Jesus our Lord.

Chapter 9

WHEN I say that there is a great grief and an unceasing anguish in my heart, I am speaking the truth as a Christian. This is no lie, and my conscience under the direction of the Holy Spirit supports me in everything I say. 2I could pray that a curse to banish me from the presence of Christ might fall upon me, if such a fate would save my brothers, my natural kith and kin. ₄For they are Israelites. God made them members of his own family. The glory, the covenants, the law, the worship of the Temple, his promises—he gave them all to them. ₅Theirs are the fathers, and in human descent it is from them that the Messiah comes. God who is over all be blessed for ever and ever! Amen.

₆And yet it is not as though the word of God had completely failed, for it is not all who are descended from Israel who are really Israel. ₇Not all are Abraham's real children because they happen to be his physical descendants. In point of fact scripture says: 'It is through Isaac that the line of your descendants will be traced.' ₈This means that it is not those who are simply physically Abraham's children who are the children of God. It is the children born as a result of God's promise who are reckoned as Abraham's real descendants. ₉The statement of the promise in fact is: 'At this time next year I will come, and Sarah will have a son.' ₁₀There is further proof to be added to this. Rebecca had two children, and our ancestor Isaac was the father of both. ₁₁Before they were even born, and before they had done anything good or bad, she was told: 'The older will be the servant of the younger.' ₁₂This was to ensure that the choice between them, involved in the purpose of God, might be permanently based, not on any human achievement, but simply on God's call. ₁₃This is exactly what scripture says: 'I loved Jacob, but I hated Esau.'

₁₄What then are we to conclude? Are we to say that this is injustice on the part of God? God forbid! ₁₅He says to Moses: 'I will have mercy on whom I choose to have mercy, and I will have pity on whom I choose to have pity.' ₁₆So then everything depends, not on man's will, or effort, but on God's pity. ₁₇Scripture says to Pharaoh: 'I have brought you on to the stage of history for the sole purpose of making you the object of the demonstration of my power, and so that the story of what I have done may be told all over the world.' ₁₈So then, if God wills to show mercy on anyone, he does so; and if God wills to make anyone more stubborn than ever, he does so.

₁₉If that is so, you may well argue, why does he blame me? Obviously no one can resist what God wills. ₂₀I might well ask you, my friend, who are you to answer God back? Surely you would not give the created the right to say to the creator: 'Why did you make me like this?' ₂₁Has the potter not the right to do what he likes with the clay? Has he not a perfect right to make out of the same lump one article which is designed for the drawing-room, and one which is designed for the kitchen? 22God must have wished to demonstrate his wrath and to display his power. In spite of that he bore very patiently with the men and women he had created, men and women who deserved nothing but his wrath and who were fit for nothing but destruction. 23What if it was for the sake of the men and women whom he had created to be the objects of his pity, the men and women he had prepared for glory before they ever came into the world, that he held his hand, because he wanted to show them the wealth of that glory of his, which he had always intended for them? 24Such are we, and it is we whom he has called, not only from among the Jews, but from among the Gentiles too. 25As he says in Hosea:

'To those who were not a people
    I will give the title of "my people";
and to her who was not loved,
    I will give the title of "the beloved";
26and in that very place where they were told:
    "You are not my people,"
they will be given the title
    "sons of the living God".'

27Isaiah's prophetic proclamation about Israel is: 'The sons of Israel may be as many in number as the sand of the sea, but it is only the remnant who will be saved. 28Finally and summarily, the Lord will do on earth what he said he would do.' 29As Isaiah said in a previous passage:

'If the Lord of hosts had not left us children,
    we would have become like Sodom,
    and we would have been like Gomorrah.'

30What then are we to conclude? We must conclude that the Gentiles who were not trying to find a right relationship with God received such a relationship, and it was a relationship which was the result of faith, 31while Israel which was looking for some kind of law through which it might enter into a right relationship with God found no such law. 32And why? Because they looked for it, not as the product of faith, but, as they believed, the product of their own performance. They stumbled over the stumbling-stone. 33As scripture says:

'I will place a stumbling-stone in Sion,
    a rock to make men trip,
but he who puts his faith in him will not be disappointed.'

Chapter 10

BROTHERS, with all my heart I long and pray to God for their
salvation. ₂This I will say for them—they have a zeal for God, but
it is superficial and ill-informed. ₃They have failed to realize that it is
God who brings men into a right relationship with himself, and they
have tried to establish such a relationship by their own unaided
efforts, and have refused to submit to God's method of bringing it
about. ₄It is Christ who completes what it was the goal of the law to
do, and who thereby opens a right relationship with God to everyone
who has faith.

₅About the right relationship with God which is based on trying to
keep the law, Moses writes that, if a man did obey the law, he would
find life in the right relationship that such obedience would bring—
an impossible task! ₆But this is how the message of the right relationship which comes through faith speaks: 'Do not say to yourself:
"Who will go up to heaven?" (that is, to bring Christ down), ₇or,
"Who will go down to the abyss?" (that is, to bring Christ up from
the dead).' ₈No! What does it say?

'The word is near you,
on your lips and in your heart.'

The word it is speaking about is the message of faith which we are
proclaiming to you. ₉For if you publicly assert with your lips your
belief that Jesus is Lord, and if you believe with all your heart that God
raised him from the dead, you will be saved. ₁₀For it is the heart's
faith which brings a man into a right relationship with God, and it is
the open assertion of that faith with the lips which brings a man to
salvation. ₁₁For scripture says: 'No one who has faith in him will
have his hope disappointed.' ₁₂For there is no difference between
Jew and Greek. The same Lord is Lord of all, and his wealth is enough
for all who call upon him. ₁₃For, 'Everyone who appeals to the name
of the Lord will be saved.'

₁₄How then can men appeal to someone in whom they have not
put their faith? And how can they put their faith in someone of
whom they have never heard? And how can they hear without someone to bring them the message of him? ₁₅And how can they bring the
message of him unless they have been sent by God to do so? As
scripture says: 'How welcome is the coming of the messengers who

bring good news!' 16But not all have accepted the good news. For
Isaiah says: 'Who has believed the message we brought?' 17So then,
faith must be the consequence of hearing the message, and the
message comes through the word which tells of Christ and which was
sent by him. 18But, I ask, have they not in fact heard? Indeed they
have, for

> 'Their voice has gone out to the whole earth,
> and their words to the limits of the inhabited world.'

19But, I ask, if that is so, did Israel not realize the meaning of the
message? First, a quotation from Moses:

> 'I will treat a nation that is no nation
> in such a way as to make Israel jealous,
> I will treat a foolish people
> in such a way as to make Israel angry.'

20Then Isaiah, greatly daring, says:

> 'I was found
> by those who were not looking for me,
> I made myself seen
> by those who were not asking about me.'

21But to Israel he says: 'All the day long I have held out my hands in
appeal to a disobedient and hostile people.'

Chapter 11

I ASK then, did God reject his people? God forbid! How could I
agree to that, I who am an Israelite, a descendant of Abraham, a
member of the tribe of Benjamin? 2God did not reject his people
whom before time began he chose to be his own. No! Do you not
know what scripture says in the story of Elijah? Do you not remember how Elijah pleads with God against Israel? 3'Lord,' he said, 'they
have killed your prophets. They have demolished your altars. I alone
am left, and they are out for my life.' 4But what is God's answer to
him? 'I have left for myself seven thousand men who have never
knelt to Baal in worship.' 5So at this present time there is a remnant,
and the choice of it is due to grace. 6And, if their choice is due to grace,
then that choice is no longer a consequence of their own performance, for, if that were so, grace would no longer be grace. 7What

then? Israel as a whole failed to obtain what it sought; the chosen few did obtain it. The hearts of the rest were made impervious to the appeal of God. 8As scripture says:

'God gave them a spirit benumbed into insensibility,
eyes designed not to see, ears designed not to hear,
a state which has lasted right down to this present day.'

9David too says:

'Let their well-spread table become a trap and a snare;
let it become the very thing which causes their ruin
and trips them up, and brings them retribution.
10Let their eyes be blinded to take away the ability to see,
let their backs be bent for ever beneath their burden.'

11So then I ask, did their error involve them in irretrievable disaster? God forbid! So far from that, it was through their sin that salvation went out to the Gentiles, and the intention was that the inclusion of the Gentiles should awaken Israel to envy. 12If their sin enriched the world, and if their failure enriched the Gentiles, how much more will it mean when no longer the remnant but the whole nation becomes the people of God?

13It is to you Gentiles that I speak. I am an apostle to the Gentiles, and I magnify my office, 14for my one aim is somehow to provoke the people of my own flesh and blood to envy the Gentiles their privilege, and so to succeed in saving some of them. 15If the rejection of the Jews results in the reconciliation of the world to God, to what can you compare their reception, except to life from the dead? 16If the first handful of dough is consecrated, then the whole lump must be consecrated, and if the root is consecrated, the branches must be consecrated too.

17If some of the original branches of the olive-tree have been lopped off, and if you, like a wild olive, have been grafted in in their place, and if you thereby become sharers in the rich root of the olive-tree, 18you must not pride yourselves on being superior to the original branches. If you do feel moved to such a pride, remember that it is not you who support the root, but the root which supports you. 19So then, you will say: 'The branches were lopped off to allow me to be grafted in.' 20Very well! It was their refusal to take the way of faith that caused them to be lopped off; it was your acceptance of the way of faith that put you where you are. Your feelings should not be feelings of pride, but of awe. 21For, if God did not spare the original branches, he will not spare you either. 22So then, remember both the kindness and the severity of God. Remember his severity to those who fell into sin; remember his kindness to you. In that kindness you must continue to trust, and not in your own achievement. Otherwise you too will be cut away. 23As for them, if they cease to persist in their refusal to take the way of faith, they will be grafted in again. For God is able to graft them in again. 24For, if you were cut out from what is naturally a wild olive-tree, and if against all nature you were grafted into a cultivated olive-tree, how much more will they who are the original olive-branches be grafted back into the stock which is their own?

25Brothers, I want you to grasp this divine secret which God has revealed to his own, because I do not want you to get the impression of your own cleverness. The insensitiveness of the hearts of the Jewish nation is not a total insensitiveness, and it will only last until the full number of the Gentiles has come in. 26After that has happened, all Israel will be saved. As scripture says:

> 'The Rescuer will come from Sion,
>   he will drive all godlessness from Jacob.
> 27This is the covenant I will make with them,
>   when I take away their sins.'

28Looked at from the point of view of the gospel, they have incurred God's hatred, and it is all for your sake. Looked at from the point of view of God's eternal choice, they are still loved by God for the sake of the fathers. 29For God cannot go back on his gifts or his call. 30You once disobeyed God, but now through their disobedience you have found God's mercy. 31Just so, in the present situation they have been disobedient, but God's purpose is that they should find mercy through the mercy which you have found. 32For God made all men prisoners to disobedience, for it was his purpose to show mercy to all.

33How deep is the wealth of the wisdom and knowledge of God! His decisions are beyond man's mind to understand! His ways of working are beyond man's power to trace!

> 34'Who has understood the mind of the Lord?
>   Or, who has been his counsellor?
> 35 What man ever gave anything to God
>   that put God in his debt?'

36For everything had its beginning from him, and owes its continued existence to him, and will find its end in him. Glory be to him for ever! Amen.

Chapter 12

So then, brothers, I urge you by the mercies of God to offer your bodies to God as a living, consecrated sacrifice, which will delight God's heart, for that is the only worship which a rational being can offer to God. ₂Stop always trying to adjust your life to the world's ways. You must get a new attitude to life; your whole mental outlook must be radically altered, so that you will be able to decide what God's will is, and to know what is good and pleasing to him, and perfect.

₃I say to everyone among you—and it is the special place which God's grace gave me which gives me the right to say it—you must not have a more exalted idea of your own importance than you have any right to have. You must use your mind to arrive at a sober estimate of yourself, an estimate based, not on your own performance, but on the measure of faith that God has given to each of you. ₄In a single body there are many parts, and each part has its own function. ₅In the same way, although we are many, our union with Christ makes us one body, and we are individually living parts of one another. ₆The grace of God has given us each special gifts, which are all different, and each man must use his gift. If a man has the gift of prophecy, he must use it in proportion to his faith. ₇If he has the gift of administration, he must use it in administration. If he is a teacher, he must use it in teaching. If by his words he can lift up men's hearts, he must use them to do so. ₈If a man can contribute to someone else's need, he must do so generously. If he has the gift of leadership, he must exercise it with enthusiasm. If he is helping those in distress, he must do so gladly.

₉Your love must not be a superficial pretence. You must hate evil, and you must give your unshakable loyalty to what is good. ₁₀Your brotherly love must make you one loving family. You must lead the way in honouring each other. ₁₁Your zeal must never flag. You must keep your enthusiasm at boiling-point. You must always be serving the Lord. ₁₂You must be filled with optimistic joy. You must meet trouble with the power to pass the breaking-point and not to break. You must persevere in prayer. ₁₃You must share what you have with God's people who are in need. You must be eager to practise hospitality. ₁₄You must bless your persecutors; you must bless them and not curse them. 15You must be joyous with the joyful, and you must be sad with the sorrowful. 16You must live in harmony with one another. You must not be haughtily contemptuous; you must be happy to seek the society of people who in the world's eyes are quite unimportant. You must avoid conceit. 17You must not live on the principle that one bad turn deserves another. You must aim only at the things which all men regard as lovely. 18If it is possible, so far as it depends on you, your personal relationships with everyone must be good. 19My dear friends, never be out for vengeance. Leave room for the wrath of God, for scripture says: 'Retribution belongs to me,' the Lord says. 'I will repay.' 20So far from that, if your enemy is hungry, give him something to eat. If he is thirsty, give him something to drink. For, if you do that, you will make him feel the pangs of burning shame. 21Never let yourself be defeated by evil, but always defeat evil with good.

Chapter 13

EVERYONE must submit to the governing authorities. All authority owes its existence to the act of God, and the existing authorities were instituted by God. 2Since this is so, to rebel against authority is to resist what God has ordered. Those who do resist will have no one to blame but themselves for any punishment they will incur. 3It is not good conduct but bad conduct which has any reason to fear the magistrates. Do you want to be in a position in which you need have no fear of those in authority? If your conduct is good, you will receive nothing but approval from them. 4The man in authority is the servant of God, and he exists for the sake of what is good. If you are guilty of misconduct, then you must necessarily be afraid. It is not for nothing that a man in authority has the power of life and death. He is the servant of God, and his function is to exercise punishment and to demonstrate the divine wrath on evil-doers. 5It is therefore necessary to submit to authority, not simply because you are afraid of God's wrath, but also because you respect your own conscience. 6For the same reason you must pay your taxes, for the magistrates are God's officers, intent on carrying on this very duty of maintaining good order. 7Pay all men what is due to them. If you are due tribute to anyone, pay it. If you are due taxes to anyone, pay them. Give respect to whom respect is due, and honour to whom honour is due.

Be in debt to no one—apart from the debt of love which you

always owe to one another, for to love your neighbour is to fulfil the whole law. ₉The commandments, 'You must not commit adultery; you must not murder; you must not steal; you must not covet'—and any other commandment there may be—are all summed up in this one sentence: 'You must love your neighbour as yourself.' ₁₀Love never wrongs its neighbour. Therefore love is the law's complete fulfilment.

₁₁Further, you are well aware what moment in history we have reached. You know that it is high time to wake from sleep, for our salvation is closer to us than when we first took the decision to believe. ₁₂The night is almost over. Day is almost here. We must therefore strip ourselves of the conduct which belongs to the dark, and we must clothe ourselves in the armour of soldiers of the light. ₁₃We must behave ourselves with propriety, as those who live in the full light of day. We must have nothing to do with revelry and drunkenness, with debauchery and shameless immorality, with quarrelling and jealousy. ₁₄You must clothe yourselves with the Lord Jesus Christ, and you must stop planning how to satisfy the desires of yourselves at your worst.

Chapter 14

WELCOME the man who is weak in the faith, but do not begin by introducing him to discussions about debatable matters. ₂One man has faith enough to believe that he may eat all kinds of food. Another, who is weaker in the faith, feels compelled to be a vegetarian. ₃The man who believes that food laws are quite irrelevant must not look down with contempt on the man who carefully observes them; and the man who carefully observes them must not think that he has the right to judge the man who thinks them unnecessary, for God has welcomed him. ₄Who are you to pass judgment on another man's servant? It is by the judgment of his own master that a man stands or falls. And, what is more, he will stand, for the Lord can make him stand. ₅One man regards one day as more holy than another day; another man regards all days as alike. Each man must make up his own mind, and reach his own conviction, on such a matter. ₆If a man feels like that about a certain day, he does so with the honour of God in his mind. If a man eats meat, he eats with the honour of God in his mind, because he says his grace for what he eats. If a man does not eat meat, he abstains from eating with the honour of God in his mind, for he too says his grace to God. ₇No man's life concerns only himself, and no man's death concerns only himself. In life we live for the Lord; ʒin death we die for the Lord. In life and in death we belong to the Lord. ₉The very reason why Christ died and came to life again was to make him Lord of the dead and of the living. ₁₀As for you, why do you pass judgment on your brother? Or, why do you regard your brother with contempt? We shall all stand at God's judgment seat. ₁₁For scripture says:

'As I live, says the Lord,
    every knee shall bow to me,
    and every tongue shall acknowledge me
    as God.'

₁₂So then, each of us will have to answer for himself to God.

₁₃So then, let us resolve to stop passing judgment on each other. Instead of that, let us resolve never to place an obstacle in any Christian's way, and never to do anything which would make it easier for him to go wrong. ₁₄My Christian faith gives me the knowledge and the conviction that there is nothing which in itself is impure. Only if a man thinks that something is impure does it become impure to him. ₁₅But, if your fellow-Christian is distressed because of the food you eat, your conduct is no longer based on love. You must not let what you eat become the ruin of a man for whom Christ died. ₁₆You must not do the right thing in such a way that it gets you a bad reputation. ₁₇For the Kingdom of God does not consist in eating or not eating, and drinking or not drinking. It consists in justice and peace and joy—and all in the atmosphere of the Holy Spirit. ₁₈To serve Christ in this way is to please God and to win the approval of men. ₁₉We must then concentrate all our efforts on the things which produce right relationships between one another and which build us into a real fellowship. ₂₀Do not for the sake of food undo all that God has done. It is quite true that all things are pure, but it is quite wrong for any man to make the Christian way more difficult for others by what he eats. ₂₁The really fine thing is to abstain from eating meat, and to abstain from drinking wine, and to abstain from anything which makes the way more difficult for your fellow-Christian. ₂₂By all means retain your faith, but retain it as a personal matter between you and God. He is a fortunate man who has no self-questionings when he comes to a decision that a thing is right. ₂₃And, if a man eats, and is still not sure whether he is doing the right thing or not, he stands condemned for eating, because his action does not spring from faith, and what is not based on faith is sin.

Chapter 15

I^F our faith is strong, it is our duty to accept the scruples of those whose faith is not so strong as ours as part of the burden which we must carry. It is not our duty to consider only ourselves. 2It is our neighbour that each of us must consider, and our aim must be his good and the upbuilding of his faith. 3For Christ certainly did not consider only himself. Far from it, for scripture says:

> 'The reproaches of those who reproached you
>   fell upon me.'

4Everything that was written long ago was written for our instruction. Its aim was to enable us, through the fortitude and the encouragement which the scriptures give, to maintain our hope. 5I pray that God, from whom fortitude and encouragement come, may grant to you to live in Christlike harmony with each other,6so that your hearts and voices may be united in a chorus of praise to the God and Father of our Lord Jesus Christ.

7Welcome each other, therefore, as Christ welcomed you—and all for the glory of God. 8I mean that Christ became the servant of the Jewish people to confirm God's promises to the fathers, and thus to demonstrate that God is true to his word, 9and also to give the Gentiles reason to praise God for his mercy. As scripture says:

> 'Therefore I will praise you among the Gentiles,
>   and I will sing to your name.'

10And again it says:

> 'Gentiles, rejoice with his people!'

11And again:

> 'Praise the Lord, all Gentiles, and let all the peoples add
>   their praise to him.'

12And again, Isaiah says:

> 'The root of Jesse shall come,
>   he who will be raised up to rule the Gentiles,
>   and on him shall the Gentiles set their hope.'

13May the God who gives you hope make your faith an experience

which is filled with joy and peace, so that by the power of the Holy
Spirit your hearts may be brimming over with hope.

₁₄I personally, my brothers, have no doubt at all that you are full of
goodness, filled with all kinds of knowledge, and well able to give
advice to each other. ₁₅All the same, in parts of this letter I have
written to you with some considerable boldness, to remind you of
what you already know. ₁₆My warrant for so doing is the special
privilege given to me by God. ₁₇This privilege made me the servant
of Christ Jesus to the Gentiles, and gave me the telling of the good
news as my priestly task. It gave me as my aim the task of making the
Gentiles an offering, consecrated by the Holy Spirit, and thus acceptable to God. ₁₈I will venture to speak only of the things in which I
was the agent of Christ to lead the Gentiles into obedience to him by
my words and by my actions, ₁₉and by the compulsion of miraculous
demonstrations of the power of God in action, and by the power
which the Holy Spirit gave me. And so from Jerusalem right round to
Illyricum I have completed the proclamation of the good news
of Christ. ₂₀My ambition has always been to tell the good news of
Christ not in places where the name of Christ is already known, for I
do not want to build on a foundation which some one else has laid.
₂₁My ambition is expressed in the words of scripture:

> 'Those to whom the story of him has never been told
>   shall see him,
> and those who have never heard of him
>   shall understand.'

₂₂That is why I was repeatedly prevented from coming to visit you.
₂₃As things now are, I have no longer any scope for work in these
parts. I have been longing to visit you for many years, and I hope to
do so now, ₂₄whenever I go to Spain. For I hope to see you on the way
through, and to have your help on my way there, after I have had the
pleasure of spending some time with you. ₂₅At the moment I am off to
Jerusalem with help for God's people there. ₂₆For Macedonia and
Achaia decided to make a contribution to the poor members of
God's people in Jerusalem. ₂₇This they decided to do, and indeed they
are in their debt. For, if the Gentiles have shared in the spiritual
blessings of the Jews, they are bound to regard it as nothing less than
a duty to give them help in material things. ₂₈So then, when I have
completed this business, and when I have delivered the proceeds of
the collection intact, I shall leave for Spain, and I shall visit you on

the way. 29I know that when I come to you, I will come with a full blessing from Christ.

30I appeal to you by our Lord Jesus Christ, and by the love which the Spirit inspires, to join with me in straining every nerve in prayer to God for me, 31that I may escape the clutches of the unbelievers in Judaea, and that God's people in Jerusalem may welcome the help I bring to them, 32because through God's will I want to come joyfully to you and so to be rested and refreshed in your company. 33God, the giver of peace, be with you all. Amen.

Chapter 16

THIS is to introduce to you our fellow-Christian Phoebe, who is active in the service of the congregation at Cenchreae, 2and to ask you to give her a Christian welcome, worthy of God's people. Please assist her in any matter in which she may need your help, for she has given help to many, myself included.

3Give my good wishes to Prisca and Aquila, who have so often shared with me in Christian work, 4for they have risked their lives for my life. Not only I, but all the Gentile congregations too, are grateful to them. 5Give my good wishes to the congregation which meets in their house. Give my good wishes to my dear Epaenetus, who was the first convert to Christ in Asia. 6Give my good wishes to Mary, who has worked so hard among you. 7Give my good wishes to Andronicus and Junias, my fellow-countrymen and my fellow-prisoners, for they are distinguished members of the apostolic company, and they were Christians before I was. 8Give my good wishes to Ampliatus, my dear Christian friend. 9Give my good wishes to Urbanus, who shares with me in the work and in the fellowship of Christ, and to my dear Stachys. 10Give my good wishes to Apelles, that sterling Christian. Give my good wishes to the Christian members of the household of Aristobulus. 11Give my good wishes to my fellow-countryman Herodion. Give my good wishes to the members of the household of Narcissus who are Christians. 12Give my good wishes to Tryphaena and Tryphosa, who are such strenuous workers in the Lord's service. Give my good wishes to my dear Persis, who has toiled so hard in the Lord's service. 13Give my good wishes to Rufus, that choice Christian, and to his mother, who was a mother to me too. 14Give my good wishes to Asyncritus, to Phlegon, to Hermes, to Patrobas, to Hermas, and to all the members of their Christian community. 15Give my good wishes to Philologus and to Julia, to Nereus and to his sister, and to Olympas, and to all God's people who are members of their Christian community. ₁₆Greet each other with the kiss of peace. All the congregations of Christ send their good wishes.

₁₇I urge you, brothers, to keep your eye on those who are trouble-makers and who make it easier for others to go wrong, in defiance of the teaching you have received. Have nothing to do with them. ₁₈For men like that are the servants, not of our Lord Jesus Christ, but of their own appetites, and with their smooth and flattering talk they seduce the hearts of innocent people. ₁₉The story of your Christian obedience is known to everyone. You make me very happy, but I want you to be experts in goodness and innocent of evil. ₂₀It will not be long until the God of peace so crushes Satan that you will trample on him. The grace of our Lord Jesus be with you.

₂₁Timothy, my colleague, sends you his good wishes, and so do Lucius and Jason and Sosipater, my fellow-countrymen. ₂₂I Tertius, who took down this letter from Paul's dictation, send you Christian greetings. ₂₃Gaius who has given me hospitality, and whose hospi-tality embraces the whole congregation, sends you his good wishes. Erastus, the city treasurer sends you good wishes and so does our Christian brother Quartus.

₂₅To him who is able to make you stand four-square,
as the good news I preach and the message Jesus Christ proclaimed promised that he can,
that good news and that proclamation which came in the revelation of the secret purpose of God,
that purpose which was for long ages veiled in silence,
₂₆but has now been full disclosed and through the writings
of the prophets and the command of God made known to
all the Gentiles, to lead them to the obedience
which is born of faith—
₂₇to the God who alone is wise be glory for ever
through Jesus Christ. Amen.

Introduction to the Letter to the Ephesians

THE Letter to the Ephesians has been called 'The Queen of the Epistles'. But it presents us with certain problems.

Some of the oldest and the best manuscripts of the Greek New Testament do not have the words *in Ephesus* in the first verse of the letter. In them the letter, as the Revised Standard Version has it, is written: 'To the saints who are also faithful in Christ Jesus.' We further note that, unlike the usual letters, it has no personal greetings at the end. The simplest explanation of these facts is that the letter we know as the Letter to the Ephesians was in fact a circular letter, which was sent out to the churches of Asia Minor, and Ephesus among them. If it is a circular letter, it is all the more important, for it was meant, not for one congregation, but for a group of congregations.

There are some who do not think that it is one of Paul's letters at all. They feel that the style and the thought are so different from Paul's usual style and thought that he cannot have written it. But it must be remembered that this letter comes from very near the end of Paul's life, and that it was written when he was in prison, and therefore had far more time to write it than he had to write the other letters which he had to dash off on the spur of the moment to meet some threatening situation in one of his churches.

The Letter to the Ephesians was written about A.D.62, and it is one of a group of letters—Colossians, Philemon and Philippians are the others—which were written when Paul was in prison in Rome. Certain that he would receive no justice from the Jews, Paul had exercised the right of a Roman citizen, and had appealed direct to the Emperor (Acts 25.10,11). We know that he was in prison for at least two years before his case came up (Acts 28.30), and during this period he wrote these letters. In the Letter to the Ephesians he more than once mentions the fact that he was in prison when he was writing (3.1; 6.1; 6.20).

The theme of the letter is simple, but very great. We may state it in four propositions.

i. This is a world of disunity. Man himself is a disunity, torn by his passions and desires. And this disunity obviously separates a man from God (2.1-10). Further, men are separated from each other. There is the dividing wall which separates the Gentile from the Jew (2.1-22).

ii. It is God's aim to bring unity into this literally distracted world. This is the purpose of God.

iii. That unity of man with himself, of man with man, and of man with God is to be brought about in and through Jesus Christ (1.9; 4.13). That is to say, God's instrument of reconciliation is Jesus Christ.

iv. But Jesus Christ has ascended to heaven, and he too needs an instrument, and his instrument, the body through which he works, is the church (1.23; 5.23).

So then the thought of the Letter to the Ephesians revolves round two closely connected propositions—God's instrument of reconciliation is Jesus Christ, and Jesus Christ's instrument of reconciliation is the church.

As a missionary, it is Paul's great privilege to bring this message to the Gentiles; and as a pastor, it is his task to lay before the church the life the Christian must live.

The Letter to the
EPHESIANS

Chapter 1

THIS is a letter from Paul, who became an apostle of Jesus Christ because God willed it so, to God's consecrated people in Ephesus, the loyal Christians there. 2Grace to you and every blessing from God our Father and from the Lord Jesus Christ.

3Praise to the God and Father of our Lord Jesus Christ, for he in the heavenly places has blessed us with every spiritual blessing, because our life is bound up with the life of Christ. 4It was through this connection with Christ that before the creation of the world God chose us to be his own consecrated people, and to live lives faultless in his sight. In his love 5he had already destined us for adoption into his own family through the work of Jesus Christ, for this was the purpose of his will. 6All this he did that men might praise that glorious grace of his which he gave to us in his Beloved and through no merits of our own. 7It is in and through Christ and the sacrifice of his life that we have been liberated, a liberation which means the forgiveness of sins. It all happened because of the wealth of his grace. 8This grace he gave us in superabundance to equip us with all wisdom and with all insight. 9He revealed to us the secret of his will, and of the purpose which long ago he had in Christ. 10This purpose is finally to bring to their conclusion all the events in history, and to make of all things, things in heaven and things on earth, one perfect whole in Christ. 11And we too have received a share in him, for this was our destiny in the intention of that God who works out everything as the purpose of his will directs. 12The purpose of all this was that we Jews, who were the first to set our hopes on Christ, should cause his glory to be praised, 13and it is through him that you Gentiles too have heard the message of the truth, the good news of your salvation. It is in him that you took your decision to believe, and received the promised Holy Spirit, who marks you out as his, 14that Holy Spirit who is the first instalment and the pledge of all that one day you will possess.

The final end of all this is the liberation of God's own people, so that his glory may be praised.

15This is why, since I heard of your faith in the Lord Jesus and your love to all God's consecrated people, 16I never stop thanking God for you, and remembering you in my prayers. 17For it is my prayer that the God of our Lord Jesus Christ, the glorious Father, may give you the Spirit to make you wise in heavenly things, and to reveal to you full knowledge of himself. 18I pray that your inner vision may be flooded with light, to enable you to see what hope the fact that he has called you gives you, to see the glorious wealth of the life that he has promised you as members of his dedicated people, 19to see how surpassingly great is his power to us who believe, that power demonstrated in the action of the mighty strength 20which was operative in the case of Christ, when he brought him back to life again, and seated him at his right hand in the heavenly places. 21There he gave him a place far above all spiritual powers, above every ruler and authority and power and lord, above every possible title of honour, not only in this world but also in the next. 22He subjected everything to him, and he gave him as the supreme head to the church; 23and the church is his body, the complement of him who completes all things everywhere.

Chapter 2

YOU Gentiles were spiritually dead in your trespasses and sins. 2It was in them that you lived an earthbound life, under the domination of the controller of those evil powers who haunt the air, of that spirit who is now active in those who are disobedient to God. 3We Jews were no different, for we too at one time lived a life dominated by the desires of our lower nature, doing what the human body wanted and what the human mind planned. We were just as much in danger of the divine wrath as anyone else. 4But God is rich in mercy, and, because of his great love for us, 5he raised us to life with Christ, even though we were spiritually dead in sins. It is to grace that you owe your salvation. 6Because of our union with Christ Jesus he raised us from spiritual death, and gave us a seat with him in the heavenly places. 7He did this to demonstrate to all future ages the surpassing wealth of his grace in his kindness in Christ Jesus to us. 8For it is to grace that you owe your salvation through faith. The whole process comes from nothing that we have done or could do;

it is God's gift. 9Any achievement of ours is ruled out to make it impossible for anyone to boast. 10It is he who made us what we are, for through Jesus Christ we have been created for that life of goodness which God already prepared for us to live.

11You will therefore do well to remember that you were once Gentiles from the physical point of view. You Gentiles were once called 'the uncircumcised' by the Jews who call themselves 'the circumcised.' The circumcision of which they speak is a physical and man-made thing. 12You will do well to remember that at that time you knew nothing of a Messiah. You were aliens with no share in the divine nation of Israel. You were complete strangers to the covenants which contain the promise of God. You lived in a world without hope and without God. 13But because of your relationship with Christ Jesus the situation has changed. You who were far away have been brought near through the death of Christ.

14It is he who has solved the problem of our relationships with God and man. He has destroyed the fence's dividing wall and made both Jew and Gentile into one. By his incarnation he destroyed the old enmity, 15for he abolished the law with its commandments and its decrees. This he did in order that their common relationship to himself might make the two into one new man, and thus their new relationship to him gave them a new relationship to each other. 16It was his purpose to make Jew and Gentile into one united body through the cross, and thus by it to kill the ancient enmity, and to bring both back to God. 17So he came and brought the good news of this new divine and human relationship both to you Gentiles, who were far away, and to the Jews, who were near, 18for through him we both possess the right of access through the one Spirit to the Father. 19So then, it follows that you are no longer foreigners and aliens; you are fellow-citizens with God's consecrated people, and members of the household of God. 20The prophets and the apostles are the foundations of the structure into which you have been built, and Christ Jesus himself is the corner-stone. 21It is he who holds the whole building together and who makes it grow into a holy temple in the Lord. 22In your union with him you too are being built in as a part with all his other people, to make you through the Spirit a dwelling-place for God.

Chapter 3

B ECAUSE of this I, Paul, Christ's prisoner for you Gentiles as I am, am praying for you. ₂I am sure that I can assume that you have heard of my divinely allotted ministry, a ministry given to me to bring to you Gentiles that grace of God which I myself have already experienced. ₃It was by direct revelation that God told me of his secret plan, about which I have briefly written to you in the earlier part of this letter, ₄and by reading it you can judge for yourselves if I have really grasped the secret of the real meaning of Christ. ₅In former times that secret was not told to men in the way in which it has now been disclosed by the Spirit to God's consecrated apostles and prophets. ₆That secret is that the Gentiles through the gospel are partners with the people of God, fellow-members of the one body, sharers in the promise in virtue of their connection with Christ Jesus. ₇Of that gospel I was made a servant, as a result of the free gift of the grace of God which I experienced, an experience which came to me through the action of his power. ₈I am the least of all God's consecrated people, and yet God in his grace gave me the privilege of bringing the good news of the wealth of Christ to the Gentiles, a wealth the limit of which no man can ever find. ₉It was my God-given task to shed a flood of light on the working out of that secret, up to now hidden from all eternity in the mind of God, the creator of all things. ₁₀The purpose of all this was through the church to make known the many-coloured wisdom of God to the demonic rulers and powers in the heavenly places, ₁₁for this was the eternal purpose that God had planned to work out in Christ Jesus our Lord. ₁₂And because of Christ Jesus and our faith in him we can enter God's royal presence with no fear and in perfect trust. ₁₃So then, it is my prayer that you will not be discouraged by the troubles that I am going through for you, for in my troubles is your glory.

₁₄For this cause I kneel in prayer to the Father, ₁₅that Father who is the origin and ideal of all fatherhood in heaven and on earth, ₁₆praying to him that in the wealth of his glory he may grant to you to be strengthened in power through his Spirit in your inner being, ₁₇praying that your faith may be such that Christ may make your hearts his home, praying that love may be that in which your life is rooted and on which it is founded. ₁₈I pray that in fellowship with all God's consecrated people you may have strength to grasp how broad and long and high and deep Christ's love is, 19to know that love of his which is greater than we can ever understand, for then your life will be filled with all God's fullness.

20Now to him who can do for us far more than our lips can ask or our minds conceive through that power of his which is at work in us, 21to God be glory in the church and in Christ Jesus from age to age, for ever and ever. Amen.

Chapter 4

PRISONER though I am, my life is still lived in the presence and power of the Lord. You have been called by God to be his own. So then, I urge you to live a life which befits such a call. 2I urge you to live a life of complete humility and gentleness, a life of patience, a life in which you always lovingly bear with one another. 3I urge you to be eager to preserve that unity which the Spirit can give, a unity in which you are bound together in a perfect relationship to one another. 4There is one body and there is one Spirit, just as the fact that God has called you has set before you one hope. 5There is one Lord; there is one faith; there is one baptism. 6There is one God and Father of all, who reigns over all, and works through all, and is in all.

7Each of you has received his own share of grace, in proportion as the free gift of Christ has given it to you. 8That is why it is said:

'He ascended on high,
    after he had taken his prisoners captive,
    and gave gifts to men.'

9What can 'he ascended' mean other than that he first descended into the lower parts of the earth? 10The one who descended is the same as the one who ascended far above all heavens, so that he might fill all things with his presence and himself. 11And these were the gifts he gave—some to be apostles, some to be prophets, some to be preachers of the good news, some to be pastors and teachers. 12Their function is to equip God's consecrated people for the service they must give; it is their function to build up the body of Christ. 13Then we shall go on to be one united band of brothers, one in our faith and in our knowledge of the Son of God. Then we shall grow into mature manhood, until we reach the stature of Christ in all his completeness. 14Then we shall no longer be infants, tossed and blown about by every chance blast of teaching, at the mercy of the slick cleverness of men, craftily calculated to lead us astray. 15We must rather speak the truth with the accent of love, and then in everything we shall become more and more closely united with him who is the head, I mean Christ. 16For it is through its connection with him that the whole body, formed into one harmonious whole through each ligament with which it is equipped, as each part of it performs its own function, develops its own growth, and so builds itself up in love.

17This I say—and in the Lord's name I solemnly call on you to listen to it—you must no longer live the kind of life the heathen live, a life of utter futility. 18For their minds are darkened and they are alienated from the life of God, because of the deliberate ignorance of their minds and the sheer imperviousness of their hearts. 19They have lost all decent feelings, and have abandoned themselves to shameless immorality, which ends in all kinds of filthy practices, in their greed for the things which no man has any right even to desire. 20This is not the way that you have learned about Christ. 21I have no doubt that you have been told about him, and that you have received Christian instruction in the truth as it is embodied in Jesus. 22You must therefore, as you have been taught, divest yourselves of that old personality, which was characteristic of the way in which you used to live, and which was rotting away, seduced by its own desires. 23You must have a completely new attitude of mind. 24You must put on that new personality, which was divinely created, and which shows itself in that justice and holiness, which are the products of the truth.

25So then, banish all falsehood from your lives. You must speak the truth to your fellowmen, because we are as closely bound up with each other as the parts of the body are. 26Sometimes it is a duty to be angry, but your anger must never be sinful anger. Never come to the end of any day still angry with anyone. 27Give the Devil no place or opportunity in your life. 28The man who stole must steal no longer. He must rather work his hardest, doing an honest day's work with his own hands. His aim must be to have enough to share it with the man who has less than enough. 29You must never use foul language. So far from that, any word of yours must be good for meeting the need of the occasion. Then it will be a means of grace to those who hear it. 30Do not bring sorrow to God's Holy Spirit, that Spirit by whom God's sign of ownership has been set upon you, to mark you out for the day of deliverance. 31All bitterness and bad temper and anger, the loud voice and the slanderous tongue must be removed from your lives, and so must all maliciousness. 32You must be kind to one another; you must be compassionate; you must forgive one another, as God in Christ forgave you.

Chapter 5

So then you must try to be like God, for you are his children and he loves you. 2Your life must be lived in love, and must have as its pattern the life of Christ, who loved us and gave himself for us, as a sacrifice and offering acceptable to God. 3Fornication and any kind of indecency or conscienceless greed should not even be so much as mentioned in your society, for it is not fitting for God's consecrated people even to talk about things like that. 4You must have nothing to do with obscene language and with stupid or frivolous talk. These things are not becoming for you. No! Gratitude to God should be the accent of your talk. 5For you are well aware that no one who is guilty of sexual excess, no one who is morally impure, no one who is characterized by that greed, which has made gain its god, has any part in the Kingdom which is Christ's and God's.

6You must not allow anyone to mislead you with empty words. It is things like that which bring God's wrath on those who disobey him. 7You must never have anything to do with people like that. 8You were once all darkness, but now your connection with the Lord has made you light. You must behave as those who are at home in the light. 9For light brings as its harvest everything that is good and right and true. 10You must submit everything to the test of the approval of the Lord. 11You must have no share in the sterile deeds of darkness; you must rather expose them. 12It is shameful even to talk about the things they do and try to keep hidden. 13Everything that is exposed by the light is lit up; and anything that is lit up itself becomes all light. 14As the hymn has it:

> 'Sleeper, awake,
> and rise from the dead,
> and Christ will shine on you!'

15Pay careful attention to the kind of life you live. Behave as sensible and not as senseless men. 16Seize each opportunity as it comes, for we are living in evil times. 17Don't behave like fools. You must always try to understand what the Lord wants you to do. 18Don't get drunk with wine—that way debauchery lies. No! Fill yourselves with the Holy Spirit. 19Speak to each other in psalms and hymns and songs inspired by the Spirit. Sing and make music to the Lord with all your heart. 20Never stop thanking God the Father for everything in the name of our Lord Jesus Christ. 21Your reverence for Christ must banish all feeling of superiority to others.

22Wives must be subject to their husbands, for that is their Christian duty. 23For a husband is head of his wife as Christ is head of the church, for he is the Saviour of the church, which is his body. 24As the church is subject to Christ, so too wives must be in everything subject to their husbands. 25Husbands, you must love your wives, as Christ too loved the church and gave himself for it. 26It was his purpose to cleanse and consecrate it by the washing of baptism and the preaching of the word, 27for he wished to present the church to himself in all its splendour, without stain or wrinkle or any such thing, for he wished it to be dedicated and faultless. 28It is thus that husbands too ought to love their own wives, as they love their own bodies. To love one's body is to love oneself. 29No one ever hated his own body. So far from that, he nourishes it and cherishes it, as Christ too nourishes and cherishes the church, 30because we are parts of his body. 31For this cause a man will leave father and mother, and will be inseparably joined to his wife, and they two will become so completely one that they will no longer be two persons, but one. 32There is here a very great symbol. As I see it, that saying is a symbol of the relationship of Christ and the church. 33I say no more, except that each one of you husbands must love his wife as he loves himself, and that every wife must respect her husband.

Chapter 6

CHILDREN, you must obey your parents. This is your Christian duty, and it is right that you should do so. 2Honour your father and mother—this is the first commandment with a promise attached to it. 3If you do, you will have a prosperous and a long life in the land. 4You fathers also have your duties. You must not make your children resentful by your treatment of them. You must bring them up in Christian discipline and training.

5As for you slaves, you must obey your human masters, with proper respect and fear, in honest loyalty, as you would obey Christ. 6You must not work only when someone is watching you, as if the only thing that matters is human approval. You must work as Christ's slaves, genuinely trying to do what God wants you to do.

7You must give your service with good-will, as if it was the Lord you were working for, and not a human master, 8for you well know that each man, whether he is a slave or a free man, will receive from the Lord the equivalent of anything good that he has done. 9As for you masters, you must act towards your slaves in the same way. You must stop using threats, for you well know that both they and you have a Master in heaven, and there is no favouritism with him.

10Finally, your union with the Lord and with his mighty power must give you a dynamic strength. 11Put on the complete armour which God can give you, and then you will be able to resist the stratagems of the Devil. 12For our struggle is not against any human foe; it is against demonic rulers and authorities, against the cosmic powers of this dark world, against spiritual forces of evil in the heavens. 13So then, take the complete armour which God can give you, and then, when the evil day comes, you will be able to see things through to the end, and to remain erect. 14So then take your stand. Buckle the belt of truth round your waist. Put on righteousness for a breastplate. 15Put preparedness to preach the gospel of peace on your feet, like shoes. 16Through thick and thin take faith as your shield. With it you will be able to extinguish all the flaming arrows of the Evil One. 17Take salvation as your helmet. Take the sword the Spirit gives. That sword is the word of God. 18Keep on praying fervently, and asking God for what you need, and on every occasion let the Spirit be the atmosphere in which you pray. To that end sleeplessly and always persevere in your requests to God for all God's consecrated people. 19Pray for me too, and ask God to give me a message when I have to speak. Pray that I may be able fearlessly to tell men the secret of the good news, 20for which I am an ambassador, though now in chains. I need your prayers to enable me to speak it with the fearlessness with which I ought to speak.

21Tychicus, our dear brother and a loyal Christian servant, will tell you everything and will let you know how things are with me, and what I am doing. 22I am sending him to you for this very purpose, to let you know what is happening to me, and to encourage your hearts.

23Every blessing to the brothers, and love and faith combined from God the Father and the Lord Jesus Christ. 24Grace be with all those who love our Lord Jesus Christ with a love which will never die.

Introduction to the Letter to the Colossians

THE Letter to the Colossians was written about A.D.62, when Paul was in prison in Rome awaiting trial (4.3,18). It has a close resemblance to the Letter to the Ephesians and was written at the same time.

Paul himself had neither founded nor visited the church at Colosse (2.1). Its founder was probably Epaphras (1.7), and it was most likely founded in the missionary activity which took place when Paul was in Ephesus (Acts 19.10).

The congregation in Colosse was in good heart (1.3-8), and the letter was written rather to meet a situation which was threatening than a situation which had actually emerged. What was that situation?

At the back of the Letter to the Colossians there was a heresy which is at the back of much of the New Testament. Its name was Gnosticism, which means wisdom, and, in order to understand this letter, we have to understand this heresy.

The Gnostic began with the basic assumption that in the world there are two realities, spirit and matter, and that both are eternal; they have both been there since before the beginning of time. Out of this matter the world was made in the beginning; but the characteristic of this matter is that it is flawed; it is bad stuff. Therefore everything made out of it is bad. The inevitable consequence is that the body is bad. If the body is essentially and incurably bad, we may do one of two things with it. We may either practise a rigid asceticism in which we starve and neglect the body, or, since the body is bad anyway, and since it does not matter what happens to it, we may give it its way, and sate and glut its passions. In regard to the body, Gnosticism issues either in asceticism or in antinomianism.

But this belief has the most important consequences for the doctrine of creation. Spirit is altogether good, and God is spirit; matter is essentially flawed and evil. It follows that God cannot touch matter, and it therefore also follows that God cannot be the creator of the world. How then was the world created? God sent out an emanation and this emanation sent out another emanation and so on and on in an endless chain, until we come to a very distant emanation, who is so far from God that he can touch and handle matter. This distant emanation is the creator of the world. Further, as the emanations grow further and further from God, they become, first, more and more ignorant of God, and, finally, more and more hostile to God, so that the emanation who created the world is both totally ignorant of, and hostile to, the true God. The world is made of bad stuff by a lesser and ignorant god, who knows nothing of the true God, and who is hostile to him.

To get from this world to God, the soul has to pass up through the endless chain of emanations. To do this it needs to know their names and the pass-words. Gnosticism is therefore only for the clever intellectuals, and simple folk cannot know true religion at all. This is the heresy which the Letter to the Colossians combats. Let us trace the combat.

i. The Gnostics did not believe in the uniqueness of Jesus. Jesus was only one in the chain of the emanations between man and God. He might stand very high in the chain, maybe highest of all, but he is no more than one link in the chain. To meet this Paul insists that Jesus is nothing less than the image of God (1.15), that in him all knowledge and wisdom dwell (2.3), that he is indeed the fullness of God (1.19; 2.9). The Gnostic would of course deny the incarnation. The body is bad; Jesus could not have a body. But to Paul Jesus is all of God in bodily form (2.9).

ii. The Gnostic said that creation was carried out by an ignorant and hostile god. Paul insists that Jesus Christ the Son of God was God's agent in creation (1.16). The true love and power which are operative in redemption are also operative in creation.

iii. The Gnostic declared that he was offering a philosophy (2.8) possible only for the intellectual élite, the chosen few. Paul insists that Christianity is for every man and that every man can become perfect before God (1.28).

iv. The Gnostic sometimes practised asceticism. He passed food laws and regulations; he prescribed days and seasons and fasts; his motto was, 'Touch not, taste not, handle not.' This is all completely unchristian and against Christian freedom (2.16-23).

v. On the other hand, the Gnostic might let the body, bad anyway, have its way, and so become guilty of gross immorality. This, says Paul, a Christian must never do (3.5).

Paul closes the letter with his usual ethical section and his greetings.

We see how in this letter Paul takes the Gnostic heretical claims one by one, and meets them with Christ. This letter defends the church against a heresy which would have wrecked Christianity.

The Letter to the
COLOSSIANS

Chapter 1

THIS is a letter from Paul, who became an apostle of Christ Jesus because God willed it so, and from our colleague Timothy, 2to the consecrated and loyal members of the Christian fellowship in Colosse. Grace be to you and every blessing from God our Father.

3We always thank God, the Father of our Lord Jesus Christ, for you in our prayers, 4because of the reports which have reached us of your Christian loyalty and of the way in which you show your love for all God's dedicated people. 5You have this loyalty and love, because of the hope which is waiting ready for you in heaven, the hope of which you have already heard, 6when the gospel arrived among you and its truth was preached to you. That gospel is spreading and producing lovely lives all over the world, just as it is among you from the day you first heard of God's grace and realized what it truly is. 7You were taught it by Epaphras, our dear fellow-servant, who is Christ's loyal worker and our representative to you. 8It was he who told us of that love of yours which the Spirit has inspired.

9That is why, from the day on which news of you reached us, we never stop praying for you, and asking that you may be given spiritual wisdom and understanding, for then you will have complete insight into what God wants you to do. 10We pray that your life and conduct will be worthy of the Lord and such as will be altogether pleasing to him. We pray that your life will be productive of all kinds of good action, and that you will continue to come to know God better and better. 11We pray that in God's glorious strength you will receive power to cope with anything, a power which will enable you gladly to meet life with fortitude and patience. 12We pray that you will be ever grateful to the Father who has made you fit to receive a share in the possession which he promised to his dedicated people in the realm of light. 13It was he who rescued us from the grip of the power of darkness, and transferred us to the Kingdom of his dear Son. 14It is through this Son that we have received the liberation which comes when sins are forgiven. 15He is the perfect likeness of the invisible God; his is the supremacy over all creation. 16For he is the agent by whom all things were created, in heaven and upon earth, visible and invisible, spiritual powers and beings, whether they be thrones or lordships or authorities or powers. He is the agent and the goal of all creation. 17He exists before everything else, and everything else holds together in him. 18The church is his body, and he is its head. He is its beginning, for he was the first to return from the dead, which means that there is no part of the universe in which the topmost place is not his, 19for by God's own decision God in all his completeness made his home in him. 20More, it was God's decision to effect through him an act of universal reconciliation to himself of everything in heaven and on earth, and it was through his death on the cross that God did bring the whole universe into a right relationship with himself.

21Once you were estranged from God; your minds were hostile; your conduct was evil. 22But now the situation has changed. God has changed your enmity into friendship to himself by the incarnation and death of his Son, and has thus brought you into his own presence, dedicated, innocent and blameless, 23provided that you remain firmly founded in your faith, immovable in the hope of the gospel which you have heard, the gospel which was proclaimed to the whole created world under heaven, the gospel of which I Paul have been made a servant.

24I am now happy to suffer for your sake. It is my privilege to fulfil the uncompleted sufferings which the work of Christ still entails, human being though I am, for the sake of his body, which is the church. 25Of that church I was made a servant because of the part in his work that God gave me to do for your sake. My particular office is to tell to men the whole message which God has sent, 26to tell the secret which only a disciple can know, the secret which has been hidden throughout the ages and the generations, and which has now been revealed to God's dedicated people. 27It was God's will to make the glorious wealth of his secret known to them, and to make it known to all nations. The secret is that Christ is in you, and therefore yours is the hope of future glory. 28It is he of whom we tell. And in so doing it is every man whom we warn; it is every man whom we instruct in all wisdom; for it is our aim to present every man as a mature Christian. 29It is for this that I toil, and it is his power working mightily in me which nerves me for the struggle.

Chapter 2

I WANT you to know the intensity of my efforts for you and for the people in Laodicea and for all those who have never personally met me. ₂I want their hearts to be encouraged. I want them to be welded together in love. I want them to experience all the wealth of conviction that insight brings, for then they will come to know and understand God's secret which only a disciple can know—and that secret is Christ. ₃In him all the treasures of wisdom and knowledge are hidden. ₄I am telling you this to prevent anyone leading you astray with speciously persuasive talk. ₅For, even if I am physically absent from you, I am with you in spirit, and it makes me very happy when I see the disciplined order and the staunch front which your Christian faith displays.

₆The tradition you have received is that of Jesus as Messiah and Lord. Your whole life and conduct therefore must be that of men who are indissolubly linked to him. ₇You must live as men who have their roots in him and whose life is founded on him and who are continually being reinforced by the faith which you were taught, and all the time you must be overflowing with gratitude. ₈You must be careful not to become the victims of an arid and misleading intellectualism, which is based on merely human tradition and on that elementary knowledge, which is all the world can supply, and not on Christ. ₉For it is in Christ that godhead in all its completeness dwells in bodily form. ₁₀It is in your union with him that your own life reaches perfected completeness. He is supreme over every demonic power and authority. ₁₁In your union with him too you were circumcised with a circumcision which was not a physical operation, but which consisted in stripping off your lower sensual nature, for that is the circumcision which Christ effects on you. ₁₂For in baptism you were buried with him, and in baptism you were also raised with him from the dead through your faith in the power of God, which was operative in raising him from the dead. ₁₃You were dead in sins; you were uncircumcised strangers to God, but God made you alive with Christ, for he forgave us for all our sins. ₁₄He cancelled the bond by which we were self-committed to the decrees of the law, and by which we stood condemned. He completely removed it and nailed it to the cross. ₁₅On the cross he stripped the demonic powers and authorities of their power, and made a public spectacle of them, as if they had been captives in a victor's triumphal procession.

16You must not therefore let anyone criticize you in matters of what it is right or wrong to eat or drink, or with regard to the alleged correct observance of festivals, new moons and sabbaths. 17These things are no more than the shadow of the things to come; the reality belongs to Christ. 18There are self-appointed umpires around who delight in asceticism and in angel worship, and who are always trying to penetrate further into their own world of fantasies. Their minds, dominated by a false idea of the importance of external things, inflate them with a senseless conceit. You must not let them disqualify you. 19They lose their grip on him who is the head, and it is only through its connection with him that the whole body, equipped and welded together by the joints and ligaments, grows as God meant it to grow.

20Your death with Christ means that the world's rudimentary teaching has nothing more to do with you. Why then go on living as if your life was dominated by the world? 21Why pay any more attention to those whose slogans are: 'Don't handle this! Don't taste that! Don't touch the next thing!'? 22All these regulations refer to things which are bound to perish in the course of being used. They move in the sphere of human regulations and human teaching. 23These things may bring a reputation for wisdom with their rigoristic piety, their deliberate self-abasement, their ascetic treatment of the body, but they are of no real value in the struggle against sensual indulgence.

Chapter 3

IF then you have been raised to life with Christ, your heart must be set on the great realities of that heavenly sphere, where Christ is seated at the right hand of God. 2Your constant concern must be with the heavenly realities, not with worldly trivialities. 3For you died to this world, and now you have entered with Christ into the secret life of God. 4When Christ, who is your life, comes again for all the world to see, then all the world will see that you too share his glory.

5Once, finally and for all you must put an end to the use of any part of your body for worldly and immoral purposes. Your new state must mean the death, as far as you are concerned, of fornication, impurity, unbridled passion, desire for the forbidden things, the spirit which makes a god of gain—for that is a kind of idolatry. 6These are the things which incur the wrath of God. 7There was a time when your life and conduct too were characterized by these things, a time when they were an integral part of your life. 8But now you too must remove them all from your life—the long-nourished anger, the blaze of temper, maliciousness, abusiveness, foul language. These must no longer stain your lips. 9There must be no more dishonesty to each other, for you have stripped off the old nature and all its works and ways, 10and you have clothed yourselves with the new nature, which is progressively renewed, until it reaches fuller and fuller knowledge of God, and comes nearer and nearer to being in the image of its creator· 11And so we have arrived at a state of things in which there is no distinction between Jew and Greek, circumcised and uncircumcised, barbarian, Scythian, slave and free man. Christ is all that matters, and there is neither person nor thing in which Christ is not.

12You are God's chosen people, dedicated and dear to him. You must therefore clothe yourselves in compassion, in kindness, in humility, in gentleness, in patience. 13You must bear with each other, and, if anyone has something to complain about in someone else, you must forgive each other. You must forgive each other as the Lord forgave you. 14And, to crown all, you must clothe yourselves in love, which holds all the other qualities together and completes them. 15Only Christ can enable men to live in a right relationship with each other. It is this unifying power of his which must dictate your every decision, for you were meant to be one united body. You must be thankful. 16You must open your hearts to the message of Christ so that in all its riches it may find its home there. You must with all wisdom continually teach and advise each other. With heartfelt gratitude to him you must sing to God in psalms and hymns and songs inspired by the Spirit. 17Whatever you do and whatever you say, you must do and say it all as the representatives of the Lord Jesus, and all the time you must be giving thanks to God the Father through him.

18You wives must accept the authority of your husbands, for this is fitting in a Christian household. 19You husbands must love your wives, and must not be harsh to them.

20You children must always obey your parents, for this is pleasing to God and proper for a Christian. 21You fathers must not make life intolerable for your children, in case you take all the heart out of them.

22You slaves must obey the orders of your human masters in every

detail. You must not be the kind of workman who works only when·
he is watched, as if the only person you have to satisfy is some human
being. You must be an honest workman, and the one person whose
verdict you must respect is the Lord. 23Put the whole of yourselves
into whatever you are doing, and do it, not as if you were doing it for
men, but as if you were doing it for the Lord, 24for you well know
that it is from the Lord you will receive the reward into which he has
promised that you will enter. The master of whom you are the slaves
is Christ. 25Wrong-doing will bring its own reward—and there is no
favouritism with God.

Chapter 4

YOU masters must treat your slaves justly and fairly, for you well
know that you too have a Master in heaven.

2You must never grow discouraged in prayer, and, when you pray,
you must be unwearied in thanksgiving. 3Pray for us too. Pray to God
to give us the opportunity to preach, to tell the secret of Christ, which
only the disciple can know, that secret for the sake of which I am in
prison. 4Pray to him to enable me to speak in such a way that I will
open that secret to all, for that is what it is my duty to do. 5You must
behave wisely to those outside the church. You must eagerly seize
every opportunity that comes to you. 6Your conversation must always have charm and wit. You must study the art of giving the right
answer to everyone you talk to.

7Tychicus, our dear Christian brother, our trusty helper, and our
fellow-servant in the Lord's service, will give you all the news about
how things are with me. 8The reason why I am sending him is to give
you all the news about us and to cheer you up. 9I am sending with
him Onesimus, our dear and trusty brother, who is one of yourselves.
They will tell you all the news from here.

10Aristarchus, my fellow-prisoner, sends you every good wish,
and so does Mark, Barnabas' cousin. You have already received instructions about him, to give him a welcome, if he comes to visit you.
11Jesus called Justus sends his good wishes too. These are the only
Jewish Christians who are working with me for the Kingdom of God,
and they have been a comfort to me. 12Epaphras, who is one of yourselves and Christ's servant, sends you his good wishes. He never stops
praying strenuously for you, asking that you should stand fast,
mature in your faith, firm in your convictions, always engaged in do-

ing the will of God. 13I can testify how hard he works for you and for the people in Laodicea and in Hierapolis. 14Our dear friend Luke the doctor sends his good wishes, and so does Demas. 15I send all my good wishes to our fellow-Christians in Laodicea, and to Nympha and the congregation which meets in her house. 16When this letter has been publicly read in your group, make arrangements for it to be read in the congregation in Laodicea too. And you too must have the letter which is on the way to you from Laodicea read to your congregation. 17Say to Archippus: 'See that you fully discharge that duty which was entrusted to you in the Lord's service.'

18In my own handwriting—every good wish from Paul. Remember my chains. Grace be with you.

Introduction to the Letter to Philemon

THE Letter to Philemon is unique among the letters of Paul for it is the only personal letter, written to an individual, that we have from his pen.

It was written about A.D.62, when Paul was in prison in Rome, and it was written to Philemon, a member of the church at Colosse. It was written to help Onesimus. Onesimus was Philemon's slave, and he had run away. He probably was a thief as well as a runaway, for Paul promised to make good any theft Onesimus had been guilty of (verse 18). Just as a modern criminal might run to London or to New York, to lose himself in the vast crowds of the great city, so Onesimus had fled to Rome. Somehow or other he had made contact with Paul there, and he had become a Christian. He had become very dear to Paul, and Paul would have liked to keep him with him, but Paul would do nothing without the good-will of Philemon.

So Onesimus had to be sent back to his master, and all the more so because a Christian must do the right thing. So Paul sent him back. Paul was taking a risk. There were as many as sixty million slaves in the Roman Empire. They clearly had to be rigidly kept down. The fate of the runaway slave was extremely hard, if he was recaptured. He might well be killed, for his master had the right of life and death over him. In the eyes of the law of Rome a slave was not a person but a thing. He might well be branded on the forehead with a red-hot iron with the letter F, standing for *fugitivus*, runaway. At the best, he would certainly expect to be cruelly beaten.

Nevertheless Paul sent Onesimus back. But he makes a request to Philemon. Philemon is to receive him, not only as a returned runaway, but as a Christian brother beloved.

The end of the story we do not know, but surely we can be sure that Philemon responded to the pleading of Paul.

It is to be noted that Paul does not mention emancipation. Any move to try to abolish slavery at this stage would have been to court disaster. A rising of the slaves could only have ended in massacre. But something had happened. If the slave has become a dear brother, then the sting of slavery is drawn, and the principle has been stated which will end sooner or later in emancipation.

So in this letter we find the great apostle concentrating all his efforts for the sake of a runaway slave.

The Letter to
PHILEMON

THIS is a letter from Paul, a prisoner for Christ Jesus' sake, and from our colleague Timothy, to our dear friend and fellow-worker Philemon, and to the congregation which meets in your house, ₂and to our sister Apphia, and to our fellow Christian soldier Archippus. ₃Grace to you and every blessing from God our Father and from the Lord Jesus Christ.

₄I never mention you in my prayers without thanking God for you, ₅for I am always hearing of your faith in the Lord Jesus and your love for all God's dedicated people. ₆It is my prayer that your fellowship with us in the faith we share may be effective in giving us an ever-deepening understanding of all the blessings which have become part of our life, and so may lead us nearer and nearer to Christ. ₇Your love has made me very happy, and has been to me a source of much courage and comfort, because, my brother, you have been the means by which the hearts of God's people have been refreshed.

₈So then, although our relationship as Christians entitles me with every confidence to order you to do what is your duty, ₉yet because we love one another I appeal rather than command. I take this line though I am such as I am—Paul, the ambassador of Christ, and now in prison for Christ Jesus' sake. ₁₀I appeal to you in regard to Onesimus, who is nothing less than my own child, because in prison I became his father in the faith. ₁₁He is living up to his name now.* For there was a time when he was useless to you, but now he is useful both to you and to me. ₁₂I am sending him to you, and with him I am sending my own heart. ₁₃I am in prison here for the sake of the good news, and I would have liked to keep him with me, to render me the service which you yourself would gladly have given me. ₁₄But I wished to do nothing without your consent, for I wanted your kindness to me to be, not a gift which you were compelled to give me, but a gift which you gave of your own free-will. ₁₅It may be that he was taken away

*Paul here makes a word-play on the name *Onesimus*, which means *useful* or *profitable*.

from you for a time so that you might get him back for eternity, 16no longer as a slave, but as something far more than a slave, as a brother, specially dear to me, and how much more dear to you as a man and as a Christian!

17So then, if you regard me as your partner in the faith, welcome him as you would welcome me. 18If he has defrauded you of anything, or, if he owes you anything, charge it to me. 19Here is my written and signed guarantee that I will repay it—(signed) Paul. It is unnecessary for me to remind you that you owe me nothing less than your very self. 20So, brother, do me this favour as a Christian duty, and, like a Christian, put an end to my anxiety.

21I write to you confident that you will agree to my request, sure that you will do even more than I ask. 22At the same time, please get a room ready for me, for I hope that your prayers will be answered, and that God will allow me to visit you.

23Epaphras, my fellow-prisoner for Christ Jesus' sake, sends you his good wishes, 24and so do Mark, Aristarchus, Demas and Luke, my fellow-workers. 25The grace of the Lord Jesus Christ be with your spirit.

Introduction to the Letter to the Philippians

THE Letter to the Philippians is another of the letters written by Paul when he was in prison in Rome, and its date is about A.D.62. When he wrote it, he had already faced one part of his trial (1.7). He is not yet in despair about his freedom (1.25,26), and yet, in spite of his hopes, he writes as if death was not very far away (1.20-23; 2.17).

There was no church to which Paul was closer than the church at Philippi. He loved the Philippians and the Philippians loved him (1.3-11). The measure of his closeness to them is seen in the fact that from his other churches Paul was too proud to accept any help. He would rather work his fingers to the bone than take charity (1 Thessalonians 2.9), but from the Philippians he was happy to take and to take more than once (4.10-18).

There were troubles in Philippi, but they were minor troubles. There is nothing in this letter of the dangers and heresies which threatened the very life of the church.

There were those who were rather his competitors than his comrades in preaching (1.15-18). There were those who tried to persuade the Christians to accept circumcision (3.1-4). There were, as might happen in any congregation, two women who had quarrelled and who would not make it up again (4.2,3). And Paul's cure for everything is to have the same attitude of humble service as Jesus Christ had in his life (2.1-18).

Through this letter the warmth of Paul's affection shines and throbs and glows, and in this letter there is the nobility of that courage of his which was ready to face death or life.

The Letter to the
PHILIPPIANS

Chapter 1

THIS is a letter from Paul and Timothy, servants of Christ Jesus, to all God's consecrated Christian people who are in Philippi, and to those who are in charge of the congregation there and those who are engaged in its service. ₂Grace to you and every blessing from God our Father and from the Lord Jesus Christ.

₃In all my memories of you I have cause for nothing but thanksgiving. ₄In my every prayer for you all it is always with joy that I pray. ₅I thank God for the way in which you have been my partners in the work of the gospel from the first day it arrived among you right up to the present. ₆And I am quite sure of this—that God who began a good work in you will continue it until it is completed on the day when Jesus Christ comes. ₇It is right for me to feel like this about you all, because of the place you have in my heart, for you are my partners in the work that God's grace gave me the privilege of doing, both in my imprisonment, and when I have to stand my trial to defend and to establish the truth of the gospel. ₈God knows that I am telling the truth when I tell you how I yearn for you with the same affection as Christ Jesus himself does. ₉It is my prayer that your love may overflow with deeper and deeper knowledge, and with a greater and greater sensitive awareness of every kind, ₁₀for then you will be able to decide between the different courses of action which present themselves to you, for I want you to be pure and blameless to meet Christ on the day when he comes. ₁₁I want you to be filled with that harvest of goodness which Jesus Christ alone can give, and which moves men to glorify and praise God.

₁₂I want you to know, brothers, that, contrary to all that might have been expected, what has happened to me has resulted in the progress of the gospel. ₁₃The result has been that the whole praetorian guard and all the others could not fail to see that it is as a Christian that I have been imprisoned. 14The very fact that I am in prison has given more and more of our fellow-Christians an ever-increasing confidence in the Lord to dare more and more fearlessly to preach the Christian message.

15It is quite true that there are some who preach Christ from motives of jealousy and controversy; but there are others who preach him in good will. 16It is love which makes some preach Christ, because they know well that it is for the defence of the gospel that I am lying in prison. 17Others proclaim Christ in a spirit of competitive rivalry with very mixed motives. Their idea is to make my imprisonment still harder to bear. 18What does it matter? Whatever else is true, it is true that in every way, whether the preaching is only an excuse for other things, or whether it is done in all sincerity, Christ is being proclaimed—and therefore I am quite happy about it. 19Yes, and I will continue to be happy, for I know that all this will end in my release, because you are praying for me and because the Spirit of Jesus Christ is generously helping me. 20It is my dearest wish and hope that I will never let myself down, but that, as always so now, I may have the courage to speak so freely that men may honour Christ because of my conduct, whether I live or die. 21For to me life is Christ, and death leads to still greater life. 22If I am to go on living life in this world, then I will have the chance to go on doing useful work. But it is not mine to know what choice I will have to make. 23I find it very difficult to decide between the two alternatives. I long to leave this world and to be with Christ—for that is far better. 24But for your sakes it is more necessary for me to go on living in this world, 25and, because I am convinced of this, I know that I am going to remain with you all, and that I am going to continue to stand by you all, to help you to make still further progress, and to have still more joy in the faith. 26I want to visit you again and so to give you the opportunity to have still more Christian pride in me.

27One thing I do want to say to you—in your day to day conduct in the ordinary life of society you must live in a way that befits the gospel of Christ. I want you to live in such a way, that whether I come and see you, or whether I am absent, I will hear that you are standing fast, one in spirit and one in heart, one in your united contest for the faith of the gospel, 28facing your opponents without a trace of nervous fear. Then your courage will be the clear proof to them that they are doomed and that you will be saved—a proof supplied by God himself. 29For you have received the privilege of serving Christ, not only by believing in him, but also by suffering for him. ₃₀You have to fight the same battle as you once saw me fight, and which, as you hear, I am still fighting.

Chapter 2

I F there is such a thing as Christian encouragement, if there is such a thing as love's comforting power, if you and I are really sharing in the partnership which only the Holy Spirit can make possible, if you really wish to show me a heartfelt sympathy which is like the mercy of God, ₂make my joy complete by being in perfect harmony of mind, by joining in a common love for God and for each other, by sharing in a common life, by taking every decision in unity of mind, ₃by never acting from motives of competitive rivalry or in the conceited desire for empty prestige. If you want to make my joy complete, instead of that each of you must humbly think the other better than himself; ₄each of you must concentrate, not on his own interest, but on the interests of others also. ₅Try always to have the same attitude to life as Jesus had.

> ₆He shared the very being of God,
>   but he did not regard his equality to God
>   as a thing to be clutched to himself.
>   ₇So far from that, he emptied himself,
>   and really and truly became a servant,
>   and was made for a time exactly like men.
> In a human form that all could see,
>   ₈he accepted such a depth of humiliation
>   that he was prepared to die,
>   and to die on a cross.
>   ₉That is why God has given him the highest place,
>   and has conferred on him
>   the name that is greater than any name,
>   ₁₀so that at the name of Jesus every creature
>   in heaven, and on earth, and beneath the earth
>   should kneel in reverence and submission,
>   ₁₁and so that everything which has a voice
>   should openly declare
>   that Jesus Christ is Lord,
>   and thus bring glory to God the Father.

12You have always been obedient. So then, my dear friends, not only as you did when I was with you, but now much more when I am not with you, keep on toiling in fear and trembling to complete your salvation. 13For it is God who is at work in you, to put into you the will to desire and the power to achieve what his purpose has planned for you. 14Do everything without grumbling and without arguing, 15and then no one will be able to question your morals or your sincerity, and you will be faultless children of God, although you live in an age in which life is twisted and perverted. Even in an age like that you must shine like stars in the world. 16You must go on offering them the word of life, for, if you do, on the day when Christ comes I will be able proudly to claim that I did not run a loser's race, and that all my toil has not gone for nothing. 17When men make their sacrifices to the gods, they pour out upon them a sacrificial cup of wine. Your faith and your service are a sacrifice to God, and it may be that my life, like that cup of wine, must be poured out to crown and complete your sacrifice. 18If it must be so, I am glad and I share my joy with you; and in the same way you must be glad and share your joy with me.

19I hope, if the Lord Jesus wills it, to send Timothy to you soon, to cheer my heart with news of how things are going with you. 20I have no one whose heart and mind are so much in tune with mine. He is the one man who will take a genuine interest in your affairs. 21For they are all self-centred instead of being Jesus Christ-centred. 22You well know his sterling worth, and you are well aware how he has served with me, like a son with a father, for the advancement of the gospel. 23I hope then to send him as soon as I see how things are going to go with me. 24I am confident that, if the Lord wills it, I myself will soon come to you.

25I thought it necessary to send back to you Epaphroditus, our fellow-Christian, who has done Christ's work and fought Christ's battles with me. He is the messenger you sent to serve me in my need, but now I send him home to you, 26because he was homesick to see you all, and because he was worried, because he knew that you had heard that he had been ill. 27And indeed he was so ill that he nearly died. But God took pity on him, and not only on him but on me too, to save me from having one grief after another. 28I am all the more eager to send him, to give you the joy of seeing him again and to relieve my own anxiety. 29Welcome him home gladly with a Christian welcome. Honour him and such as him, 30because for the sake of Christ's work he narrowly escaped death, for he risked his life to give to me for you the service which you yourselves could not give.

Chapter 3

NOTHING remains, brothers, but for me to wish you the joy that comes from being united with the Lord. To me it is no trouble to repeat what I have already written, and to do so will help to keep you safe.

2Beware of these dogs! Beware of these manufacturers of wickedness! Beware of those whose circumcision is no better than mutilation! 3It is we who are really circumcised, for we offer God a worship directed by his Spirit. Our pride is in Christ Jesus. We place no reliance on human externals, 4although I might well base my claims on such things. If anyone thinks that he can rely on physical marks and human achievements, I have an even stronger claim. 5I was circumcised on the eighth day after I was born. I am a pure-blooded Israelite. I belong to the tribe of Benjamin. I am a Hebrew and the son of Hebrew parents. In my attitude to the Jewish law I was a Pharisee. 6So enthusiastic was my devotion to the law that I was a persecutor of the church. As far as the goodness which the law prescribes and demands is concerned, I was beyond criticism. 7But whatever achievements in my life and career I would once have reckoned among the profits of life, I have written off as a dead loss for the sake of Christ. 8Yes, and more than that—I am prepared to write off everything as a dead loss for the sake of getting to know Christ Jesus my Lord, for that knowledge is something which surpasses everything in the world. For his sake I have abandoned everything, and I regard all else as of no more value than filth for the garbage heap. For me the only thing of value in the world is to gain Christ, 9and to make my life one with his. I am not right with God through any legalistic achievement of my own. All I want is the relationship with God which only God himself can give me, all founded on faith in Christ. 10My one aim is to know Christ, and to experience the power of his resurrection, and to share with him in his sufferings. My aim is to die the death he died, 11so that, if it may be, I may reach the resurrection from the dead.

12I do not claim that I have already attained this, or that I have already reached perfection. I press on to try to grasp that for which Christ Jesus has already grasped me. 13Brothers, I do not regard myself as having already grasped the prize. But I have one aim in life—to forget what lies behind, and to strain every nerve to reach what lies ahead. 14And so I press on to the goal to win the prize to which God in Christ Jesus calls me upward and onward. 15This must be how all of us who are mature Christians feel about life. If there is any point on which you feel differently, God will make it clear to you too. 16This one thing I say, let us never fall below the standard of conduct we have already reached.

17Brothers, make a united effort to follow the example I have given you, and keep watching those who model their conduct on the pattern they have seen in us. 18For there are many of whom I have often spoken to you, and of whom I now speak even with tears, whose conduct makes them the enemies of the cross of Christ. 19They are doomed to destruction. They worship their own appetites. They glory in their shame. They have never a thought beyond the horizons of this world. 20We are citizens of heaven, and we eagerly wait for the Lord Jesus Christ to come from heaven as our Saviour. 21He will change the form of the body which we now possess, with all its earthly limitations and humiliations, and will make it exactly like his own glorious body; and he will do so by the exercise of that power of his, which enables him to bring that and everything else under his sway.

Chapter 4

MY brothers, I love you and I long for you. You are my joy and you will be my crown. And in view of all that I have said to you, this, my dear friends, is how you must demonstrate your unswerving loyalty to the Lord.

2I urge Euodia and I urge Syntyche to settle their differences in Christian unity. 3And I make a special appeal to you, my dear partner, to do all you can to help these women, for they have shared with me in the strenuous work of the gospel, along with Clement too, and with the rest of my fellow-workers whose names are in the book of life. 4Never lose your Christian joy. Let me say it again! Never lose it! 5You must make it common knowledge that you never insist on the letter of the law. It will not be long now until the Lord comes. 6Don't worry about anything. In every circumstance of life tell God about the things you want to ask him for in your prayers and your requests to him, and bring him your thanks too. 7And God's peace, which is beyond both our understanding and our contriving, will stand guard over your hearts and minds, because your life is linked for ever with the life of Christ Jesus.

8It only remains to say, brothers, that your thoughts must continually dwell on everything that is true, on everything that is nobly serious, on everything that is right, on everything that is pure, on everything that is lovely, on everything that is honourable, on all that men call excellence, and on all that wins men's praise. 9You must keep putting into practice the lessons you have learned from me, the instruction you have received from me, and the example I have given you in speech and in action. And then the God of peace will be with you.

10It is my great and truly Christian joy to know that, after so long an interval, your care for me has flowered again. I know that your care has always been there, but you never had the opportunity to show it. 11Don't think that I am saying this because I am thinking of all the things I have to do without. I have learned how to be content in any circumstances. 12I know how to live with less than enough, and I know how to live with more than enough. I have learned the secret of how to live in any situation and in all circumstances, of how to eat well and of how to go hungry, of how to have more than enough and how to have less than enough. 13He who fills me with his dynamic power has made me able to cope with any situation. 14All the same, I am very grateful to you for sharing with me when I am in trouble.

15You yourselves well know, my Philippian friends, that in the earliest days of the gospel, when I had left Macedonia, you were the only church by whom in partnership I was offered, and from whom I accepted, any financial help. 16Even when I was in Thessalonica you more than once sent help for my needs. 17It is not the gift that I am concerned about. What I am concerned about is the heavenly profit which accumulates to your account! 18You owe me nothing! You have more than paid your debt! I have all that I could possibly want now that I have received from Epaphroditus the gifts you sent. These gifts of yours were like a sweet-smelling offering to God, a sacrifice which he is glad to accept, and in which he delights. 19My God will supply everything you need out of the splendour of his wealth given you in Christ Jesus. 20Glory be to our God and Father for ever and ever! Amen.

21Give my good wishes to every one of God's dedicated people. Our fellow-Christians who are here with me send their good wishes to you. 22All God's people send you their good wishes, especially those on the imperial staff. 23The grace of the Lord Jesus Christ be with your spirit.

Spirit and Matter
A Note on the Background of Thought
in New Testament Times

THERE is a certain line of thought which was very common in the pagan world in New Testament times, and which invaded the thought of the church. We shall meet it in the Pastoral Epistles, that is, in First and Second Timothy and Titus, in Second Peter and in Jude, which are closely connected, and in First and Second John. Instead of explaining it each time we meet it in these various letters, it will be better if we outline it in the one place, so that the one account of it can be referred to in the introduction to all of these letters.

Greek thought was always suspicious of the body. So many of man's sins and troubles could be traced to the fact that he had a physical body, with all the weakness and all the tendency to sin, which are, so to speak, inherent in the body. So Plato could say that the body is 'the prison-house of the soul'. Epictetus could refer to himself as 'a poor soul shackled to a corpse'. Seneca could speak of 'the detestable habitation of the body'. This line of thought regarded the body, not as something to be saved, but as something to be destroyed, whereas from the very beginning Christian thought regarded man as body, soul and spirit, all of which had their place in God's plan, and all of which could be saved. Christian thought never regarded salvation as being the end of one half of man, the physical half; it regarded salvation as being the saving of the total man.

This line of Greek thought is the basis of Gnosticism, of which we have already spoken in the introduction to the Letter to the Colossians. A Gnostic was a man who, as they claimed, had *gnōsis*, which is wisdom, and Gnosticism is the way of wisdom.

Gnosticism is based on a complete dualism. That is to say, it is based on a complete opposition between spirit and matter. It held that from the beginning spirit, that is God, and matter had existed. Creation was, therefore, not creation out of nothing, but creation out of already existing matter. The trouble was, as they saw it, that this matter was essentially flawed and evil; it was bad stuff; and it was out of this bad stuff that the world was created.

Since God is pure spirit and altogether good, he cannot himself touch this evil matter at all. He therefore put out a series of emanations or aeons, as they called them. There were many of these aeons. Each one in the series was a little further from God. Each one in the series was a little more ignorant of God. Finally, at the end of the series you come to aeons who are not only ignorant of God, and distant from God, but also hostile to God. It was by such an aeon, the Demiurge, the world-maker they called him, that this world was created. The world then was not created by the true God, but by an ignorant and hostile god. All this had certain consequences.

If matter is bad, then the body is bad as such. It cannot be reformed, or cured, or amended; it is bad as such. Such a belief will issue in one of two things.

a) It can issue in asceticism, in which the body is to be neglected and starved and held down, and in which all the things of the world are to be despised and used as little as possible. This line can become tied up with the Jewish Law, which with its food laws and regulations can be taken to be at least part of the rigid asceticism which is demanded.

b) It can equally issue in antinomianism, the complete neglect of all laws of morality. For, if the body is already evil, it does not matter what you do with it. Since it is in any event bad, its passions and desires may be sated and glutted, and it will make no difference.

It must be noted that this antinomian line of thought can pervert the doctrine of grace into its ally. In Romans 6 Paul deals with those who advocate sinning to give grace more and more chances to abound. The argument is that the grace of God is the greatest thing in the world; it can forgive every sin; therefore the more you sin, the more you give this wonderful grace the chance to operate. Sin then is a good thing, for it simply brings more and more grace.

So then, there was a line of thought which argued, either that sin did not matter, or that sin was a good thing in that it produced more and more grace.

All this line of thought has obvious repercussions about what will be believed about Jesus. If matter is evil, and if Jesus is the Son of God, then it follows that Jesus cannot have had a human body, so they argued. This produced the belief called Docetism. *Dokein* means *to seem*; Docetism is *Seemism*. They believed that Jesus only *seemed* to be a man. He had no real body; he was a phantom in human shape. So they said that he left no footsteps on the ground, when he walked. When you touched him there was nothing there to touch. There was no such thing as the incarnation, because it was impossible for the

Son of God to take an essentially evil body. The manhood and the humanity of Jesus were destroyed.

It also, of course, impinges on the doctrine of the resurrection. If Jesus had nothing but a phantom body, he did not ever really suffer; and if the body is essentially evil, then clearly there was no bodily resurrection. It becomes easy to see how very dangerous this teaching was.

But this Gnosticism produced something else. It also disturbed human relationships. If matter is evil, then the supreme aim is for the spirit of man to escape from the evil of the body and to rise to God. But, as we have seen, between this world with its evil matter and the God who is pure spirit there stretch a whole series and ladder of aeons. Each of these aeons was equipped with a name and with a genealogy. Long and complicated histories and stories were attached to each of them. Further, to get past them, a whole series of pass-words was required. To learn these myths and genealogies, to acquire these pass-words, needed high intellectual power. It was not possible for simple people. And so full salvation, full escape from matter to spirit, from the world to God, was only possible for an intellectual élite. And so Gnosticism, instead of enabling Christians to love one another, produced a situation in which Christians learned to despise one another, and the fellowship of the church was broken and interrupted.

Continuous glimpses of this line of thought will be seen behind the New Testament books, and especially behind the Pastoral Epistles, Second Peter and Jude, and First and Second John. The reader should watch for these signs as he reads.

Introduction to the First and Second Letters to Timothy and the Letter to Titus

THESE three letters are always called the Pastoral Epistles, a title which was given to them by Paul Anton in 1726. Prior to that they had been called the Ecclesiastical Epistles because they had so much instruction to give about the church. They are called the Pastoral Epistles, because they have so much to say about the character and the duty of those who are the pastors of the church. It has been said that their message can be summed up in the words of 1 Timothy 3.15: 'How to behave in the household of God'.

As we read them, one thing must always be remembered. They come from a time when the church was like a little island in a surrounding sea of paganism. It was so short a time since the converts had come into the church from paganism; the influences of paganism were so strong. The danger of relapse was insistent and constant. That is why it has been said that these letters are the most relevant of all New Testament letters in the mission field to this day. It is then only to be expected that they will have much to say about the Christian duty.

There is a duty to those outside the church. The Christian office-bearer must be well spoken of by people outside (1 Timothy 3.7). Religion must be no conventional thing which has no dynamic in it (2 Timothy 3.-19). A profession which practice denies is not to be tolerated (Titus 1.16).

The Christian has a duty to the state. He must pray for those who rule, and he must himself be a good citizen (1 Timothy 2.1,2; Titus 3.1).

The duties and the necessary characteristics of the various people within the church are laid down. The elders and the bishops are described (1 Timothy 3.1-8; 5.17-22; Titus 1.5-9). The deacons are described (1 Timothy 3.8-13). By this time the church had in it an order of widows (1 Timothy 5.3-16). The place of women is laid down, and they are forbidden to teach, a necessary restriction in Greek society, in which a forward woman would have automatically been regarded as an immoral woman (1 Timothy 2.11-15).

The duties of slaves are laid down, for the Christian slave must be a good slave (1 Timothy 6.1,2; Titus 2.9,10). The danger of riches is stressed (1 Timothy 6.6-10, 17-19).

There is much stress on keeping the faith, that is, on maintaining strict orthodoxy (2 Timothy 1.13,14; 3.14; Titus 1.9; 2.1).

This is all the more necessary, because at the back of these letters there is a heresy and a mistaken teaching to which continuous reference is made. It has myths; it has endless genealogies; it has speculations. It is given to argument and to discussion; it has a morbid craving for controversy; it has no true knowledge. It forbids people to marry, and tries to lay down ascetic food laws and is connected with Judaism. It declares that the resurrection is already past (1 Timothy 1.3-11; 4.1-5; 4.7; 6.4,5; 2 Timothy 2.14-16; 2.18; 4.2; Titus 1.10; 1.14; 3.9). It is easy to see that this is just the kind of situation that Gnostic speculations produced.

There are a great many scholars who do not think that these letters come from the hand of Paul as they stand. The style is different, much more matter of fact. The church with its elders and bishops and deacons and widows seems a much more highly developed institution than ever it was in the missionary days of Paul. Faith tends to be orthodoxy rather than personal relationship with Jesus Christ. In Paul's life as we know it there is no room for a ministry to Crete (Titus 1.5), unless Paul was released after his arrest and was free to work for some time before he was finally martyred. This is possible, but, if it was so, we have no information.

And yet in these letters there are a number of passages which are very personal to Paul and his life (1 Timothy 1.1-20; 2 Timothy 1.11,12; 1.15-18; 3.10,11; 4.6-21; Titus 3.12,13). It is just possible that what happened was that, after Paul's death, a devoted friend and follower of his took certain personal letters he had from Paul and added a message for the church of his day, and sent it out in the name of his great missionary master.

The First Letter to
TIMOTHY

Chapter 1

THIS is a letter from Paul, who is an apostle of Christ Jesus by the command of God our Saviour and of Christ Jesus our hope, ₂to Timothy his own true son in the faith. Grace, mercy and every blessing to you from God the Father and from Christ Jesus our Lord.

₃When I set out for Macedonia, at my urgent request you stayed on in Ephesus. What I wanted you to do was to give my orders to certain individuals to stop teaching doctrines which are a contradiction of the Christian faith, ₄and to give up spending their time and energy in the study of myths and genealogies to which there is no end, and which only provide recondite and abstruse speculations instead of helping to further God's scheme of salvation, the central principle of which is faith. ₅This order of mine has no other object than to promote the love which issues from a clean heart, a good conscience, and a sincere and genuine faith. ₆There are some people who have aimed at all the wrong things. They have lost the right way, and have ended up in a welter of arid and futile speculative discussions. ₇They would like to be instructors in the Christian ethic, but in fact they do not know what they are talking about, and they have no proper understanding of the things on which they lay so much stress.

₈We know that the law is a splendid thing, when it is used as it ought to be used. ₉We know very well that the law is not directed against the good man; it is directed against the lawless and the law-defying, against the impious and the sinner, against the irreligious and the irreverent, against patricides and matricides, against murderers, ₁₀fornicators, homosexuals, kidnappers, liars, perjurers, against anyone or anything which is hostile to sound teaching, ₁₁the teaching which agrees with the glorious good news sent by the blessed God to mankind, the teaching with which I have been entrusted.

₁₂It was Christ Jesus our Lord who gave me the strength for the responsibility of this task. My gratitude goes out to him because he believed that he could trust me, and appointed me to do this service for him, ₁₃in spite of the fact that I formerly abused and persecuted and wantonly insulted him. But he treated me with mercy, because I acted in ignorance in the days before I came to believe. ₁₄My sin was great, but the grace of our Lord was still greater, and with it there came the faith and love which are to be found in Christ Jesus. ₁₅Christ Jesus came into the world to save sinners—this is a saying which you can believe and accept absolutely—and I am the worst of them. ₁₆But I received mercy, and it was for this reason. Christ Jesus wanted me to be the first in whom he might display all his patience for everyone to see, because he wanted me to be an example of those who were going to believe in him, and so find eternal life. ₁₇To the eternal King, immortal, invisible, the only God, be honour and glory for ever and ever. Amen.

₁₈Such are the instructions which I entrust to you, son Timothy, and I do so with confidence, because I remember how what the prophets said about you first directed me to you. I want you to remember what they said, and to wage a good campaign, ₁₉armed with faith and a clear conscience. It is because they defied conscience that there are some who have made shipwreck of their faith. ₂₀Among these are Hymenaeus and Alexander. I have consigned them to Satan. They must be taught by discipline not to insult God.

Chapter 2

FIRST of all, I urge you to offer petitions, prayers, intercessions, thanksgivings for all men. ₂Pray for kings and for all who hold high office. Thus we will be able to live a quiet and peaceful life, in all reverence to God and in all dignity to man. ₃Such prayer is a lovely thing. It is the kind of prayer that God our Saviour wants to hear, ₄for he wants all men to be saved and to arrive at a knowledge of the truth. ₅There is one God, and one Mediator between God and man, Christ Jesus in his humanity, ₆for he sacrificed himself as the price of freedom for all men. And that sacrifice of his is the proof and guarantee, given in his good time, that God's desire is indeed the salvation of all mankind. ₇Of this truth I was appointed a herald and apostle—it is the truth I am telling you and no lie—to teach the Gentiles the true faith.

₈I would therefore wish that wherever you meet for public worship prayers should be offered by the men of the congregation. The hands they lift to God in appeal must be pure. Angry arguments must have no place in your meeting. ₉In the same way, women must dress neatly, modestly and soberly. They must not use elaborate hair-styles; they must not wear jewellery of gold and pearls; they must not dress in extravagantly expensive clothes. ₁₀They must be clothed in good conduct, as befits women who profess to be worshippers of God. ₁₁It is a woman's duty to learn quietly and to live submissively. ₁₂I do not allow a woman to teach or to have authority over men. A woman must keep quiet, ₁₃for Adam was made first, then Eve. It was not Adam who was led astray. ₁₄It was the woman who was led astray, and who became the victim of sin. ₁₅But women will be saved by motherhood, if they continue to live faithfully and lovingly, modestly walking the way to holiness.

Chapter 3

IT has been said, and said truly, that to be ambitious to be the leader and guardian of the community is to set one's heart on a noble task. ₂The superintendent of the community must therefore be a man whom no one can criticize. He must be the faithful husband of one wife. He must be abstemious, wise in the art of living, with an ordered beauty in his life. He must be hospitably inclined and he must be skilled in teaching. ₃He must not be too fond of wine. He must be gentle and not pugnacious. He must be peaceable and money must have no attraction for him. ₄He must preside well over his own family, with children who give him complete obedience and perfect respect. ₅If a man does not know how to preside over his own household, how can he look after one of God's congregations? ₆He must not be a new convert, in case he should become inflated with a sense of his own importance, and so incur the same judgment that was passed on the Devil for his pride. ₇He must have a good reputation among those who are not members of the church, for he must never incur the risk of making himself a target for abuse, and he must never provide ammunition for the slanderer.

₈In the same way, the deacons must be serious men. They must not be the kind of men who say one thing to one person and another to another. They must not be too fond of wine, nor must they be prepared to make money by disreputable methods. ₉They must combine a disciple's knowledge of the Christian faith with a clear conscience. ₁₀They must first undergo a period of probation. If they emerge from it with a clear record, they must then enter upon the work of a deacon. 11Their wives too must be serious women. They must not be given to malicious scandal-mongering. They must be abstemious and completely trustworthy. 12Deacons must be the faithful husbands of one wife. They must control their children, and preside well over their own households. 13Deacons who successfully carry out their office win for themselves a high standing in the church, and they receive the right to speak very freely in matters of the Christian faith.

14I am writing this letter to you, although I hope to come to see you fairly soon. 15I am sending it to you, because, if I am delayed, I want you to know how to behave in God's household, and God's household is the church of the living God, a pillar and buttress of the truth. 16No one can deny the greatness of the truth of our religion, the truth which only a disciple can understand:

> He appeared in a human body;
> was vindicated in the spirit;
> was seen by angels;
> was preached among the nations;
> was believed in all over the world;
> was taken up in glory.

Chapter 4

THE Spirit expressly says that in later times there will be some who will become deserters from the faith, and who will listen to spirits, who will lure them from the right way, and to the teaching of demons. 2The demons will operate through men whose teaching is a mixture of insincerity and lies, men whose own conscience bears the brand-mark of the Devil burned into it. 3Such teachers try to stop people marrying. They try to teach them to abstain from certain foods, foods which God created to be received with gratitude by those who are believers and who know the truth. 4For everything that God created is good. Nothing is to be rejected. Everything is to be received with thanksgiving, 5for it is consecrated by God's word and by prayer.

6If you remind the Christian fellowship of these basic truths, you will be a good servant of Christ Jesus, and all the time you will continually nourish your soul on the words of faith, and on that fine teaching of which you have become a follower. 7You must have nothing to do with myths, which are quite profitless for religion, and which are no better than old wives' tales. Train yourself for the life whose goal is God. ₈Physical training has a limited usefulness, but to live the life whose goal is God has an unlimited usefulness, for it promises life now and life to come. ₉This is a saying which you can believe and accept absolutely. ₁₀It is for that reason that we accept both the strict discipline of training and the stern struggle of the contest, because we have set our hope on the living God, who is the Saviour of all men, and above all the Saviour of those who believe.

₁₁Hand on these instructions and this teaching. ₁₂It would be wrong for anyone to look down on you because you are young. It is rather your duty to provide an example of what a believer should be, in your speech, in your conduct, in love, in reliability, in purity. ₁₃While you are waiting for me to come, give your attention to the public reading of scripture, to the exhortation of the congregation, and to teaching. ₁₄Do not neglect the special gift the Spirit gave you. It was given to you through the words of the prophets, when the elders as a body laid their hands on you. ₁₅Give your continuous attention to these things. They must be your whole life, and then no one will be able to fail to see your all-round progress. ₁₆Pay attention to yourself and to your teaching. If you do, you will save both yourself and your hearers.

Chapter 5

IF you have occasion to find some fault with an older man, do not do so harshly. Appeal to him, as you would to a father. Treat younger men as your brothers, ₂older women as your mothers, younger women as your sisters. Then your relationship with them will be completely pure.

₃You must honour widows, who are genuinely widows. ₄If a widow has children or grandchildren, her own younger relatives must first learn to discharge what is a religious duty to their own family, and to repay the debt which they owe to their parents and grandparents, for this is what God approves. ₅But a genuine widow, who is left all alone in the world, has no other hope than God, and night and day she spends all her time telling him her needs and praying to him. ₆As for a widow who lives a life of extravagant luxury, although she may be physically alive, she is spiritually dead. ₇Pass on these instructions, for the widows must be beyond criticism. ₈To make no provision for one's own people, and especially for one's own family, is to deny our

Christian faith, and to be worse than an unbeliever. ₉To be enrolled, a widow must be at least sixty years old. She must have been the faithful wife of one husband. ₁₀She must have a reputation for good works. She can only be enrolled, if she has brought up children, if she has practised hospitality, if she has been prepared to render the most menial service to God's people, if she has been in the habit of helping people in trouble, if good works of every kind have been the aim and object of her life. ₁₁Do not place younger widows on the roll. For, when passion makes them grow restive under the discipline of Christ, they want to marry, ₁₂and so stand condemned, because they have broken their pledge to him. ₁₃At the same time they learn to be idle, and to spend their time on a continual round of social visits. They learn not only to be idle; they learn to gossip, and to poke their noses into everyone's business, chattering about things that should not be talked about at all. ₁₄I would like the younger widows to marry, to have children, to preside over a house and home, and to give none of those who are hostile to us an opportunity to spread their slanders about us. ₁₅Some of them have already lost the way, and gone to the Devil. ₁₆Any Christian man or woman who has widows within the family circle must personally support them. The congregation must not be asked to carry a burden of responsibility for people like that; it must be left free to support those who are genuinely widows.

₁₇Elders who exercise an efficient leadership should be reckoned as worthy of double pay, especially those strenuously engaged in preaching and teaching. ₁₈For scripture says: 'You must not muzzle the ox when it is treading the corn,' and, 'The workman deserves his pay.' ₁₉Do not accept any charge against an elder, unless it is supported by the evidence of two or three witnesses. ₂₀Consistent sinners must be publicly convicted to make the others healthily afraid. ₂₁Before God and Christ Jesus and the holy angels I charge you to keep these rules, and never to prejudge an issue or to act other than impartially. ₂₂Do not be in too big a hurry to ordain anyone to the eldership. Do not get yourself involved in the sins of others. Keep yourself clean. ₂₃Don't go on drinking nothing but water. Use a little wine for the sake of your stomach and your frequent attacks of sickness.

₂₄Some men's sins are so notorious that the court knows all about them long before they come up for trial. The sins of others have not caught up with them yet. ₂₅In the same way good deeds are evident for all to see, and, even if they are not, they cannot in the end be hidden.

Chapter 6

A LL those who are under the yoke of slavery must recognize that their masters have a right to all respect. If they fail to see this, the name of God and the Christian teaching will get a bad reputation. ₂If their masters happen to be believers, they must not treat them with any the less respect because they are brothers within the Christian community. So far from that, they must try to be all the better slaves, because those who are receiving their service are their brothers in faith and love.

This is what you must teach, and this is what you must urge upon your hearers. ₃If anyone's teaching is at variance with this, and if he does not take his stand on sound instruction—and by that I mean the instruction which our Lord Jesus Christ gave—and on truly religious teaching, ₄he is inflated with conceit. Instead of having a real grasp of the truth, he has an unhealthy passion for speculations and for hair-splitting arguments, which are bound to issue in jealousy and in controversy, insults, and in an atmosphere poisoned with suspicion ₅and in continuous friction, which are all characteristic of men who have become mentally depraved and deprived of the truth. They are characteristic of men who regard their religion as a profit-making concern. ₆And indeed there is great profit in religion for the man who has learned the secret of needing nothing outside himself. ₇For we brought nothing into the world, for the very good reason that, when we come to leave it, we can take nothing out of it. ₈Given food to eat and clothes to wear, we have quite enough to be going on with. ₉Those who want to be wealthy run the risk of encountering many a temptation, and falling into many a trap, and of developing a great many senseless, and even hurtful, ambitions, which are liable to plunge men into wreck and ruin. ₁₀For the love of money is the root from which all evils grow. It is this uncontrolled craving for money which has made some people lose the way, and caused them to experience the sting of many a bitter pang.

₁₁You are a man of God, and therefore you must have nothing to do with these things. Justice, godliness, fidelity, love, fortitude, gentleness—these you must make the object of all your endeavour. ₁₂Strain every nerve, as the noble athlete of faith, to win the prize of eternal life. It was to this you were called, when you nobly and publicly confessed your faith in the presence of many witnesses. ₁₃I charge you in the presence of God, the universal giver of life, and of Christ Jesus, who before Pilate nobly witnessed to his faith, 14never to blot your copy-book, never to lay yourself open to criticism, but to obey your orders, until the Lord Jesus Christ appears. 15And that appearance will be displayed in his own good time by the blessed and only Sovereign, the King of kings, the Lord of lords, 16the One who alone possesses immortality, whose home is in the light that no man can approach, whom no man has ever seen or can see. To him be honour and might that knows no end! Amen.

17Tell those who are wealthy in this world's goods not to be arrogant, and not to place their hopes on money with all its uncertainty, but on God who richly provides us with everything to enjoy. 18Tell them to be kind, to find their wealth in lovely deeds, to be quick to give and ready to share. 19Then they will provide themselves with a treasure on which they can build well for the future. Thus they will grasp the life which is real life.

20My dear Timothy, keep what has been entrusted to you safe. Turn your back on godless and meaningless chatter, and on the contradictory statements of that knowledge, which it is a lie to call knowledge. 21There are some who profess to have knowledge, but, as far as the faith is concerned, they have missed the mark.

Grace be with you all.

The Second Letter to
TIMOTHY

Chapter 1

THIS is a letter from Paul, who is an apostle of Christ Jesus, to his dear son Timothy. I am an apostle because God willed that I should be, and my work is to bring to men the promised life which Christ Jesus can give them. ₂Grace, mercy and every blessing to you from God the Father and from Christ Jesus our Lord.

₃I serve God with a good conscience as my forefathers did before me, and I thank him, when night and day I continually remember you in my prayers. ₄I remember the tears you shed when we parted, and I am longing to see you again. Nothing could make me happier than that. ₅I am reminded of the sincerity of your faith. It was a faith like that, which long before this had its home in the heart of your grandmother Lois and your mother Eunice—and I am quite sure that it is in your heart too. ₆That is why I want to remind you to kindle to a flame God's gift, which came to you, when I laid my hands upon you at your ordination. ₇For God did not give us the spirit of cowardly fear; he gave us the spirit of power, of love, and of self-discipline. ₈Don't be ashamed publicly to declare your loyalty to our Lord. Don't be embarrassed that I am in gaol for his sake. Join the company of sufferers for the gospel, and God will give you strength. ₉It is that same God who saved us and called us to a life dedicated to himself. He did not call us because we had done anything to deserve it. He called us because it was his purpose to do so. He called us in the grace which has been given to us in Christ Jesus. That grace existed in God's purpose before time began, ₁₀and has now been fully displayed for all to see through the coming to earth of our Saviour Christ Jesus, who destroyed death and brought life and immortality to light through the good news. ₁₁For the service of the good news I was appointed a herald, an apostle and a teacher. ₁₂That is the reason why I am in the situation in which I now am. But I am not ashamed of it. I know the person to whom I have entrusted my life, and I am absolutely sure that he can protect what I have placed in his safe-keeping, until the great day comes. 13Take as the standard by which you live the sound instruction which you received from me. Live in that loyalty and love which come into life when Christ Jesus becomes the very atmosphere in which you exist. 14By the help of the Holy Spirit, who has his home within you, keep safe the noble gift which has been entrusted to you.

15You already know that everyone in the province of Asia has deserted me, including Phygelus and Hermogenes. 16I pray for God's mercy for the family of Onesiphorus. His visits have always been like a breath of fresh air to me. He was not ashamed to visit me in gaol. 17So far from that, when he arrived in Rome, he made every effort to search for me until he found me. 18The Lord grant him to find mercy from the Lord on the great day! And you know even better than I do all the service he rendered to the church in Ephesus.

Chapter 2

FORTIFY your life with the dynamic influence of that grace which enters life, when Christ Jesus becomes the atmosphere in which we live. 2Take the instruction I gave you in the presence of many witnesses, and hand it over to men on whom you can rely, and who are such that they will be competent to communicate to others what they themselves have learned. 3Like a good soldier of Christ Jesus, join the company of those who are prepared to suffer for their faith. 4No soldier on active service gets involved in civilian affairs; he has no other aim than to satisfy his commanding officer. 5No athlete will win the victor's laurel crown, unless he keeps the rules of the game. 6The farmer who has done all the hard work has the first right to share in the crops. 7Think over what I am saying to you. The Lord will make you able to understand all about it.

8Remember Jesus Christ, risen from the dead, descended from David. This is what my gospel teaches. 9It is for the sake of that gospel that I am at present suffering, even to the length of being imprisoned as a criminal. But no one can put the word of God in prison. 10It is for the sake of God's chosen ones that I can pass the breaking-point and not break. I want them too to win that salvation which is ours because of what Christ Jesus has done for us, and with it the glory that is eternal. 11It has been said, and said truly:

If we have died with him,
  we shall live with him;
12if we endure,
  we shall reign with him;
if we deny him,
  he too will deny us;
13if we are faithless,
  he remains faithful,
  for he cannot deny himself.

14Keep on reminding them of all this. Charge them before God not to engage in pugnacious debates about verbal niceties. Debates like that are an unprofitable occupation, and do nothing but undermine the faith of the hearers. 15Do your best to present yourself to God as a man of sterling worth, a workman who has no need to be ashamed of his work, a sound expositor of the true word. 16Avoid empty and irreverent chatter. Those who indulge in it make fast and excellent progress in irreligion. 17The damaging effects of their teaching will spread like a cancerous ulcer. Hymenaeus and Philetus are men like that. 18Their idea of the truth is well off the mark, for they say that our resurrection has already taken place, a statement which upsets some people's faith. 19The firm foundation God laid still stands, sealed with this inscription: 'The Lord knows those who are his,' and, 'Everyone who takes the name of the Lord on his lips must turn his back on wickedness.' 20In any great house there are utensils not only of gold and silver; there are utensils of wood and earthenware too. Some are put to an honourable use, and some to a menial use. 21Anyone who cleanses himself from the things we have been talking about will be a utensil fit for honourable use, dedicated to God, useful to his master, equipped to render every useful service. 22Leave the hot passions of youth behind. Consistently take as your aim justice, fidelity, love, right relationships with those whose appeal is sincerely to the Lord. 23Refuse to take any part in senseless and illiterate speculations, for you are well aware that they can result in nothing but controversies. 24The Lord's servant must not be quarrelsome; he must be characteristically kindly. He must be a good teacher. He must have a mind above resentment. 25When he has to exercise discipline upon those who oppose him, he must do so in the strength of gentleness, for it may be that God will lead them to repentance and to a knowledge of the truth. 26True, they were captured alive by the Devil, but it may be that they will come to their senses and escape from his trap, and end up by accepting God's will.

Chapter 3

YOU must realize that in the last days difficult times will come. ₂There will be men who love nothing but self and money. They will be boastful, arrogant and abusive. They will have no respect for parents, and no gratitude to any man. They will be without reverence to God ₃and without natural affection to men. They will be implacable in their enmities and slanderous in their words. They will be intemperate and savage. They will see nothing to love in goodness. ₄They will be treacherous, reckless, inflated with conceit. They will love pleasure more than they love God. ₅They will retain the outward conventions of religion, but they will consistently deny its dynamic. Refuse to associate with people like that. ₆It is people like that who insinuate themselves into houses and thus get into their clutches silly women, who are burdened by their sins of the past and driven by all kinds of desires, ₇women who go from teacher to teacher, and who remain quite incapable of ever arriving at a knowledge of the truth. ₈Jannes and Jambres rebelled against Moses, and they too rebel against the truth. They are men with corrupt minds and a counterfeit faith. ₉But they will not get very far. Their folly will be publicly exposed as that of Jannes and Jambres was.

₁₀But you have been my comrade in my teaching, my way of life, my purpose, my faith, my patience, my love, my fortitude. ₁₁You have been my partner in my persecutions and my sufferings. You know what happened to me in Antioch, in Iconium, in Lystra. You know what persecutions I had to go through. The Lord rescued me from all of them. ₁₂All who choose to live a godly life as Christians will be persecuted. ₁₃Malicious men and impostors will go from bad to worse, deceiving others and themselves deceived. ₁₄You must refuse to move from the things you have been taught and have accepted as true, and you must never forget from whom you learned them. ₁₅Nor must you forget that from your childhood days you have known the sacred scriptures, which, if you have faith in Christ Jesus, can give you the wisdom that leads to salvation. ₁₆Every divinely inspired scripture is also useful for the teaching of the truth, for the refutation of error, for moral correction, and for training in the good life. ₁₇Its aim is to make the man of God fit for his task, and to equip him for every kind of useful work.

Chapter 4

I CHARGE you before God and Christ Jesus, who will judge the living and the dead, I charge you by his coming appearing and his coming reign, ₂proclaim your message. Urge it upon people whether you can take an opportunity or have to make an opportunity. Use argument, rebuke, appeal, with all the patience that good teaching needs. ₃The time will come when they will refuse to listen to sound teaching. They will collect a motley assortment of teachers to tickle their ears by telling them the things they want to hear. ₄They will deliberately shut their ears to the truth, and will wander down the byways of mythology. ₅You must retain your sanity of mind. You must be prepared to suffer. You must act like a man who has good news to tell. You must leave no part of your Christian service incomplete.

₆Men pour out a cup of wine as a sacrifice to their gods, and the last drops of my life are being poured out on the altar of sacrifice. The time for me to strike camp has come. ₇My wrestling days are over, and I have fought well. For me the race is finished now. And I have kept my pledge. ₈Now there awaits me the victorious athlete's laurel crown, which is the prize of life lived well. The Lord, the just Judge, will give it to me on that great day, and not only to me, but to all who lovingly longed for him to appear.

₉Do your best to come to see me soon. ₁₀Demas has left me. He fell in love with this world. He has gone to Thessalonica. Crescens has gone to Galatia, and Titus to Dalmatia. ₁₁Only Luke is with me. Get Mark and bring him with you. He can render me useful service. ₁₂I have sent Tychicus to Ephesus. ₁₃When you come, bring me the cloak I left in Carpus' house at Troas. Bring me the books, and specially the parchments. ₁₄Alexander the coppersmith did me a lot of harm. The Lord will give him what he has earned for what he has done. ₁₅You too must watch him, because he bitterly opposed our message.

₁₆At my first appearance in court on trial, no one supported me. Everyone deserted me. I pray that it may not be held against them. ₁₇But the Lord stood by me and gave me strength, and so through me the Christian message in all its fullness was proclaimed, and all the Gentile world heard it, and I was rescued from the lion's mouth. ₁₈The Lord will rescue me from every wicked attack on me. He will keep me safe until his heavenly kingdom comes. Glory be to him for ever and ever! Amen.

19Give my good wishes to Prisca and Aquila, and to Onesiphorus' family. 20Erastus stayed on at Corinth. I left Trophimus ill at Miletus. 21Do your best to come before winter sets in. Eubulus sends you his good wishes, and so do Pudens and Linus and Claudia and all your fellow-Christians. 22The Lord be with your spirit. Grace be with you all.

The Letter to
TITUS

Chapter 1

THIS is a letter from Paul, God's servant and Jesus Christ's apostle.
It was to awaken faith in God's chosen people and to bring them
the knowledge of the truth, as it is contained in our religion, that I
was made both servant and apostle. ₂That religion is founded on the
hope of eternal life. Long ago God—and he cannot lie—promised this
life. ₃Now in his own good time God has displayed his message for all
to see, through the proclamation of it, with which I was entrusted by
the direct command of God our Saviour. ₄I am writing to you Titus,
for you are my true son in the faith which we both share. Grace to
you and every blessing from God our Father and Christ Jesus our
Saviour.

₅My intention in leaving you behind was that you should tidy up
the loose ends of things which I did not manage to finish, and that
you should appoint elders in every town. In any such appointments
you are to follow my instructions, ₆and you are to appoint only men
who are above suspicion of moral fault, men who are the faithful
husbands of one wife, men whose own children are Christian believers, not open to any charge of loose living or out of control.
₇The superintendent of the community is God's servant, and as such
he must necessarily be a man who is above suspicion of moral fault.
He must not be self-opinionated or violent in temper. He must not
be too fond of wine or pugnacious. He must not be prepared to make
money by disreputable methods. ₈He must keep open house for
strangers. He must be ready to welcome goodness wherever he sees it.
He must be wise in the art of living, just, devout, master of himself.
₉He must never lose his grip of the message which he has been taught
and on which he must rely, for thus he will have the ability to appeal
to his hearers with sound doctrine, and to refute opponents.

₁₀There are many, especially among the Jewish members of the
church, who are a law to themselves. Their talk is wild and futile,

and they produce nothing but error and confusion in the mind of their hearers. 11It is essential that they should be silenced, for they are upsetting whole families by teaching things that should not be taught, and by doing so for motives which are shamefully mercenary. 12It was one of themselves, one of their own prophets, who said: 'The Cretans are always liars, vicious beasts, lazy gluttons.' 13This statement is true. You must for that very reason sternly convict them of the error of their ways. Only thus will they return to a sound faith, 14and stop devoting themselves to Jewish myths and to rules and regulations imposed by men who turn their back on the truth. 15To the pure everything is pure; to the corrupt and unbelieving nothing is pure. They are corrupt both in mind and conscience. 16They profess to know God, but by their conduct they deny him. They are detestable, disobedient, disqualified for any good activity.

Chapter 2

As for yourself personally, what you say must be in keeping with sound doctrine. 2You must instruct the older men to be abstemious, serious, wise in the art of living, sound in faith, in love and in fortitude. 3In the same way the older women must live as if every act in life is an act of worship. They must not indulge in scandal-mongering. They must not be so addicted to drink that they cannot do without it. They must be teachers of all that is fine, 4and so train the younger women to love their husbands and their children, 5to be wise in the art of living, to be chaste, to be domesticated, to be kind, to accept the authority of their own husbands. This is the way to ensure that no one can spread bad reports about the message of God. 6In the same way you must urge the younger men to live wisely and well. 7You must yourself provide in everything an example of fine living. In your teaching you must show integrity and dignity. 8Your speech must be wholesome, and such that no one can find fault with it. Then your opponent will be shamed into silence, when he can find nothing discreditable to say about us. 9Slaves must try to give complete obedience and satisfaction to their masters. They must not answer back. 10They must never be guilty of pilfering. They must show themselves to be completely honest and reliable, for to work like that is the way to become ornaments of the teaching we have received from God our Saviour.

11For the grace of God has broken into history for the salvation of all men. ₁₂It is training us to renounce the life in which God is banished from the scene, and in which the world's desires hold sway, and in this age to live a well-ordered, upright and godly life, ₁₃while all the time we are waiting for our blessed hope to be realized, when the splendour of our great God and Saviour Jesus Christ bursts upon the world. ₁₄He gave himself for us, to liberate us from all wickedness, and to make us a people purified to be his own, and eager to live a noble life. ₁₅This is your message. Plead with men and argue with men to accept it, and always with the accent of authority. Don't allow anyone to look down on you.

Chapter 3

MAKE it a regular part of your teaching to remind your people to submit to the government and the authorities, to obey them, and to be ready to undertake any honest work. ₂Consistently remind them that they must not use insulting language, or be quarrelsome; that they must always be fair and more than fair to others, and that in their dealings with everyone they must show themselves to be men and women whose strength is always in their gentleness. ₃We too were once foolish and disobedient and astray. We too were the slaves of all kinds of passions and pleasures. Malice and envy were the characteristics of our daily life. We were detested by others and we hated each other. ₄But, when the kindness and the generous love of God our Saviour appeared upon the scene, ₅not in consequence of anything that we had done in any goodness of our own, but solely in his own mercy, he saved us through the water of rebirth and that renewal which the Holy Spirit gives. ₆Through Jesus Christ our Saviour he poured out the Spirit richly upon us. ₇For it was his purpose to put us, through his grace, into a right relationship with himself, and to enable us to enter into possession of the eternal life which God had promised and for which we hope. ₈This has been said, and said truly.

These are the points that I want you to stress, for I want to make sure that those who have come to believe in God will make it their object to engage in honest work. Such work is not only honest; it is also useful to society. ₉Avoid senseless speculations and genealogies, dissension and wordy battles about legalistic points. They are a waste of time and get nowhere. ₁₀If a man disregards the beliefs of the community and goes his own way, you must warn him a first time and a second time. After that have nothing to do with him. ¹¹You can be sure that a man like that is a perverted sinner who stands self-condemned.

¹²When I send Artemas or Tychicus to you, come and join me at Nicopolis as soon as you can. It is there that I have decided to spend the winter. ¹³Do your best to help Zenas the lawyer and Apollos on their way, and see to it that they have everything they need. ¹⁴Our people must be instructed to engage in honest work. They must earn the necessities of life, and they must not contribute nothing to the common good.

¹⁵All the people who are with me send their good wishes. Give my good wishes to all our faithful friends. Grace be with you all.

Introduction to the Letter to the Hebrews

THE Letter to the Hebrews might well be called the letter of the great unknown. No one knows who wrote it. Away back in the third century Origen had said: 'Who wrote the Letter to the Hebrews God alone knows.' How then did it get attached to the name of Paul? When the New Testament came to be put together as a book, the test of whether or not any single book was to get into it was whether or not the book had been written by an apostle, or at least by an apostolic man, a man who had been in contact with the apostles. No one knew who had written the Letter to the Hebrews, but it was far too great and far too valuable a book to omit and to lose. So it was, as it were, put under the protection of Paul, the great letter-writer, and was included with his letters.

Five hundred years before the writer to the Hebrews wrote his letter, Plato the great Greek had spoken of a doctrine which had left a deep mark on Greek thought. He had spoken of the *forms* or *ideas*. There were, he said, the perfect ideas, the perfect forms, the perfect patterns, the perfect archetypes of all things laid up in heaven. Everything on earth was a pale and imperfect copy of these forms and ideas; and the task of life was to get from the world's imperfections to heaven's perfections, to get from earth's unreality to heaven's reality. As the writer to the Hebrews saw it, in Jesus heaven's perfection had come to earth.

Before Jesus everything had been fragmentary and evanescent (1.1), but Jesus is greater than everything that went before. He is greater than the angels (chapter 1). He is greater than Moses (chapter 3). He is greater than Joshua (chapter 4). Everything that had been foreshadowed and hinted at came to its perfection in Jesus.

But in one respect, in the greatest of all things, this was specially true. The priest had a very special position in ancient religion. The Latin for priest is *pontifex*, which means a bridge-builder. The priest was the person who built a bridge between God and man. In particular the Jewish High Priest had a very special function on the Day of Atonement. No human being ever went into the Holy of Holies in the Temple, except the High Priest, and even he on only one day in the year, the Day of Atonement. The priest on behalf of the people went into the presence of God. To the writer to the Hebrews the ancient priesthood is only the imperfect shadow of the real thing.

Jesus is the real priest, the priest who himself can go into the presence of God, and who can open the way for others to follow.

So the writer to the Hebrews tells how Jesus is the perfect priest. Two things are necessary for any priest—he must have sympathy with men, and he must be divinely appointed (chapter 5). That was supremely true of Jesus.

There are things which show the obvious imperfection of the old priesthood. The old priesthood had to offer sacrifice for its own sins before ever it offered sacrifice for the sins of the people. Jesus does not need to do that, because he has no sin (7.27). The old sacrifices had to be made over and over again, day in and day out throughout the years. But the sacrifice Jesus made is made once and for all and never needs to be made again (10.1-3).

The imperfection of the old sacrifices is obvious. If they were really effective, they would not need to be made over and over again. The blood of animals can never really make atonement. But Jesus is not only the perfect priest, he is the perfect offering too; and the offering he brings is himself, and his perfect obedience (10.5-14).

There is nothing surprising in this, because the new covenant, the new relationship to God had already been foretold (Jeremiah 31.31-34; Hebrews 9.15-18), and the new kind of priesthood, the priesthood after the order of Melchizedek (Genesis 14.17-21; Psalm 110.4; Hebrews 7) had already been foretold too.

So Jesus is both the perfect priest and the perfect offering, and therefore in him the way to God is open wide. So for the writer to the Hebrews two things are to be said to the Christian.

First, *Let us go in*. The access to God is wide open, because of what Jesus the great High Priest has done. Let us then draw near (4.16; 10.19-22).

Second, *Let us go on*. Those to whom he was writing had become a little weary, a little regretful for what they had left, a little discouraged and they were on the verge of turning back. But to them there comes the invitation, to go, not backwards, but forwards, and to go in faith (5.11–6.12; chapter 11).

Let us go in, and, Let us go on, are the twin rallying-calls of the great unknown who wrote the Letter to the Hebrews.

The Letter to the
HEBREWS

Chapter 1

LONG ago God spoke to our ancestors by means of the prophets,
but the revelation which was given through them was fragmentary and varied. 2But now, as time as we know it is coming to an
end, he has spoken in one whose relation to himself is that of Son,
that Son into whose possession he gave all things, and by whose
agency he created the present world and the world to come. 3This
Son is the radiance of his glory, just as the ray is the light of the sun.
He is the exact impression of his being, just as the mark is the exact
impression of the seal. It is he who sustains all things by the dynamic
power of his word. And, after he had effected the cleansing of men
from their sins, he took his place at the right hand of the Majesty in
the heights of heaven, 4for he was as much superior to the angels as
the title he had been given as his possession by God was greater than
theirs.

5To which of the angels did God ever say:

'You are my Son;
today I have begotten you'?

And again:

'I will be his Father,
and he will be my Son'?

6Again, when he leads his firstborn Son on to the stage of world
history, he says:

'Let all God's angels worship him.'

7Of the angels he says:

'God makes his angels winds,
and his servants a flame of fire.'

173

8But of the Son he says:

'Your throne, O God, will last for ever and ever;
  the righteous sceptre is the sceptre of your kingdom.
9You have loved justice, and you have hated lawlessness.
  That is why God, your God, has singled you out
    from your fellows,
  and has given you the thrilling joy
    of being anointed for kingship.'

10And again:

'It was you, O Lord, who in the beginning
  laid the foundations of the earth;
and it was your hands
  which made the heavens.
11They will be destroyed, but you remain.
  They will all grow old, as clothes grow old.
12You will fold them up like a cloak,
  and they will be changed, as clothes are changed.
But you are always the same,
  and your years will never come to an end.'

13To which of the angels has he ever said:

'Sit at my right hand,
  until I make your enemies a footstool for your feet'?

14Clearly, the angels are serving spirits, despatched each on his own errand, to help those who are to receive the salvation which God has promised.

Chapter 2

IT is therefore necessary that we should pay all the more attention to what we have been told. Otherwise, we may well be like a ship which drifts past the harbour to shipwreck. 2For, if the message delivered through angels, as the law was, was valid, and, if every transgression of it, and disobedience to it, carried its just penalty, 3how can we escape, if we disregard so much greater a way to salvation? For the way of salvation offered to us had its origin in the Lord's own words, and its validity was guaranteed to us by those who actually heard it from his own lips. 4God too continuously supplied further evidence of its truth in events in which his own power is plainly visible, in all kinds of acts of supernatural power, and in the distribution of the gifts the Holy Spirit gives, as God decides.

₅For it was not to angels that God subjected the new order of which we are speaking. ₆There is a passage of scripture, in which one of the sacred writers puts it on record:

'What is man that you should remember him,
   or what is the son of man that you should be concerned with him?
₇You made him for a little time lower than the angels.
   But afterwards you crowned him with glory and honour,
   ₈and you subjected all things beneath his feet.'

When it says that he subjected all things to him, it means that he left nothing unsubjected to him. But as things are we do not in fact yet see all things in a state of subjection to man. ₉What we do see is Jesus. For a short time he was made lower than the angels. But now we see him crowned with glory and honour, because of the death he suffered, for it was the gracious purpose of God that Jesus should experience death for all.

₁₀God will be the end of all things as he was the beginning, and it was fitting for him, in bringing many sons to glory, to make the pioneer of their salvation perfect through his sufferings. ₁₁For the consecrating priest and the consecrated people have one Father That is why he does not hesitate to call them brothers:

   ₁₂'I will tell of your name to my brothers,
      I will sing your praises in the assembly of God's people.'

₁₂And again he says, as any man might say:

      ₁₃'I will put my trust in God.'

and again:

      'Here am I and the children God gave me.'

₁₄The children share in a flesh and blood human nature, and he too in exactly the same way shared in the same things. The purpose of his doing so was to destroy him who had death in his control, I mean, the Devil, ₁₅and so to liberate those for whom life was a kind of slavery, because of their fear of death. ₁₆For obviously it is not angels that he is out to help; it is, as scripture says, the children of Abraham whom he helps. ₁₇He therefore had to be completely identified with his brothers, for only then could he become in divine things a compassionate high priest on whom men can rely, and so bring forgiveness to the people for their sins. 18For, because he himself went through the ordeal of suffering, he is able to help others who are now going through that same ordeal.

Chapter 3

So then, brothers in consecration, sharers in the calling which comes from heaven and calls to heaven, fix your attention on Jesus. Jesus is the Apostle and High Priest of the faith which we profess, 2and he was faithful to God who appointed him to that office. Moses too was faithful to God in all God's house. 3The founder of a house has always greater honour than the house itself. So then Jesus is deemed to be worthy of greater honour than Moses. 4Every house is founded by someone; it is God who founded all things. 5It was in the capacity of a servant that Moses was faithful in God's house. His function was to point to the things which God was going to say in the future. 6But it was as a son that Christ was faithful over the house of God. And we are God's house, if we retain our courage, and our pride in the hope that is ours.

7So then, as the Holy Spirit says:

'Today I plead with you, listen to his voice.
8Do not be stubborn,
    as you were when you rebelled against him,
    on the day when you sorely tried his patience
        in the desert.
9There your ancestors tried me,
    and put me to the test,
    and saw what I could do 10for forty years.
That was why I was angry with that generation.
I said: "In their hearts they always go astray,
    and they never learned my ways."
11As I swore in my anger,
    they shall never come in to me,
    and share my rest.'

12Brothers, you must be very careful to avoid a situation in which the heart of any of you becomes so wicked in its refusal to believe that he thereby becomes a deserter from the living God. 13So long as it is possible to use the word 'Today' in that appeal of God, you must rather daily urge one another not to allow any of you to be made stubborn against God by sin's seductive influence. 14For we have been made partners with Christ, if only we preserve firm the confidence we had at the beginning. 15When it was said:

> 'Today I plead with you, listen to his voice.
> Do not be stubborn,
>   as you were when you rebelled against him,'

16who was it who heard God's appeal, and who rebelled? Who but all those who came out of Egypt under Moses' leadership? 17With whom was God angry for forty years? Was it not with those who sinned, and who fell dead in the desert? 18To whom did he swear that they would never enter his rest, if it was not to those who disobeyed him? 19So we see that it was their refusal to believe which made it impossible for them to enter.

Chapter 4

So then, so long as the promise of entrance into his rest remains open to us, the one thing we must dread is that any of you should be judged to have missed it. 2We too have heard the good news, just as they did, but the message they heard did them no good, because there was no faith in those who heard it for it to be blended with. 3It is we who have believed who are entering that rest. What he said was:

> 'I swore in my anger
>   that they should never enter into my rest.'

This is said, although God's work has been completed since the creation of the world. 4For somewhere scripture has said about the seventh day: 'God rested from all his work on the seventh day.' 5Let me repeat it. In the passage we have already quoted we find: 'They shall never enter into my rest.' 6Those who in the old days received the good news of that rest never did enter into that rest because of their refusal to believe. It therefore remains for someone to enter this rest. 7God therefore again fixes a day, for in David, so long a time afterwards, he says 'Today,' for in the passage we have already quoted he says:

> 'Today I plead with you, listen to his voice.
> Do not be stubborn.'

₈If Joshua had in fact given them rest, God would not afterwards have spoken to them about another day. ₉The deduction therefore must be that there still remains a Sabbath rest for the people of God. ₁₀For, if anyone enters into God's rest, he too rests from his work, as God did from his. ₁₁Let us then make every effort to enter into that rest, so that no one may make the mistake of being guilty of the same kind of disobedience.

₁₂For the word of God is effectively alive; it is sharper than any double-edged sword; it penetrates right to the division of soul and spirit, of joints and marrow. It scrutinizes a man's thoughts and intentions. ₁₃There is no created thing or being which is out of sight to him. Everything is stripped and exposed to the eyes of the one to whom we have to render account of ourselves.

₁₄Since then we have a great high priest, who has passed through the heavens, Jesus the Son of God, we must never lose our grip of the faith we have publicly professed. ₁₅It is not a high priest who is unable to sympathize with the weaknesses that we possess; it is a high priest who in every respect has gone through the same ordeal of temptation as we have to go through, and who emerged sinless. ₁₆We must then fearlessly and confidently come to the throne of grace, and then we will find mercy and grace to help us in every situation when we need them.

Chapter 5

EVERY high priest who is selected from his fellowmen is appointed to act for them in matters concerning God. His function is to offer to God gifts and sacrifices for men's sins. ₂Because he himself is clothed in weakness, he can deal gently with those who do not know the truth and who lose the way. ₃Because of this weakness he is under obligation to offer sacrifices for his own sins, just as he does for the sins of the people. ₄No one takes this honour upon himself; he is called to it by God, just as Aaron was.

₅So Christ too did not give himself the glory of becoming high priest; that glory was given to him by God, who said to him:

'You are my Son;
today I have begotten you.'

₆In the same way he says in another passage:

'You are a priest for ever
in the order of Melchizedek.'

₇In the days of his human life, with loud cries and tears, he brought his prayers and requests to God, who was able to save him from death, and his prayers were heard because of his reverence for God. ₈Son though he was, for him suffering was the way to learn obedience. ₉So he became perfect, and thus became the source of eternal salvation for all who obey him, ₁₀and he was given by God the title of a priest in the order of Melchizedek.

₁₁On Melchizedek I have a great deal to say, and it is not easy for me to put it in a way that you will understand, for you have become dull of hearing. ₁₂By this time you ought to be teaching others. But in point of fact you need someone to teach you all over again the elementary principles of God's message to you. It is milk you have come to need, not solid food. ₁₃If a man is still being fed on milk, he is unable to take in instruction on the good life, for he is still a baby. ₁₄Solid food is for mature men; it is for those whose faculties are disciplined by practice to distinguish between right and wrong.

Chapter 6

So then, we must leave behind elementary Christian instruction, and move on to mature teaching. There is no point in laying the foundations all over again. I mean the basic teaching about repentance from the way of life the end of which is death, and about faith in God, ₂teaching about purificatory rites, the laying on of hands, the resurrection of the dead, and eternal judgment. ₃And move on we shall, if God allows us. ₄For, once people have been enlightened, once they have experienced the heavenly gift and have received a share of the Holy Spirit, ₅once they have experienced the goodness of God's word and the dynamic powers of the age to come, ₆if they then fall away, it is impossible again to renew their repentance, for they are personally crucifying the Son of God all over again, and are publicly treating him with cynical contempt. ₇So long as the ground, which drinks in the rain which often falls upon it, produces a useful crop for those by whom it is cultivated, it continues to receive its share of blessing from God. ₈But if it produces a crop of thorns and thistles, it is no use to anyone; it is in danger of being cursed by God; and it will end up by being burned.

9My dear friends, even if we do use language like this, we remain convinced that you are not as bad as this, but that you still possess the necessities of salvation. 10God is not unjust; he will not forget all that you did, and the way in which you showed your love for him in your past and present service of his dedicated people. 11It is our earnest desire that each of you should show the same eagerness in your efforts to reach the full and final realization of your hope. 12You must not become lazy. You must take as your examples those who through faith and perseverance are entering into the possession of the promises of God.

3For, when God made his promise to Abraham, since he had nothing greater by which to swear, he swore by himself. 14'I pledge myself to bless you,' he said, 'and to give you many descendants.' 15And thus Abraham patiently waited, and so received what God had promised. 16Men swear by someone greater than themselves, and an oath is a guarantee which ends all dispute. 17So then, when God wished to give to those who are destined to receive what he promised an even more compelling proof of the unalterable character of his purpose, he introduced an oath, as well as a promise, between himself and them. 18Thus by means of two unalterable things, in which it is impossible that he should lie, God wanted those who have sought safety with himself to have a powerful incentive to hold fast to that hope which is set before us. 19That hope we hold, and it is for us the anchor of the soul. It is both sure and certain. It enters with us into the inner sanctuary behind the curtain. 20There Jesus has already gone, to make it safe for us to follow, for he has become a priest for ever in the order of Melchizedek.

Chapter 7

THIS Melchizedek was King of Salem, and priest of the most high God. He met Abraham, when Abraham was returning from the defeat of the kings, and blessed him. 2Abraham assigned to him as his share a tenth part of everything. In the first place, the translation of his own name, Melchizedek, is King of Righteousness. In the second place, he is King of Salem, and that means King of Peace. 3There is no mention of his father; there is no mention of his mother; no ancestor of his is ever mentioned. His days are never said to have had any beginning, and his life is never said to have had any end. He is like the Son of God; he remains a priest for ever.

₄Look how outstanding this man is! Abraham the patriarch gave him a tenth part of the best of the spoils. ₅Those of Levi's sons, who receive the priestly office, possess with it an injunction which legally entitles them to exact tithes from the people, that is, from their own fellow-countrymen, although they are descendants of Abraham. ₆Melchizedek was not of Levitical descent at all, and yet he exacted tithes from Abraham, and blessed the man who was the possessor of the promises of God. ₇There can be no question that it is the inferior who is blessed by the superior. ₈Further, in the case of the Levitical priesthood it is mortal men who receive tithes. In the case of Melchizedek the evidence of scripture is that he is alive. ₉Further, it would be possible to say that in the person of Abraham Levi too, who has the right to exact tithes, had tithes exacted from him, ₁₀for he could be said to be in the body of his forefather Abraham when Melchizedek met him.

₁₁It was on the basis of the levitical priesthood that the people had received the law. If that priesthood had been perfectly able to do what it was designed to do, there would obviously have been no need for a different kind of priest to emerge, a priest of the order of Melchizedek, and not of the order of Aaron. ₁₂Now, if the priesthood is changed, then of necessity there is a change of the law too, ₁₃for Jesus Christ, of whom we are speaking, belonged to a different tribe, from which no one ever served at the altar, ₁₄for it is clear that our Lord sprang from the tribe of Judah, and Moses said nothing about priests in connection with that tribe. ₁₅This is still clearer, when another priest emerges, a priest like Melchizedek. ₁₆This priest became a priest, not through any regulation based on the rule of physical descent, but through the force of an indestructible life. ₁₇The evidence for this is that it is said of him:

'You are a priest for ever
in the order of Melchizedek.'

₁₈There has been a cancellation of the previous rule, because it was weak and ineffective. ₁₉The law was unable to do what it was designed to do, but a better hope has been brought on to the scene, and through it we can find the way to approach God.

₂₀The levitical priests became priests without any oath being taken. ₂₁He became a priest after an oath had been taken, because God said to him:

'The Lord has taken his oath,
and will never change his mind.'

22And in as far as it was with an oath that Jesus became priest, in so far he has become the surety of a better relationship between God and man. 23Under the levitical system, a great many became priests, because death would not allow them to remain for long in the priesthood. 24But, because he remains for ever, he is a priest who needs no successor. 25That is why he is for all time able to save those who come to God through him, for he is always alive to intercede with God for them.

26This is the kind of priest we need, holy, untainted with evil, stainless, quite different from sinners, exalted above the heavens. 27Unlike the levitical high priests, he has no need first daily to offer sacrifices for his own sins, and then to offer them for the sins of the people. He did this once and for all when he offered himself. 28The law appoints as high priests men who are characteristically weak creatures, but the sworn statement, which came later than the law, appointed a Son, who remains perfect for ever.

Chapter 8

Now the point of what we have just been saying is that it is just such a high priest that we actually have. He has taken his seat at the right hand of the throne of the Majesty in heaven. 2He serves God in the Holy of Holies, I mean, in the real tabernacle, which the Lord, not man, set up. 3Every high priest is appointed to offer gifts and sacrifices. It is therefore necessary for this high priest too to have something to offer. 4If he was on earth, he would not be a priest at all, for there already are priests, who offer the gifts which the Jewish law prescribes. 5The service that such priests render is no more than a shadowy copy of the heavenly reality. That it is a copy is shown by the fact that, when Moses was about to build the tabernacle, God's instructions to him were: 'See that in everything you copy the pattern which was shown to you on the mountain top.' 6But in the new situation our high priest has been given a ministry which is as much superior to that of the levitical priests as the covenant of which he is the mediator is a better covenant, for this covenant was established on the basis of better promises.

7If that first covenant had been beyond criticism, there would have been no necessity to introduce a second into the situation. 8But that it is not beyond criticism is shown by the fact that God says in criticism of those who acknowledge no other:

'The time is coming, the Lord says,
    when I will establish a new and different covenant
    with the house of Israel and the house of Judah.
9It will not be like the covenant which I made with their fathers,
    at the time when I took them by the hand
    to bring them out of the country of Egypt.
The new covenant is necessary,
    because they did not abide by the covenant which I made
        with them.
So I let them go their own way, the Lord says.
10This is the covenant which I will make with the house of Israel,
    when that time comes, the Lord says.
I will put my laws into their minds,
    and I will write them on their hearts.
I will be their God, and they will be my people.
11There will be no necessity for any of them to teach his fellow-
        citizen,
    or for any of them to teach his brother,
    and to say to him: "Know the Lord,"
For from the humblest to the greatest everyone will know me.
12I will forgive their iniquities,
    and I will not remember their sins any more.'

13When God speaks of a new covenant of a different kind, he makes
the first covenant obsolete, and what is obsolescent and aging is not
far from extinction.

Chapter 9

THE first covenant had indeed a ritual of worship laid down, and
it had a sanctuary, although a this-worldly one. 2For a tabernacle
was constructed, in the outer part of which there stood the lampstand and the table with the bread of the presence. It was called the
Holy Place. 3Beyond the second curtain there was the part of the
tabernacle called the Holy of Holies. 4It had in it the golden altar of
incense and the sacred chest of the covenant, which was completely
encased in gold. Inside the sacred chest there was a golden jar con-
taining the manna. There was also Aaron's staff, which once budded.
And there were the two stone tablets of the covenant with the ten
commandments written on them. 5Above it were the cherubim of

the glory of God, with their wings over-arching the mercy-seat, as the lid of the chest was called. It is not possible for me at present to enter into a detailed discussion of all this.

6This then is the way in which these things were arranged. Into the outer part of the tabernacle the priests continually enter in the course of carrying out the various acts of the ritual of worship. 7But into the inner part of the tabernacle only the high priest goes, and that only once a year. He never enters without taking blood with him. This he offers to God for himself and for the sins which the people have committed, without even knowing that they had committed them. 8By this the Holy Spirit makes it clear that the way into the inner sanctuary is not disclosed so long as the first tabernacle still exists. 9The first tabernacle symbolically stands for this present age, and the gifts and sacrifices which are offered in it are such that they cannot give the worshipper perfect peace of conscience. 10Founded as they are upon laws about food and drink and different kinds of ritual washings, they are no more than external regulations, remaining in force only until the time when by the action of God religion is totally reformed and reconstructed.

11, 12When Christ appeared on the scene, he came as a priest of the good things which were to come. The tabernacle in which he serves is greater and more perfect. It is not made by human hands. That is to say, it is not part of the created world at all. Once and for all he went right through it into the Holy of Holies. It was not the blood of goats and calves that he took with him as a sacrifice. It was his own blood. And thus he secured eternal deliverance for us. 13For, if sprinkling with the blood of goats and bulls, and with the ashes of a heifer, so physically purifies those who have become ritually unclean that they are rendered fit to enter God's presence in worship, 14how much more will the blood of Christ, who offered himself to God as a victim without blemish in a spiritual and eternal sacrifice, cleanse our conscience from the conduct which leads to death, and fit us for the service of the living God?

The point in the passage which follows depends on a play on words. The Greek word *diathēkē* means two things. It means both *covenant* and *will*. The writer to the Hebrews plays on these two meanings. The switch from one meaning to the other is made in verse 16, and the argument is that the benefits of a *diathēkē*, *covenant*, *will*, cannot be received until the testator has died. So for the new *diathēkē*, *covenant*, *will*, to become operative and effective the death of Christ had first to happen. A play on words is seldom translatable from one language into another, and this one is not. But it has to be kept in mind that the word for *covenant* is the same as the word for *will*.

15Christ has therefore become the connecting link between God and man, and through him the new covenant has come into being. A death has occurred—the death of Christ—as a result of which men have been rescued from their sins committed under the first covenant. And so those who have been called by God are enabled to receive the gift which God promised from all eternity. 16In the case of a will, it is essential that the death of the testator should be established. 17It is only upon death that a will becomes valid and effective, for a will cannot be operative while the testator is still alive. 18It was for this very reason that even the first covenant was not inaugurated without blood. 19For, after every commandment in the law had been announced to all the people, Moses took the blood of calves and goats, together with water, scarlet wool and hyssop, and sprinkled the book itself and all the people. 20'This,' he said, 'is the blood of the covenant which God enjoined you to keep.' 21In the same way he sprinkled the tabernacle too and everything that was used in worship. 22In fact, it would almost be true to say that in the regulations of the law everything must be cleansed by blood, and that there can be no forgiveness, unless blood has been shed.

23These are only copies of the heavenly things and they have to be cleansed by these rites. The heavenly things themselves need greater sacrifices than these. 24For it was not into a manmade sanctuary that Christ entered, a mere symbol of the real sanctuary; it was into heaven itself, now to appear before God on our behalf. 25Nor is he there to repeat the sacrifice of himself over and over again, as year after year the high priest goes into the sanctuary with blood that is not his own. 26For, if that had been the way of it, he would have had to suffer over and over again, ever since the world was created. In actual fact he appeared once and for all, at the consummation of history, to wipe out sin through the sacrifice of himself. 27For men it is appointed to die once—and after that comes judgment. 28So Christ was once and for all sacrificed to bear the sins of all. And, now that sin has been dealt with, he will appear a second time, this time not to deal with sin, but to bring salvation to those who are eagerly waiting and watching for him.

Chapter 10

THE Jewish law was no more than a shadow of the good things which are to come; you will not find in it the true expression of these realities. By going on making the same sacrifices which are offered year after year for ever the law can never perfect those who are trying to find the way into God's presence. 2If these sacrifices could have done this, they would obviously have ceased to be offered, because the worshipper would have been once and for all cleansed, and would no longer be haunted by the sense of sin. 3So far from that, these sacrifices do no more than keep reminding a man of his sins year after year. 4For it is not in the power of the blood of bulls and goats to take sins away.

5This is why Christ, as he was coming into the world, said to God:

'You had no desire for sacrifice and offering.
You prepared a body for me.
6Animal sacrifices burned whole on the altar
and offerings for sin
brought no pleasure to you.
7Then I said: "Here I am.
As scripture says of me in the roll of the book,
I have come, O God, to do your will."'

8First he said: 'You neither wish for, nor find any pleasure in, animal sacrifices and offerings, in sacrifices burned whole on the altar, in offerings for sin'—and these are the offerings which the law prescribes. 9Then he said: 'Here I am. I have come to do your will.' Thus he cancels the first, that is, animal sacrifice, to establish the second, that is, perfect obedience. 10And it is by that will of God that we have been made fit to enter God's presence through the once and for all sacrifice of the body of Jesus Christ.

11Every Jewish priest stands every day carrying out the ritual of worship, and offering the same sacrifices over and over again, and these sacrifices are such that they never take sins away. 12But Christ offered one sacrifice for sins, a sacrifice which is effective for ever, and then took his seat at the right hand of God, 13where he awaits the complete subjection of his enemies. 14For by one sacrifice, valid for ever, he enabled men to enter into perfect communion with God.

15We have the declaration of the Holy Spirit that this is true. 16For after he had said:

> 'This is the covenant which I will make with them
>   after these days, the Lord says;
> I will put my laws into their hearts,
>   and I will write them upon their minds,'

17he then goes on to say:

> 'And their sins and their disobedience
>   to my laws I will completely forget.'

18And, when these have been forgiven, there is no longer any need for an offering for sin.

19Through the sacrificial death of Jesus we, brothers, have complete freedom to enter the Holy of Holies by a new and living way, 20which he inaugurated for us. We can pass right through the curtain, for as the curtain was rent, so his body was rent for us. 21We have a great high priest, who presides over the house of God. 22Let us then come to him in complete sincerity of heart and conviction of faith, with our hearts so sprinkled with the blood of his sacrifice that we no longer have a guilty conscience, and with our bodies washed with pure water. 23Let us hold inflexibly to the hope which we tell the world we possess, for we can rely on the word of him who promised it to us. 24We must think how to stimulate each other to love and to lovely living. 25We must not, as some do, abandon meeting together; we must rather encourage each other to do so, and all the more because you see that it will not be long now until the great day comes.

26For, if we go on deliberately sinning after receiving the knowledge of the truth, there is no longer any possible sacrifice for sin left. 27All that is left is to await in terror the judgment, and the fury of fire which will destroy the opponents of God. 28If anyone treats the law of Moses as if it did not exist, the penalty is death without pity on the evidence of two or three witnesses. 29How much more severe, do you think, must be the punishment deserved by the man who has spurned the Son of God, who has regarded as a common thing the covenant blood through which he was made fit to enter God's presence, and who has wantonly insulted the Spirit through whom God's grace has come to us? 30For we know who said: 'The right of just punishment is mine; I will repay.' And again: 'The Lord will judge his people.' ₃₁It is a terrifying thing to fall into the hands of the living God.

₃₂Cast your minds back to your early days. At that time, when you had seen the light, you met with gallantry a hard struggle with sufferings. ₃₃Some of you had abuse and torture heaped upon you, to provide a public spectacle. Some of you deliberately chose to share the experiences of those who were involved in those troubles. ₃₄You voluntarily shared the sufferings of those who were in prison. You gladly accepted the violent confiscation of your possessions, for you knew that you possessed something better and more lasting. ₃₅You must not throw away your confidence, for it will bring you a rich reward. ₃₆What you need is the power to see things through. If you have that, you will obey the will of God, and so receive what he has promised.

> ₃₇'Soon, very soon now,
> he who is to come will come,
> and will not delay.
> ₃₈ And by his fidelity the good man who is mine
> will find life.
> But, if he is afraid to face things,
> I have no pleasure in him.'

₃₉We are not afraid to face things; we are not men destined to be lost; we are men of faith destined to save our souls.

Chapter 11

FAITH is the confidence that the things which as yet we only hope for really do exist. It is the conviction of the reality of the things which as yet are out of sight. ₂It is because of this faith that the heroes of the past received the approval of God.

₃It is by faith that we understand that the universe was constructed by the word of God, for the seen had to take its origin from the unseen.

₄It was through faith that Abel offered to God a better sacrifice than Cain did. It was because of his faith that he was approved as a good man, for God showed his approval of the gifts he offered. His faith made him, even after his death, a living and speaking example to us. ₅By faith Enoch was removed from this world without experiencing death. He vanished from this world because God removed him. We can rightly attribute this to his faith, because it is recorded in scripture that before his removal his life had pleased God, 6and without faith it is impossible to please God, for anyone who wishes to come to God must believe that God exists, and that he rewards those who search for him. 7It was through faith that Noah received from God a message about events which were still out of sight. He received it reverently, and built an ark to save his household. Through his faith he proved the error of the world's ways, and entered into possession of that goodness in the Lord's sight which comes through faith.

8It was through faith that Abraham obeyed the call of God, and went out to a land which he was to receive, because God had promised it to him. He set out, although he did not know where his journey was going to take him. 9It was through faith that he lived like an alien in a foreign country in the land that had been promised to him. He had his home in tents, and so had Isaac and Jacob who shared possession with him of the promise God had made, 10for he was waiting for the city with its foundations, the city of which God is the architect and builder. 11It was through faith that he received the power to beget a child, even although Sarah was unable to have children, and even although he himself was beyond the age to become a father, for he had made up his mind that, since God had made a promise, he could depend on God to keep it. 12The result was that from one man, and that a man who from the point of view of begetting children was as good as dead, there came descendants as many as the stars in the sky in number, and as countless as the grains of sand on the sea-shore.

13These all died in faith. They never received what God had promised. They only saw and greeted God's promises in the far-off distance. They never denied the fact that they were strangers, and that they had no permanent home anywhere on earth. 14When people speak like that, they make it clear that they are looking for a country of their own. 15If their thoughts had always been turning back to the country they had left, they could easily have found an opportunity to return to it. 16But in point of fact they are reaching out to a better country, I mean a heavenly one. That is why God is not ashamed to be called their God, for he had prepared a city for them.

17, 18It was through faith that Abraham, when he was tested, as good as offered up Isaac as a sacrifice to God. Isaac was his only son, and God had told him that the line of his descendants would descend through Isaac, and yet he was ready to offer him in sacrifice to God.

19He had reasoned it out that God could raise his son to life again even from the dead—and symbolically he did indeed receive him back again. 20It was through faith that Isaac called down future blessings on Jacob and Esau. 21It was through faith that the dying Jacob blessed each of Joseph's sons, and bowed in worship before God, leaning on the top of his staff. 22It was through faith that Joseph, when the end was near, spoke about the time when the Israelites would leave Egypt, and gave instructions as to what was to be done with his bones, when that time came.

23It was through faith that, when Moses was born, he was hidden by his parents for three months, because they saw that he was an exceptionally beautiful child, and so disregarded the king's edict. 24It was through faith that, when Moses grew up, he refused to be called the son of Pharaoh's daughter. 25He preferred to share their ill-treatment with the people of God than to enjoy the short-lived pleasure sin can bring, 26for he regarded the insults and injury, which God's Anointed One must suffer, as greater wealth than the treasures of Egypt, for his eyes were fixed on his reward. 27It was through faith that Moses left Egypt. He was not afraid of the king's anger. He held inflexibly to his chosen course, as one who sees the invisible God. 28It was through faith that he kept the Passover, and carried out the sprinkling of the doors with blood, to keep the Destroying Angel from touching the eldest sons of the Israelite families. 29It was through faith that they crossed the Red Sea, as if it had been dry land. But, when the Egyptians attempted the same crossing, they were drowned. 30It was through faith that the walls of Jericho collapsed, after the Israelites had marched round them each day for seven days. 31It was through faith that the prostitute Rahab did not share in the destruction of those who did not believe in Israel's God, because she had given the spies a kindly welcome.

32What more need I say? There is no time for me to tell of Gideon, Barak, Samson, Jephthah, David, Samuel and the prophets. 33It was through faith that they conquered kingdoms, established justice, found God's promises come true. It was through faith that they muzzled the mouths of lions, 34quenched raging flames, escaped the threat of the sword. It was through faith that their weakness was changed into power, that they became strong in battle, that they routed the serried ranks of foreign armies. 35It was through faith that women received back their dead resurrected to life again. Some were battered to death in torture. They refused to accept release, for they wanted to win a better resurrection. 36Some had to face mockery and the lash, and the even worse fate of chains and imprisonment. ₃₇They were stoned; they were sawn in two; they died murdered by the sword. They went about clad in sheepskins and goatskins. They had not even the bare necessities of life. Life was for them a series of crushing blows; they lived in constant ill-treatment. ₃₈The world did not deserve people like that. They wandered in the lonely places and among the hills; caves and holes in the ground were their homes.

₃₉All these through their faith won the approval of God, but they did not receive what God had promised to his people, ₄₀because God in his providence had a better plan for us. His purpose was that we and they should reach the final blessedness together.

Chapter 12

So then, in the arena of life we are surrounded by a vast crowd of spectators. We must therefore, as an athlete strips for action, strip off every encumbrance and the sin which clings to us, and we must run with gallant determination the race which stretches in front of us. ₂And all the time we must concentrate on nothing but Jesus, in whom our faith had its beginning and must have its end, for he, for the joy that lay ahead of him, courageously accepted the cross, with never a thought for the shame, and has now taken his seat at the right hand of God. ₃The way to avoid the failure of your nerve and heart is to compare your situation with the situation of him who met the opposition of sinners with such constancy and courage.

₄In your struggle with sin you have not yet had to resist to the point of having to die for your faith. ₅Have you forgotten that challenging passage of scripture, which speaks to you as sons?

'My son, always remember the value of the discipline
    which comes to you from the Lord,
and never be depressed and discouraged,
    when he corrects you.
₆The Lord disciplines the man he loves,
    and punishes every son
    whom he accepts into his family.'

₇You must accept it as discipline. God is treating you as sons. Is there any son whom his father does not discipline? ₈If you are left without the discipline in which all sons share, then you are bastards and not real sons. ₉Again, we had human fathers who disciplined us, and we respect them for it. Should we not be much more ready to submit to a spiritual Father in order to learn to live? 10They exercised discipline over us for a short time, and as they thought best; but he disciplines us for our good, and his aim is to make us fit to share his holiness. 11No discipline seems pleasant at the moment; it is always painful. But afterwards it repays those who were trained by it with the happy harvest of a good life.

12So then, fill the listless hands with energy; strengthen the trembling knees; 13make straight paths for your feet to walk in, so that the lame limb may not be dislocated, but cured.

14Aim at right relationships with everyone. Set your heart on that consecration without which no one can see the Lord. 15See to it that no one deprives himself of the grace of God. See to it that no poisonous weed grows up to make trouble for you and to contaminate the whole community. 16See to it that no one is guilty of sexual immorality, or lost to all religious feeling, as Esau was, for he sold his birthright for a single meal. 17You know that, when he afterwards wished to claim the blessing he had sold, he was rejected. There was no possibility for him to think again, although he tried with tears to undo what he had done.

18It is not to Mount Sinai that you have come, to a material and blazing fire, to gloom and thick darkness, to a hurricane of wind, 19to the blare of the trumpet, to a voice which spoke such terrible words that those who heard it pled that it should say no more. 20For they were appalled by the order that, if even a beast touched the mountain, it should be stoned to death. 21The sight was so terrible that Moses said that it left him trembling and afraid. 22No! You have come to Mount Sion and to the city of the living God, to the heavenly Jerusalem and to thousands upon thousands of angels. 23You have come to the firstborn sons of God's family registered in heaven, in worshipping assembly. You have come to God who is the judge of all, to the spirits of good men who have reached the goal of life, 24to Jesus the mediator of the new covenant, to the sprinkled sacrificial blood, which has a greater message than the blood of Abel.

25Take care not to refuse to listen to him who speaks. Those who refused to listen to the man Moses, who on earth was the messenger of God's truth, did not escape. Still less will we escape, if we turn our backs on Christ, the one who comes from heaven. 26At that time his voice shook the earth, but now he has promised: 'Once again I will shake, not only the earth, but heaven too.' 27That phrase, 'once— and only once—again', can only mean the complete removal of the things that are shaken—for they are only created things—and then only the things that cannot be shaken will remain. 28Since then we are receiving a kingdom that cannot be shaken, we must be grateful to God, and, to show our gratitude, we must worship him in the way that pleases him, with reverence and fear, 29for our God is a devouring fire.

Chapter 13

CHRISTIANS must never stop loving their fellow-Christians. 2Do not forget the duty of hospitality, for there are those who through it have entertained angels without being aware that they were doing so. 3Remember those who are in prison with a sympathy which shares their chains with them. Do not forget those who are being ill-treated, for you have not yet left this life, and the same fate can happen to you. 4You must regard marriage as an honourable state. Nothing must violate the marriage bond. Fornicators and adulterers have God as their judge. 5Never let the love of money dominate your life. Be content with what you have. God himself has said: 'I will never let go my grip of you; I will never abandon you.' 6If that is so, we can meet life fearlessly, for we can say:

'The Lord is my helper.
I shall not be afraid.
What can any man do to me?'

7Remember those who were once your leaders. It was they who brought God's message to you. Look back on the way in which they left this life, and make their loyalty your example. 8Jesus Christ is the same yesterday, today and for ever. 9Do not allow yourselves to be swept away by all kinds of strange teachings. The best thing to fortify your souls is the grace of God, not regulations about what we may eat and not eat, which have never been of the slightest use to those who use them as rules of life. 10The Jewish priests, who carry out the ritual of the earthly tabernacle, get as the perquisite of their office their share of the sacrificial meat to eat, but we have an altar from whose sacrifices they have no right to eat. 11The high priest brings the blood of the animals into the Holy of Holies as a sin-offering, but the bodies of these animals are burned outside the camp. 12That is why Jesus had to suffer outside the city, in order, through his own blood, to make the people fit to enter the presence of God. 13So then, we must go out to him outside the camp, and we must accept the same abuse as he accepted. 14For here we have no permanent city; we are looking for the city which will come. 15Through him then we must bring a sacrifice of continual praise to God. The sacrifice I mean is given by lips which publicly affirm their faith in him. 16Never forget to live a life of goodness and sharing. It is sacrifices like that which delight God.

17Obey your leaders, and accept their leadership. Their care for you is ceaseless and unsleeping. They look after you as men who will answer for the responsibility placed upon them. Make their task of leadership a happy and not a distressing experience. To make their task an unhappy one would do you no good at all.

18Keep praying for us, for we believe that our conscience is clear, for our only desire is to live a good life. 19I urge you all the more strenuously to pray for us, so that you and I may meet again all the sooner.

20God brought our Lord Jesus back from the dead, and his sacrificial death made him the great shepherd of the sheep and the inaugurator of the eternal covenant. 21And may that God of peace equip you with every good thing you need to enable you to do what he wants you to do, and may he make us and our life such as he would wish us and it to be through Jesus Christ, to whom be glory for ever and ever! Amen.

22I ask you, brothers, please to bear with this message of encouragement and comfort, for indeed it is a short letter that I have sent you. 23I would like you to know that our brother Timothy has been released from prison, and, if he arrives in time, he will be with me when I see you.

24Give my best wishes to all your leaders and to all God's consecrated people. The people from Italy send you their good wishes. 25Grace be with you all.

Introduction to the Letter of James

IT is not by any means certain who the James is who wrote this letter, but he may well have been James the brother of Jesus.

The Letter of James has always suffered from the fact that Luther called it 'a right strawy epistle', and would have banished it from the New Testament altogether. Luther's objection to it was that he thought that it contradicted Paul. Paul had said that no man could ever be justified by works, that every man had to be justified, had to be put right with God, by faith alone. But James seems to say, and to say with vigour, that what matters is works (2.14-26). To Paul Abraham was justified by faith (Romans 4.1-12); to James Abraham was justified by works (2.21). But Paul and James are not really at variance. They are not saying contradictory things; they are saying complementary things. It has been well put this way: 'A man is not saved *by* works, but he is saved *for* works.' No man can earn the love of God, but once a man knows through faith that God loves him, he knows, or he knows nothing of the meaning of Christianity, that he must spend all his life trying to live a life that is worthy of that love. We are not saved by works; but the only proof that we are saved is that we live a life a little more like that of our Saviour and our Lord.

In many ways this is a strange letter. In the Greek it only mentions the name of Jesus twice (1.1; 2.1). It is an intensely practical letter, and is the very essence of practical Christianity.

One of the strange things about it is that it is impossible to make a connected analysis of it. It consists of a series of disconnected paragraphs of advice and admonition. It speaks of the necessity of constancy in trial (1.2-4); of the necessity of doing as well as hearing (1.22-25); of the dangers of partiality and of snobbish respect of persons (2.1-7); of the necessity of adding works to faith (2.14-26); of the terrible dangers of the tongue (3.1-12); of the true wisdom (3.13-18); of the folly of planning without God (4.13-17); of the necessity of steadfastness, because Christ is coming (5.7-11); of the power of prayer (5.13-18); and it has a special sense of the danger of riches (2.6,7; 5.1-6). It is a series of cameo-like utterances, with no logical connection with each other, and simply set down one after another.

This is the fact which may tell us what this letter may well have begun by being. When the Jewish rabbis gave instruction in preaching, their instruction always was that the preacher must never linger long on any one subject. To keep and to maintain the interest of the hearer he must move quickly from subject to subject. The Hebrew word for preaching is in fact *charaz*, which is literally the word for stringing beads or pearls. Preaching was like stringing a series of pearls together.

This is exactly what James is. It is like a series of pearls of wisdom strung together with no connection. So we may well believe that this letter was originally a sermon, either a synagogue or a church sermon, preached by James, and afterwards taken down and made into a general letter of advice.

The Letter of
JAMES

Chapter 1

GREETINGS from James, servant of God and of the Lord Jesus Christ, to the twelve tribes scattered in exile from their homeland.

2My brothers, you must regard it as nothing but joy when you are involved in all kinds of trials, 3for you must realize that when faith has passed through the ordeal of testing the result is the ability to pass the breaking-point and not to break. 4This ability must go right on to the end, and then you will be perfect and complete, without a weak spot. 5It is characteristic of God to give generously and ungrudgingly to all. So then, if anyone is lacking in wisdom, he must ask God for it, and it will be given to him. 6But he must ask in faith and with no doubts, for the man who doubts is like a wave of the sea, blown about at the mercy of every wind. 7That kind of man need not think that he will receive anything from God. 8A man like that can never make up his mind, and is quite unable to steer a steady course.

9The brother who is nobody in the eyes of the world must take pride in the way that the hard experiences of life, rightly accepted, raise him to new heights of character. 10The brother who is wealthy must take pride in the way in which life brings him low, for he will last no longer than a wild flower blooms. 11For the sun rises, and the sirocco blows and withers the grass, and the flower wilts, and its beauty is gone. So the life of the rich man is a journey to decay.

12Happy is the man who meets trial with the unbreakable spirit, for, after he has come through the ordeal, just as the victorious athlete in the games receives the laurel crown, so he will receive as his prize the life which God has promised to those who love him. 13If in his ordeal a man is tempted to sin, he must not say: 'I am being tempted by God.' God cannot be tempted by evil, nor does he ever tempt anyone else. 14Each man is tempted when he is seduced and enticed by his own desire. 15Then the next thing that happens is that this desire conceives and becomes the mother of sin. And then, when sin is full-grown, it spawns death.

16My dear brothers, don't be misled. 17All God's giving is good, and every perfect gift comes down from above, from the Father of the lights of the heavens. In him there is no change, nor does he turn away from us and leave us in the shadows. 18By an act of his own will, through the word of truth, he brought us into being, for, just as the first-fruits of the harvest are specially dedicated to him, so he intended us to have the first and highest place in all creation.

19My dear brothers, there is something that you must bear in mind. Everyone must be quick to listen, slow to speak, and slow to become angry. 20Human anger can never produce the kind of conduct God desires. 21So then, you must strip off everything that would soil life and all that malice that is like an alien growth on life, and in a teachable spirit you must receive implanted in your heart the word which is able to save your souls.

22You must not only listen to the word; you must act on it. Otherwise, you indulge in self-deception. 23To listen to the word and not to act on it is to be like a man who looks in a mirror at the face that nature gave him. 24He looks at himself, and then he goes away, and immediately forgets what he looks like. 25It is the man who looks into the perfect law, which is the source of liberty, and who takes his stand on it, the man who is not simply a forgetful listener, but who is an active doer, who will be blessed by God, because he is a man of action.

26A man may regard himself as religious, but, if he has no control over his tongue, he is deceiving himself, and his religion is futile. 27The religion which in the sight of God the Father is pure and stainless consists in helping orphans and widows in their distress, and in keeping oneself from becoming contaminated by the world.

Chapter 2

MY brothers, you cannot at one and the same time believe in our glorious Lord Jesus Christ and be a snob. 2Suppose a man elegantly dressed and wearing a gold ring on his finger comes into your meeting, and suppose a poor man dressed in soiled and shabby clothing comes in at the same time. 3And suppose you pay special attention to the elegantly dressed man. Suppose you say to him: 'Would you be kind enough to sit there?' while you say to the poor man: 'Stand there!' or, 'Squat on the floor at my feet!' 4Do you not thereby inconsistently introduce class distinction into your fellowship, and does this not mean that you arrive at your judgments of people from the wrong motives altogether?

₅Listen, my dear brothers! Didn't God choose those who by the world's standards are poor to be rich in faith, and to enter into possession of the kingdom which he has promised to those who love him? ₆But you dishonour the poor man. Is it not the case that the rich treat you as tyrants treat their slaves? Is it not true that it is they who drag you to the law-courts? ₇Is it not they who hurl their insults at the fair name of Jesus, which was pronounced over you, when you became his in baptism? ₈The law of the Kingdom is stated in the passage of scripture: 'You must love your neighbour as yourself,' and perfectly to obey that law is to do well. ₉But, if you continue to allow snobbery to dictate your attitude to other people, you are committing a sin, and you stand condemned by the law as law-breakers. ₁₀To keep the rest of the law in its entirety, but to fail to keep it in one particular part, is legally to become guilty of breaking the law as a whole. ₁₁For the same person said both: 'You must not commit adultery' and: 'You must not commit murder.' It may be that you do not commit adultery, but, if you commit murder, you have become a law-breaker. ₁₂You must so speak and you must so act as men who are going to be judged by the law that makes men free. ₁₃Judgment will be merciless for the man who acted mercilessly. But mercy can laugh at judgment.

₁₄My brothers, what good is it for a man to say that he has faith, if he never does anything to prove it? Can faith save him? ₁₅Suppose a fellowman or woman has no clothes to wear and no food for a daily meal, ₁₆and suppose one of you says to a person in such a situation: 'Go and God bless you! May you have a fire to warm yourself and a meal to eat!' And suppose you do not give that person even enough to keep body and soul together, what use is that? ₁₇Faith is like that. If faith does not issue in action, if it is all alone by itself, it is dead.

₁₈But someone will say: 'You get different kinds of people. One man may well claim to be a man of faith, while another man may equally well claim to be a man of action.' I challenge you to prove to me that you have faith in any other way than by actions. For my part, I am perfectly willing to prove my faith to you by my actions. ₁₉You believe that there is one God? Excellent! The demons believe so too—and shudder with terror. ₂₀You poor fool! Do you want proof that faith is useless without action? ₂₁Take the case of our ancestor Abraham. Was it not because of his actions that he was accepted by God as a good man? Was it not in fact by his action in offering Isaac on the altar? ₂₂It must be obvious to you that his faith and his actions combined to act together, and that his faith was completed by his actions. ₂₃So the passage of scripture which says: 'Abraham had faith in God, and that faith made him accepted by God as a good man' came true, and he was called God's friend. ₂₄It must be clear to you that it is in consequence of his actions that God reckons a man to be a good man, and not only in consequence of faith. ₂₅In the same way, was it not as a consequence of her actions that the prostitute Rahab was reckoned to be good? Was it not because she welcomed the Jewish messengers, and helped them to escape by a different route? ₂₆The body is dead when there is no breath in it, and faith is dead when it has no actions to accompany it.

Chapter 3

MY brothers, you ought not to try to become teachers in large numbers, for you are well aware that we teachers will be judged by a sterner standard than ordinary people. ₂We all make many a slip, but, if a man does not slip up in his words, he is a perfect man, able to control every part of himself. ₃We put bits into the mouths of horses to make them obey us, and thus we turn their whole body in any direction we wish. ₄Take the case of ships. In spite of their size, and even when they are being driven by fierce winds, by a very small rudder they can be guided to change course, just as the steersman's wish directs. ₅Just so, the tongue is a small part of the body, but it makes great claims.

Take the case of a forest fire. A tiny spark can set a whole forest ablaze. ₆The tongue is a fire. Among the parts of the body the tongue represents this wicked world. It infects the whole body with the taint of evil. It sets the whole course of our existence on fire with a fire that is fed from the flames of hell. ₇Every kind of beast and bird, every kind of reptile and fish, can be, and has been, brought under control by mankind. ₈The tongue is the one thing that no man can control. It is an evil which is out of all control, full of deadly poison. ₉With it we bless the Lord and Father, and with it we curse men made in the likeness of God. ₁₀Blessing and cursing issue from the one mouth. My brothers, it is all wrong that this should happen. ₁₁Obviously, a spring cannot gush out sweet and bitter water from the same opening. ₁₂Clearly, my brothers, a fig-tree cannot produce olives, or a vine figs. No more can salt water produce fresh water.

13Have you a wise and understanding man in your society? He must demonstrate by the excellence of his life and conduct that all he does is done in that gentleness which is the hall-mark of wisdom. 14If in your heart there is a zeal which is bitter and fanatical, if you are actuated by selfish ambition, you must not treat others with arrogant conceit, and you must not defeat the truth with your falsehoods. 15This is not the wisdom which comes down from above. This is a wisdom which never sees beyond the horizons of this world, which is quite unspiritual, and which is demon-inspired. 16Where there is fanaticism and personal ambition, there is bound to be a chaotic state of affairs, in which every kind of evil flourishes. 17The wisdom which comes from above is in the first place pure. Then it produces harmony between man and man; it never stands on the letter of the law; it is never obstinate; it is characteristically merciful; it produces a rich crop of kindly acts; it is free from doubts and hesitations; it never acts a part. 18Goodness has its own harvest. But the harvest grows only when its seed is sown where harmony holds sway, and it is for those who are the makers of such a harmony.

Chapter 4

WHAT causes feuds and fights in your society? Are they not the outward expression of that inner warfare which results from your instinctive desire for pleasure? 2You want something; you cannot have it; you are ready to commit murder. You passionately desire something; you are unable to get it; you fight and feud. The reason why you do not have what you want is that you do not ask God for it. 3And when you do ask, you do not get what you ask for, because you ask for the wrong reasons. All you want to do with what you get is to spend it on your own pleasure. 4You have broken all your vows! Do you not know that friendship with the world means enmity to God? If a man chooses to be a friend of the world, he thereby makes himself an enemy of God. 5Or, do you think that scripture is meaningless when it says: 'God yearns jealously for the loving devotion of the spirit he implanted in us'?* 6But to meet the greater need he gives the greater grace. That is why scripture says:

'God is hostile to the arrogant,
but favours the humble.'

*An alternative translation of this passage is: 'The spirit which God implanted in us is envious in its desires.'

₇So then, accept the authority of God. Take a stand against the devil, and he will run away from you. ₈Come to meet God, and he will come to meet you. You are sinners; you must therefore cleanse your hands from evil deeds. Your loyalty is divided; you must therefore purify your heart from false loves. ₉You will be well to be wretched, to mourn and to weep. Your laughter must change to mourning, and your gladness to gloom. ₁₀Come in self-abasement to the Lord, and he will lift you high.

₁₁Brothers, you must stop your habit of disparaging criticism of each other. To disparage a brother or to criticize him is to disparage Christ's law of love and to criticize it. And, if you criticize the law, then you are not obeying the law; you are critics of it. ₁₂There is one law-giver and judge—the One who is able to save and to destroy. Who then are you to judge your fellowman?

₁₃'Today or tomorrow,' some of you say, 'we will travel to this or that town, and we will spend a year there, trading and making money.' Stop and think a minute! ₁₄You do not know what life will be like for you tomorrow. Your life is like a mist—seen for a moment, then vanishing for ever. ₁₅Instead of speaking as you do, what you ought to say is: 'If it is the Lord's will, we shall live to do this or that.' ₁₆In point of fact, you take a pride in your self-confident assertions—and all such self-confident pride is wrong. ₁₇So then, for a man to know the right thing and not to do it is sin.

Chapter 5

Yᴏᴜ who are rich must stop and think! You must weep and wail for the miseries that are hastening on you! ₂Your wealth has rotted; your splendid garments are the food of moths; ₃your gold and silver are eaten with rust. That rust is the proof of the real value of these things—and it will eat into your own bodies like fire. You have piled up wealth in a world that is coming to an end. ₄The pay that you never paid to the workers who reap your fields cries out against you. The clamorous protests of those who harvested your fields have reached the ears of the Lord of hosts. ₅You have lived in this world in the luxury which saps a man's moral fibre and in dedication to wanton pleasure. You fattened yourselves like specially fattened cattle—and the day of slaughter has come. ₆You condemned the innocent man; you murdered him; and he does not resist you.

₇So then, brothers, you must be patient until the Lord comes. Take the case of the farmer. He waits for the ground's precious crop in patience, until it has received the autumn and the spring rain. 8You too must be patient, and you must hold inflexibly to your purpose, for it will not be long now until the Lord comes. 9Brothers, you must not spend your time lugubriously blaming one another for your troubles, if you want to escape God's judgment. The Judge is here— standing at the door. 10Brothers, take the prophets, who spoke as the representatives of the Lord, as an example of patience in suffering. 11We have no doubt of the ultimate bliss of those who met suffering with the power to see things through. You have heard the story of Job, and of how he had this power, and you know how the Lord brought Job's sufferings to a triumphant conclusion. For the Lord is compassionate and merciful.

12Above all, my brothers, when you make a promise you must not use an oath. In such circumstances you must not swear by heaven, or by earth, or by anything else. If you mean Yes you must say Yes, and if you mean No you must say No, if you do not wish to become liable to judgment.

13Is there anyone in your society who is in distress? He must pray. Is there anyone happy? He must sing a hymn. 14Is there anyone in your society who is ill? He must call in the elders of the congregation, and they must pray over him, and anoint him with oil in the name of the Lord. 15Such a prayer, offered in faith, will cure the sick man, and the Lord will put him on his feet again, and whatever sins he has committed will be forgiven. 16Confess your sins to each other, and pray for each other, for that is the way to be cured. The prayer of a good man is powerfully effective. 17Elijah was a man every bit as human as we are. He prayed earnestly that there should be no rain, and for three years and six months no rain fell on the land. 18Then he prayed again, and the rain fell from the sky, and the ground produced its crops again.

19My brothers, if anyone wanders away from the truth, and someone turns him back again, I want you to know that the man who turns a sinner back from his wandering way will save that sinner's soul from death, and will draw a veil over a host of sins of his own.

Introduction to the First Letter of Peter

IT is just possible that the First Letter of Peter is two letters joined together into one. In 4.11 we find a doxology, and the usual place for a doxology to come is at the end. In 3.21 we find a reference to baptism. So some people have thought that from the beginning down to the doxology we have a sermon preached on the occasion of a baptismal service, and that from 4.12 to the end we have a separate address given when trial and persecution were threatening the church. This could well be so, but for the purposes of this introduction we shall treat the letter as one whole.

The First Letter of Peter might well be called the letter of Christian responsibility.

i. It stresses the responsibility of the Christian to God and to Jesus. It is characteristic of this letter that it never mentions a Christian privilege without also mentioning a Christian responsibility. You have received the good news. *Therefore* gird your minds (1.12,13). The good news has been preached to you. *Therefore* put away all malice (1.25–2.1). Christ has suffered. *Therefore* live well (4.1-6). The end is near. *Therefore* live the Christian life (4.7-11). And always this has to be done with the example of Jesus Christ before us (2.21). In First Peter privilege and responsibility go hand in hand.

ii. It stresses the duty of the Christian to the person outside the church. This letter never forgets the propaganda value of a Christian life, and that the best argument for Christianity is a Christian. The Christian is to prove the falsity of the charges against Christianity by the excellence of his life (2.12,15). The Christian wife is to win her pagan husband for the faith without a word being spoken (3.1,2).

iii. It stresses the duty of the Christian to the state. The Christian is to be a good citizen (2.13-17). He is to be a good servant, even when he is treated with injustice, for then he will be like Jesus (2.18-25).

iv. It stresses the Christian's duty to family and to community (2.1-12). Christianity begins at home, and in the community in which a man lives.

v. It stresses the Christian's responsibility to the church, of which he must be a good and willing servant (5.1-5).

The other great line of this letter is its encouragement in the face of coming trial. The Christian will suffer, but his suffering must never be as an evil-doer, but always as a Christian (4.12-19), and the end is sure (5.6-11).

From beginning to end the First Letter of Peter is the letter of Christian responsibility in every sphere of life.

There are many scholars who doubt whether this letter was written by Peter at all. The only persecution which took place in Peter's lifetime was the persecution set on foot by Nero in Rome about A.D.64, and that persecution did not extend to the provinces, and to the places to which this letter is written (1.1). This did not happen until the time of Domitian about A.D.95 or of Trajan about A.D.111. This is true, but the news of the persecution at Rome instigated by Nero could well have reached Asia Minor and could have sent through the Christians a shudder of terror, when they thought of what had not yet happened, but at any time might happen to them. It is not necessary to abandon Peter's authorship of this letter.

The First Letter of
PETER

Chapter 1

THIS is a letter from Peter, Jesus Christ's apostle. I write to the exiles scattered all over Pontus, Galatia, Cappadocia, Asia and Bithynia, ₂to those who have been chosen in the providence of God the Father, who are travelling on the road to holiness in the power of the Spirit, who are destined to obey Jesus Christ and to share in the new relationship with God which God made possible by his sacrificial death. May more and more of God's grace and blessing be with you.

₃Praise be to the God and Father of our Lord Jesus Christ, who in his great mercy made our lives begin all over again, and who through the resurrection of Jesus Christ from the dead gave us a living hope, ₄and the certainty that one day we will enter into that immortal, undefiled and unfading life which he promised to you, and which he is keeping in heaven for you. ₅Your faith has made the power of God the guardian of your lives, until you reach that salvation which will burst upon the world, when time comes to an end. ₆You must rejoice in all this, even if at the moment you are involved in a situation in which you are bound to be distressed by all kinds of troubles. ₇Even gold which has stood the test of the refiner's fire perishes in the end. But the purpose of all this is that you should emerge with a tried and tested faith, which is more valuable than gold, for such a faith will find praise and glory and honour, when Jesus Christ dawns upon the world again. ₈You have never seen him, yet you love him. You do not see him now, yet you believe in him, and your faith makes you rejoice with a joy which is beyond words to tell, and which is tinged with glory. ₉And the secret of your joy is that, as the final result of your faith, you are on the way to receiving the salvation of your souls.

₁₀This salvation was the subject of the searching and the investigating of the prophets, who prophesied about the grace which was to come to you. 11They tried to find out to what person and to what time Christ's Spirit within them pointed, when that Spirit declared beforehand the sufferings Christ would have to endure, and the glories which would follow the sufferings. 12It was revealed to them that their search was not for their own sakes, but for yours, for the things they foretold have now been announced to you through those who brought the good news to you through the Holy Spirit sent from heaven. And these are things which even the angels long to see into.

13So then your minds must be stripped for action. You must live soberly. You must set all your hope on the grace which is coming to you when Jesus Christ will appear again. 14You must live like obedient children, and you must not allow your lives to be shaped by the influence of the passions which used to dominate you in the days of your ignorance. 15So far from that, you must show yourselves holy in all your conduct, as he who called you is holy, 16for it stands written: 'You must be holy, because I am holy.'

17The God whom in your prayers you call Father does not arrive at his verdict on any man by favouritism; he judges each man by his actions. You are exiles of eternity, and you must therefore spend your time on this earth in reverent living, 18for you know well what it cost to liberate you from the slavery of that life of futility which you inherited from your fathers. The price did not consist of things which are doomed to decay, of silver and gold. 19The price was the precious life-blood of Christ, who was, as it were, the sacrificial lamb with no flaw or blemish. 20He was destined for this task before the creation of the world, and for your sakes he came for all men to see as time comes to its end. 21It was for the sake of you he came, for you who through him believe in God, who raised him from the dead and gave him glory. So then, your faith and your hope look to God.

22Now that obedience to the truth has purified your souls, and now that you have reached a genuine love for your brother-Christians, you must love each other sincerely and intensely, 23for you have been born all over again through the agency of the living and lasting word of God, and this time your father is not a mortal man but the immortal God. 24For:

> 'Human life is like grass,
> and all its splendour is like the grass's flower.
> The grass withers; the flower fades;
> but the word of the Lord remains for ever.'

25And this word is the word of good news which has been preached to you.

Chapter 2

So then, you must strip yourselves of all malicious and twisted conduct, of two-faced and envious behaviour, of all slanderous gossiping. 2As newly-born children want nothing but their mother's milk, so you must set your heart on the pure milk that flows from the word of God, for it is by it that you will grow up in a steady progress towards salvation. 3Surely, in the psalmist's words, you have experienced the kindness of the Lord. 4He is the living stone, rejected as worthless by men, yet chosen and precious to God. So then, you must come to him, 5as if you yourselves were living stones, and you must let yourselves be built into a living temple, in which you will become a holy priesthood, to offer spiritual sacrifices, which God will be glad to accept through Jesus Christ. 6For, as scripture has it:

'See! I am laying in Sion
a chosen and precious corner-stone,
and whoever believes in him will never
have his hope disappointed.'

7His preciousness is for you who believe in him. But to those who refuse to believe,

'The very stone which the builders rejected
has become the corner-stone,'

8and he becomes

'A stone over which men will stumble,
and a rock which will trip them up.'

They stumble because they refuse to obey the word—a fate for which they were destined.

9But you are a chosen race, a royal priesthood, a nation different from other nations, a people designed by God to be his own, and it is your task to proclaim the noble deeds of him who called you out of darkness into his wonderful light.

₁₀'Once you were not a people at all;
  now you are the people of God.
  Once there was no mercy for you;
  now you have received mercy.'

₁₁My dear friends, I plead with you as exiles of eternity and strangers in this world, to abstain from those passions which are part of sinful human nature, for they wage a continuous campaign against your soul. ₁₂Live a lovely life among the heathen, and then, when they spread their malicious stories about you as bad men, they will see the lovely way you live, and end up by praising God on the day God comes to judge.

₁₃Accept the authority of the institutions of human society for the Lord's sake, whether it be that of the emperor, who is the supreme authority, ₁₄or of governors, on the ground that they are sent by him to punish criminals and to praise good-living citizens. ₁₅For it is God's will that by your good behaviour you should silence the ignorant accusations of senseless men. ₁₆You must live like free men, but not like men who use their freedom as a pretext for vice. So far from that, you must use your freedom to become God's slaves. ₁₇You must honour all men; you must love the members of the Christian community; you must reverence God; you must continue to honour the emperor.

₁₈You slaves must accept the authority of your masters with all respect, not only in the case of those who are kind and considerate, but also in the case of those who are perversely unfair. ₁₉For a man indeed deserves praise, if, because of his continual consciousness that he is living in the presence of God, he uncomplainingly bears pain, even when he is suffering undeservedly. ₂₀What credit is it to you if you get a beating for doing wrong, and bear it uncomplainingly? But to suffer when you have behaved well, and to bear it uncomplainingly, is something which is a credit to you in the sight of God. ₂₁This is the very situation to which you have been called, for Christ too suffered for you, and in so doing, he left you an example, for he wanted us to follow in his steps.

₂₂'For he committed no sin,
  and no one ever heard him speak a twisted word.'

₂₃He did not answer insult with insult. He did not answer ill-treatment with threats of revenge. No! He committed himself and his cause to the Judge whose verdict is just. ₂₄In his own body he carried our sins to the cross, for he wanted us to be able to die to sin and to live to goodness. It is by his wounds that you have been healed. 25Once you were straying away like sheep, but now you have turned to the shepherd and guardian of your souls.

Chapter 3

IN the same way, you wives must accept the authority of your husbands. Your aim must be that any of them who refuse to believe will be won over by the conduct of their wives, without a word being spoken, 2when they see how reverent and pure your conduct is. 3Your beauty must not be the superficial beauty which depends on elaborate hair-styles and expensive jewellery and the wearing of fashionable clothes. 4No! Your beauty must be the beauty of your inner character and personality. It must consist of the beauty of a gentle and serene character, a beauty which the years cannot wither, for in God's sight that is what is really precious. 5This was the beauty with which once upon a time consecrated women, whose hopes were set on God, adorned themselves. They accepted the authority of their husbands. 6It was in this way that Sarah obeyed Abraham, calling him master. And you have now become Sarah's daughters, if you continue to live well, and if you refuse to allow anything to reduce you to frightened panic.

7In the same way, you husbands must live understandingly with your wives. You must treat them with special respect, for women are the weaker sex. They too, you must remember, are sharers with you in God's gift of life eternal. For only if you live like that will there be no barrier between your prayers and God.

8Finally, you must be one in your attitude to life, and one in your sympathy with each other. Love must be the hall-mark of your society. You must be deeply concerned for others. There must be no pride in you. 9You must never repay injury with injury, or abuse with abuse. You must ask God to bless people who treat you badly. It is to act like that that you were called and that is the way in which you will receive for yourselves the blessing God has promised you.

10'For, if a man wants a life he can love,
and if he wants to experience good fortune,
he must restrain his tongue from evil,
and his lips from twisted speaking.

11He must turn away from what is wrong, and do what is right.
He must make right relationships with his fellowmen
the object of all his endeavour and his search,
12for God looks with favour on the good,
and is always ready to hear their prayer,
But his face is set against wrong-doers.'

13Who can harm you, if you make what is right the object of all your endeavour? 14Even if you have to suffer because of doing the right thing, you will still have joy. Don't allow their threats to terrify or distress you. Make Christ your Lord, and give him a unique place in your hearts. 15Always have your answer ready, when anyone asks you to give an account of the hope all Christians share, 16but do so with gentleness and with reverence. Keep your conscience clear, for then, when slanderous stories are spread about you, those who abuse your fine Christian life will be ashamed of what they said about you. 17For, if it is God's will, it is better to suffer for doing the right thing than for doing the wrong thing. 18For Christ too died once and for all for our sins. He, the good, died for us, the bad, and he died to open the way to God for you. He underwent physical death, but in his spirit he was brought to life, 19and in his spirit he went and preached to the spirits in prison. 20These were the spirits of men, who long ago refused to obey God, when in the time of Noah God in his patience withheld his hand, while the ark was being built. In the ark a few people, eight souls in all, were brought safely through the water. 21That water was the symbol to which the water of baptism, which now saves you, corresponds. For baptism is not simply the removal of physical dirt from your bodies; it is a confession of faith to God by a good conscience—and it is the resurrection of Jesus Christ that makes this saving process possible. 22And he is at God's right hand, for he went to heaven after angels and demonic authorities and powers had been made subject to him.

Chapter 4

WHEN he was here in the body Christ accepted suffering, and you must arm yourselves with the same resolution, for in this earthly life the way to be done with sin lies through suffering. 2The object of such suffering is to enable a man to live the rest of his earthly life in obedience, not to human passions, but to God's will. ₃In your past life you had ample time to follow the heathen way of life. Your conduct was characterized by shameless immorality, by giving your passions their way, by habitual drunkenness, by carousals and drinking parties, and by idolatries which outrage common decency. ₄Your former associates therefore find it strange when you no longer join them in their headlong rush into the maelstrom of debauchery, and their surprise makes them abusive. ₅But they will have to answer for their conduct to him who is ready to judge the living and the dead. ₆For the object of preaching the good news to the dead was that, although in this human life they had received the judgment of death which all men receive, they might yet in their spiritual existence learn to live as God wants them to live.

₇It will not be long now until the end of the world comes. Keep calm and keep sober—you will pray all the more effectively, if you do. ₈Above all, love each other intensely, for love draws a veil over many a sin. ₉Keep open house for all, and never grudge it. ₁₀Each of you has his own special gift, and all of you must use your gifts in the service of one another. Only thus will you use as you ought the varied grace which God has entrusted to you. ₁₁If any of you speaks to the fellowship, he must speak as a man with a message from God. If anyone is called upon to undertake some service, he must do so in the strength which God supplies. All your actions must be designed to bring glory to God through Jesus Christ, for his is the glory and the power for ever and ever. Amen.

₁₂My dear friends, do not be surprised at the ordeal by fire in which you find yourselves involved, as if something strange was happening to you, for it has been sent to test you. ₁₃So far from that, rejoice in so far as you are sharing in the sufferings of Christ, for, if you do so, when his glory flashes upon the world, you will greet it with a surge of joy. ₁₄If they throw the name of Christ in your teeth as an insult, it is all joy, because then the Spirit of God in all his splendour rests upon you. ₁₅I say this because none of you must ever have to suffer as a murderer, or as a thief, or as a criminal, or as unjustifiably interfering with other people's affairs. ₁₆But if any of you has to suffer for being a Christian, he must not be ashamed to do so. He must make the name of Christian a name which brings honour to God. ₁₇For the time has come for judgment to begin, and to begin from the house of God. And if it begins with us, what will be the end for those who refuse to accept the good news that God has sent?

₁₈'And if it is going to be difficult
for the good man to be saved,
what will happen
to the impious and the sinner?'

₁₉Those for whom suffering is the will of God must continue to live well, and must commit their lives to the Creator on whom they can rely.

Chapter 5

IT is to the elders in your fellowship that I address my appeal. I too am an elder. With my own eyes I saw Christ suffer, and I will share with you in the glory which is destined to flash upon the world. ₂Be true pastors of the flock of God which is in your charge. Exercise your oversight over them, not like men who have been conscripted into office, but like willing volunteers, as God would have you to do; not for the mean motive of what you can get out of it, but as men eager for the task; ₃not with any desire to domineer over those allotted to your charge, but as examples to the flock. ₄And when the chief shepherd appears, you will receive the glorious crown, which will never wither.

₅In the same way, you younger men must submit to the authority of your elders. All of you in your service of each other must put on the apron of humility, because:

'God is hostile to the arrogant,
but favours the humble.'

₆Submit yourselves with no thought of self-assertion to the strong control of God, and then in his good time he will honour you. ₇Bring all your worries to him to carry for you, for he is always concerned about you.

₈You must be abstemious. You must be on the alert. Your enemy the Devil prowls around, like a roaring lion, looking for someone to devour. ₉You must resist him with a rock-like faith, and you must realize that, so long as they are in the world, all members of that Christian brotherhood of which you are a part must right to the very end experience the same kind of suffering. ₁₀For a short time you will have to suffer, but the God of all grace who through Christ called you into his eternal glory will restore you, establish you, strengthen you, and give you a firm foundation for your life. 11To him be power for ever and ever. Amen.

12I am writing this letter to you with the help of Silvanus, who is in my estimation a brother in whom you can have every confidence. I write to encourage you, and to add my personal testimony that this is the true grace of God. Stand fast in it.

13The Christian church in its modern Babylon—chosen just as you have been chosen—sends its good wishes, and so does my son Mark.

14Greet each other with the kiss of Christian love. Every blessing be on you all who belong to Christ.

Introduction to the Second Letter of Peter

THE writer of this letter is not out to tell his readers anything new; he is out to remind them of what they already know and of what they should never have forgotten (1.12,13).

In particular they should have known that the great promise of Christianity is that through it men can escape from the corruption of this world (1.4). But false teachers have come in, and have brought with them eternal danger, for the whole lesson of history, as exemplified in the cases of Noah and Lot, is that God destroys the sinner and rescues his own from the evil of their age (2.4-10).

The description of these false teachers is vivid. By implication we learn that they dealt in myths (1.16), that they interpreted scripture to suit themselves (1.20,21), and that they twist the meaning of things to their own destruction (3.16). They are utterly licentious and immoral (2.2; 2.13-18). They promise freedom, but they themselves are the slaves of corruption (2.17-19). They escaped the defilement of sin only to plunge into it again. It would have been better for them never to have known the right, than to have known it, and then to have relapsed into gross immorality (2.20-22).

This was only to be expected, for it was prophesied that evil men would arrive on the scene (3.1-3). They think that Christ will not come again; but he is coming. The delay is only God's way of giving men a further chance to amend their lives, and in any case they must remember that in the sight of God a thousand years is as a day (3.1-10). The prospect of Christ's coming and God's judgment demands a life of goodness (3.11-18).

Here, clearly, we have still another case of men who taught that sin did not matter, and who perverted the grace of God into an excuse for sinning as they pleased (pp. 148-150).

'Lilies that fester smell far worse than weeds,' and the corruption of the best always results in the worst. These men were threatening to turn the Christian gospel into an excuse for sin, and the writer of this letter is fighting a battle to keep the Christian faith and life as they ought to be.

It has to be said that a very great many scholars, from John Calvin onwards, have been very doubtful if Peter really is the author of this letter. There are three main reasons for this doubt.

First, the style of this letter is so different from the first letter which bears Peter's name that it is next to impossible that the same man could have written both. This is one of the most florid, rhetorical and flamboyant pieces of style in the New Testament.

Second, in 3.15, 16, the writer writes to his readers as if the letters of Paul were well known to them. This seems to imply that the letters of Paul had been collected and published and were part of the literature of the church. But Paul's letters were private letters, and they were not collected and edited and published for all to read until at least A.D.90. In the early sixties, when Peter died, it would hardly have been possible to write like this.

Third, he talks of the people who said that the Second Coming was not going to happen, because things have been just the same 'since the fathers fell asleep' (3.4). This seems to mark out the readers of this letter as at least second generation Christians, whose fathers, who had first heard the Christian message, are now dead.

It may be that the writer of this letter was someone who knew well what Peter had said in his preaching and his writing, and who knew well what he would say in the present situation, and who wrote in his great teacher's name.

The Second Letter of
PETER

Chapter 1

THIS is a letter from Simon Peter, Jesus Christ's servant and apostle to those who through the justice of our God and Saviour Jesus Christ have been privileged to receive a faith as precious as our own. ₂May God's grace and every blessing be given ever more richly to you, and may you enter ever more and more deeply into the knowledge of God and of Jesus our Lord.

₃This I can pray with confidence, for his divine power has gifted us with everything necessary for life and godliness, because we have come to know him who called us to share his own glory and excellence. ₄It was through the excellence of his glory that we received the precious and very great gifts he promised to us, and it is through these gifts that you are enabled to escape the world's corruption, which is the fruit of unbridled passion, and so to become sharers in the divine nature. ₅And this is the very reason why you must make up your minds to make every effort to equip your faith with virtue, your virtue with knowledge, ₆your knowledge with self-mastery, your self-mastery with fortitude; your fortitude with godliness, ₇your godliness with Christian friendliness; your friendliness with love. ₈For, if you possess these virtues, and if you keep on growing in them, it will keep you from being ineffective and unproductive on your road to an ever deeper knowledge of our Lord Jesus Christ. ₉If such virtues are lacking in a man's life, he is blind and short-sighted, and he has forgotten that his life has been cleansed from the sins that once defiled it. ₁₀Brothers, you must be all the more eager to confirm the fact that you really have been called and chosen. If you live like this, you will never collapse on the march, ₁₁for then the way into the everlasting Kingdom of our Lord and Saviour Jesus Christ will open ever more generously to you.

₁₂I therefore propose to keep on constantly reminding you of these things, although you know them already, and although you are well grounded in the truth which you already possess. 13I regard it as my duty, so long as this transient life remains to me, to keep on reminding you of these things, for I want to prevent you from falling into a sleepy lethargy, 14for I am well aware that my earthly pilgrimage has not long to go now, because our Lord Jesus Christ himself has told me so. 15And I will make every effort to see to it that after my death you will be able to call these things to mind, whenever need arises.

16It is not skilfully contrived fictions that we made use of to tell you about the power and the coming of our Lord Jesus Christ. So far from that, we were eye-witnesses of his majesty. 17There was a time when he received honour and glory from the Father, a time when there came to him, sent from the majestic glory, that voice which said: 'This is my Son, the beloved and only one in whom I have found my delight.' 18At that time we too heard that voice sent from heaven, for we were with him on the sacred mountain. 19This makes us even more sure of the message of the prophets. You will be wise to pay attention to it, for it is like a lamp shining in a dark place, until the day dawns, and the morning-star rises in your hearts. 20But it is of the first importance that you should realize that no prophecy in scripture is a matter for one's own individual interpretation, 21for no prophecy came through some man's will. No! Prophecy came because men were moved by God to speak, under the influence of the Holy Spirit.

Chapter 2

FALSE prophets emerged in Israel, and there will be false teachers among you too. They will introduce pernicious heresies by underhand methods, and they will repudiate the Master who bought them for himself. Their conduct will result in their own speedy destruction. 2They will have many followers in their blatant immoralities, and through them the true way will be brought into disrepute. 3They will be out for what they can get, and they will use plausibly constructed stories to exploit you. Long ago sentence was passed on them, and it has never been revoked. Their doom is not asleep.

4We know that God did not spare the angels who sinned. We know that he committed them to hell in pits of darkness to be kept for judgment. 5We know that God did not spare the ancient world, and we know that, when he despatched the flood on the world of impious men, he saved Noah, the preacher of righteousness, along with seven others. 6We know that God reduced the cities of Sodom and Gomorrah to ashes, and sentenced them to complete destruction. We know that in that catastrophe God provided an example of what is going to happen to the impious. ,We know that he rescued Lot, who was a good man, and who was distressed by the blatantly immoral conduct of the wicked. ₈For to that good man in his life amongst them the sights he saw and the things he heard made their lawless conduct a daily agony to his law-abiding soul. ₉We can therefore be sure that the Lord knows how to rescue God-fearing men from their ordeal, and equally he knows how to keep the wicked under punishment to await the day of judgment, ₁₀especially those whose conduct is dominated by the polluted passions of their lower nature, and characterized by contempt for all authority.

Foolhardy and self-opinionated, they have no compunction in insulting the celestial glorious ones, ₁₁whereas angels, who are their superiors in strength and power, do not attack other celestial beings with insults, even when they are seeking judgment against them in the presence of the Lord. ₁₂They are no better than brute beasts, born by nature to be caught and killed. They heap their insults on anything they do not understand. And like beasts they will certainly be destroyed. ₁₃Injury they inflicted, and injury they will receive in return. To revel in broad day light is their idea of pleasure. They are disfiguring blemishes on your society. Even when they share your meals with you, they are luxuriating in the deceptions which they practise. ₁₄They strip with their eyes every woman they look at. They are insatiable in looking for sin. Those whose moral defences are weak are the victims of their seductions to sin. They are stripped for action in the race to get. God's curse is on them! ₁₅They have left the straight road and have gone wandering. They have taken the same road as Balaam, the son of Bosor, who loved ill-gotten gain. ₁₆But Balaam was forcibly brought face to face with his disobedience to God. A dumb animal spoke to him with a human voice, and halted the prophet in his mad career.

₁₇These men are wells with no water in them. They are mists driven by a squall of wind. The depths of darkness are reserved for them. ₁₈With their bombastic and empty talk they use the seductions of physical passion and blatant immorality to make victims of those who are just beginning to escape from the errors of the society in which they used to live. ₁₉They promise them freedom, while they themselves are enslaved by corruption; for a man is a slave to that by which he has been mastered. ₂₀If through coming to know our Lord and Saviour Jesus Christ they escaped the defilements of the world, and if they again became involved in them, and were again mastered by them, they finish up worse than they began. 21For it would have been better for them never to have known the way of goodness than to have known it and then to have abandoned the sacred commandment which they were taught. 22In their case the proverb has turned out to be true: 'A dog returns to his own vomit,' and: 'The sow that has been washed returns to rolling in the mud.'

Chapter 3

MY dear friends, this is the second letter which I have now written to you. In both of them it has been, and is, my aim to stimulate you to do some straight thinking by reminding you of what you already know. 2My aim is to compel you to remember the words already spoken to you by God's dedicated prophets, and the command of the Lord and Saviour which you received from your apostles. 3Right at the beginning you must realize that in the last days there will come men who will pour cynical scorn on the faith, and who know no law but their own desires. 4'What has happened to his promised coming?' they will demand. 'Already a generation has passed to its rest, and the situation remains exactly as it always has been since the world was created.' 5Such men have chosen to shut their eyes to the fact that long ago the heavens existed, and an earth was formed out of water and through water by the word of God. 6And it was by these waters that that ancient world was inundated and destroyed. 7But the present heavens and earth are by that same word reserved for fire. They are being kept for the day of judgment, when godless men will be destroyed.

8My dear friends, there is one fact you must never forget. One day to the Lord is the same as a thousand years, and a thousand years are the same as one day. 9It is not dilatoriness—although some people think it is—which keeps the Lord from fulfilling his promise; it is his patience with you. He does not want any to be destroyed; he wants them to find their way to repentance. 10The day of the Lord will come as unexpectedly as a thief. When it comes the heavens will vanish with a sound like roaring fire. The heavenly bodies will disintegrate in flames. The earth, and everything in it that man has made, will be laid bare.* 11In view of this coming dissolution of the universe, ask

*The reading is uncertain here. Some manuscripts have *will vanish*; others have *will be burned with fire*.

yourselves what kind of people you ought to be! Think in what consecrated godliness of conduct you ought to live! 12Think how you ought to live in constant expectation of the coming of the day of God, and how you ought to do everything possible to hasten its coming! For on it the heavens will be dissolved in fire, and the heavenly bodies will melt in flames. 13But, because God has promised that it shall be so, we await the new heavens and the new earth, in which justice will have its home.

14So then, my dear friends, since this is what you are waiting for, make up your minds to exert every effort to see to it that that day will find you spotless and blameless, at peace with God. 15You must regard our Lord's patience as your opportunity of salvation. This is what our dear colleague Paul too wrote to you in the wisdom God gave him. 16This is what he says in all his letters, when he speaks of this subject in them. In his letters there are some passages which are not too easy to understand, passages which men, whose knowledge of the faith is inadequate and who lack stability, twist to suit themselves, as they do with the rest of the scriptures—to their own ruin. 17So then, my dear friends, you have been warned in advance. You must therefore take every precaution not to become involved in, and swept away by, the error of men who disregard the laws of God, for, if that happens, you will have no firm ground left to stand on. 18You must steadily grow in grace and you must steadily come to know more and more of our Lord and Saviour Jesus Christ. Glory be to him now and for all eternity!

Introduction to the Letter of Jude

JUDE, or Judas, was a common name, and we cannot be quite sure who the Jude is who wrote this letter. But there is one very interesting possibility. He describes himself as the brother of James. The only James who was great enough to be called simply James with no further description was the James who was the head of the Jerusalem church. He was the brother of Jesus, and so it may well be that the writer of this letter is Jude, the brother of Jesus (Mark 6.3).

The letter is obviously an emergency production. Jude was going to write a treatise on the faith, but faced with this threatening situation he took up his pen to deal with it (verse 3), and what he has to deal with is the perversion of the truth (verse 4).

Anyone who reads the two letters carefully will see that the contents of this letter are very nearly the same as the second chapter of the Second Letter of Peter. The same danger is threatened; the same licentiousness and ungodly immorality is there; the same prophecy is cited. There is little doubt that the writer of the Second Letter of Peter found this little letter of Jude so cogent and so eloquent and so powerful that he incorporated it into his own.

In the end Jude pleads with his readers to keep themselves in the love of God (21), and to exert every effort to rescue those who had gone so far astray (22,23), and then he comes to the end with the most magnificent doxology in the New Testament (24,25).

Once again we see a Christian teacher wrestling with the perversion of the Christian gospel into an excuse to sin (pp. 148-150).

There is only one other notable thing in this little letter. It does what the New Testament writers very, very seldom do. It quotes books outside the Old Testament and outside scripture altogether. The passage about the argument of Michael with the devil about the body of Moses comes from an apocryphal book called *The Assumption of Moses* (verses 8 and 9), and later on he goes on to quote a passage from the Book of Enoch, which was a book of the same kind (verses 14 and 15). This could mean that Jude comes from a time so early that the canon of Old Testament scripture was not yet finally fixed.

The Letter of
JUDE

THIS is a letter from Jude, Jesus Christ's servant and James' brother, to those who have been called by God, and whose lives are lived in the love of God and under the protection of Jesus Christ. ₂It is my prayer that you should experience more and more of the mercy and the love of God, and that you should be blessed ever increasingly with every good thing.

₃My dear friends, while I was devoting all my energies to writing a treatise for you on the salvation we all share, I felt the necessity to write to you here and now to urge you strenuously to defend the faith which was once and for all handed over to God's dedicated people. ₄I regard this as necessary because there are some who have insinuated themselves into your fellowship—they were long ago marked out for this judgment—godless men they are, who pervert the grace of God into an excuse for blatant immorality, and who deny our only Master and Lord, Jesus Christ.

₅You have already been given full and final knowledge of the Christian faith. Nevertheless I want to remind you that the Lord* who rescued the people of Israel from their slavery in the country of Egypt later destroyed those who were guilty of unbelief. ₆The angels too who did not observe their own rank, and who left their proper place, he keeps under guard in eternal chains beneath darkness, to await the judgment of the great day. ₇You have another instance of this in Sodom and Gomorrah and the neighbouring towns. They in the same way practised sexual immorality and pursued un-natural vice. They provide an example of what happens to people who live like that, for they were subjected to the penalty of eternal fire.

₈So too these men today with their so-called visions defile their bodies, and treat the Lord's authority with contempt, and insult the glorious celestial ones. ₉When Michael the archangel was arguing

*Some manuscripts here have *God*; others have *Jesus*, which may be the Greek form of *Joshua*, as in Acts 7.45 and Hebrews 4.8.

with the Devil in their dispute about who was to get possession of Moses' body, he did not venture to add insult to condemnation. All he said was: 'The Lord rebuke you.' 10These men attack with their insults everything they do not understand. The things which, like brute beasts, they instinctively do understand are the very things which ruin them. 11Tragic will be their fate, for they have walked in the footsteps of Cain, they have flung themselves into Balaam's error for pay, they rebelled like Korah, and like Korah they are doomed. 12These men are blots on your Love Feasts; they bring no reverence to the sacred meals they share with you. They are supposed to be shepherds of the flock, but the only people they look after are themselves. They are clouds, driven by the wind, yet giving no rain. They are trees, fruitless in autumn, doubly dead, torn up by the roots. 13They are wild sea-waves foaming out their shameless acts. They are wandering stars, and the deepest depths of hell for ever and ever await them.

14It was of these too that Enoch prophesied in the seventh generation after Adam. 'The Lord will come,' he said, 'with tens of thousands of his holy angels 15to execute universal judgment, and to convict the godless of the godless conduct of which they have been guilty, and of the wild words they have spoken against him in their sin and their godlessness.' 16These men are filled with smouldering discontent. They are in a state of chronic resentment against life. Their conduct is determined by nothing but their own desires. Their talk is insolent and arrogant. They give their fulsome admiration to those out of whom they think they can get something.

17As for you, my dear friends, you must remember the statements already made by the apostles of our Lord Jesus Christ. 18During the last time, they said, there will be men to whom religion is a matter for a jest, and who have no principle of action other than their own godless desires. 19They are the kind of men who are a disruptive influence. They know no life beyond the life of this world. They are completely unspiritual. 20As for you, my dear friends, you must continue to build your life on the foundation of your most sacred faith. You must live lives of prayer in the atmosphere of the Holy Spirit. 21You must keep yourselves in the love of God. You must await the mercy of our Lord Jesus Christ, through which you will receive eternal life. 22Some, who cannot make up their minds, you must treat with pity. 23Some you must rescue by snatching them from the fire. With some you must deal with mingled pity and fear. You must hate even clothes stained by contact with a sensual man.

₂₄And to him who is able to keep you from falling, and to bring you blameless into his glorious presence with glad rejoicing, ₂₅to the only God our Saviour, through Jesus Christ our Lord, be glory, majesty, dominion, authority, before time began, and now, and until time ends.

Introduction to the First Letter of John

IT has been well said that a suitable title for this letter would be *The Tests of Life*. In it there is a phrase which occurs again and again—By this we know. In each case there is a test of what the true Christian is, and by inference an indication of the mistakes of the misguided people who are threatening to wreck the Christian community. Let us then look at these tests.

i. The first test is that we can only prove that we really do know God by keeping his commandments (2.3; 2.5; 5.2). This is clearly a rebuke to the Gnostics who said that sin does not matter, and to the Christians who twisted the grace of God into an excuse for sinning. We can only prove that we are Christians by walking as Jesus walked (2.5).

ii. The second test is that we can only prove the reality of our faith by doing right, by believing in Jesus, and by loving our fellow men (3.10,16,19,24). John is quite clear that to hate your brother is to be as bad as a murderer (3.15). Forthrightly he lays it down that to say that we love God, and at the same time to hate our brother, is to be a liar (4.20). The most correct theology and the most faultless morality without love are not Christian. Once again, the Gnostics who despised their fellow men stand condemned.

iii. The third test is that the real Christian must believe that Jesus really did come in the flesh (4.2). The Christian must believe in the real flesh and blood manhood of his Saviour. He must believe in a real and genuine incarnation. Once again, the Gnostics who said that Jesus was no more than a phantom in human form and who denied him a flesh and blood body are condemned.

iv. The fourth test is willingness to listen to the word and the message of God (4.6). The Gnostics claimed to have special and private information, to have, indeed, a gospel of their own. The real Christian never thinks that he knows better than the gospel.

v. The fifth test is the possession of the Holy Spirit (4.13). The true Christian lives in the guidance and in the strength of the Spirit.

To love and to obey God, to believe in Jesus and to be convinced of his true manhood, always to love our fellow men, and to live in the Spirit, these for John are the tests of the truly Christian life.

The First Letter of
JOHN

Chapter 1

OUR theme is the Word which is life. We tell you of what was
there from the beginning, of what we heard, and saw with our
own eyes, of what we looked at, and touched with our own hands.
₂This life was full displayed for all to see. We saw it, and we speak
from personal experience. It is news of this eternal life, which was
with the Father, and which was full displayed to us, that we are now
bringing to you. ₃We bring you the message of what we saw and heard.
We do so because we have fellowship with God and with his Son Jesus
Christ, and we want you to share with us in that fellowship. ₄We are
writing this to you, because we want our joy to be complete.

₅The message which we have heard from him and which we are
transmitting to you is this—God is light and there is no darkness in
him. ₆To claim to have fellowship with God, and at the same time to
walk in darkness, is to speak and act a lie. ₇To walk in the light, as he
is in the light, is to have fellowship with each other. And the blood of
Jesus his Son purifies us from all sin. ₈To claim that we have no sin is
an act of self-deception, and a proof that we have no idea of the truth.
₉If we confess our sins, we can depend on him, even although he is
just, to forgive us our sins, and to purify us from every kind of wickedness. ₁₀To say that we have never committed a sin is as good as to call
him a liar, and to prove that we have no idea what his message means.

Chapter 2

MY dear children, I am writing like this to you to keep you from
committing any sin. But, if anyone does sin, we have one to
plead our cause with the Father, I mean Jesus Christ—and he is good.
₂He himself is the sacrifice, by which the defilement of our sins is

227

removed, and not only the defilement of our sins but also of those of the whole world. ₃The only test by which we can really know that we do know him is this—do we obey his commandments? ₄If anyone claims to know him, and does not obey his commandments, that man is a liar, who does not know what truth is. ₅But in anyone who obeys his message, love for God has reached perfection. Here is the one test which proves that our lives are indissolubly bound to his. ₆Anyone who claims that his life is indissolubly linked to the life of Christ must live the same kind of life as he did.

₇My dear friends, it is not a new commandment that I am writing to you about. It is an old commandment which you have possessed from the beginning of your Christian life. The old commandment is the message which you have heard. ₈But there is a sense in which it is a new commandment that I am writing to you about. What I am writing to you about came true in him and in your own experience. It is new because we are now in a situation in which the darkness is passing away, and in which the real light is already shining. ₉If a man claims to be in the light, and at the same time hates his brother, he is still in the dark. ₁₀To love your brother is to live in the light; it is to live a life in which there is nothing to make a man stumble. ₁₁To hate your brother is to be in the dark, and to walk in the dark. For a man to live like that is to have no idea where he is going, because his eyes are blinded by the dark.

₁₂I write to you, my dear children,
    because your sins have been forgiven for his sake.
₁₃I write to you, fathers,
    because you know him who existed when the world began,
        and who still exists.
I write to you, young men,
    because you have conquered the Evil One.
₁₄I have written to you, my children,
    because you know the Father.
I have written to you, fathers,
    because you know him who existed when the world began,
        and who still exists.
I have written to you, young men,
    because you are strong,
        because God's word has its home in you,
            and because you have conquered the Evil One.

₁₅You must not be in love with the world, and the things of the world. No one can be in love with the world and in love with God at one and the same time. ₁₆Everything that is characteristic of the world, the desires of the passions, the way in which the sight of what we have not got kindles our desires for it, the tawdry glamour of this world's life, has its source, not in the Father, but in the world. ₁₇There is no permanence in the world and the things it sets its heart upon, but to do God's will is to last for ever.

₁₈Children, it is the last hour. You were told that Antichrist is coming, and now many Antichrists have arisen. This is how we know that it is the last hour. ₁₉They left our fellowship, but they never really belonged to it. If they had really belonged to our fellowship, they would have remained with us. They left us to make it clear that none of them belong to us. ₂₀They speak as if they were the only ones anointed by God with his Holy Spirit. But you too have had that experience, and all of you possess knowledge. ₂₁It is not because you do not know the truth that I have written to you; it is because you do know it, and you are well aware that no lie has its source in the truth. ₂₂Surely the supreme lie is to deny that Jesus is the Messiah. The one who denies the Father and the Son is Antichrist. ₂₃To deny the Son is to deny the Father too; to acknowledge the Son is to have the Father too. ₂₄What you heard when you first became Christians must remain immovably in you. If what you heard when you first became Christians remains immovably in you, then you too will remain in indissoluble union with the Son and the Father. ₂₅And the promise that he made to us is eternal life.

₂₆I have written to you about those who are trying to lead you astray. ₂₇As for you, the anointing with the Spirit, which you received from him, remains with you, and you do not need anyone to teach you. So far from that, the fact that you were anointed with the Spirit gives you all knowledge. His teaching is the truth itself and no lie. Therefore, you must remain united with Christ, as he taught you.

₂₈My dear children, your life must be indissolubly united with his even here and now, and then, whenever he appears, we will have nothing to fear, and we will not try to hide in shame from him, when he comes. ₂₉You know that he is good, and therefore you must be well aware that everyone who practises goodness draws his life from him.

Chapter 3

THE fact that we have been called the children of God must compel us to see how great a love the Father has given us. We are not only called his children; we are his children. The world does not recognize us, because it did not recognize him. ₂My dear friends, already here and now we are God's children, but what we shall be has not yet been revealed. What we do know is that, when Christ appears, we shall be like him, because we shall see him as he is. ₃If any man has this hope, the hope that is founded on Christ, he purifies himself as Christ is pure.

₄To commit sin is to break God's law. Sin is in fact the breaking of that law. ₅Christ himself was completely free from sin, and he appeared, as you are well aware, to remove sins altogether. ₆If a man's life is linked with the life of Christ he stops sinning. If a man goes on sinning, this is the proof that he has neither seen nor known Christ. ₇Dear children, you must not allow anyone to lead you astray. The man who does the right thing is a good man, just as Christ is good. ₈The man who goes on sinning is a child of the Devil, for there never was a time when the Devil was not a sinner. The reason why the Son of God appeared was to destroy the Devil's work. ₉No one who has God for his father continues to sin, because God's seed is a permanent part of him. He cannot go on sinning, because God is his father. ₁₀The test which makes it evident who are God's children and who are the Devil's children is that, if a man does not do what is right, and if a man does not love his fellowman, he is not God's child.

₁₁This is so because from the beginning the one thing that you have been taught is to love one another. ₁₂We must never be like Cain, who was a child of the Evil One, and murdered his brother. And why did he murder him? Because his own conduct was bad and his brother's was good. ₁₃Do not be surprised, brothers, if the world hates you. ₁₄It is because we love our fellowmen that we know that we have crossed the boundary between death and life. Not to love is to remain in the realm of death. ₁₅To hate one's fellowman is to be a murderer, and you know well that no murderer possesses eternal life as a permanent part of his being. ₁₆The action of Christ in laying down his life for us has shown us what love is; and we too are bound to lay down our lives for our fellowmen. ₁₇If a man is comfortably equipped with this world's necessities, and if he sees a brother man in need, and shuts his heart against him, how can he claim that God's love is an integral part of his life? 18Dear children, our love must not be a thing of words and of fine talk; it must be a thing of action and of sincerity.

19It is when we have a love like that that we will know that our life has its source in the truth, 20and, if there are times when our conscience condemns us, we will be able to assure ourselves before him by remembering that God is greater than our conscience, and that he knows all about us. 21My dear friends, if our conscience does not condemn us, we can come to God with confidence, 22and receive from him whatever we ask, because we keep his commandments and do what pleases him. 23It is his command that we should accept the claims of his Son Jesus Christ, and that we should love one another, for this is the commandment he gave us. 24If a man keeps God's commandments, God enters into his life, and he enters into God's life. It is through the Spirit, whom he gave us, that we know that he has entered into our life.

Chapter 4

My dear friends, do not trust every man who claims to be inspired by the Spirit. You must test such claims to inspiration to see if they really do have their origin in God, for many prophets inspired by false spirits have gone out into the world. 2The test by which you can recognize God-given inspiration is this. Everyone who claims to be inspired, and who accepts and states as an article of faith that Jesus Christ came in a human flesh and blood body, does draw his inspiration from God. 3Everyone who claims to be inspired, and who denies this article of faith about Jesus Christ, does not draw his inspiration from God. This is in fact the spirit of Antichrist. You were told that Antichrist was to come; but he is already in this world, here and now. 4But, my dear children, your life has its source in God, and yours is the victory over them, because the Spirit who is in you is greater than the spirit who is in the world. 5Their life has its source in the world. Therefore, their message has its source in the world. That is why the world listens to them. 6Our life has its source in God. If a man knows God, he listens to us; if a man does not belong to God, he does not listen to us. That is how we recognize which spirit is the spirit of truth, and which is the spirit of error.

7My dear friends, we must love one another, for love's source is

God, and to love is to be God's child and to know God. 8Not to love is not to know God, because God is love. 9As far as we are concerned, God's love was displayed in all its splendour by his action in sending his only Son into the world, and so through him giving us life. 10The wonder of love is not that we loved God but that he loved us enough to send his Son to remove the barrier that our sins had erected between us and him. 11My dear friends, if God loved us like that, it is our bounden duty to love each other. 12No one has ever seen God. But, if we love each other, God becomes an integral part of our lives, and his love is perfected in us.

13The proof that our life is joined to God's life, and his to ours, is to be found in the share of the Spirit which he has given to us. 14Further, we declare from personal knowledge, because we were eye-witnesses of the facts, that God sent his Son to be the Saviour of the world. 15If any man accepts, and states as an article of faith, that Jesus is the Son of God, God enters into his life, and he into God's. 16As for us, we have personal knowledge of, and faith in, the love which God has for us.

God is love. So then, if a man lives a life of love, he enters into the life of God, and the life of God enters into him. 17As far as we are concerned, love reaches its peak in that we are certain that on the day of judgment we have nothing to fear, because our relationship to this world is the same as his was. 18In love there is no fear. So far from that, perfect love banishes fear. Fear is connected with punishment. If a man is still afraid, he has not yet experienced love in all its perfection. 19Our love has its source and origin in God's love, for God loved us before we loved him. 20If anyone claims that he loves God, while at the same time he hates his brother, he is a liar. For, if a man does not love his fellowman, whom he has seen, he cannot possibly love God, whom he has not seen. 21And indeed the commandment that he has given us is that the man who loves God must love his fellowman too.

Chapter 5

To believe that Jesus is the Messiah is to be a child of God. To love the father is to love his child. 2We are therefore bound to realize that to love God and to obey his commandments must mean to love his children too. 3To love God is to obey his commandments, and his commandments are not burdensome, 4because to be a child of God is to be victorious over the world, and the victory which conquers the world is our faith. ₅Surely the man who is victorious over the world is none other than the man who believes that Jesus is the Son of God.

₆This is he who came through the water of his baptism and the blood of his cross—I mean Jesus Christ. It was not only by the water that he came; it was by the water and the blood. It is the Spirit who is the witness to this, because the Spirit is truth. ₇That truth is guaranteed because there are three witnesses, ₈the Spirit, the water, and the blood, and the three agree. ₉We accept human evidence on these terms, and surely the evidence of God has still greater weight, and this evidence is the evidence of God. This is the evidence that he has given in regard to his Son. ₁₀If a man believes in the Son of God, he finds his evidence in his own heart. If a man refuses to believe God, by that very action he as good as calls God a liar, because he has refused to accept the evidence which God gave in regard to his Son. ₁₁The evidence in question is this—that God gave us eternal life, and that his Son is the source of this life. ₁₂To have the Son is to have life; not to have the Son is not to have life.

₁₃My purpose in writing this letter to you is to give you the assurance that you do possess eternal life. I am writing to you who already know who and what the Son of God is, and who have committed yourselves to him. ₁₄The reason why we can approach God with complete confidence is that, if we ask for anything that is in accordance with his will, he listens to us. ₁₅If we know that he listens to us, whenever we ask him for anything, we know that the things for which we have asked him are already ours.

₁₆If anyone sees his fellowman committing a sin which is not a deadly sin, he must pray to God for him, and he will be the means whereby the sinner receives life. This is in the case of those whose sin is not deadly sin. There is such a thing as deadly sin. To pray about that is a different matter. ₁₇All wrong-doing is sin, but there is sin which is not deadly sin.

₁₈We know that no child of God keeps on sinning. We know that the Son of God keeps him safe, and that the Evil One cannot touch him. ₁₉We know that, although the whole world lies in the power of the Evil One, we belong to God. ₂₀We know that the Son of God has come, and has given us understanding to know the One who is real. Our lives are indissolubly bound to the One who is real, because they are indissolubly bound to his Son Jesus Christ. This is the real God, and this is eternal life. ₂₁My dear children, be on your guard against false gods.

Introduction to the Second Letter of John

THIS little letter does no more than reiterate the advice and the warnings of the first letter. The recipients are commanded to love one another, to be obedient to the commandments of God, and never to move from the belief that Jesus came to this world in full flesh and blood manhood. The letter is not so much a rebuke for any past mistakes; it is rather a warning to put its readers on their guard, should any of the false teachers visit them.

The only problem in the letter is who the elect lady is. She may have been a person and an individual, but the tone of the letter makes it much more likely that John is writing to a group and a community, and it is more likely that the phrase the elect lady stands for a church and not a person, and that the elect sister in verse 13 is a sister church.

The Second Letter of
JOHN

THIS is a letter from the Elder to the Lady chosen by God, and to her children, whom I truly love. Nor am I the only person to love you and yours. All who know the truth love you too. ₂It is for the sake of the truth, which has its home among us, and which will always remain with us that I write. ₃Grace, mercy and every blessing to you from God the Father and from Jesus Christ, the Father's Son, in truth and in love.

₄It made me very happy to find that some of your children are making truth the rule of their lives and are thus obeying the commandment we have received from the Father. ₅And now, dear lady, it is not as if I was pressing some new commandment on you. I am reminding you of a commandment we have known since the very beginning of our Christian life. I have only one thing to urge on you— that we should love one another. ₆To love means to live in obedience to God's commandments. This is the commandment which you have been taught from the beginning, and it must be for you the rule of life. ₇I say this because many deceivers have gone out into the world, who do not acknowledge Jesus Christ as coming in flesh and blood manhood. Such a teacher is a deceiver and Antichrist. ₈Be on your guard. You must be careful not to lose all that you worked for. Rather, you must see to it that you receive your reward in full. ₉Every so-called progressive who ceases to take his stand on the teaching of Jesus Christ has lost God. But, if a man continues to take his stand on that teaching, he has both the Father and the Son. ₁₀If anyone visits you, and does not bring this teaching, refuse to have him in your house. Give him no greeting. ₁₁For to give a man like that your good wishes is to become a partner in his evil work.

₁₂There are many things about which I could write to you, but I do not want to communicate with you by paper and ink. I hope to visit you soon, and to talk with you face to face, for then our joy will be complete. ₁₃The children of your sister, chosen by God, send you their good wishes.

Introduction to the Third Letter of John

BEHIND this little letter there is one of the most interesting and important situations in the New Testament.

In the early days of the church there were two kinds of ministry. There was the settled ministry, the ministry of the local congregation, the elders and the deacons. This kind of ministry did its work in one place and within one congregation, much as the ministry functions now. But there was also an itinerant ministry. The prophets and the apostles were not confined to one congregation. They moved throughout the whole church. Their authority was, so to speak, universal and not confined to any one place or any one congregation. *The Teaching of the Twelve Apostles* is the earliest book of Church Order which we possess. It must date back to very early in the second century, to a time very near that at which this little letter was written. This book gives the order for the Eucharist, and then at the end it says: 'But allow the prophets to hold the Eucharist as they will' (*The Teaching of the Twelve Apostles* 10.7). That this itinerant ministry was not without its problems is seen in the passage which immediately follows: 'Concerning the prophets and apostles, act thus according to the ordinance of the gospel. Let every apostle who comes to you be received as the Lord, but let him not stay more than one day, or if need be a second as well; but if he stays three days, he is a false prophet. And when an apostle goes forth let him accept nothing but bread; but, if he asks for money, he is a false prophet' (11.3-6). From this we can see that the itinerant apostles and prophets brought their own problems.

In particular they brought one big problem. They brought the inevitable clash between the itinerant and the settled ministry. The stronger the institution of the settled congregation became, the less it liked the invasions of the nomadic prophets and apostles, especially when these wanderers tried to tell them what to do. And after years of authority the wandering prophets and apostles found it hard to understand that they were no longer welcome.

This is exactly the situation we have in this letter. John is one of the old school. In fact, he was probably the last survivor of the old school. The essence of the situation is in verses 5-10. John pleads for the welcome and the support of those wandering prophets and apostles, who have given up everything to undertake this itinerant ministry.

He pleads that they should be welcomed and supported and helped on their way. But in verses 9 and 10 we read of Diotrephes who wanted nothing to do with these wanderers, who will not receive them, and who would actually debar them from the congregation. Diotrephes is the representative of the settled ministry and he finds the arrival of these wanderers nothing less than a nuisance and a disturbance. Demetrius (verse 12) is presumably still prepared to accept the old order.

So then, in this little letter we see the clash between the itinerant and the settled ministry, with the settled ministry resenting the invasion of these incomers with their claim to special and universal authority. In this letter the aged John throws all his weight on the side of the wandering prophets and apostles. But it was a losing battle and before very long the wandering evangelists had vanished from the scene, and the local ministry became the backbone of the structure of the church.

The Third Letter of
JOHN

THIS is a letter from the Elder to my dear Gaius, whom I truly
love.

₂My dear friend, it is my prayer that everything is going well with
you, and that you are in good health. I know that it goes well with
your soul. ₃It made me very happy, when some of our fellow-
Christians came and told me of your devotion to the truth. I am well
aware that you make the truth the rule of your life. ₄Nothing gives
me greater pleasure than to know that my children are making the
truth the rule of their lives.

₅My dear friend, you show your loyalty in what you do for your
fellow-Christians, strangers though they are to you. ₆They have told
to the congregation here the story of your Christian love. Please help
them on their way in a way that is fitting for servants of God. ₇It
was for the sake of Christ's name that they set out, and it is their
custom to accept nothing from pagans. ₈It is our duty to support
such men, for by so doing we will become their fellow-workers in
the truth.

₉I sent a letter about this to the congregation, but Diotrephes
cannot stand any interference with what he thinks is his place, and
he refuses to recognize our authority. ₁₀So, if I come, I will take occasion to remind the congregation of his conduct. He spreads malicious and untrue stories about us. Not content with that, he refuses
to accept our fellow-Christians who wish to visit your congregation.
He tries to stop those who would gladly receive them and tries to
expel them from the congregation.

₁₁My dear friend, do not imitate a bad example; imitate what is
good. The man who does good belongs to God; the man who does
evil has never seen God. ₁₂Everyone speaks well of Demetrius, as does
the truth itself. We too affirm his worth, and you know that our
evidence is true.

13There are many subjects on which I could write to you, but I do not want to communicate with you by pen and ink. 14I hope to see you soon, and we will talk face to face. 15Every blessing to you! The friends here send you their good wishes. Give our good wishes individually to all our friends with you.

Introduction to the Revelation

To a modern reader the Revelation is the strangest book in the New Testament. In the New Testament it stands alone, and there is nothing like it. But in point of fact it is a specimen of a kind of book which was very common between the Testaments, and of which many other examples exist. It is often called by another name; it is often called the Apocalypse. The Greek word *apokalupsis* means a revealing, an unveiling, a drawing of the curtain aside. And many Apocalypses were written both by Jews and Christians in the years before and after Jesus came. What then were these strange books, and what did they tell of?

The Jews never forgot that they were God's chosen people, and they never lost their faith and hope that some day this would be proved for all to see, and that they would become masters of the world, for they tended to think that they were chosen for power and for glory rather than for service and responsibility.

At first they believed that they would become great when there emerged a king of David's line to lead them to conquest. This was the Messiah whom they expected, and they thought of him in human terms. As time went on they began to think in terms of a supernatural instead of a human leader. But as time passed, and as they were subject in turn to the Babylonians, the Assyrians, the Persians, the Greeks, the Romans, as they realized their own smallness and the world's vastness, they began to see that their greatness could never be achieved by human means at all. After all, Palestine was only one hundred and twenty miles from north to south, and less than fifty miles from east to west. So they began to believe, not in any human leader, but in the direct intervention of God. The day would come when God himself would come striding into history and lead them to greatness and to glory.

So they began to have the belief that all time is divided into two ages. There is this present age, which is wholly bad, wholly under the domination of Satan, and quite beyond cure and reformation. There is the age which is to come, which was the golden age of God and of his people. But how was the one to turn into the other? It would happen on the Day of the Lord, the great day when God himself would enter history. It would be a day of cosmic disintegration, when the sun would be turned into darkness and the moon into blood, and

240

the mountains hurled into the sea, and when all order would become chaos. It would be a day of dreadful judgment; and then the new world would be born, and all would be well.

The Apocalypses were the books in which seers and visionaries set out what they believed would happen on the Day of the Lord. All Apocalypses therefore tend to be unintelligible, because they are trying to describe the indescribable, to express the inexpressible, to put into signs and symbols the terrors and the glories of the end time.

Now this is what our Apocalypse does. Only for it the end is not the Day of the Lord, but the coming again of Jesus Christ in majesty and glory and victory. To paint this picture it takes over much of the imagery and the dramatic apparatus which had attached to the Day of the Lord. Old Testament passages like Isaiah 24, Joel 2, Zephaniah 1 are the basis of the picture. This is a typical Apocalypse, describing the indescribable events which will happen when this world vanishes and the new world is born. We have only to see this to see that it cannot be taken literally. It is a poet's vision far more than it is an historian's story. It is the word of a prophet and a visionary (1.3; 22.9,10), not a literal time-table and description of celestial events.

It begins with the letters to the seven churches, which were the churches in which the seer John's writ ran (1.3). But from chapter 4 onwards it is a series of visions of the end time. The opening of the seven seals (6.1–8.1), the sounding of the seven trumpets (8.2–13.18), the pouring out of the seven bowls (15.1–18.24), the vision of worship and judgment (19.1–20.15), the picture of the new order (20.1–22.5) are all symbolic visions of the end time.

It shows us nothing of the Jesus of the Gospels; it shows us the warrior Christ. It has been said that the Revelation is the most Jewish book in the New Testament. This is true. There is hardly anything in it which cannot be paralleled from the Old Testament. In one thing it is very strange to us, but very Jewish. It calls Jesus the Lamb oftener than any book in the New Testament (eg. 5.8; 6.1; 7.17; 8.1; 14.1). But it is a strange picture, for we hear of the wrath of the Lamb and the victory of the Lamb and the might of the Lamb. This is a Jewish picture. The great Jewish heroes like David and Judas Maccabaeus were depicted as horned lambs. There is no gentleness here at all, only ineluctable power.

And what is at the back of all this? When we read the Revelation, one thing strikes us straight away. Its attitude to the state is quite different from any other book in the New Testament. The other books respect the state and tell Christians to be good citizens (Romans 13.1-7;

1 Timothy 2.2; 1 Peter 2.13-17). But in the Revelation Rome is the great harlot, drunk with the blood of the saints and the martyrs, for in it Babylon stands for Rome (17.1-6). What had gone wrong?

Bit by bit the Roman Emperor had come to be regarded as a god. He embodied the spirit of Rome, and in very gratitude for good rule people had first worshipped the spirit of Rome, and then the Emperor as the incarnation of that spirit. At first the Emperors were embarrassed by this, for they had not sought it. But they began to see how they could use it. Rome stretched from Britain to the Euphrates and from the Danube to North Africa. What could give some kind of unity to this vast polyglot Empire which comprised most of the world? The one thing that could unify it was Caesar worship. So the day came, when once a year every citizen had to burn a pinch of incense to the godhead of Caesar and say: 'Caesar is Lord.' This the Christians would never do. Christ and Christ alone was Lord. And that was why they were persecuted. If they had conformed and had burned the incense and said the sentence, they could have gone off and worshipped anything. But they would not, and so they became what the poet called 'the panting, huddled flock, whose crime was Christ.'

The Revelation comes from that time when men had to choose between Caesar and Christ, when to be true to Christ was to be liable to die. That is why it hates Rome, and that is why it looks so eagerly forward to the end of the present evil age, and the time when Christ's enemies will be vanquished and he will reign for ever and ever.

THE REVELATION TO JOHN

Chapter 1

THIS is the record of the revelation given by Jesus Christ. God gave it to him to show to his servants what must soon happen, and he through his angel sent and made it known to his servant John. ₂John publicly proclaimed the message given to him by God and affirmed by Jesus Christ, telling all that he had seen.

₃God's joy will come to the man who reads
    the words of this prophetic message
      to the assembled people,
and to those who listen to them,
and to those who obey what is written in it,
for it will not be long now until the crucial moment
    of fulfilment comes.

₄This is John's message to the seven churches in the province of Asia.

Grace to you and every blessing,
    from him who is and was and is coming,
    and from the seven spirits before his throne,
    ₅and from Jesus Christ,
      who declared God's truth and whose word can be trusted,
      who was the first to rise from the dead,
      who is the ruler of all earthly kings.
To him who loves us,
    and who liberated us from our sins
      at the cost of his blood,
    ₆and who made us a kingdom
      every member of which is a priest
        to his God and Father,
to him be glory and dominion for ever and ever. Amen.
₇Look! he is coming with the clouds.
    Everyone will see him,
    and so will those who pierced him,
      and all the nations of the earth

will weep in remorse for what they did to him.
Even so! Amen!

8I am Alpha and Omega, the one who is the beginning and the end,
says the Lord, who is and who was and who is coming, the one who
holds all things in control.

9I, John, your fellow-Christian, and your partner in the trouble, in
the Kingdom, and in the gallant endurance which being a follower of
Jesus involves, was in the island called Patmos, because I had preached
God's word and had publicly declared my faith in Jesus. 10On the
Lord's Day I fell into a trance, in which I heard behind me a voice
like the sound of a trumpet. 11'Write what you are seeing on a scroll,'
it said to me, 'and send it to the seven churches, to Ephesus, to
Smyrna, to Pergamum, to Thyatira, to Sardis, to Philadelphia, and to
Laodicea.'

12I turned to see
whose voice it was that was speaking to me,
and, when I had turned,
I saw seven golden lampstands.
13And in the middle of them
there was a figure like a man.
He was wearing a robe
that reached down to his feet,
and he had a golden girdle
encircling his breast.
14The hairs of his head were as white
as snow-white wool;
his eyes were like flaming fire;
15his feet were like burnished brass,
refined in a furnace;
his voice was like the sound
of torrents of waters.
16In his right hand
he had seven stars;
and out of his mouth
there came a sharp double-edged sword,
and his face
shone like the sun in full blaze.

17When I saw him, I fell at his feet like a dead man. He laid his right
hand on me. 'Have no fear,' he said. 'I am the first and the last. 18I am

the living one. I was dead, and now I am alive for ever, and the keys of death and Hades are mine. 19Write down what you have seen, what is and what will be hereafter. 20This is the secret meaning of the seven stars, which you saw in my right hand, and of the seven golden lamp-stands. The seven stars are the angels of the seven churches, and the seven lampstands are the seven churches.'

Chapter 2

WRITE this message to the angel of the church at Ephesus. This is a message to you from the one who holds the seven stars in his right hand, and who walks among the seven golden lamp-stands. 2I know the life that you have lived. I know how hard you have toiled, and how gallantly you have met your troubles. I know how impossible you find it to tolerate evil men. I know that there was a time when you tested those who claim to be apostles, and who have no right to that title, and proved them liars. 3Indeed you have met your troubles with gallantry. Indeed you have suffered for your Christian loyalty, and you have never abandoned the struggle. 4But I do have this criticism of you to make. You have lost the love that once you had, when you first became Christians. 5Think back to the standards that once you had, and repent, and live again the life you lived, when you first became Christians. If you do not, I am coming to you, and, unless you repent, I will remove your lampstand from its place. 6But you do have this in your favour—you hate the practices of the Nicolaitans, and so do I. 7It is the duty of anyone who can hear to listen to what the Spirit is saying to the churches. I will give the victor in the battle of life the right to eat the fruit of the tree of life, which is in the garden of God.

8Write this message to the angel of the church at Smyrna. This is a message to you from the one who is the first and the last, the one who was dead and who rose to life again. 9I know the troubles you are going through. I know you are destitute of this world's goods. But for all that you are rich in true wealth. I know the slanders of those who call themselves Jews, but who are Satan's synagogue. 10Do not be afraid of what is going to happen to you. The Devil will throw some of you into prison. It will be to test you, and you will have a ten day time of trouble. Prove yourself to be willing to die for your faith, and I will give you life as your victor's crown. 11It is the duty of everyone who can hear to listen to what the Spirit is saying to the churches. The second death can never hurt the victor in the battle of life.

12Write this message to the angel of the church at Pergamum.

This is a message from the one who has the sharp, double-edged sword. 13I know where your home is. I know that it is where Satan has his seat of power. And yet I also know that you never lose your grip of me, and that you did not deny your loyalty to me even in the time of Antipas, who was so steadfast in declaring his loyalty to me that he was put to death among you, where Satan has his residence. 14But I do have a few criticisms of you to make. You have among you some who have accepted the teaching of Balaam, who taught Balak to lay a trap for the Israelites, by teaching them to eat meat which has been part of a sacrifice to a heathen idol, and to practise sexual immorality. 15So you too have some who have accepted the very similar teaching of the Nicolaitans. 16You must repent. If you do not, I am coming to you soon, and I will make war on them with the sword of my mouth. 17It is the duty of everyone who can hear to listen to what the Spirit is saying to the churches. To the victor in the battle of life I will give a share of the manna that was hidden away, and I will give him a white stone, and on the stone a new name will be inscribed, a name undisclosed to anyone except to the person who receives it.

18Write this message to the angel of the church at Thyatira.

This is a message from the Son of God, from the one whose eyes are like flaming fire, and whose feet are like burnished brass. 19I know the life you have lived. I know your love, your loyalty, your service, and the gallantry with which you have met your troubles. I know that your conduct was good, when you first began the Christian life, and that it is even better now. 20But I do have this criticism to make of you. You tolerate that Jezebel of a woman who claims to be a prophetess, and whose teaching seduces my servants into committing fornication, and eating meat which has been part of a sacrifice to a heathen idol. 21I gave her time to repent, and she refuses to repent of her fornication. 22I will lay her on a bed of pain, and I will hurl her partners in adultery into terrible trouble, unless they realize how wrong her conduct is, and stop participating in it. 23I will strike her children dead, and all the churches will know that the most secret thoughts of men's minds and the most secret feelings of their hearts are no secrets to me. Each man's conduct will decide what reward or punishment I will assign to him. 24But on all the rest of you in Thyatira, who have not accepted this teaching, and who have no knowledge of 'the deep secrets of Satan,' as they call them, I make no other demand 25than to order you not to relax your grip on what you have, until I come. 26To the victor in the battle of life, and to the man who to the end lives the kind of life I have commanded him to live, I will give authority over the nations. 27He will shatter them with a rod of iron; they will be smashed like broken pieces of pottery. 28His authority will be like the authority I received from my Father. And I will give him the morning star. 29It is the duty of everyone who can hear to listen to what the Spirit is saying to the churches.

Chapter 3

WRITE this message to the angel of the church at Sardis. This is a message from the one who has the seven spirits of God and the seven stars. I know the life that you have lived. I know that you have the reputation of being alive, but you are in fact dead. 2Awake from your sleep, and strengthen what is left, for it too is on the way to death, for, as far as I can see, in the sight of God nothing that you should have done has been done. 3So then, keep remembering the faith you have received, and the instruction you were given. Keep on obeying it, and make up your mind to repent. If you do not awake from your sleep, I will come like a thief, and you will not know the moment when I will come upon you. 4In spite of it all, you still have a few people in Sardis who have not stained their clothing, and they will walk with me, dressed all in white, because they deserve to do so. 5The victor in the battle of life will be thus clothed in white robes. I will never erase his name from the book of life. I will acknowledge him as mine before my Father and his angels. 6It is the duty of everyone who can hear to listen to what the Spirit is saying to the churches.

7Write this message to the angel of the church at Philadelphia. This is a message from the one whose nature is holiness and truth, the one who has the key of David. When he opens, no one can shut; when he shuts, no one can open. 8I know the life that you have lived. A door of opportunity, which no man can shut, stands open in front of you, and it is I who have given it to you. I know that you have only a little strength, but you have been obedient to my instructions, and did not disown your loyalty to me. 9I am going to deliver into your hands those who belong to the synagogue of Satan, those

who claim to be Jews, but who are liars, and who are not. I will make
them come and do homage to you, and I will make it clear to them
that you are dear to me. ₁₀You have kept my instructions to face your
troubles gallantly. I will therefore keep you safe from the crisis time
of ordeal which is going to descend on the whole world to test all the
inhabitants of the earth. ₁₁I am coming soon. Never relax your grip on
what you have, and then no one will be able to take away your
victor's crown. ₁₂I will make the victor in the battle of life a pillar in
the temple of my God. Never again will he leave it. I will write on
him the name of my God, and the name of the city of my God, the
name of the new Jerusalem, which is to come down from heaven
from my God. ₁₃It is the duty of everyone who can hear to listen to
what the Spirit is saying to the churches.

₁₄Write this message to the angel of the church at Laodicea.
This is a message from the one who is the guarantor of all God's
promises, the witness on the truth of whose word you can rely, the
moving cause of God's creation. ₁₅I know the life that you have lived.
I know that you are neither cold nor hot. If only you were either cold
or hot! ₁₆So, because you are tepid, and neither hot nor cold, you
make me want to be sick! ₁₇You claim to be rich and wealthy. You
claim to have everything you need. You are not aware that in your
destitution and blindness and nakedness you are in fact a wretched
creature who is to be pitied. ₁₈I therefore strongly advise you to buy
from me gold refined in the fire, to make you really rich; and white
clothes in which to dress yourself, to keep you from becoming a
public spectacle, naked and ashamed; and ointment to put on your
eyes, to make you able really to see. ₁₉My way of showing that I love
people is to reprove and discipline them. Make up your mind to
repent. Make a lasting enthusiasm of your religion. ₂₀I am standing
at the door knocking. If anyone hears my voice, and opens the door,
I will come in and we will share our meal together, I with him, and
he with me. ₂₁To the victor in the battle of life I will give the privilege
of sitting with me on my throne, just as I won the victory, and took
my seat with my Father on his throne. ₂₂It is the duty of everyone
who can hear to listen to what the Spirit is saying to the churches.

Chapter 4

AFTER this I had another vision. There in front of me a door
stood open in heaven, and the voice like the sound of a trumpet,
which I had heard speaking to me before, spoke to me. 'Come up
here,' it said, 'and I will show you what must happen in the future.'
₂Immediately I fell into a trance. I had a vision of a throne standing in
heaven, and of someone sitting on the throne. ₃When I looked at the
one sitting on the throne, it was like looking at the sheen of a jasper
or carnelian stone, and all around the throne there was a rainbow,
gleaming like an emerald. ₄In a circle surrounding the throne I saw
twenty-four thrones. And on the thrones I saw twenty-four elders
sitting. They were wearing white robes, and they had victors' golden
crowns on their heads. ₅Out from the throne there came flashes of
lightning and peals of thunder. In front of the throne there were
burning seven blazing torches, which are the seven spirits of God.
₆The space in front of the throne looked like a sea of glass, like crystal.
  In the middle of the scene, round about the throne, there were four
living creatures, covered with eyes, back and front. ₇The first living
creature was like a lion; the second living creature was like an ox;
the third living creature had a man's face; the fourth living creature
was like an eagle in flight. ₈Each of the four living creatures had six
wings, and they were covered all over with eyes, inside and out. Day
and night they never rested from singing:

> 'Holy, holy, holy is the Lord God,
>   he who holds all things in control,
>   he who was and who is and who is coming.'

₉Whenever the four living creatures give glory and honour and
thanksgiving to the one who sits on the throne, and who lives for
ever, ₁₀the twenty-four elders throw themselves down in front of the
one who sits on the throne, and worship him who lives for ever and
ever. They lay their crowns before the throne, and this is their song:

> ₁₁'Our Lord and God, yours is the right
>   to receive glory and honour and power,
>   for you created all things,
> and it was through your will
>   that they came into being, and were created.'

Chapter 5

THEN in the right hand of the one who was sitting on the throne I saw in my vision a scroll, covered on both sides with writing, front and back. It was sealed with seven seals. ₂Then I saw a strong angel and heard him announcing for all to hear: 'Is there anyone here fit to open the scroll and to break its seals?' ₃No one in heaven or on earth or under the earth was able to open the scroll or to see what was in it. ₄I began to cry bitterly, because no one could be found who was fit to open the scroll and to see what was in it. ₅One of the elders said to me: 'Stop crying! The victory of the Lion from the tribe of Judah, the Root of David, has given him the right to open the scroll and to break the seven seals.'

₆Then I saw in my vision a Lamb standing in the middle of the throne, in the centre of the circle of the four living creatures and of the twenty-four elders. The Lamb had all the marks of a victim slain for sacrifice. He had seven horns and seven eyes. The seven eyes are the seven spirits of God, which are sent by him all over the earth. ₇The Lamb went and received the scroll from the right hand of the one who was sitting on the throne. ₈When he had received the scroll, the four living creatures and the twenty-four elders threw themselves down in front of him. Each of the elders had a harp. And they had golden bowls filled with incense, which is the prayers of God's dedicated ones. ₉They sang a new song, and this is what they sang:

'You have the right to take the scroll,
and to break its seals,
because you were slain,
and at the cost of your life-blood
you bought for God
men out of every tribe and language
and people and nation,
₁₀and you made them into a kingdom
every member of which is a priest to serve God,
and they will reign on earth.'

₁₁The vision continued, and I heard the voice of many angels encircling the throne, and of the living creatures and the elders. There were myriads and myriads, and thousands and thousands of them. ₁₂And this is what they were saying for all to hear:

'The Lamb who was slain
 has the right to receive
power and wealth and wisdom and strength,
 honour and glory and thanksgiving.'

13And I heard the whole of the created world in heaven and on earth and under the earth and in the sea and everything they contain speaking, and this is what they were saying:

'Blessing and honour and glory and power
 to the one who is sitting on the throne,
 and to the Lamb for ever and ever.'

14The living creatures said Amen, and the elders threw themselves down and worshipped.

Chapter 6

IN my vision I saw the Lamb open the first of the seven seals, and I heard one of the four living creatures say in a voice like thunder: 'Come!' 2In my vision I saw a white horse. Its rider had a bow. He was given a victor's crown, and he rode out conquering and to conquer.

3When the Lamb opened the second seal, I heard the second living creature say: 'Come!' 4Another horse came out, blood-red in colour. Its rider was given the right to take peace from the earth, and to make men slaughter one another. And he was given a great sword.

5When he opened the third seal, I heard the third living creature say: 'Come!' And in my vision I saw a black horse. Its rider was holding a pair of scales in his hand. 6I heard what sounded like a voice speaking from the middle of the four living creatures. 'It will take a whole day's wages to pay for a quart of flour,' the voice said. 'It will take a whole day's wages to pay for three quarts of barley. But you are forbidden to damage the olive and the wine.'

7When he opened the fourth seal, I heard the voice of the fourth living creature say: 'Come!' 8And in my vision I saw a horse blanched and pale. Its rider's name was Death, and with him as his follower came Hades. He was given power over a quarter of the earth. He was allowed to kill by the sword, by famine, by pestilence, and by the wild beasts of the earth.

9When he opened the fifth seal, I saw at the foot of the altar the souls of those who had been slaughtered, because they had preached the word of God, and had publicly declared their belief in it. 10They shouted their appeal to God: 'Sovereign Lord, holy and true, how long is it going to be until you act in judgment, and take vengeance for our murder on the inhabitants of the earth?' 11Each of them was given a white robe. They were told to rest a little while longer, until there should be completed the number of their fellow-servants who were to be killed, as they had been.

12In my vision I saw what happened, when the Lamb opened the sixth seal. There was a violent earthquake. The sun became as black as black sackcloth. The moon looked as if it was all made of blood. 13The stars fell from the sky to the earth, like figs from a fig-tree shaken by a gale of wind. 14The sky vanished like a scroll being rolled up. Every hill and island was removed from its place. 15The kings of the world, and the great ones, and the generals, and the wealthy, and the powerful, all men, slave and free alike, hid themselves in the caves and among the rocks of the hills. 16They said to the hills and the rocks: 'Fall on us, and hide us from the one who is sitting on the throne, and from the wrath of the Lamb. 17For the great day of their wrath has arrived, and who can survive it?'

Chapter 7

THE vision continued, and in it I saw four angels standing at the four corners of the earth. They were holding back the four winds of the earth, to stop any wind blowing on the earth or on the sea, or against any tree. 2In my vision I saw another angel coming up from the east. He had the living God's seal. He shouted to the four angels who had been given power to damage the land and the sea. 3'You must not damage the land or the sea or the trees,' he said, 'until we have marked the foreheads of the servants of God with God's seal.'4I was told the number of those who were marked with the seal. The number was one hundred and forty-four thousand, sealed from all the tribes of the Israelites:

5Of the tribe of Judah, twelve thousand were sealed;
   of the tribe of Reuben, twelve thousand;
   of the tribe of Gad, twelve thousand;
   6of the tribe of Asher, twelve thousand;
   of the tribe of Naphtali, twelve thousand;

of the tribe of Manasseh, twelve thousand;
7of the tribe of Simeon, twelve thousand;
of the tribe of Levi, twelve thousand;
of the tribe of Issachar, twelve thousand;
8of the tribe of Zebulun, twelve thousand;
of the tribe of Joseph, twelve thousand;
of the tribe of Benjamin, twelve thousand were sealed.

9The vision continued, and in it I saw a vast crowd of people, too
many for anyone to count. They came from every nation and from
all tribes and peoples and languages. They were standing in front of
the throne, and in front of the Lamb. They were wearing long white
robes, and they were holding palm branches in their hands. 10They
were shouting:

> 'It is our God who is seated on the throne,
>   and the Lamb,
> who have brought us in safety
>   through all our troubles.'

11All the angels stood in a circle round the throne and the elders and
the four living creatures. They threw themselves down on their faces
in front of the throne and worshipped God, 12and this is what they
said:

> 'Amen! Blessing and glory and wisdom
> and thanksgiving and honour and power
> and strength belong to our God for ever and ever.
> Amen!'

13One of the elders said to me: 'These men who are wearing the
long white robes—who are they and where did they come from?'
14'Sir,' I said, 'you will have to tell me.' 'These,' he said to me, 'are the
men who have come through the terrible time of trouble. They have
washed their robes, and have made them white through the blood of
the Lamb. 15That is why they are there before God's throne.

> Night and day they serve him in worship
>   in his temple,
> and he who sits on the throne will company with them
>   in all his glory.
> 16Never again will they hunger or thirst;
>   the sun will not beat down on them,
>   nor any scorching heat,

17because the Lamb who is in the centre of the throne
will be their shepherd.
He will be their guide
to the springs of the water of life,
and God will wipe away all tears from their eyes.'

Chapter 8

WHEN the Lamb opened the seventh seal, there was a silence
in heaven for about half an hour. 2In my vision I saw the
seven angels who stand in the presence of God being given seven
trumpets.

3Another angel came and stood beside the altar. He was carrying
a golden censer. He was given a large quantity of incense to mingle
with the prayers of all God's dedicated people, as he offered them on
the golden altar in front of the throne. 4The smoke of the incense
went up before God from the angel's hands with the prayers of God's
dedicated people. 5Then the angel took the censer and filled it with
fire from the altar and hurled it at the earth, and there were peals of
thunder and flashes of lightning and an earthquake.

6Then the seven angels with the seven trumpets prepared to sound
them.

7The first angel sounded a blast on the trumpet, and there came
hail and fire mingled with blood, and it was hurled on the earth. A
third of the land was burned up, and a third of the trees were burned,
and all the green grass was burned.

8Then the second angel sounded a blast on the trumpet, and what
looked like a great mountain blazing with fire was hurled into the
sea. A third part of the sea turned into blood, 9and a third of
the living creatures in the sea died, and a third of the ships were
wrecked.

10Then the third angel sounded a blast on the trumpet, and a great
star, flaming like a torch, fell from heaven. It fell on a third of the
rivers and the springs of water. 11The name of the star was Wormwood. A third of the waters turned into wormwood, and the waters
brought death to many men because of their bitterness.

12Then the fourth angel sounded a blast on the trumpet, and a
third of the sun was struck, and a third of the moon, and a third of the
stars, with the result that a third of them were darkened, and the day
lost a third of its light, and so did the night.

13In my vision I saw an eagle in flight in the middle of the sky, and I heard it shout: 'Tragic, tragic, tragic will be the fate of the inhabitants of the world, when the trumpets speak which the rest of the angels are to sound.'

Chapter 9

THEN the fifth angel sounded a blast on the trumpet, and in my vision I saw a star which had fallen from the sky to the earth. To this star was given the key of the shaft of the Abyss. 2The star then opened the shaft of the Abyss. From the shaft there rose smoke, like the smoke of a vast furnace, and the sun and the air were darkened by the smoke rising from the shaft. 3Out of the smoke locusts spread all over the ground. They were given the same power as normal scorpions have. 4They were instructed not to damage the grass of the earth, or any of the green things or of the trees. They were to do no damage to anything except to men who did not have God's seal on their foreheads. 5They were not permitted to kill them, but they were to torture them for five months. The pain they were to inflict was to be like the pain a scorpion inflicts, when it stings a man. 6At that time men will search for death and will not be able to find it; they will long to die, but death will evade them.

7In appearance the locusts were like horses caparisoned for battle. On their heads they had what looked like golden crowns. Their faces were like human faces. 8They had hair like women's hair. Their teeth were like lions' teeth. 9They had breastplates like iron breastplates. The sound of their wings was like the sound of many chariots and horses charging into battle. 10They had tails like scorpions, with stings. It was in their tails that their power to hurt men for the five month period lay. 11They had the angel of the Abyss as their king. In Hebrew he is called Abaddon; in Greek his name is Apollyon, which means the Destroyer.

12The first woe has passed. There are still two more woes coming.

13Then the sixth angel sounded a blast on the trumpet. Then I heard a voice, coming from the horns of the golden altar, which stood in the presence of God. 14'Release the four angels who are held bound at the great river Euphrates,' it said to the sixth angel with the trumpet. 15So the four angels who were there, all ready for that very hour and day and month and year, were released to kill a third of mankind. 16Their squadrons of cavalry numbered two hundred million. I was told the number of them. 17In the vision this was how I saw the horses and their riders. The riders were wearing breast-plates of flame colour, blue and sulphur-yellow. The horses had heads like lions' heads, and flames and smoke and sulphur issued from their mouths. 18A third of mankind were killed by these three plagues, by the flames and the smoke and the sulphur, which issued from their mouths. 19The power of the horses lay in their mouths and in their tails, for their tails were like snakes with heads, and with them they inflicted wounds.

20But the men who were left, and who had not been killed by these plagues, did not repent. They did not abandon their manmade gods. They did not stop worshipping demons and idols of gold and silver and bronze and stone and wood, which cannot see or hear or move. 21They did not repent of their murders, their sorceries, their im-morality, their thefts.

Chapter 10

IN my vision I saw another strong angel coming down from heaven. He was wrapped in a cloud; the rainbow was on his head; his face was shining like the sun; and his legs were like pillars of fire. 2He was holding in his hand a little scroll which was unrolled. He placed his right foot on the sea, and his left on the land. 3Then he shouted with a shout like a lion's roar, and, when he shouted, the seven thunders spoke with their voices. 4When the seven thunders spoke, I was about to write down what they said. But I heard a voice speaking from heaven. 'You must seal with secrecy what the seven thunders said,' I was told, 'and you must not write it down.' 5The angel, whom I saw standing on the sea and on the land, raised his right hand to heaven, 6and swore by him who lives for ever and ever, by him who created heaven and everything in it, and earth and everything in it, and the sea and everything in it, that there would be no more delay, 7but that at the time of the trumpet blast which the seventh angel was to sound, the secret purpose of God would be completed, as he had told his servants the prophets.

8Then the voice I had heard from heaven spoke to me again. 'Go,' it said, 'and take the scroll, which the angel who is standing on the sea and on the land is holding open in his hand.' 9So I went to the angel, and asked him to give me the little scroll. 'Take it,' he said to me, 'and eat it. Your stomach will find it bitter, but your mouth will find it as sweet as honey.' 10So I took the little scroll from the hand of the angel, and ate it. In my mouth it tasted as sweet as honey; but, when I ate it, it turned my stomach sour. 11I was told: 'Once again you must prophesy about many peoples and nations and languages and kings.'

Chapter 11

I WAS given a cane like a measuring-rod. 'Up!' I was told, 'and measure the temple of God, and the altar, and count those who worship in it. 2Omit the outer court from your calculations, and do not measure it. It has been given to the Gentiles, and they will trample on the holy city for forty-two months. 3I will give my two witnesses the task of proclaiming my message, dressed in sackcloth, throughout the one thousand two hundred and sixty days.' 4It is these witnesses that the two olive trees and the two lampstands, which stand in the presence of the Lord, represent. 5If anyone tries to harm them, fire will issue from their mouths, and will devour their enemies. This is the death that anyone who tries to harm them must die. 6These witnesses possess the power to shut up the sky, and to stop any rain falling during the period they are proclaiming the message of God. They also possess power over the waters, to turn them into blood, and to smite the earth with every kind of plague, as often as they wish. 7When they have completed their declaration of the truth, the beast who rises from the Abyss will make war on them, and will conquer them, and kill them. 8Their dead bodies will lie on the street of the great city, which is symbolically called Sodom and Egypt, the city in which their Lord also was crucified. 9Men of all peoples and tribes and languages and from all nations will see their dead bodies for three and a half days, and they will refuse to allow their bodies to be buried. 10The whole population of the world will be so glad to see them dead that they will celebrate their death, and give presents to each other to mark it, because these two prophets were responsible for the merciless and universal castigation of all men. 11After the three and a half days the breath of life from God went into them. They stood up, and those who saw them were terrified at the sight of them. 12Then they heard a shout from heaven. 'Come up here!' it said to them. And they went up into heaven in a cloud as their enemies watched. 13At the same moment there was a violent earthquake, and a tenth part of the city collapsed in ruins. Seven thousand people lost their lives in the earthquake. Those who were left were terrified, and praised the God of heaven.

14The second woe is over. The third woe is coming soon.

15The seventh angel sounded a blast on the trumpet, and voices in heaven began to shout:

> 'Our Lord and his Messiah
> have become the sovereigns of the world,
> and he will reign for ever and ever.'

16The twenty-four elders, who sit on their thrones in the presence of God, flung themselves down and worshipped God, 17and this is what they said:

> 'We give you thanks, Lord God,
> you in whose power are all things,
> you who are and who were,
> that you have taken your great power
> and entered upon your royal rule.
> 18The nations raged;
> your wrath went out,
> for the time for the dead to be judged has come,
> the time to give their reward
> to your servants the prophets,
> and to your dedicated people,
> and to those who reverence your name,
> both great and small,
> the time to destroy those who are destroying the earth.'

19God's temple in heaven was opened, and within the temple the ark of the covenant could be seen. The lightning flashed and the thunder pealed, and there was an earthquake and a violent storm of hail.

Chapter 12

THEN a sight full of meaning appeared in the sky. It was a woman, clothed with the sun, standing on the moon, and with a crown of twelve stars on her head. 2She was pregnant, and in her labour and her agony she cried aloud for her child to be born. 3Then another sight full of meaning appeared in the sky. It was a huge flame-coloured dragon, with seven heads and seven horns, with a royal crown on each of its heads. 4Its tail swept from their places a third of the stars in the sky, and hurled them to the earth. The dragon stood waiting in front of the woman, who was waiting for her child to be born, for he intended to devour the child as soon as he was born. 5So the woman had her baby, a boy, who is destined to rule all nations with an iron rod. Her child was snatched up to God and to his throne. 6The woman fled to the desert, where there was a place prepared by God, waiting for her. She was to be cared for there for one thousand two hundred and sixty days.

7War broke out in heaven, in which Michael and his angels fought against the dragon. The dragon with his angels put up a fight, 8but he was not strong enough to win, and in the end no place was any longer left for them in heaven. 9So the great dragon, the ancient serpent, who is called the Devil and Satan, and who is responsible for leading the whole world astray, was hurled to the earth, and his angels with him. 10I heard a voice speaking in heaven for all to hear, and this is what it said:

'Now our God has won the victory;
    now God has displayed his power and his sovereignty,
    and the authority of his Messiah,
because the accuser of our brothers,
    who accused them night and day in the presence of God,
    has been hurled out of heaven.
11The blood of the Lamb,
    and their fearless declaration of their faith,
    have won for them the victory over him,
    for they did not love their lives
    enough to refuse to die for their faith.
12So then, rejoice, you heavens,
    and you who live in them!
But tragic is your fate, earth and sea,
    for the Devil has come down to you,
    and great is his wrath,
    for he knows that his time is short.'

13When he saw that he had been hurled to the earth, the dragon pursued the woman who had had the boy baby. 14But the woman was given two great eagle's wings, to enable her to fly away to her place in the desert, where she was to be cared for for a time, times and half a time, that is, three and a half years, where the serpent could not reach her. 15Out of his mouth the serpent hurled after the woman a stream of water like a river, in an attempt to sweep her away in the torrent. ₁₆But the earth came to the help of the woman. It opened its mouth and drank up the river which the dragon had hurled from his mouth. ₁₇The dragon was infuriated with the woman. He went off to make war on the rest of her children, I mean, on those who obey God's commandments, and who declare their loyalty to Jesus. ₁₈He stood on the sea-shore.

Chapter 13

IN my vision I saw a beast rising from the sea. It had ten horns and seven heads. On each of its ten horns there was a royal crown, and on each of its heads there was a name which was a deliberate insult to God. ₂The beast which I saw in my vision was like a leopard; its feet were like a bear's feet; its mouth was like a lion's mouth. The dragon assigned to the beast his power and far-reaching authority. ₃I saw that one of its heads looked as if it had been fatally injured, but its mortal wound had been healed. The whole earth went after the beast in fascinated wonder. ₄They worshipped the dragon, for he had assigned his authority to the beast, and they worshipped the beast. 'The beast,' they said, 'is unique and irresistible.'

₅The beast was allowed to use grandiloquent language which was a deliberate insult to God. It was given the right to exercise authority for forty-two months. ₆It poured out a torrent of insults against God. It insulted his name, and the place where he lives, and the inhabitants of heaven. ₇It was allowed to make war on God's dedicated people, and to conquer them, and it was given authority over people of every tribe and nation and language and race. ₈The whole population of the world will worship it, except those whose names were inscribed before the world began in the roll of the living, which belongs to the Lamb who was killed.

₉If a man can hear, he must listen to this message.

> ₁₀'If a man is destined for captivity,
>   to captivity he goes;
>   if a man is to be slain by the sword,
>   by the sword he is to be slain.'

This is where the gallantry and loyalty of God's dedicated people must be displayed.

₁₁Then in my vision I saw another beast rising from the land. It had two horns like a lamb, and, when it spoke, it was like a dragon speaking. 12It exercised all the authority of the first beast, while the first beast looked on. It made the earth and all its inhabitants worship the first beast, the beast whose mortal wound had been healed. 13It performed great miracles. It even made fire come down from heaven to earth while people looked on. 14Through the miracles that it was allowed to do in the presence of the beast it led astray the inhabitants of the earth. It told the inhabitants of the earth to make an image in honour of the beast who was wounded by the sword and came to life again. 15It was allowed to give breath to the image of the beast, and thus it made the image of the beast able to speak, and it was allowed to cause all who refused to worship the image of the beast to be put to death. 16It caused everyone, important and unimportant, rich and poor, free men and slaves to be branded with a mark on their right hand or on their forehead. 17Without this mark, the name or the number which stands for the name, no one was allowed to buy or sell. 18To solve this problem needs wisdom. An intelligent man can calculate for himself the number of the beast, for the number represents a man's name, and, if you count the letters of his name, their value as numbers is six hundred and sixty-six.

The point of this obscure passage is that neither Greek nor Hebrew has any signs for the numbers. The letters of the alphabet do duty for the numerals as well, as if A were to equal 1; B,2; C,3, and so on. Since that is so, if the letters in any name are given their numerical value, they can be added up and so give a sum total. In point of fact, 666 is the sum of the Hebrew letters in the Hebrew form of Nero Caesar, who was the first and the most notorious persecutor of the church.

Chapter 14

IN my vision I saw the Lamb standing on Mount Sion. With him there were one hundred and forty-four thousand people with his name and the name of his Father inscribed on their foreheads. 2I heard a sound from heaven, like the sound of cataracts of water and like a crashing peal of thunder. The sound I heard was like the music of harpers playing on their harps. 3They were singing a new song before the throne and before the four living creatures and the elders. No one could learn that song except the hundred and forty-four thousand, who had been ransomed from the world. 4These are men who never soiled their lives with women, for they kept themselves in virgin purity. These are men who follow the Lamb wherever he goes. They were ransomed, and thus separated from the rest of men, as the first-fruits of that harvest which God and the Lamb will gather in. ₅They have never been known to tell a lie; they are faultless in their purity.

₆In my vision I saw another angel, flying in mid-heaven, with an eternal gospel to proclaim to the inhabitants of the earth, to every nation and tribe and language and people. ₇'Reverence God,' he shouted for all to hear, 'and give him the glory, for the hour of his judgment has come! Worship him who made heaven and earth, the sea and the springs of water!'

₈Another angel followed the first angel. 'Fallen, fallen is Babylon the great,' he said, 'Babylon who made all the nations drink the wine of her fornication, the wine doomed to the wrath of God.'

₉Another angel followed the first two. 'Anyone who worships the beast and his image,' he said for all to hear, 'and anyone who accepts the mark of the beast on his forehead or on his hand ₁₀will also drink of the wine of the wrath of God, poured undiluted into the cup of his anger. He will be tormented with sulphurous fire in the presence of the holy angels and in the presence of the Lamb. ₁₁The smoke of their torture rises to all eternity. Those who worship the beast and his image, and anyone who receives the mark of his name, have no rest, day or night!' ₁₂A situation like this demands the gallantry of God's dedicated people, of those who continue to maintain their obedience to the commandments of God and their loyalty to Jesus.

₁₃Then I heard a voice from heaven. 'Write,' it said, 'God's joy will come to the dead who from now on die with their connection with their Lord unbroken.' 'Yes, indeed,' said the Spirit, 'for after their toil they will have their rest, and the record of what they did goes with them.'

₁₄In my vision I saw a white cloud. Sitting on the cloud I saw one like a human figure, wearing a victor's crown of gold on his head, and carrying a sharp sickle in his hand. ₁₅Another angel came out of the temple, and shouted to him who was sitting on the cloud: 'Set to with your sickle and reap. The time to reap has come, for earth's harvest is ripe, and more than ripe.' ₁₆So he who was sitting on the cloud swung his sickle on the earth, and the earth was reaped.

₁₇Then another angel came out of the temple in heaven. He too had a sharp sickle. ₁₈Then still another angel came from the altar. He was the angel who controls fire. He shouted to the angel with the sickle. 'Set to with your sharp sickle,' he said, 'and gather in earth's grape harvest from the vine. Its clusters are ripe.' ₁₉So the angel swung his sickle on the earth, and gathered its grapes, and threw them into the great winepress of God's wrath. ₂₀The juice was squeezed out of the grapes outside the city, and blood flowed from the winepress as high as the horses' bridles for two hundred miles round about.

Chapter 15

THEN I saw another great and astonishing sight in heaven, a sight which was full of meaning. I saw seven angels with seven plagues. These were the last plagues of all, because in them the wrath of God reached its climax and its consummation.

₂Then I saw what looked like a sea of glass, mingled with fire. I saw, standing beside the sea of glass, those who had emerged victorious from their struggle with the beast, and with his image, and with the number of his name. ₃They were singing the song of Moses, the servant of God, and the song of the Lamb, and this is what they were singing:

'Lord God, you hold all things in your power,
    and great and marvellous are your deeds.
Just and true are your ways, King of the nations.
₄Who will not reverence you, Lord,
    and who will not glorify your name?
    For you alone are holy.
All the nations will come,
    and will worship in your presence.
because the justice of your decrees
    has been made plain for all to see.'

₅My vision continued. The sanctuary of the Tent of Witness in heaven was opened. ₆Out of the sanctuary there came the seven angels with the seven plagues. They were robed in linen, clean and shining. They were wearing golden girdles round their breasts. ₇One of the four living creatures gave the seven angels seven golden bowls, full of the wrath of God, who lives for ever and ever. ₈The sanctuary was filled with smoke from the glory of God and from his power. No one could enter the sanctuary, until the seven plagues of the seven angels were completed.

Chapter 16

THEN I heard a voice shouting from the sanctuary to the seven angels. 'Go,' it said, 'and pour out on the earth the seven bowls of the wrath of God.'

₂So the first angel went and poured out his bowl, and ulcerous and malignant sores attacked the men who had the mark of the beast, and who worshipped his image.

₃The second angel poured out his bowl on the sea, and the sea turned into blood, like the blood of a corpse, and every living creature in the sea died.

₄The third angel poured out his bowl on the rivers and the springs of water, and they turned into blood. ₅Then I heard the angel who presided over the waters saying:

'You who are and were, the Holy One,
  it is in your justice
    that you have pronounced this sentence.
  ₆Because they poured out
    the blood of God's dedicated people
      and of the prophets,
  you have given them blood to drink.
  They have got what they deserved.'

₇Then I heard the altar saying:

'Yes, Lord God,
  you hold all things in your control;
  your judgments are true and just.'

₈Then the fourth angel poured out his bowl on the sun, and the sun was allowed to burn men with its flame. ₉Men were dreadfully burned. They hurled their insults at the name of God, who has the power to unleash such plagues, and they refused to repent and to give him glory.

₁₀Then the fifth angel poured out his bowl on the throne of the beast. His kingdom was enveloped in darkness. They tried to bite out their tongues in their agony. ₁₁They hurled their insults at the God of heaven for their pains and their sores, but they did not repent for what they had done.

₁₂Then the sixth angel poured out his bowl on the great river

Euphrates, and its waters were dried up to prepare the way for the kings from the east. 13In my vision I saw issuing from the mouth of the dragon and the mouth of the beast and the mouth of the false prophet three evil spirits like frogs. 14They were the spirits of demons, and they were able to perform miracles. They went out to the kings of the inhabited world to muster them for the battle which is to be fought on the great Day of God, who holds all things in his control. 15I am coming like a thief. Happy is the man who stays awake, and who keeps his clothes beside him, for then he will not have to walk naked and thus have all men see his shame. 16So they mustered the kings in the place called in Hebrew Armagedon.

17Then the seventh angel poured out his bowl in the air. Then there came a shout out of the sanctuary from the throne: 'It is done!' 18Then there came flashes of lightning and peals of thunder, and an earthquake of such violence that there never was an earthquake like it for violence, since men came into being on the earth. 19Then the great city was split into three parts. The cities of the nations collapsed. Babylon the great did not escape her fate, for God gave her the cup of the wine of his furious wrath. 20Every island vanished, and the mountains disappeared. 21Huge hailstones, weighing as much as a hundredweight, rained down on men from the sky. Men hurled their insults at God for the plague of the hail, because the plague was devastating in the extreme.

Chapter 17

ONE of the seven angels, who had the seven bowls, came and spoke to me. 'Come!' he said. 'I will show you the sentence of condemnation which has been passed on the great prostitute, that city which is built on many waters. 2She has acted the prostitute with the kings of the earth, and the inhabitants of the earth have become drunk with the wine of her fornication.' 3So he carried me away to the desert in a trance. In my vision I saw a woman seated on a scarlet beast. The beast was covered with names which are a deliberate insult to God. It had seven heads and ten horns. 4The woman was robed in purple and scarlet. She was bedecked with gold and jewels and pearls. She had a golden cup in her hand, filled with obscenities and with the filth of her fornication. 5On her forehead there was inscribed a name with a secret meaning—Babylon the great, mother of prostitutes and of earth's obscenities. 6In my vision I saw the woman drunk with the blood of God's dedicated people and with the blood of those who had declared their faith in Jesus.

To me the woman was a most astonishing sight. 7The angel said to me: 'What is so astonishing to you in all this? I will explain to you the secret meaning of the woman and of the beast she is riding, the beast with seven heads and ten horns. 8The beast which you saw was once alive and is not now alive. It will rise from the Abyss, and it is on the way to destruction. Those of the inhabitants of the earth whose names were not written, since the world was created, in the roll of the living will look in wonder at the beast. They will stand astonished at it, because it was once alive, and is not now alive, and will appear. 9The solution of this requires a mind equipped with wisdom. The seven heads are seven hills on which the woman sits enthroned. They are also seven kings. 10Five of them have already fallen; one is the king now in existence; the other has not yet come. And, when he does come, he is destined to remain for only a short time. 11The beast which was once alive, and which is not now alive, is itself also an eighth. At the same time it belongs to the seven, and it is on its way to destruction. 12The ten horns which you see in your vision are ten kings, who have not yet entered upon their reigns. They are to receive authority for one hour and are to exercise it in co-operation with the beast. 13These kings share one common purpose—to hand over their power and their authority to the beast. 14They will go to war with the Lamb, and the Lamb will conquer them, because he is Lord of lords, and King of kings. Sharing the Lamb's battle and victory are those who are called and chosen and loyal.

15'The waters, on which the prostitute sits, which you saw in your vision,' the angel said to me, 'are crowds of peoples and nations of every language. 16The ten horns, which you saw, and the beast will come to hate the prostitute. They will leave her stripped and desolated. They will devour her flesh. They will burn her in flames to ashes. 17For God put it into their minds to carry out his purpose by coming to a common decision to hand over their sovereignty to the beast, until all that God has said should be completed and done. 18The woman you saw is the great city which has sovereignty over the kings of the earth.'

Chapter 18

MY vision continued, and in it I saw another angel coming down from heaven. He was an angel of great authority, and the earth was lit up by his splendour. ₂He shouted in a resounding voice:

'Fallen, fallen is Babylon the great.
She has become the home of demons,
the haunt of every unclean spirit,
the haunt of every unclean and loathsome bird,
₃because she made all the nations
drink of the wine of her fornication,
the wine doomed to the wrath of God.
The world's kings committed fornication with her,
and the demands of her wanton luxury
have made the world's merchants rich.'

₄I heard another voice from heaven, and this is what it said:

'Come out of her, my people,
if you do not wish to be partners in her sins,
and if you do not wish
to share in her plagues.
₅For her sins are heaped as high as heaven,
and her crimes are not forgotten by God.
₆Give her what she gave to others;
repay her twice over for all that she has done.
In the cup that she mixed for others
mix her a drink that is twice as strong.
₇Give her torment and grief,
to match the splendours and the luxury
that once she gave herself.
She says in her heart:
"I am a queen on a throne!
I am no widow forlorn!
Sorrow will never touch me!"
₈Because of all this, in one single day
her plagues will assail her—
pestilence and sorrow and famine—

she will be burned to ashes in flames,
for mighty is the Lord,
and he has pronounced her doom.'

₉The world's kings were her companions in fornication and in
wanton luxury. Now they will weep and lament over her, when they
see the smoke of the conflagration in which she will be burned. ₁₀In
their terror at her torment they will stand far away and say:

'Tragic, tragic is the fate of the great city,
of Babylon the mighty city!
For in one brief hour her doom has come!'

₁₁The world's merchants too will weep and mourn for her, because
there will be no one now to buy their cargoes any more, ₁₂cargoes of

gold and silver and jewels and pearls;
cloths of fine linen and purple and silk and scarlet;
all kinds of perfumed woods, ornaments made of ivory,
all kinds of things made of precious wood
and bronze and iron and marble;
₁₃cinnamon and spice, incense and myrrh and
frankincense;
wine and oil and fine flour and wheat;
cattle and sheep, horses and chariots;
slaves and human lives.

₁₄'Gone is the fruit of your heart's desire!
Perished your brilliance and your splendour!
And no one will ever see them again.'

₁₅The merchants who dealt in these things, and who grew rich because of their trade with her, will stand far away in their terror at her
torture, in tears and in sorrow. ₁₆They will say:

'Tragic, tragic is the fate of the great city,
she who was robed in fine linen and purple
and scarlet,
she who was gilded with gold,
and bedecked with jewels and pearls,
₁₇for in one brief hour,
wealth so great was turned into a desert!'

And every ship's captain, and every sea-faring man, all sailors, and
all whose trade is on the sea, stood far away, ₁₈and shouted as they

watched the smoke of the conflagration in which she was burning:
'Truly the great city was unique!' ₁₉They flung dust on their heads,
and in their tears and sorrow they cried:

'Tragic, tragic is the fate of the great city,
the city by whose wealth,
all who had ships at sea grew wealthy,
for in one brief hour
she has become a desert!'

₂₀'Rejoice over her, O heaven,
rejoice you dedicated people of God,
you apostles and you prophets,
because God has passed on her,
the sentence she passed on you!'

₂₁Then a strong angel took a stone like a huge millstone, and hurled
it into the sea, and, as he did so, he said:

'Thus will Babylon the great city
be hurled violently down,
and will disappear from sight for ever.
₂₂Never again will the melody
of harpers and minstrels,
of flute-players and trumpeters,
be heard in you.
Never again will craftsmen of any trade
be found in you.
The sound of the mill
will never again be heard in you.
₂₃The light of a lamp
will never again be seen in you.
The voice of the bridegroom and the bride
will never again be heard in you.
Your merchants were once
the world's commercial aristocrats.
Your sorceries led
all the nations astray.
₂₄She stands exposed as the murderer
of the prophets,
and of God's dedicated people,
and of all the world's slaughtered martyrs.'

Chapter 19

M Y vision continued, and in it I heard what sounded like the roar of a vast crowd in heaven, and this is what they were saying:

> 'Alleluia!
> Victory, glory and power belong to our God,
>   2for his judgments are true and just.
> He has sentenced the great prostitute,
>   who was the corrupter of the earth with her fornicati on
>   and he has taken vengeance on her
>   for the murder of his servants.'

3A second time they shouted:

> 'Alleluia!
> The smoke rises from her for ever and ever.'

4The twenty-four elders and the four living creatures threw them :elves down, and worshipped God as he sat on his throne. 'Amen they said. 'Alleluia!'
    5Then a voice came from the throne, and this is what it said:

> 'Praise our God,
>   all you servants of his,
>   all you who reverence him,
>   both great and small!'

6Then I heard what sounded like the sound of a vast crowd, and like the sound of cataracts of water, and like the crash of thunder, and this is what they were saying:

> 'Alleluia!
> For the Lord our God,
>   who holds all things in his control,
>   has begun his reign.
>   7Let us rejoice and thrill with gladness,
>   and let us give him glory,
>   for the wedding day of the Lamb has come
>   8and his Bride has prepared herself for it.
>   Fine linen, dazzlingly white,
>   has been given to her for her dress.'

The fine linen stands for the good deeds of God's dedicated people.

₉Then he said to me: 'Write this—God's joy will come to those who have been invited to the Lamb's wedding banquet!' He went on to say to me: 'This is a genuine message from God.' ₁₀I threw myself down at his feet to worship him. 'This is what you must not do,' he said. 'I too am a fellow-servant with you and your brothers, for we both possess the declaration of the truth which Jesus brought to us. It is God alone whom you must worship. For the same Spirit speaks in the declarations of Jesus and in the words of the prophets.'

₁₁Then I saw heaven standing open, and on to the scene there came a white horse. Its rider's name was Faithful and True, for both as a judge and as a warrior he is just. ₁₂His eyes were like flaming fire; on his head he had many royal crowns. Inscribed on him, he had a name known only to himself. ₁₃The robe he was wearing was soaked with blood. The name by which he is called is The Word of God. ₁₄The armies of heaven followed him, mounted on white horses, and dressed in fine linen, white and clean. ₁₅A sharp two-edged sword issued from his mouth. With it he was to smite the nations, for he will rule them with an iron rod. He treads the winepress of the anger of the wrath of God, who holds all things in his control. ₁₆He has a name inscribed on his robe and on his thigh—King of kings and Lord of lords.

₁₇Then I saw an angel standing in the sun. He shouted to all the birds flying in mid-sky. 'Come!' he said. 'Gather for God's great banquet! ₁₈Come and eat the flesh of kings and the flesh of generals, the flesh of strong men, the flesh of horses and their riders, the flesh of all men, free men and slaves, small and great.' ₁₉Then I saw the beast and the world's kings and their armies mustered to join battle with the rider of the horse and his army. ₂₀The beast was captured, and so was the false prophet, who in the presence of the beast had performed miracles, by which he had led astray those who had received the mark of the beast, and those who worship his image. These two were hurled alive into the lake of fire with its sulphurous flames. ₂₁The rest of them were killed by the sword, which issued from the mouth of the rider of the horse, and the birds all gorged themselves with their flesh.

Chapter 20

THEN I saw in my vision an angel coming down from heaven. In his hand he was holding the key of the Abyss and a huge chain. ₂He seized the dragon, the ancient serpent, who is the Devil or Satan, and bound him for a thousand years. ₃Then he hurled him into the Abyss, and locked him in, and sealed the opening over him, to keep him from leading the nations astray any more, until the thousand year period had been completed. Following on that period, he has to be released again for a short time.

₄Then in my vision I saw thrones. Sitting on them were the souls of those who had been executed, because they had declared their faith in Jesus, and for the sake of the word of God. They had not worshipped the beast or his image, and they had not received his mark on their foreheads and on their hands. To them the right of judgment had been given. They came to life again, and they shared Christ's reign for a thousand years. ₅The rest of the dead did not come to life again until after the thousand year period had been completed. This is the first resurrection. ₆God's joy will come to the man who has a share in the first resurrection! He is one of God's dedicated people. The second death has no power over these. They will be priests of God and of Christ, and they will share his reign for a thousand years.

₇Then, when the thousand year period has been completed, Satan will be released from his imprisonment. ₈He will go out to lead astray the nations all over the world, in all its four quarters. He will muster Gog and Magog, all God's enemies, for battle. In number they will be like the sand of the sea. ₉They covered the whole breadth of the world as they marched up, and they surrounded the camp of God's dedicated people and the city he loves. Then fire came down from heaven and devoured them. ₁₀Then the Devil who led them astray was hurled into the lake of sulphurous fire, into which the beast and the false prophet had already been thrown. Day and night they will be tortured for ever and ever.

₁₁Then I saw a great white throne and someone sitting on it. Earth and heaven fled from his presence, and not a trace of them remained. ₁₂Then in my vision I saw the dead, great and small, standing in front of the throne. The record books were opened. Another book was brought—the register of the living. The dead were judged on the basis of what was written in the books, by the record of what they had done. 13The sea gave back its dead. Death and Hades gave back their dead. And each man was judged by the record of what he had done. 14Death and Hades were hurled into the lake of fire. The lake of fire is the second death. 15Everyone whose name was not found to be recorded in the book of the living was hurled into the lake of fire.

Chapter 21

THEN I saw in my vision a new heaven and a new earth, for the first heaven and the first earth were gone. The sea no longer existed. 2I saw the holy city, new Jerusalem, coming down out of heaven from God, made ready like a bride, dressed in all her finery for her husband. 3Then I heard a voice speaking from the throne for all to hear. 'The home of God in all his glory is with men,' it said, 'and he will live with them. They will be his people and God himself will be with them, and he will be their God. 4He will wipe away every tear from their eyes. Death will cease to exist. There will no longer be any sorrow or crying or pain. The old order of things has gone!'

5Then he who was seated on the throne said: 'See! I am making everything new. Write this down,' he said, 'because you can believe what I am saying, for it is true.' 6Then he said to me: 'It is done! I am Alpha and Omega, the beginning and the end. I will allow the thirsty to drink from the spring of the water of life—and all as a free gift. 7The victor in the battle of life will enter into possession of all this. I will be his God and he will be my son. 8But for the cowards, for those who refuse to believe, for those whose lives are an abomination, for murderers and fornicators, for sorcerers and idolaters and for liars of every kind, their fate is the lake, burning with sulphurous fire, which is the second death.'

9Then one of the angels, who held the seven bowls which were filled with the seven last plagues, came and spoke to me. 'Come here,' he said, 'and I will show you the bride, the Lamb's wife.' 10He took me away in a trance to a great high mountain, and showed me the holy city Jerusalem coming down out of heaven from God, 11with the sheen of God's splendour on it. Its radiance was like the radiance of a very precious stone, like a jasper, clear as crystal. 12It had a huge high wall with twelve gates. At the gates there were twelve angels. Names were inscribed on the gates, and the names were

the names of the twelve tribes of Israel. 13There were three gates on
the east, three gates on the north, three gates on the south, and three
gates on the west. 14The city wall had twelve foundation stones, with
the twelve names of the Lamb's twelve apostles on them.

15The angel who was speaking to me had a golden measuring-
rod to measure the city and its gates and its wall. 16The city was built
in the shape of a square. The length and the breadth were equal. He
measured the city with his rod, and the length of the sides was fifteen
hundred miles. Its length and breadth and height were all equal.
17He measured the height of the wall, and it came to two hundred
and sixteen feet. (This is in human figures, which the angel was using.)
18The wall was constructed of jasper. The city was of pure gold, as
clear as glass. 19The foundations of the city wall were adorned with
jewels of every kind. The first foundation stone was a jasper; the
second, lapis lazuli; the third, chalcedony; the fourth, emerald; 20the
fifth, sardonyx; the sixth, carnelian; the seventh, chrysolite; the eighth
beryl; the ninth, topaz; the tenth, chrysoprase; the eleventh, tur-
quoise; the twelfth, amethyst. 21The twelve gates consisted of twelve
pearls. Each gate was made of a single pearl. The city streets were of
pure gold, like translucent glass.

22I saw no temple in the city. Its temple is the Lord God, who holds
all things in his control, and the Lamb. 23The city has no need of the
sun or the moon to shine in it, for the splendour of God illumines it,
and its lamp is the Lamb. 24The nations shall walk by its light. The
world's kings will bring their splendour to it. 25Its gates will never be
shut in the day-time—and it will never be night there. 26The splendour and wealth of the nations will be brought to it. 27Nothing unclean will ever be allowed into it, nor anyone whose conduct is foul
and false. Only those whose names are written in the Lamb's roll of
the living will be allowed to enter it.

Chapter 22

THEN he showed me the river of the water of life, sparkling like
crystal. It issues from the throne of God and of the Lamb. 2It
flows down the middle of the city street. On each side of the river
grows the tree of life. The tree produces twelve crops of fruit. It
gives a crop for each month in the year. The leaves of the tree are
meant to be a cure for the nations. 3No accursed thing shall exist any
more. The throne of God and the Lamb will be there, and his servants

will worship him. ₄They will see him face to face; his name will be on their foreheads. ₅There will be no night any more. They do not need the light of any lamp or even the light of the sun, because the Lord God will give them light. And they will be kings for ever and ever.

₆Then he said to me: 'You can believe what I am saying to you because it is true. The Lord, the God who inspired the prophets, has sent his angel to show his servants what must soon happen. ₇I am coming soon! God's joy will come to the man who obeys the prophetic message of this book!'

₈It was I John who heard these messages and saw these visions. When I heard and saw them, I threw myself down in worship at the feet of the angel who showed them to me. ₉'That is what you must not do,' he said to me. 'I am your fellow-servant, and the fellow-servant of your brothers the prophets, and of all who obey the words of this book. It is God alone whom you must worship.' ₁₀He went on to say to me: 'Do not seal up as secret the prophetic message of this book, for the crisis time is near. ₁₁The evil man must continue in his evil-doing. The filthy man must continue in his filthiness. The good man must continue to live the good life. The man who is dedicated to God must continue in his dedication.'

₁₂'I am coming soon,' Jesus says, 'and I am bringing my reward with me. I will settle accounts with each man on the basis of the life he has lived. ₁₃I am Alpha and Omega, the first and the last, the beginning and the end.'

₁₄'God's joy will come to those who wash their robes, for then they will have the right to the tree of life, and to entry through the gate into the city. ₁₅Outside there are dogs and sorcerers, forni-cators and murderers and idolaters, and everyone who loves and acts a lie.'

₁₆'I Jesus have sent my angel to give you this solemn message from me to bring it to the churches. I am the Root of David and my descent is from him. I am the bright morning star. ₁₇The Spirit and the bride say: "Come!" If any man hears the invitation, he must answer: "Come!" If anyone is thirsty, he must come. Here is the invitation, to everyone who wants the water of life, to come and take it—and all for nothing.'

₁₈I make a solemn declaration to everyone who hears the prophetic message of this book. If anyone makes any addition to it, God will add to him the plagues recorded in this book. ₁₉If anyone removes anything from the words of this book's prophetic message, God will take away his share in the tree of life and in the holy city, described in this book.

20He who has sent this solemn message says: 'Yes indeed! I am coming soon!' So be it! Come, Lord Jesus!

21The grace of the Lord Jesus be with you all.

New Testament Words
Notes on Passages

New Testament Words

ABBA. This is the word by which the Christian is said to be able to address God through the action and the help of the Holy Spirit (Romans 8.15; Galatians 4.6). It is the word by which Jesus addressed God in the hour of his sorest trial (Mark 14.36). It is the familiar form of the Hebrew word *ab*, which means father. *Abba* was the word used by the child in the intimacy of the family circle, the word by which the child called his father in the home. The normal English equivalent would be Daddy. What the word shows is the loving intimacy made possible between the Christian and God through the work of Jesus Christ.

ACCESS: *prosagōgē* (Romans 5.2; Ephesians 1.5; 2.18). *Prosagōgē*, and the corresponding verb *prosagōgein* (1 Peter 3.18), can mean generally *to bring in*. But the words have the special and technical sense of introducing someone into the presence of a king. Anyone who wished anything from Cyrus the Persian king had to get a *prosagōgē* to him, an introduction to the royal presence (Xenophon, *Cyropaedia* 7.5.45). Ancient kings had an official called the *prosagōgeus, the introducer*, whose task it was to bring the right people into the presence of the king, and to keep the wrong people out. So, when it is said that through Jesus we have access to God, the idea is that of subjects receiving the privilege of entry into the presence of the King.

ADOPTION: *huiothesia* (Galatians 4.5; Ephesians 1.5; Romans 8.15). When Paul speaks of adoption, it is Roman adoption of which he is thinking. Roman adoption was a far-reaching process, involving religious and legal ceremonial. What made it so difficult in Roman law was the conception of the *patria potestas*, the father's power. The Roman father had absolute power over his son and his whole family so long as he lived, even theoretically the power of life and death. So long as the father was alive, the son never came of age, and never emerged from this power. If therefore a man's parents were alive, adoption meant the momentous step of passing out of one *patria potestas* into another. In his new family the adopted son had absolute rights as a son. Further, he was literally a new person. Debts, legal charges in which he was involved in his previous life were all cancelled. He began a new life detached from the past. It is this radical renewing of which Paul is thinking when he speaks in terms of adoption.

ADULTERER: *moichalis* (James 4.4). Normally this word, when it appears in lists of vices, has its usual physical meaning. But there are times when it has a different meaning. In the Gospels we find the phrase, An evil and adulterous generation (Matthew 12.39; 16.4; Mark 8.38). And James 4.4 likely falls within this special category. In these cases the word describes, not physical, but spiritual, infidelity. This usage comes from the idea of Israel as the bride of God (Hosea 3.1; Jeremiah 3.9; 9.1). If then Israel is unfaithful to God and strikes up an association with some false god, she may be said to be guilty of spiritual adultery. Thus we hear of Israel awhoring after strange gods (Exodus 34.25; Leviticus 17.7; Deuteronomy 31.26; Judges 8.27). So in the James passage it is this spiritual adultery which is in question.

ALLELUIA: *allelouia* (Revelation 9.1,3,6) (RSV, Hallelujah). This is the transliteration of a Hebrew expression which means, Praise Jahweh.

ALMIGHTY: *pantokratōr* (Revelation 4.8; 11.17; 15.3; 16.7,14; 19.15; 21.22). This word is almost confined to the Revelation. It comes from two Greek words, *panta*, all things, and *kratein*, to hold in control. It therefore describes God as the one who holds all things in control. The very use of the word is a declaration of faith. The Revelation was written at a time of savage persecution, when the apparently irresistible might of the Roman Empire had been directed against the church. No one had ever been able to withstand Rome, but for the Christian, not Rome, but God, is the one who holds all things in control.

ALPHA AND OMEGA. This is the first title of God in Revelation 1.8; 21.6; 22.13. *Alpha* is the first letter of the Greek alphabet, and *omega* the last. In English we speak of knowing something from A to Z. *Aleph* is the first letter of the Hebrew alphabet, and *tau* the last. So the Jews said that Abraham kept the law of God from *aleph* to *tau*. The idea is that of comprehensive completeness.

AND: *kai*. There are in Greek two uses of the common word *kai*, which means *and*. There is the use in which it simply adds one thing to another. We might call this the *additive* use of *kai*, and it is of course by far the commonest. But there is also what is called the *epexegetic* use of *kai*. In this use the words which follow *kai* do not simply add something to what goes before; they explain or define what goes before. There is a good example of this epexegetic use in Revelation 2.2: 'I know thy works, and thy labour, and thy patience . . .' But the meaning is that all that comes after the first *and* is an explanation and a definition of what is meant by works. So the translation should read literally: 'I know your works. I mean your labour and your patience . . .' There is another example of the use of this epexegetic *and* in Revelation 2.19.

ANSWER: *eperōtēma* (1 Peter 3.21) (RSV, NEB, appeal). The word occurs in 1 Peter in connection with baptism. It is a word with a technical business usage. Every deal was completed with a question as to whether the terms were accepted and an affirmation that they were. So we get such phrases as: In answer to the formal question they declared their assent. It is therefore most likely that in 1 Peter the word *eperōtēma* refers to the question put to the Christian at baptism and his assent to it. Just as a human pledge was ratified by question and answer, so was the pledge of the Christian to God.

APPEARING: *epiphaneia* (2 Thessalonians 2.8; 1 Timothy 6.14; 2 Timothy 4.1,8; Titus 2.13). In ordinary Greek *epiphaneia* had two technical usages. It was used of the appearance of a god to a human person, whether in the form of a vision or of a manifestation in nature, and it was used of the accession of an emperor to the imperial power. In the New Testament the word is regularly used of the Second Coming of Jesus. The idea is that that coming will be the demonstration of his divine majesty and his kingly power. It is used once of his appearance in the flesh (2 Timothy 1.10).

BABYLON. In the Old Testament, Babylon with all its pagan splendour and power stood for everything that was hostile to God. In the New Testament (1 Peter 5.13; Revelation 14.8; 16.19; 17.5; 18.2,10,21) Babylon stands for Rome, which, especially to the writer of the Revelation, stood for everything that was anti-Christian and anti-God. It may be worth pointing out that this use of the word Babylon refers to the Roman Empire and has nothing whatever to do with the Roman Church.

BEGIN and END: *enarchesthai* and *epiteleisthai*. Twice Paul uses these words in close association, and both times of beginning and ending the Christian life, of embarking on the Christian life and of bringing it to a successful conclusion. The interesting thing is that these two words are technical sacrificial words. *Enarchesthai* is used of taking the first step in the sacrificial process, of 'taking the barley from the basket', and *epiteleisthai* is used of fully discharging a religious duty, of bringing a sacrifice to its sacred and proper conclusion. So then, to use them of beginning and ending the Christian life is to say by implication that the Christian life is a sacrifice offered by the Christian to God. The Christian should thus regard all life as a sacrificial offering to God (Galatians 3.3; Philippians 1.6).

BEGUILE: *katabrabeuein*. The AV translates Colossians 2.18: Let no man beguile you of your reward. The word beguile loses the flavour of the original. *Brabeus* is the Greek for an umpire in a game, or for an arbitrator. *Katabrabeuein* means to give a decision against, or to rob a person of the prize which he ought to have received. The idea is that the Christian must allow no false teacher to make him accept teaching which will rob him of his reward. The RSV and the NEB both have *disqualify*.

BEHOLD: *epopteuein* (1 Peter 2.12; 3.2); *epoptēs*: eyewitness (2 Peter 1.16). Both these words had in Greek a special use. They were used in connection with the ceremonies of the Mystery Religions. The Mystery Religions had secret rites and symbols which the candidate was only allowed to see after a long course of instruction and ascetic discipline. After that preparation the candidate became an *epoptēs*, one with the right to behold the sacred things, and the verb used for the act of seeing was *epopteuein*. These words therefore have in them the idea of seeing something wonderful, splendid and sacred. In 1 Peter 2.12 and 3.2 they are used of the heathen beholding the Christian life. And in 2 Peter 1.16 *epoptēs* is used of being an eyewitness of the glory and the majesty of Jesus, especially on the Mount of Transfiguration. They mean more than merely to see; they mean to see that which is sacred and splendid. The Christian life is regarded as a revelation of God.

BELIAR. This word also exists in the form Belial, but in the one place in the New Testament where it appears (2 Corinthians 6.15) the correct reading is Beliar. Beliar means *worthlessness*, and is another name for the Devil.

BISHOP: *episkopos*; THE OFFICE OF A BISHOP: *episkopē* (Philippians 1.1; 1 Timothy 3.2; Titus 1.7; 1 Peter 2.25; 1 Timothy 3.1). The word bishop has today an ecclesiastical sound which the word *episkopos* did not have in New Testament times at all. The word literally means an overseer or a superintendent; the oversight may be with a view to discipline or it may be with a view to protection. So the gods are said to be the *episkopoi* of contracts, that is, to be the guardians of promises and pledges. The tutor is said to be the *episkopos* of his pupil, that is, the pupil's guardian. The Athenians sent *episkopoi*, that is, *inspectors*, to examine the states which were subject to them. Usually in New Testament times the word bishop will give a quite wrong impression of what the *episkopos* was. He was the superintendent of the congregation. The NEB well recognizes this in 1 Timothy 3.1,2: 'There is a popular saying, "To aspire to leadership (*episkopē*) is an honourable ambition." Our leader, therefore, or bishop, must be above reproach.' It has been said with truth that the word *elder* in the New Testament describes the church leader in his *person*, while the word *episkopos* describes him in his *function*.

BLAMELESS. There are few New Testament words which better illustrate the problems of translation than the word blameless. There are four words which are on occasions translated blameless.

i. *Amōmos* (Ephesians 1.4: AV, without blame; RSV, blameless; NEB, without blemish; Ephesians 5.27: AV, RSV, NEB, without blemish; Philippians 2.15: AV, without rebuke; RSV, without blemish; NEB, faultless; Colossians 1.22: AV, unblameable; RSV, blameless; NEB, without blemish; 1 Peter 1.19 (of a sacrifice): AV, RSV, NEB, without blemish; Revelation 14.4: AV, without fault; RSV, spotless; NEB, faultless).

ii. *Amōmētos* (2 Peter 3.14: AV, blameless; RSV, without blemish; NEB, above reproach).

iii. *Anegklētos* (1 Corinthians 1.8: AV, blameless; RSV, guiltless; NEB, without reproach; Colossians 1.22: AV, unreprovable; RSV, irreproachable; NEB, innocent; 1 Timothy 3.10: AV, RSV, blameless; NEB, no mark against them; Titus 1.6,7: AV, RSV, blameless; NEB, of unimpeachable character).

iv. *Anepilēmptos* (1 Timothy 3.2: AV, blameless; RSV, NEB, above reproach; 1 Timothy 5.7: AV, blameless; RSV, without reproach; NEB, above reproach; 1 Timothy 6.14: AV, unrebukeable; RSV, free from reproach; NEB, irreproachable).

It is worthwhile to make this detailed examination of the use of these words, in order to see the problem of translation in the case of fairly simple words, and in order to see the variation which can exist. And now to define the words more closely.

They are all negative words. They all begin with *a-*, which in Greek is called *alpha privative*, and which has the same effect on a word as the addition in English of the suffix *-less*. That is to say, the *a-* and the *-less* negative a word.

Each of the words has its special background. *Amōmos* and the less common *amōmētos* are both sacrificial words. A sacrificial victim had to be perfect, and both words are technical words to describe such a victim. In their case *without blemish* gives the literal meaning.

Anegklētos is connected with the verb *egkalein*, which means to bring a charge or accusation against. *Anegklētos* describes the man against whom it is impossible to bring a charge and its background is legal.

Anepilēmptos is connected with the verb *epilambanesthai*, which means to attack with words, to try to fasten something on a person, and the person who is *anepilēmptos* is the person who is morally unassailable, to whom no charge will stick. So this word blameless describes the person who in sacrificial terms is without blemish, who in legal terms is unimpeachable, and who in general terms is morally unassailable.

BLINDED, BLINDNESS: *pōroun, pōrōsis*. The verb *pōroun* occurs in Romans 11.7 and 2 Corinthians 3.14; the noun *pōrōsis* occurs in Romans 11.25 and Ephesians 4.18. In all cases the AV translates in terms of *blindness*. But this is not the real meaning of the word. The real meaning is insensitiveness, loss of feeling. The modern translations indicate this when they translate in terms of *hardness*. In Greek the words are used, for instance, of a callus, in which the skin has been hardened and rendered insensitive; they are used of marble which is impenetrably hard; they are used of a person who has reached a physical condition in which feeling is gone. The idea is therefore not that of blindness, but of a moral and spiritual insensitiveness to which not even God can appeal, an impenetrability of mind and heart which is impervious to the voice of God.

BLOT OUT: *exaleiphein*. The word literally means to wipe off and to wipe away. It is so used of wiping away tears in Revelation 7.17 and 21.4. It is used in Colossians 2.14 of blotting out the record of the debt which our sins have incurred (RSV,NEB, cancel); and in Revelation 3.5 of blotting out a name from the book of life (NEB, strike off).

There is a special point in this word. Ancient ink had no acid in it, and therefore did not bite into the papyrus on which ancient letters and books were written. It simply lay on the surface of the papyrus, and it could be literally wiped or sponged off, leaving no mark at all. Part of the flavour of the word is the completeness of the erasure. In particular, the debt is as if it had never been.

BOAST. There is a group of inter-related words which occur fairly frequently in the New Testament, and with special frequency in 2 Corinthians. There is the verb *kauchasthai*, which is usually translated to boast (2 Corinthians 5.12; 7.14; 10.8,13,15,16,17). There is the passive noun *kauchēma*, which means a boast (2 Corinthians 1.14; 5.12; 9.3). There is the active noun *kauchēsis*, which means the act of boasting (2 Corinthians 1.12; 7.4,14; 11.10). In many cases it would get the meaning better to translate to claim proudly, and sometimes even, to claim with legitimate pride.

BOASTER, BOASTING: *alazōn* (Romans 1.30; 2 Timothy 3.2). The translations vary between boaster and proud: *alazoneia* (James 4.16, where the NEB has brag; 1 John 2.16, where both the AV and the RSV have the pride of life, and the NEB, glamour).

These words are in fact not as simple to translate as that. The word *kauchasthai* describes the act of a man who boasts about what he has or about what he has done. But the whole point about the word *alazōn* is that it describes the man who, in order to impress people, lays claim to what he does not possess. The *alazōn* is the man who is always trying to impress people by making himself out to be a more wealthy, more influential, better connected, bigger man than he actually is. Theophrastus in his *Characters* has a character study of such a man. A. D. Knox calls him the pretentious man. A. D. Knox's translation runs:

'Pretentiousness, of course, will seem to be a laying claim to advantages a man does not possess. The pretentious or snobbish man will stand at the Mole and tell strangers of the great sums he has ventured at sea, and descant about the greatness of the usury trade and his own profit and losses in it; and while he thus outruns the truth, will send off his page to the bank, though he have there but a shilling to his name. He loves to make sport of a fellow-traveller by the way by telling him that he served under Evander (Alexander the Great), and how he stood with him, and how many jewelled cups he brought home; and will have it that the artificers of Asia are better craftsmen than those of Europe; —all this talk though he has never set foot out of his own country. Moreover, he will say that he has no fewer than three letters from Antipater (the regent of Macedonia after the death of Alexander) requesting his attendance upon him in Macedonia, and although, so he says, he has been offered free exportation of timber, he refused to go.... He is like to say also that during the famine he spent more than twelve hundred pounds in relieving distress, —he cannot say no.... He will go to the horse-market and pretend to the dealers that he wishes to buy thoroughbreds.... And though he lives in a hired house, he tells anyone who knows no better that he had it from his father, and is about to put it up for sale because it is too small for the entertaining of his friends.'

There the *alazōn* is sketched, and his distinguishing characteristic is that in order to impress he boasts about things he does not possess.

BOLDNESS: *parrēsia*. The word appears fairly frequently in the New Testament, and it is a word with an interesting history. Originally it meant the exercise of freedom of speech, which in the ancient world was a thing which required courage, and which was greatly admired as heroic, since tyrants were apt simply to eliminate the man who was brave enough to tell the truth. It appears in this sense in the New Testament, especially of that freedom of speech which Paul fearlessly used, no matter what the consequences (2 Corinthians 3.12; 1 Thessalonians 2.2, the verb *parrēsiazesthai*, to use freedom of speech; Ephesians 6.19; Philippians 1.20).

The second meaning of *parrēsia* is confidence and courage, especially that confidence which is born of faith, and particularly the confidence which knows that the way to God is open (Ephesians 3.12; 1 Timothy 3.13; Hebrews 3.6; 4.16; 10.19,35; 1 John 2.28; 3.21; 4.17; 5.14). *Parrēsia* is the word of courage before men and confidence before God.

BOOK OF LIFE (Revelation 3.5; 13.8; 17.8; 20.12; 21.27; Philippians 4.3). The NEB has the roll of the living. It was the case that ancient kings and rulers kept a roll of their subjects, from which a man's name was removed, if he died or if he became a traitor to the state. The book of life or the roll of the living is the record of those who are living and faithful citizens of the Kingdom of God.

BORN OUT OF DUE TIME: *ektrōma*. This is the phrase which Paul applies to himself in 1 Corinthians 15.8. The word *ektrōma* literally means an untimely birth, a miscarriage, an abortion. It can even mean a monstrous birth. Paul means that his entry into the Christian faith came with such violence and so unexpectedly that it had all the characteristics of an untimely birth.

BOUGHT WITH A PRICE. In 1 Corinthians 6.19,20 Paul tells the Corinthians that they are not their own, but that they are bought with a price. In Greece there was one way in which a slave might obtain his freedom. He might for a long time earn a few pence here and there by doing odd jobs in such time as was his own. Every time he earned a little he took it and deposited it in the temple of a god. After perhaps years of saving, when he had accumulated his purchase price, he took his master to the temple. The money was then paid to the master, and the slave became technically the property of the god, and therefore free from all men. He was no longer his own; he no longer belonged to any man; he belonged to the god. So Paul thinks of the Christian as a man purchased by Christ, who had paid the price to set him free. He was not his own; he belonged to God, because the Son of God had paid the price.

BOWELS: *splagchna* (2 Corinthians 7.15; Philippians 1.18; 2.1; Colossians 3.12; Philemon 7,12,20; 1 John 3.17). We locate the seat of the feelings and emotions in the heart; the Greeks located it in the liver and the kidneys and the larger viscera. When, then, *splagchna* occurs in this emotional sense, modern English will always translate it by heart, or by some word which signifies deep sympathy and compassion.

BUT: *alla*. *Alla* in Greek, which is usually translated *but*, is strongly adversative. It can also be elliptically used and the translation *but* in English can be awkward. Three things can be done with it in translation.

(a) The two clauses can be placed side by side with no connecting link, so that the force of the juxtaposition brings out the contrast (e.g. 1 Corinthians 2.7).

(b) The second clause can begin No! to underline the contrast (e.g. Ephesians 5.4).

(c) The second clause can begin, So far from that..., once again to emphasize the contrast (e.g. Romans 11.11; 1 John 2.27).

CALL, CALLED. The idea of the call of God, and of the Christian being called, is so universal in the letters of the New Testament that particular instances do not need to be quoted. Specimen examples are in Romans 8.28 and 1 Corinthians 1.1. The word call is a word which has acquired all kinds of theological overtones and implications. It might be well to remember that the word which is translated call is the word *kalein*, which is the normal Greek word for to invite. Quite simply God's call is God's invitation, and the called are those who have answered that invitation.

CAPTAIN: *archēgos* (Hebrews 2.10; 12.2: RSV, pioneer; NEB, leader, the one on whom faith depends). This word has three meanings. It can mean chief captain or leader. It can mean the founder of a city or of a family. It can mean the first cause or the originator of anything, as for instance of a philosophy and a way of life. It has the flavour of doing something so that others can follow in safety. Jesus is the pioneer who blazes the way to salvation for others to follow.

CHASTENING, CHASTEN: *paideia*, *paideuein*. *Pais* is the Greek for a child and basically these words have to do with the training of children. They have to do with the training of the child's mind and character as distinguished from *trophē*, which has to do with the child's physical nurture and upbringing. The words have three stages in meaning.

They begin by meaning simply upbringing in general.

They go on to have the meaning of training and instruction (Ephesians 6.4; 2 Timothy 3.16).

They finally go on to mean that correction, discipline, chastening, even punishment which is essential for the formation of character (1 Corinthians 11.32; 2 Corinthians 6.9; Hebrews 12.6,7,8,11), whether that correction is applied by God or by man (1 Timothy 1.20).

These are the words of Christian education in character.

CHRISTIAN: *Christianos*. The word Christian occurs only three times in the New Testament, twice in Acts (Acts 11.26; 26.28), and once in 1 Peter (1 Peter 4.16). -*ianos* is the regular suffix to denote a supporter of a person, or one who belongs to a person's party. So the *Herōdianoi* (-*oi* is the Greek plural form) are the supporters of Herod, and the

Kaisarianoi are Caesar's party. The name was first given to the Christians at Antioch, and the people of Antioch were notorious for their habit of attaching nicknames to people. The word Christian may therefore well have originated as a nickname—these Christers.

CHURCH: *ekklēsia*. *Ekklēsia* has two uses in the New Testament.

First, it is used for the church at large, for the whole church (Galatians 1.13; Ephesians 1.22; Philippians 3.6).

Second, it is used for an individual congregation of the church (1 Thessalonians 2.14; 2 Thessalonians 1.4; 2 Corinthians 8.18). In this second case it is usually better to speak of the congregation rather than the church. 1 Timothy 3.5 is a doubtful case. The AV has: 'If a man know not how to rule his own house, how shall he take care of the church of God?' The NEB has: 'If a man does not know how to control his own family, how can he look after a congregation of God's people?' It is the NEB rendering which is most likely right.

In the New Testament the word church never means a building. At the stage of the New Testament the church did not possess any buildings. We therefore hear of house-churches (Romans 16.5; 1 Corinthians 16.19; Philemon 2).

A typical Pauline phrase is the church of God which is at Corinth (1 Corinthians 1.2). The local congregation is that part of the whole church of God which is located in a certain place. It has been suggested, and it may well be true, that the Roman Empire presented Paul with an analogy for the church. The Roman Empire was one great whole which spread all over the known world. So too the church was one great whole. But Rome planted in strategic places colonies. These colonies were like little bits of Rome. Wherever they were located, Roman dress was worn, Roman manners and customs were observed, the Latin language was the official language, the magistrates and officials had Roman titles. They were like little Romes all over the world; wherever they were, Rome existed in them. So the church was on the way to becoming a worldwide institution, but at the same time, wherever the local congregation existed, there the church of God existed in that place.

COMFORT. A number of words are translated comfort in the New Testament.

Paraklēsis, the noun, and *parakalein*, the verb. These words occur very frequently (Romans 15.4; 2 Corinthians 7.7; Ephesians 6.22; Colossians 4.8; 1 Thessalonians 3.2). The one thing to remember about these words is the strength of them. In English the word comfort has now limited its meaning to comfort in sorrow, and sometimes these words are translated consolation. But the word comfort has in it as its root the Latin word *fortis*, which means brave, and these words have in them the comfort which is also courage. They speak of the comfort which not only soothes but also inspires.

Parēgoria (Colossians 4.11); *paramuthia* (1 Corinthians 14.3); *paramuthion* (Philippians 2.1); *paramutheisthai* (1 Thessalonians 2.12; 5.14). All these words are translated comfort, but they do have their individual flavour. Bengel suggested that *parēgoria* refers to *forensic* comfort, when a man is in legal trouble, and *paramuthia* refers to *domestic* comfort in the ordinary troubles of life. But it is very doubtful if this distinction will hold.

Parēgoria has a medical background; we still use the term paregoric; and it means that which soothes pain, in this case the pain of the heart. *Paramuthia, paramuthion, paramutheisthai* all have in them *para*, which means aside, and *muthos*, which means a story. It is therefore suggested that the idea behind these words is the story, perhaps the mother's or the nurse's tale, which draws the mind (perhaps originally of the child) away from its own trouble and sorrow. If this is so, these words in a Christian context would be thinking of the Christian comfort, which comforts by drawing a man's thoughts away from himself to God, away from his condition to God's grace.

COMING: *parousia*. The word *parousia*, which has come into English as it stands, is the technical word for the Second Coming of Jesus Christ, for his advent in glory. The word has three stages.

(a) It can mean simply the presence of a person. So the Corinthians say that Paul's *parousia*, his bodily presence, is weak (2 Corinthians 10.10).

(b) It can mean an ordinary person's coming or arrival (2 Corinthians 7.6; Philippians 1.26).

(c) But its main use is for the Second Coming of Jesus Christ (1 Corinthians 15.23; 1 Thessalonians 3.13; 4.15; 2 Thessalonians 2.1,8; James 5.8; 2 Peter 1.16; 3.4; 1 John 2.28). The word *parousia* had acquired certain technical uses before Christian language annexed it. It was used for the presence and the appearance of a god to his worshippers, and it was used of the visit of a king or a governor to his country or to his province. It therefore, even as a secular word, has about it the atmosphere of royalty and divinity.

COMMIT, THAT WHICH IS COMMITTED: *paratithenai, parathēkē*. In the Pastoral Epistles there is a characteristic conception in which the Christian, and especially the Christian leader, is a person to whom the Christian faith has been committed in sacred trust that he may pass it on pure and undamaged (1 Timothy 1.18; 6.20; 2 Timothy 1.12,14; 2.2). The word *parathēkē* is a technical term for something entrusted to, or deposited with, a person. And in the ancient world it was one of the most sacred duties in life, a duty over which the gods watched, to return such an entrusted deposit safe and unharmed. So if a man commits himself to God, God will not fail him; and if God has committed and entrusted the truth of the Christian faith to a man, that man must not fail in his trust.

CONCISION: *katatomē* (Philippians 3.2). In this passage Paul urges the Philippians to beware of the concision. The RSV has it that Paul urges them to beware of those who mutilate the flesh; the NEB, to beware of those who insist on mutilation. Paul is here playing on words. The Jews insist on *peritomē*, which is circumcision. But *katatomē* means an incision or a cutting in pieces. The AV got its translation through the Vulgate which simply literally translates *katatomē* as *concisio*. What Paul is saying is : 'The Jews insist on *peritomē*, circumcision, but in effect what they are insisting on is nothing other than *katatomē*, which is no better than mutilation.'

CONTENT: *autarkēs* (adjective, Philippians 4.11; *autarkeia*, noun, 2 Corinthians 9.8; 1 Timothy 6.6). The AV and the RSV both translate in terms of content; the NEB translates in terms of having adequate resources within oneself to meet any situation

The words *autarkēs* and *autarkeia* are made up of two Greek words, *autos*, which means self, and *arkein*, which means to be sufficient. To be *autarkēs*, then, is to be completely self-sufficient. *Autarkēs* was one of the great words of the Stoic philosophy and *autarkeia* was its greatest aim. The Stoic aimed at making himself entirely self-sufficient. He aimed to do this by not allowing anything or any person to become necessary to him; and he aimed to achieve this by teaching himself not to care what happened to anyone or anything. He aimed to reach *autarkeia* by developing insulation against all feeling.

This is a good example of how Paul could take a word familiar to his readers and charge it with a new meaning. Paul was self-sufficient, but not in the sense that he had insulated his heart by teaching himself never to allow himself to care; he was self-sufficient because he was God-dependent, and his dependence on God gave him the inner resources to cope with any situation. It was said of the Stoics that they made a desert of the heart and called it a peace; Paul found that peace by opening his heart to the grace of God.

CONTENTION: *eritheia*. It occurs six times in the New Testament, and it is illuminating to look at the different translations. It will be simplest to tabulate them.

	AV	RSV	NEB
Romans 2.8	contention	faction	selfish ambition
2 Corinthians 12.24	strife	selfishness	personal rivalry
Galatians 5.20	strife	selfishness	selfish ambition
Philippians 1.17	contention	partisanship	personal rivalry
Philippians 2.3	strife	selfishness	rivalry
James 3.14	strife	selfish ambition	selfish ambition

Eritheia is a word with a very interesting history. Aristotle in the *Politics* (5.3,4,14) defines it as the self-seeking pursuit of political office by unfair means. Let us see how the word arrives at that meaning.

The AV comes down heavily on the meaning strife. *Eritheia* looks as if it might well be connected with *eris*, which is the normal Greek word for strife, and this is the connection that the AV translators made. This connection is not impossible. But more likely *eritheia* is connected with *erithos*, a day-labourer, which in turn is connected with *erion*, wool, and an *erithos* was originally a spinner or weaver. It widened its meaning to mean a worker of any kind in the day-labouring class. Clearly, at this stage there is nothing wrong with the word. It first meant a man who works for wages. But then it went on to mean a man who works *only* for wages, a man who is concerned only with what he can get, and the more he gets, the better he is pleased. It then entered the political world to describe the man who is obsessed, not with the desire to serve the state, but only with the desire to satisfy his own ambitions. It thus comes to mean canvassing for office, political intriguing, and all the twisted and self-seeking ingenuity of the man who is driven by personal ambition. The modern translations are therefore right with their stress on selfish ambition and personal rivalry.

CONVERSATION: *anastrophē, anastrephein, politeuesthai.* The AV consistently uses the word *conversation* in the translation of these words (2 Corinthians 1.12; Hebrews 13.5,7; Ephesians 2.3; James 3.13; 1 Timothy 4.12; 1 Peter 1.15,18; 2.12; 3.1,16; 2 Peter 2.7). In modern English this is misleading. Today the word *conversation* is confined to speech, and means a person's talk with other people. But in the sixteenth century it meant a person's life and conduct, his behaviour, his way of carrying himself in his relationship with others, not only in word, but also in deed. It derives from the Latin *conversari*, which means to move about, to go to and fro amongst people. For instance, pagan husbands are to be won, without the word, by the conversation of their wives (1 Peter 3.1). That is to say, the daily beauty of the Christian life is to be a wordless argument for Christianity. The words should always be translated in terms of life and conduct and behaviour.

COVENANT: *diathēkē*. The conception of the covenant is basic to the New Testament and the word *diathēkē* occurs all over it (Romans 9.4; 2 Corinthians 3.6,14; Galatians 3.15,17; Ephesians 2.12). The idea of the covenant plays a specially big part in the thought of Hebrews (Hebrews 7.22; 8.6,8,9,10; 9.4,15,16,17,20; 10.16,29; 12.24; 13.20).

The idea of a covenant is that God approaches his people with the offer to be their God and with the invitation to become his people. In the Old Testament this relationship with God is dependent on the keeping of the Law (Exodus 24.3-8). In the New Testament it is dependent on the acceptance of the grace and love which came in Jesus Christ.

Thus a new relationship is established between God and his people. One thing must be avoided. The covenant must not be thought of as an agreement, a bargain, a treaty between God and man. In the case of any such agreement the two parties to the agreement operate on an equal footing, and can thus discuss terms on a level. But in the covenant the whole initiative is with God. It is he who makes the approach; it is he who offers, and man can only take. The covenant is not an agreement between God and man, it is an offer by God to man out of God's free grace.

This basic truth is conserved in the word itself. The ordinary Greek word for an agreement, made by two parties with equal rights, is *sunthēkē*; *diathēkē* is the normal word for a will, and it is chosen by deliberate choice by the New Testament writers, because a will is the one kind of agreement in which the two parties do not discuss the terms of the agreement, but in which the one party gives and the other party takes. The covenant has its root and origin solely in the free grace of God, and this is contained in the word *diathēkē*.

COVETOUSNESS, COVETOUS: *pleonexia, pleonektēs, pleonektein*. The vice signified by these words was a vice hated not only by the Christians but also by the Greeks. The Greek moralists declared that it was the greatest of all vices and responsible for more harm than any other vice. In Ephesians 4.19 the AV translates it *greediness*, but elsewhere it consistently calls it *covetousness* (Ephesians 5.3; Colossians 3.5; 2 Peter 2.3,14; 1 Thessalonians 2.5). The *pleonektēs* is the *covetous* man (1 Corinthians 5.10,11; 6.10; Ephesians 5.5). The verb *pleonektein* is translated *to defraud, to make gain of, to take advantage of*.

It is a difficult word to translate, for it is more than covetousness. The Latin moralists called it 'the accursed love of having'. Cicero defined *avaritia*, which is the Latin equivalent, as 'the unlawful desire for things which belong to others'. Lightfoot defined it as 'the disposition which is ever ready to sacrifice one's neighbour to oneself'.

The real meaning of the word is the desire for that which no honourable man has the right to desire. It can be, and often is, used not only for the desire for material things, but for the forbidden sexual desire and the forbidden ambitious desire. It therefore has in it the idea of the exploitation of one's fellowmen. In English it is possible to use the word *covet* in a good sense; but *pleonexia* can never be used except of the desire for the forbidden thing.

CROWN: *stephanos*, noun; *stephanoun*, verb; *diadēma*. There are two words for crown in the New Testament.

The first is *stephanos* (1 Corinthians 9.25; 2 Timothy 2.5; 4.8; James 1.12; 1 Peter 5.4; Revelation 2.10; 3.11). *Stephanos* is characteristically the victor's crown, given to a man as a result of some athletic or dramatic or political contest. The common phrase, the crown of life, very likely means the crown which consists of life. The reward of living life well is God's life.

The second is *diadēma* (Revelation 4.4,10; 6.2; 12.3; 13.1; 19.12). *Diadēma* is characteristically the royal crown, and the symbol of majesty.

CUT OFF: *apokoptein* (Galatians 5.12). The AV translates Galatians 5.12: 'I would that they were cut off who trouble you.' This translation conceals the meaning. The RSV substitutes mutilate themselves for cut off. The NEB correctly has: 'As for these agitators, they had better go the whole way and make eunuchs of themselves!' The point is that the false teachers are urging circumcision. Paul says that as far as he is concerned they might as well go the whole way and castrate themselves, for this is what the word *apokoptein* here means. This is the sense in which it means to cut off.

DAY. In different forms the New Testament has a great deal to say about the Day. Sometimes it is simply called the Day (Hebrews 10.25); sometimes it is that Day (2 Thessalonians 1.10; 2 Timothy 1.12,18); sometimes it is the last time or the last day (1 Peter 1.5); sometimes it is the Day of God (2 Peter 3.12; Revelation 16.14); sometimes it is the Day of the Lord (1 Thessalonians 5.2; 2 Thessalonians 2.2; 2 Peter 3.10). In the New Testament the Day is the day when Jesus Christ will return to earth, to judge the quick and the dead and to enter upon his lordship.

But the interesting and the significant fact is that the Day of the Lord is a basic Old Testament conception, which is an integral part of the message of the prophets. The Old Testament Jews divided time into two ages, this present age which is wholly and incurably bad, and the age to come which is to be the golden age of God and goodness. This present age is so essentially evil that it is beyond reformation. How then is the one age to turn into the other? It can only do so by the direct intervention of God, and the time when God will intervene is in the Old Testament the Day of the Lord. The Day of the Lord would come as suddenly as a thief in the night; it would be a terrible time of cosmic disintegration and destruction; it would be a time of judgment; it would involve the complete destruction of things as they are, and then the birth of the new age.

The significant fact is that the New Testament has taken over the idea and the pictures and the apparatus of the Old Testament Day of the Lord, and has attached them to the day of the Second Coming of Jesus Christ. The Old Testament Day and the New Testament Day, although they are different, coalesce into one.

DEACON: *diakonos*, with the corresponding verb *diakonein*. *Diakonos* has two meanings, one general and one technical. In general, the word means a helper, a servant. The AV very commonly translates it minister, which in this sense is now archaic (Colossians 1.23; Ephesians 3.7; 2 Corinthians 3.6). In its technical sense, the word means the church official known as the deacon (Philippians 1.1; 1 Timothy 3.8,12; Titus 1.9).

The technical Christian usage was prepared for by secular usage. The word is used for a state official, and in particular it is used of a temple official. For instance, in the worship of Serapis we read of a body or college of deacons presided over by a priest. The way was already prepared for the use of the word to describe an official of the church.

The significant fact about the flavour of the word is that the service which it describes is characteristically personal service.

DEAD: *nekros*. The literal sense of this word (e.g. Revelation 1.18) needs no comment. But it has three special usages.

(a) To say that a man is dead to something is to say that that man is completely detached from the thing to which he is dead, and that it has no power and no influence upon him. So the Christian is dead to sin (Romans 6.11).

(b) To say that a man is dead in something is to say that that thing has gained such a power and an ascendancy over him that he is morally helpless. So the sinner is dead in sin or in his sins (Ephesians 2.1; Colossians 2.13; Revelation 3.1).

(c) More than once in the New Testament we find the phrase *dead works* (Romans 7.8; James 2.26). It is the works of the law which are dead. The word dead could here mean, either, completely in-effective to set a man right with God, or, deadly, in the sense that persistence in them can lead to nothing but final death, that they are the way to death rather than to life.

DEPART: *analuein* (Philippians 1.23; 2 Timothy 4.6). The interesting thing about this word is the possible picture behind it. It can mean either to strike camp or to cast off moorings.

DEVIL: *diabolos*. This is the common word for the Devil (Ephesians 4.27; 6.11; Hebrews 2.14; James 4.7; 1 Peter 5.8; 1 John 3.8,10; Jude 9; Revelation 2.10,13; 12.12; 20.10). *Diabolos* is the normal Greek word for a slanderer, and is used in its normal secular sense in 1 Timothy 3.11 and in Titus 2.3. It may be that the picture behind it is that the Devil is the one who seeks to slander God to men and men to God, in his attempt to bring about enmity between man and God instead of friendship.

DIASPORA. The word *diaspora*, although it has become an accepted English word, is not used in the ordinary translations of the New Testament. In the Greek it occurs in James 1.1 and 1 Peter 1.1. There it is used of the people to whom the letters are addressed. The AV translates it, those who are scattered abroad; the NEB, those who are dispersed throughout the world, and, God's scattered people; the RSV, the Dispersion.

The *diaspora* was the word technically used for the Jews scattered throughout the world, either because they had been forcibly taken into exile, or because they had voluntarily emigrated from Palestine to other lands. It was the term for all that great body of Jews who were exiled from their native land. In the New Testament it is appropriated by James and Peter to describe the Christians scattered throughout the world in their various groups. Just as the scattered Jews were ex-iles from Palestine, so the scattered Christians are the exiles of eternity.

DISANNUL: *athetein, athetēsis*. *Athetein* is a word which occurs quite frequently in the New Testament, in a number of different connec-tions and with a variety of translations. The AV *disannul* comes from Galatians 3.15, where it is used of cancelling a will (RSV, annul; NEB, set aside). In Galatians 2.21 it is used of *frustrating* the grace of God (RSV and NEB, nullify). In Hebrews 10.28 it is used of *despising* the moral law (RSV, violate; NEB, disregard). In 1 Timothy 5.12 it is used of *casting off* a pledge (RSV, violate; NEB, break troth). In Jude 8 it is used of *despising* authority (RSV, reject; NEB, flout).

In secular Greek the adjective *athetos* can be used, for instance, of corn or barley which is *rejected* for food.

In the New Testament the word regularly has the meaning of rejecting, cancelling, disregarding that which should have remained authoritative and binding.

DISOBEDIENCE: *parakoē, apeitheia*. Both these words are used for disobedience, but the idea behind them is different.

Parakoē (Romans 5.19; 2 Corinthians 10.6) has a curious history. Originally it meant a failure to hear, a hearing amiss, either because the hearer is deaf or because the statement is not clearly made. There is no kind of fault implied. But then it goes on to mean a deliberate refusal to hear, a shutting the ears to, an ignoring of something which should have been listened to. It is the disobedience of the person who chooses not to hear.

Apeitheia (Ephesians 2.2; 5.6; Colossians 3.6; Romans 11.30,32; Hebrews 4.6,11) is connected with *peithein*, which means to believe, and it describes the disobedience which comes from unbelief, the disobedience which is based on the fact that it does not accept the claims or the authority of the person who gives the order. In its Christian context it describes the attitude of the man who does not obey Christ because he does not accept Christ.

DISORDERLY. There is a group of words which occur in the Thessalonian letters into which the newer translations import a new idea. There is the verb *ataktein* (2 Thessalonians 3.7); the adverb *ataktōs* (2 Thessalonians 3.6,11); the adjective *ataktos* (1 Thessalonians 5.14). The AV regularly translates by the idea of disorderly or unruly. The RSV and the NEB equally regularly translate in terms of idleness or carelessness.

The words all come from the same root as the verb *tassō*, to draw up or to arrange in order, and the word *taxis*, order, rank, orderly arrangement. It is from this line of thought that the AV is working, and it takes the words to mean unruly, disorderly conduct, conduct which is like an undisciplined breaking of the ranks.

But new light was thrown on the meaning of these words by their use in the papyri. They occur there, for instance, in a contract of apprenticeship. It is there said that the apprentice must serve for so long, and for every day that *ataktei* (the third person singular, present indicative of the verb) he must serve an equivalent number of additional days at the end of his apprenticeship period. Here the word clearly means to absent oneself from work, to play truant, to be idle.

So what Paul is insisting is that the Thessalonians must not make their religion an excuse for playing truant from work or for living in idleness.

DISTRESS: *stenochōria* (Romans 2.9; 8.35; 2 Corinthians 6.4; 12.10).

This is a particularly vivid word. The AV varies between anguish and distress; the RSV, between distress and calamity; the NEB has grinding misery (in connection with *thlipsis*), hardship, dire straits, frustration. The idea of the word is *narrowness*. It describes the condition of the man who is shut up in a narrow place with no means of escape, the situation of the man on whom the walls of life are closing in.

DIVERS: *poikilos* (Titus 3.3; Hebrews 2.4; 13.9; James 1.2; 1 Peter 1.6; 4.10). Divers is now archaic, except in the form diverse, and the modern translations regularly have many, and varied.

The basic idea of the word is many-coloured, so it can be used for the plumage of a bird, the skin of a leopard, an embroidered robe. The interesting thing is that in the New Testament both the trials of men and the grace of God are said to be *poikilos*; that is to say, in the grace of God there is that which can match any difficult situation in life.

DIVIDE RIGHTLY: *orthotomein* (2 Timothy 2.15). This is an almost unique phrase. The AV has rightly dividing the word of truth; the RSV has rightly handling the word of truth; the NEB has driving a straight furrow in your proclamation of the truth.

Orthotomein literally means to cut straight. In the Old Testament it is twice used in Proverbs of making straight paths (Proverbs 3.6; 11.5). There may be two pictures in the word.

(a) There is the more commonly accepted picture of cutting a straight path across country, through woods and thickets, and across bogs and rivers and moors and hills to the goal, the picture of driving a road undeviatingly from its beginning to its goal. This would mean that the Christian expounder of the scriptures must refuse to be lured down trivial side-roads, and heretical byways, and must as it were, as it was said of a famous preacher, cut straight across country to Christ.

(b) It has also been suggested that to cut rightly could be a reference to the mason's cutting and shaping of stones so that they fit accurately into the edifice which he is building. So the expounder of scripture has to see to it that his teaching fits into true belief and builds up the edifice of the faith.

EARNEST: *arrabōn*. The word *arrabōn* is three times used by Paul in connection with the Holy Spirit. The three passages in which it is used are 2 Corinthians 1.22; 5.3; Ephesians 1.14. The AV speaks of the Christian receiving the *earnest* of the Spirit; the RSV speaks of the *guarantee* of the Spirit; the NEB speaks of the *pledge* of the Spirit, in the sense of a pledge of that which is to come.

The word *arrabōn* was a very common word in business and commercial Greek. An *arrabōn* was an instalment of the purchase price of a thing, paid in advance. It laid upon the payer the obligation to continue the future payments, and it laid upon the seller the duty of delivering in due time that for which he had accepted the advance instalment. So in the papyri we find a troop of castanet dancing-girls being engaged to dance at a village's festivities, and they are paid so much in advance as *arrabōn*, as a guarantee that they will appear and that the full fee will be paid when they have given their performance. We find a mouse-catcher being paid so much as *arrabōn* so that he can get on with the job at once, with the guarantee that he will get his full fee in due time.

So when Paul speaks of the *arrabōn* of the Spirit he means that the gift of the Spirit is the pledge and the guarantee and the first instalment of the life into which in all its fullness the Christian will some day enter.

EARNEST EXPECTATION: *apokaradokia* (Romans 8.19; Philippians 1.20). Eager longing and eager expectation are the standard translations of this word. But in the Philippians passage the NEB speaks in terms of passionate hope. The word has the flavour of an intense concentration of hope and expectation. *Apo* means *away from*; *kara* is the *head*; and the word has the idea of turning away the head from everything else to concentrate all thought and attention on one thing. The word denotes the intense concentration of the Christian hope.

ELDERS: *presbuteroi* (1 Timothy 4.14; 5.17,19; Titus 1.5; James 5.14; 1 Peter 5.1; 2 John 1; 3 John 1). The elders were—and in many forms of church government still are—what may be called the basic officials of the Christian church.

The Christian church was by no means the first institution to appoint elders. The elder, the older man, always acquires a special position in the counsels of every community. The Jews had their elders, whom they traced back to Moses (Numbers 11.16,17). Every village had its elders, who administered community justice, and the elders were the lay members of the Sanhedrin. In the non-Jewish world the village elders were just as influential, and we find references to the elders of the fishermen and the elders of the cultivators, who were the representative men of their trade or profession. When the Christian church took over the eldership, it took over an institution which was practically universal.

END: *telos*. In Romans 10.4 Paul writes that Christ is the *telos* of the law. Both the AV and the RSV translate: 'Christ is the end of the law.'

The NEB has: 'Christ ends the law.' Both these translations can be misleading. To say that Christ is the *telos* of the law is not to say that he made an end of the law, that he put an end to the law, that he abolished the law. *Telos* is not the end which destroys something; it is the end and goal to which something moves. It is that for which something existed. And to say that Christ is the *telos* of the law means that Christ is the end for which the law existed; the goal to which the law moved and pointed; in him all that the law aimed at was achieved and realised.

ESPOUSED. In 2 Corinthians 11.2 Paul writes to the Corinthians: 'I have espoused you to one husband, that I may present you as a chaste virgin to Christ.' The RSV and the NEB substitute *betrothed* for *espoused*. But behind this phrase there is a Jewish custom. In a Jewish wedding a person called the friend of the bridegroom made all the arrangements and was the go-between between the bridegroom and the bride. And one of his duties was to be guarantor to the bridegroom of the chastity and the virginity of the bride. Paul sees himself as the friend of the bridegroom in the marriage between the Corinthian church and Jesus Christ; and as such it is his duty to guarantee the chastity of the bride. He, the pastor, is responsible to Jesus Christ for the purity and fidelity of the church in his care.

EXCESS: *asōtia*. The word *asōtia* occurs three times in the NT. The AV translates *excess*, *riot*, and *excess of riot* (Ephesians 5.18; Titus 1.6; 1 Peter 4.4). The adverb *asōtōs* is the word which is used of the prodigal son spending his substance in *riotous living*. The RSV translates in terms of debauchery and profligacy. The NEB uses the translations reckless dissipation and loose living.

Aristotle deals with *asōtia* at the beginning of the fourth book of the Nicomachean Ethics. Aristotle defined all virtues as the mean between two extremes, an extreme of defect and an extreme of excess. So he describes the virtue of liberality as the mean between its defect, which is meanness, and its excess, which is prodigality. He says: 'We call these men prodigal (*asōtos*) who are incontinent and who spend money on self-indulgence.' Such a man destroys both his substance and himself. The word can be derived from the prefix *a-* which means *without*, and the verb *sōzein* which means to save. The *asōtos* is the man who spends so recklessly on his pleasures that he is unable to save himself or anything else.

EVIL. The New Testament uses three main adjectives for evil. It is not claimed that the distinction between them is always observed; they tend to be used as synonyms; but each has its own flavour.

(a) There is the word *kakos*, which is the most general term. In secular Greek it can mean anything from ugly or ill-born, to worthless, unskilled and evil. It can mean a *bad* servant, both in the sense of an inefficient servant and a wicked servant. In the New Testament it is used of a bad deed (Romans 13.3), of bad company (1 Corinthians 15.33), of people who are morally bad (Philippians 3.2), and of that which is injurious and pernicious (Titus 1.12; Revelation 16.2). It has all the range of meanings that the English word bad has.

(b) There is the word *ponēros*. In secular Greek it can mean painful, useless, base, cowardly. But it can be specially used of a man who is a rascal and a rogue, and whose conduct is pernicious and malicious. In the New Testament it is so used in Hebrews 3.12; 10.22; 2 Thessalonians 3.2; 2 Timothy 3.13; James 2.4; and in Revelation 16.2 it is used of a painful ulcer.

The main characteristic of this word is that it means not only bad, but also injurious and harmful; it describes the badness which affects, and even ruins, others. That is why it is specially used of the Devil, who is described as the Evil One (Ephesians 6.16; 1 John 2.13; 5.18,19).

(c) There is the word *phaulos*. In secular Greek it can mean low, common, slight, trivial, paltry, and thus mean or bad. The basic idea in it is that of inferiority, meanness. In the New Testament it is used, for instance, in Romans 9.11; Titus 2.8; 1 Corinthians 5.10.

So the three word *kakos*, *ponēros*, *phaulos* denote that which is bad, that which is not only bad, but also actively injurious to others, and that which is mean, inferior and low, far below the Christian standard.

EVIL-SPEAKING: *blasphēmein*, verb, *blasphēmia*, noun. These Greek words naturally lead the mind to the English word *blasphemy*. What is to be noted is that in Greek, and in the New Testament, they have a human as well as a divine reference. Their basic meaning is to speak about a person in such a way that his character is injured, to defame the person, to use abusive speech about him (Romans 3.8; 1 Corinthians 10.30; Ephesians 4.31; Colossians 3.8; Titus 3.2). When such speech is used against God, when it is God who is insulted and defamed and reviled, then they mean blasphemy (1 Timothy 1.20; 1 Peter 4.4; Revelation 16.11). What is significant is that in Greek the defamation of man and of God are both 'blasphemy'.

EXAMPLE: *hupogrammos* (1 Peter 2.21). Peter calls Jesus our *hupogrammos*, our example, model, pattern. The *hupogrammos* was either the perfect line of writing at the top of the page of a child's writing exercise-book, which the child had to copy, or it describes semi-outlined letters which the child had to complete and fill in. So the Christian has to 'copy' Jesus.

EYE-SERVICE: *ophthalmodoulia* (Ephesians 6.6; Colossians 3.22). This is a very unusual word. The NEB translates it 'the outward show of service'. The dictionary definition is that the word describes service which is done only to attract attention and to impress men, not for its own sake, not to satisfy conscience, and not to please God. *Ophthalmos* is the *eye*; *doulia* is *service*. The meaning we have given is quite certainly possible and even probably correct. But as far as the construction of the word goes, it could also describe the service of the man who will only work when his master's eye is on him, and who otherwise will idle his time and shirk his work.

FAITH: *pistis*. In the NT faith is a word with more than one meaning. We may distinguish five main lines of thought.

(a) The main meaning of faith, the characteristically Pauline meaning, is total commitment to Jesus Christ (Galatians 2.16; 3.26; 3.34). It is accepting Jesus Christ at his word, both in his demands and in his promises.

(b) Faith in the meaning of faithfulness, fidelity, occurs frequently in the NT. This is the sense in which we use it in English when we speak of keeping faith with a person, or being faithful to a person (Galatians 5.23; Revelation 13.10).

(c) Faith sometimes means unshakable hope, the hope which is so sure that it is the equivalent of certainty (Hebrews 11.1).

(d) There is sometimes a quite strongly intellectual element about faith. It is the acceptance of certain propositions about God as true (Hebrews 11.6).

(e) At least sometimes in the NT, faith is used as when in English we speak of the faith, meaning the Christian religion (Galatians 1.23; 3.7; Jude 3.20).

Of these meanings the first and the second are the commonest.

FEAR: *phobos* (noun), *phobeisthai* (verb). Some care must be taken in the translation of this apparently simple word. In the NT it is used in three ways.

(a) It means *fear* in the bad sense (Hebrews 2.15; 1 John 4.18).

(b) It means *respect*, such as the respect of a slave for his master (Ephesians 6.5).

(c) It is very commonly used in respect to God and means reverence rather than fear (Ephesians 5.21; Colossians 3.22; 1 Peter 1.17; Revelation 14.7).

There are two other words which the AV translates in terms of fear. *Deilia* (2 Timothy 1.7) is always a bad word. The RSV translates it *timidity* and the NEB *craven fear*. Its adjective *deilos* occurs in Revelation

21.8, where it is translated *fearful*; the RSV and the NEB have *cowardly*. *Deilia* and *deilos* never express something which is good.

The second word is the word *eulabeia* with its verb *eulabeisthai*. *Eulabeia* occurs twice. In Hebrews 12.28 the AV, RSV, and NEB all have *reverence*. In Hebrews 5.7 it is used of Jesus and it is said of him in the AV that his prayers were heard *in that he feared*. The RSV has *godly fear* and the NEB *humble submission*. The verb *eulabeisthai* is used of Noah in Hebrews 11.7. It is said in the AV that Noah built the ark *moved with fear*. Both the RSV and the NEB say that Noah *took heed*. Quite clearly the fear described in *eulabeia* and its verb is a good fear. The idea of the words may be seen from their derivation. *Eu* means *well*, and *labeisthai* means *to take hold of*. The words describe the attitude of the man who, as it were, takes hold of a situation cautiously and carefully, and whose caution and care are the result of a reverent attitude to God.

FELLOWSHIP: *koinōnia*. *Koinōnia* (Philippians 1.5; 2.1; 1 John 1.3,6) is one of the great words of the NT. Allied words are *koinōnos* (Philemon 17) and *sugkoinōnos* (Philippians 1.7; Revelation 1.9), which both mean *partner*. It may be that in English the word *fellowship* is a threadbare word with a very conventionally religious sound about it. It is well to remember that the original idea is partnership, and that in Greek the words can be used to describe any partnership from marriage to partnership in a commercial and business undertaking.

FILTHY LUCRE, GIVEN TO: *aischrokerdēs*. Twice in the Pastoral Epistles it is laid down that the Christian who is to serve the church must not be greedy for or given to filthy lucre (1 Timothy 3.8; Titus 1.7). The corresponding adverb, *aischrokerdōs*, is used in 1 Peter 5.2, where the Christian is urged to serve the church willingly, and not for filthy lucre. The RSV translates *greedy for gain*; the NEB speaks of the money-grubber.

The Greeks also hated this sin, and Theophrastus in his *Characters* sketched the actions of the mean man, as A. D. Knox translates the word. When the mean man is entertaining his friends, he never gives them enough to eat; if he is carving the joint, he says that the carver deserves a double share, and takes it; if he has a friend staying with him, he borrows money from the friend. When he sells wine, he waters it; when he measures out grain, he does so in a measure of which the bottom has been punched up to make it hold less. When he is on state business abroad, he will leave his travel allowance at home, and borrow from his colleagues. He demands a share of his servants' tips, and, if one of his slaves finds a penny on the pavement, he claims half of it. In the baths he says that his anointing oil is rancid, and borrows someone else's. He sends his coat to the laundry, borrows someone else's, and then keeps on wearing the borrowed coat, when his own has come back. If his children are off school for a day, he deducts something from their fees. He always tries to pay his accounts half a crown short. After a dinner party he will count even the half radishes that are left to see that his servants do not take them. When his friends join to give a subscription party in his house, he charges them for even the salt and the oil for the lamp. When a friend's daughter is to be married, he goes abroad to avoid giving a wedding present. So the character of the *aischrokerdēs* is sketched. He is the man who is out for what he can get, it does not matter how little or how much, and he has no shame about how he gets it.

FIRST-BORN: *prōtotokos*. In certain occurrences of this word a problem of meaning arises. In Hebrews 11.28 it is used of the first-born sons of the Egyptians, who were slain at the first Passover, and there is no problem there, for the meaning is the literal meaning.

The problem arises when, as in all the other instances of it, the word is used in connection with Jesus. In Hebrews 1.6 Jesus is called simply the *first-begotten* (AV), the first-born (RSV, NEB). In Romans 8.29 he is called the first-born among many brethren, as the AV and the RSV have it, and, as the NEB has it, the eldest among a large family of brothers. This is natural enough for the idea is that of Jesus as the founder of the new humanity. In Colossians 1.18 he is called the first-born from the dead, for which the NEB has the first to return from the dead. Again this is natural, for it means that Jesus was the first to conquer death. It is the one remaining instance which presents the problem. In Colossians 1.15 the AV has it that Jesus is the first-born of every creature, and the RSV that he is the first-born of all creation. The trouble about this is that it seems to imply that there was a time before the Son was born, and that he is therefore not eternal, and it also seems to involve and include him in creation as a part of it. The NEB here has two translations. In the margin, it translates that Jesus was born before all created things, but in the text it has that his is the primacy over all created things. It is this last translation which gives by far the best sense. And it is perfectly possible. The first-born is obviously the first in place and power, and *prōtotokos* tends to come to describe a person, not in his temporal relation to others, but in his superiority to others, and his place above others to which his birth entitles him. It tends to come to mean, not that a person was born before others, but that he is greater and higher than others, and this is the way in which the word is here used of Jesus.

FLESH: *sarx*. The flesh is one of the most characteristic Pauline conceptions, and the word *sarx* is one of the most difficult of all NT words to translate. We may note the following facts about it.

i. The flesh is not equal to the body. Paul lists the sins of the flesh in Galatians 5.19-21 and they include strife, jealousy, anger, selfishness, sedition, heresy, and these are not 'bodily' sins. The flesh cannot be equated with the body.

ii. Paul does use *sarx* of the body, when, for instance, he contrasts the circumcision of the flesh with the circumcision of the heart (Romans 2.28).

iii. He sometimes uses the word flesh as we would use the phrase humanly speaking. Humanly speaking, Jesus is descended from David; humanly speaking, Abraham is the forefather of the Christian (Romans 1.3; 4.1).

iv. He sometimes uses flesh to describe a thing from human standards. Not many influential by human standards have entered the church (1 Corinthians 1.26).

v. He sometimes uses flesh to mean man or humanity, which is a Hebrew usage. No flesh, that is, no human being, can be justified by works of the law (Romans 3.20).

vi. These usages are easy enough to understand and translate, but they are not the characteristic Pauline usage. In the special Pauline usage we can distinguish the following aspects of the flesh.

(a) The flesh is the precise opposite of the spirit (Romans 8.9; Galatians 5.17).

(b) To be in the flesh is the precise opposite of being a Christian; to be in the flesh is to be under sin; the Christian has crucified the flesh (Romans 7.5,14; 8.5; Galatians 5.24).

(c) The flesh is the enemy of the good life and of God. It is that in man which makes goodness impossible (Romans 7.18,25; 8.3,7,8).

In one sense the flesh is human nature without God. In another sense the flesh is that which gives sin its bridgehead. It is that in man which answers and responds to temptation. The translation is very difficult. Sometimes *lower nature* serves the purpose. 'Do not turn your freedom into licence for your lower nature' (NEB, Galatians 5.13). But the idea of *sarx* is not so much that man has a higher and a lower nature, either of which he can choose to obey, but rather that without God human nature is all vitiated. The *sarx*, the flesh, is that which the accumulated influence of generations of sinning has made human nature, and that which human nature remains, at the mercy of sin, so long as it is without God.

FORERUNNER: *prodromos*. This word is applied to Jesus in Hebrews 6.20. A *prodromos* was one who went first to make it safe for others to follow.

It is, for instance, used of reconnaissance troops who go ahead of the main army to see that the way is safe; it is used of a pilot boat which goes ahead of a ship to guide it into a harbour. Jesus is the one who went on ahead to make it possible and safe for others to follow.

FORM, FASHION: *morphē*, *schēma*. Philippians 2.1-11 is one of the most important theological passages in the NT, and both these words occur within it (Philippians 2.6,8). The AV distinguishes between them. Jesus was in the *form*, *morphē*, of God. He was found in *fashion*, *schēma*, as a man. The RSV unfortunately makes no distinction, and uses *form* in both places. The NEB says that the divine nature belonged to Jesus from the first, and then that he bore the human likeness, and was revealed in human shape, a translation which makes it clear that there is a difference.

The difference is this. A person's or a thing's *morphē* is that which never changes and which he or it always is; the *schēma* is the outward form which can vary from place to place and from time to time. A man's *morphē* is humanity; always and at all times he is a man. But his *schēma* will be different at the age of seven, seventeen and seventy, or it will be different if he is a European, an African or an Asian. All flowers have the same *morphē*; they are flowers. But the *schēma* of the flower varies in the rose, the tulip, the daffodil and so on. The *morphē* is the unchanging essence of a person; the *schēma* is the form which on different occasions the *morphē* may take. The Philippians passage therefore by its choice of words lays it down that Jesus is eternally and essentially divine in his being, but that for the sake of men that deity took the *schēma* of humanity for a period. This does not for one moment say that the manhood was not real, but it was an episode in the divinity, which even in the manhood was still there.

GENTLE, GENTLENESS: *epieikēs*, *epieikeia*. The adjective *epieikēs* occurs five times in the NT, and the noun *epieikeia* twice. The AV has *gentle* for the adjective three times (Titus 3.2; James 3.17; 1 Peter 2.18), *patient* once (1 Timothy 3.3), and *moderation* once, when the neuter of the adjective is used as a noun (Philippians 4.5). For the noun the AV has *clemency* once (Acts 24.4) and *gentleness* once (2 Corinthians 10.1). The RSV sticks consistently to the idea of gentleness, except in Philippians 4.5 where it uses *forbearance*. The NEB has *forbearance* in Titus 3.2 and 1 Timothy 3.3, *considerate* in James 3.17 and 1 Peter 2.18, and *magnanimity* in Philippians 4.5 and 2 Corinthians 10.1. The difficulty of translating this word may be seen from the fact that in the seven instances Moffatt has six different translations—*conciliatory* (Titus 3.2); *forbearing* and *for bearance* (James 3.17; Philippians 4.5); *reasonable* (1 Peter

2.18); *lenient* (1 Timothy 3.3); *courtesy* (Acts 24.4); *consideration* (2 Corinthians 10.1).

The fact is that no one English word gives the meaning of these words. Aristotle discusses *epieikeia* in the Nicomachean Ethics (5.10.6). He says that *epieikeia* corrects the law when the law is deficient because of its generality. He contrasts the man who is *akribodikaios*, who stands up for the last tittle of his legal rights, with the man who is *epieikēs*, who knows that there are times when a thing is legally right and equally morally wrong. The man who is *epieikēs* knows when to relax the law under the compulsion of a force which is greater and higher than law. He knows that there is a time when to stand on his rights would be unquestionably legal and just as unquestionably quite unchristian. Equity comes some distance towards the idea. The man who is *epieikēs* knows when to apply the law and when not to apply it, and his first instinct is not to stand on his rights in law, but to take Christian love to each situation.

GODLINESS: *eusebeia.* *Eusebeia* is one of the great Greek words. The AV consistently translates it godliness (1 Timothy 2.2; 3.16; 4.7,8; 6.3,5,6, 11; 2 Timothy 3.5; 2 Peter 1.3,6,7; 3.11). The RSV has *godliness* except in 1 Timothy 3.16 and 2 Timothy 3.5, where it has *religion.* The NEB does not use the translation *godliness* at all; it most frequently uses *religion,* or *the practice* or *observance of religion,* and three times it uses *piety* (1 Timothy 6.11; 2 Peter 1.6,7).

We shall best see the meaning of the word by seeing what the Greeks said about it. In so far as Greek has any word for religion *eusebeia* is that word. Plato defined *eusebeia* as right conduct in regard to the gods; the Stoics defined it as knowledge of how God should be worshipped. Lucian said that the man who is *eusebēs* (the adjective, Acts 10.2,7; 2 Peter 2.9) is a lover of the gods; Xenophon said that he is wise concerning the gods. Plutarch defined *eusebeia* as the perfect mean between *atheotēs* which is *atheism* and *deisidaimonia* which is *superstition.* Plato urged all men to have *eusebeia,* and thus to become the friends of God, which would also inevitably issue in the right attitude to men. *Eusebeia* is the word for true religion, for true religion may well be defined as the right attitude to God and men.

GREED: see COVETOUSNESS

HERESY, HERETIC: *hairesis, hairetikos.* The word *hairesis* occurs three times in the NT. The AV consistently translates in terms of heresy. The RSV translates *factions* in 1 Corinthians 11.19; *party spirit* in Galatians 5.20; *heresies* in 2 Peter 2.1. The NEB consistently translates by the idea of *dissension.* *Hairetikos* (Titus 3.10) is translated *heretic* by the AV and the NEB, and *factious* by the RSV.

In modern language the word *heretic* means always one who is guilty of theological error in his thinking; but the Greek word *hairesis* has a wider meaning than that. It comes from the verb *hairein*, which can mean *to choose*, and *hairesis* is literally *an act of choosing*. So from the NT point of view a heretic is a man who chooses what he believes instead of accepting the belief of the church. He is a man who is arrogant enough to prefer what he believes to what the church believes. This of course divorces him from his fellow-Christians, and thus the idea of dissension and faction come in.

HOLY: *hagios, hosios, hieroprepēs*. More than one word is translated *holy* in the NT.

i. There is the word *hagios*. This is the commonest word for *holy* (e.g. Ephesians 5.27; Colossians 3.12; Hebrews 3.1; 1 Peter 1.15,16; Revelation 6.10). This is the word which is used in the basic OT commandment in which God tells his people to be *holy* because he is *holy* (Leviticus 11.44; 19.2). This is the word which is used of Israel, when Israel is said to be the *holy* people (*hagion ethnos*).

The basic meaning of *hagios* is *separate, different*. The temple is holy because it is different from other buildings. The Sabbath is holy because it is different from other days. God is supremely the Holy One because he is different from men. This idea of separation and difference very easily develops a moral and ethical idea, because it comes to imply separation from the world's impurity in order to share God's purity. So the idea comes to be that of being separated from the world and dedicated to God, not in the sense of withdrawal from the world, but in the sense of difference from the world.

Hagios has one special usage. It is the word which the AV translates *saints*, which is the commonest of all words for the Christian in the NT (e.g. 1 Corinthians 1.2; 16.1; 2 Corinthians 8.4; Ephesians 1.1,4; Colossians 1.2; Philippians 1.1; Hebrews 6.10; Revelation 13.10; 14.2). It is to the *saints* in such and such a place that Paul writes most of his letters. The word *saint* is now misleading, because it gives an atmosphere of exceptional and abnormal piety, and it is clear from Paul's letters that the *saints* to whom he was writing were by no means perfect. When we remember the basic meaning of the word we will see that to call the Christians saints is to say that they had dedicated and consecrated their lives to God, and they were committed to live in the world a life that was *different* from the world. The saints are the people who are different, and the difference lies in their dedication to God, however imperfectly that dedication is carried out.

Hagios has a kindred word which we shall also consider here, the word *hagiasmos*. The AV translates *hagiasmos* by the word *holiness* five times (Romans 6.19,22; 1 Thessalonians 4.7; 1 Timothy 2.15; Hebrews 12.14), and by the word *sanctification* four times (1 Corinthians 1.30; 1 Thessalonians 4.3,4; 2 Thessalonians 2.13; 1 Peter 1.2). The RSV moves within the same two translations. The NEB introduces two new words, *consecration* (1 Corinthians 1.30; 2 Thessalonians 2.1,13) and the idea of *hallowing* (1 Thessalonians 4.4; 1 Peter 1.2).

Greek nouns which end in *-asmos* commonly describe a process, and *hagiasmos* is the process by which a person becomes *hagios*. *Hagiasmos* is therefore *the road to holiness*. Sanctification is therefore more an ongoing process than it is a final state.

ii. The second word for *holy* is *hosios*. It occurs five times in the NT (1 Timothy 2.8; Titus 1.8; Hebrews 7.26; Revelation 15.4; 16.5). The AV and the RSV both consistently translate *holy*; the NEB has *holy* in the Revelation passages, which both refer to God; it has *devout* in Titus and Hebrews, and it translates in terms of *pure intention* in the 1 Timothy passage.

In classical Greek *hagios* is very rare, but *hosios* is one of the great Greek words. The man who is *hosios* is the man who obeys the eternal laws which were and are before any manmade laws, what R. C. Trench calls the 'eternal sanctities'. The meaning of the word can be seen by what the Greek called *anosios*, unholy—the Egyptian custom of marriage between brother and sister, still more the Persian custom of marriage between son and mother, the refusal to allow burial to the dead. The man who is *hosios* is the man who never fails to observe the laws which are built into the structure of the universe.

iii. The third word is the word *hieroprepēs*, which occurs only once, in Titus 2.3. The AV translates it *as becometh holiness*, the RSV *with reverent behaviour*, and the NEB *with reverent bearing*. The word *hieroprepēs* is composed of two words, *hieros* which means *sacred*, and *prepein* which means *to befit*. In this sense to be holy means to live as befits a sacred person. The world is like a temple and the Christian is continually discharging a priestly duty to God.

HONEST, HONESTLY: *semnos, kalos, euschemonōs*. Here is one of the cases where the AV is now definitely misleading. In modern English the word *honest* means *truthful* and *sincere*. But in the seventeenth century this was not the main meaning of the word. It then meant *noble, honourable, distinguished, respected, illustrious, eminent* and even *beautiful*. It was not till later that it was confined to the narrower meaning of truthful. So a passage like 1 Peter 2.12 is doubly misleading: 'Having your conversation honest among the Gentiles.' It means: 'Having your conduct and behaviour honourable and beautiful among the Gentiles.' It is not the talk of the Christian which is an invitation to Christianity, it is his whole life. So then we look at these words.

i. We begin with *kalos*. *Kalos* is translated *honest* four times in the NT (Romans 12.17; 2 Corinthians 8.21; 13.7; 1 Peter 2.12). The modern translations translate in terms of honourable, noble, good. Here the word is used to describe that in which beauty and goodness are combined.

ii. *Euschemonōs* is an adverb and in the AV is translated *honestly* (Romans 13.13; 1 Thessalonians 4.12). The modern translations have *becomingly, with decency, in a way to command respect*. Once again the idea is that of something which is both morally good and winsomely attractive.

iii. Of the three words *semnos* is by far the greatest. It occurs four times in the NT (Philippians 4.8; 1 Timothy 3.8,11; Titus 2.2). In the Philippians passage the AV translates *honest*; in all the others *grave*. The RSV translates *honourable* in Philippians, and *serious* in all the others. The NEB translates *noble* in Philippians, and *of high principle*, or *high-principled* in the others.

We are once again with this word presented with something for which there is no exact equivalent. In Greek the word is often applied to the gods. Ethically, Aristotle makes *semnotēs* (the noun) the perfect mean between *areskeia*, which is the flatterer's desire to please, and *authadeia*, which is stubborn boorishness. The man who is *semnos*, says R. C. Trench, 'has a grace and dignity not lent by earth.' There is in the word something of 'the majestic and the awe-inspiring'. The life which is *semnos* is the life which is lived in reverence and which itself begets reverence.

HOSPITALITY: *philoxenos, philoxenia*. *Philoxenia* (Hebrews 13.1) is *hospitality*, and *philoxenos* (Titus 1.8; 1 Peter 4.9) describes the hospitable man.

It is interesting to note the stress that the NT lays on the simple virtue of hospitality. To the Greek the stranger was a very special person under the care of Zeus himself. In a Christian society the slave had no home of his own and to have a home open to him must have been a priceless privilege. Inns in the ancient world were notoriously bad, and therefore hospitality to the traveller was all the more important. The Christian has always a duty to the stranger in a strange place.

IMAGE: *eikōn*. *Eikōn* can have a bad meaning when it refers to an image in the sense of an idol (Revelation 13.14,15; 14.9,11). It can have a normal meaning, as when it is said that the new man is the image of God, his Creator (Colossians 3.10). The important use of this word is when it is used to describe Jesus in relation to God, as it is twice (2 Corinthians 4.4; Colossians 1.15).

Clearly, when this word is used of Jesus it becomes of first-class theological importance. Of what does the *likeness* in this word consist? There are two lines of approach.

i. *Eikonion*, the diminutive form of the word, is colloquial Greek for a portrait. There is a papyrus letter in which a young soldier says that he is sending home an *eikonion* which he has had made. In modern language, he is sending home a photograph of himself in uniform! This word *eikonion* may be the word for an identification portrait of a Roman soldier. It is therefore at least an exact reproduction.

ii. But, as R. C. Trench points out, the early church theologians saw one special thing in the word *eikōn*. *Eikōn* implies that a thing is not only like something, but that it is also essentially connected with that other thing. An artificial flower is like a real flower, and an artificial diamond is like a real diamond, but there is no connection between the two. On the other hand the reflection of the sun in a pool of water, the king's head on a coin, and above all the child of a father, are not only like the sun and the king and the father; they are indissolubly connected with that which they are like. *Eikōn*, as Trench says, 'always assumes a prototype which it not merely resembles, but from which it is drawn.' So then to call Jesus the *eikōn* of God is to say, not only that he resembles God, but that he is also integrally and indissolubly connected with God.

IMAGE: *express image ; charaktēr*. This word is used once of Jesus (Hebrews 1.3). The *charaktēr* is the impression that a seal leaves in the wax, and the point is that such an impression is an absolutely exact replica of the seal. The word stresses the perfect likeness of Jesus to God.

INHERIT, INHERITANCE: *klēronomein, klēronomia*. These words are common in the NT (e.g. 1 Corinthians 6.9,10; 15.50; Galatians 5.21; Hebrews 6.12; 12.17; 1 Peter 3.9; Revelation 21.7; Ephesians 1.14; 5.5; Colossians 3.24; 1 Peter 1.4). They can tend to be misleading. In ordinary English an *inheritance* is something into which a man enters only when the previous owner has died. To inherit is always consequent on someone's death; it is the result of the instructions contained in the will of a deceased person. But this is not the NT meaning of the words at all. To inherit in the NT sense is to enter into the possession of a promise given by God, and, since the promise is God's promise, the fulfilment of it is certain; but clearly there is no hint of the previous death of the one who made the promise.

INSTRUCT: *muein*. This word occurs only once in the NT, in Philippians 4.12 where Paul says that 'he is *instructed* both to be full and to be hungry.' The interesting thing is that *muein* is the technical word for initiating a candidate into the secrets of the Mystery Religions. So the

RSV has: 'I have learned the secret of facing plenty and hunger,' and the NEB has: 'I have been very thoroughly initiated into the human lot with all its ups and downs.' The point is that there is more than instruction here; there is initiation into the secret which only an initiate can know.

JESTING: *eutrapelia*. This word occurs only once in the NT (Ephesians 5.4). It requires comment because in ordinary Greek it is a good word, but in the NT it is a bad word. Aristotle (Nicomachean Ethics 2.7,13) as usual describes the virtue as the mean between two extremes. In this case the extremes are the extreme of excess, *bōmolochia*, which means *buffoonery*, which is the kind of humour which knows no restraint, and the extreme of defect, *agroikia*, which is *boorishness*, which has no sense of humour at all. In between there is *eutrapelia*, which is *wit*. But in the NT *eutrapelia* is not a good word. The RSV translates it *levity* and the NEB *flippant talk*. The word is not to be understood or translated in its secular sense.

JESUS. In Hebrews 4.8 *Jesus* is Joshua, of which it is the Greek form.

JOY, EXCEEDING, REJOICE: *agalliasis, agallian*. The noun *agalliasis*, which the AV translates *exceeding joy*, occurs in Jude 24; and the verb *agallian*, to rejoice or be glad with exceeding joy, occurs in 1 Peter 1.6,8; 4.13; Revelation 19.7.

These are words of the very greatest interest. They derive from a verb *agallō* which means to adorn, and they mean, as it were, as Bultmann has it, to preen or plume oneself. The idea is that of a joy which fills a man with a pride that all can see.

An even more interesting suggestion has been made. The verb is *agallian*. Verbs which end in *-ian* are at least sometimes 'sickness' verbs. *Ophthalmos* is the eye and *ophthalmian* is *to have eye trouble*. It has therefore been suggested, as it has been put, that *agallian* means *to be glad to the point of madness*. The joy of the Christian in this word is so vivid and so visible that he seems to be a man who has taken leave of his senses.

JUSTIFY, JUSTIFICATION, JUSTICE, JUST: *dikaioun, dikaiōsis, dikaiosunē, dikaios*. Since justification by faith is of the very essence of reformed religion, it is very necessary that we should have a clear idea of the meaning of these terms.

The verb *dikaioun*, which the AV translates *to justify* occurs frequently in Paul's letters, in particular in Romans and Galatians (e.g. Romans 2.13; 3.20, 24; 5.1; Galatians 2.16; 3.11). The noun *dikaiōsis*, the act of justifying, occurs twice (Romans 4.25; 5.8).

We may start our investigation of the meaning of these words from Romans 4.5. There Paul speaks of God *iustifying* the ungodly. In ordinary language to justify a person means to produce reasons why that person was right to act as he did. Clearly, that cannot be the meaning here. God is not going to produce reasons to prove that the ungodly man is right to be ungodly.

The key lies in the meaning of the verb *dikaioun*. Greek verbs which end in *-oun* do not mean to make a person something; they mean to treat, reckon, account someone as something. *Hosioun* means *to treat as holy*. So *dikaioun* means *to treat as just*. What justification by faith means is that, if a man trusts God, God treats that man as if he was a good man, hell-deserving sinner though he may be. This is exactly what the father in the story did with the prodigal son. Justification by faith means that we must believe Jesus when he tells us that the love of God is such that it treats us as loved sons even when we are sinners.

Now we come to the word *dikaiosunē*. *Dikaiosunē* has two meanings.

i. It is the normal Greek word for *justice*, which is defined as giving man and God their due. The AV usually translates it *righteousness*, but the NEB correctly often has *justice* (e.g. Romans 6.18,20; Ephesians 5.9; 1 Timothy 6.11; 2 Timothy 2.22; James 1.20; 1 Peter 2.24; 1 John 2.29). There is no difficulty about this meaning. The man who has this quality of justice is the man who is *dikaios*, the just man.

ii. Righteousness is the state of being right with God; and therefore *dikaiosunē* is the state of the man whom God has justified; this man is right with God. He knows God loves him and is at peace and at one with God. This is what righteousness so often means in Paul's letters (e.g. Romans 4.3-22; 10.4; Galatians 2.21).

We can now very easily see that the word justification is misleading. What *dikaioun* really means is that God in his grace puts us into a right relationship with himself; and to be justified, justification, means being in a right relationship with God. The words are not really legal words; they are words of man's personal relationship with God, made possible by Jesus Christ.

LAMB: *arnion*. The title *arnion* for Jesus is characteristic of, and peculiar to, the Revelation where it occurs twenty-seven times (e.g. 5.6,12,13; 6.1; 7.9,10,14,17; 12.11; 14.1,4; 15.3; 17.14; 19.7,9; 21.9,27; 22.1,3). Elsewhere in the NT Jesus is sometimes called the Lamb (John 1.29,36; 1 Peter 1.19). But the word is different and the picture is different. The word is *amnos*, and the picture is the picture of the sacrificial lamb. But in the Revelation we read of the wrath of the Lamb, and the triumph of the Lamb, and the marriage of the Lamb, and the great doxologies sing the praise of the Lamb as the sharer of the throne of God.

We are here in an area of thought which is strange to us and strange to the rest of the NT, but by no means unfamiliar to the Jews. The Jews not infrequently talked of their great warrior chieftains as horned lambs. This, for instance, was the way in which Judas Maccabeus was depicted. The picture is not of the helpless sacrificial lamb but of the warrior lamb.

It would seem that in the Revelation the two ideas are fused, because the Lamb of the Revelation still bears the wounds of sacrifice; but the picture mainly comes from the use in Judaism of the horned lamb to signify a great warrior leader.

LASCIVIOUSNESS: *aselgeia*. *Aselgeia* occurs frequently in the NT. *Lasciviousness* is the commonest translation in the AV (2 Corinthians 12.21; Galatians 5.19; Ephesians 4.19; 1 Peter 4.3; Jude 24). Twice the AV translates *wantonness* (Romans 13.13; 2 Peter 2.18), and once by means of the adjective *filthy* (2 Peter 2.7). The RSV consistently translates *licentiousness*. The NEB has wide variation—*sensuality* (2 Corinthians 12.21); *indecency* (Galatians 5.19); *vice* (Ephesians 4.19); *licentiousness* (Jude 24); *dissolute habits* (2 Peter 2.7). On three occasions the NEB introduces the idea of *debauchery* in cases where it has a kind of combined translation with the context (1 Peter 4.3; Romans 13.13; 2 Peter 2.18).

The word has a particular flavour. It is by no means confined to fleshly sins. It is defined by Basil as the spirit 'which does not possess and cannot tolerate discipline'. It is connected with *hubris*, that sin of all sins to the Greek, that wanton, insolent arrogance which has no respect for God or man. Lightfoot grasps the essence of *aselgeia*. *Aselgeia* knows no restraint from outside or in. The sinner usually tries to hide his sin, but *aselgeia* does not care if it shocks public decency; it has no shame whatever; it does not care what others think or say; it is blatant immorality. Josephus has two instances of it which perfectly illustrate it. He uses it of Jezebel when she wanted to build a temple to Baal in Jerusalem, and he uses it of the Roman soldier who produced a riot by committing an act of gross indecency in the temple courts at a Passover time (*Antiquities* 8.13.1; 20.5.3). *Aselgeia* is the conduct which is lost to shame.

LAW: *nomos*. The problem of translation in regard to *nomos* is to know when it means the Jewish law and when it means law, legalism, in general. A working rule, although by no means an infallible rule, is that when *nomos* has the definite article, *the* law, it is the Jewish law which is in question, and when it has not, it is law in general. So in Romans 2.14 Paul writes: 'When the Gentiles who have no legal system at all (*nomos* without the article) do what the law (*nomos* with the definite article, and therefore the Jewish law) prescribes, those who have no law are a law to themselves.' In Romans 7.1 Paul writes: 'Do you not know, brothers, for I am speaking to those who know what law is (no definite article) that the law (*nomos* with the definite article) has authority over a man during his lifetime?' In the famous phrase: 'By the deeds of the law shall no flesh be justified in his sight' (Romans 3.20) there are in fact no definite articles. The AV translation is possible, even without the articles, but what Paul may well be saying is: 'No human being will ever get into a right relationship with God by attempting to satisfy the demands of any legal system.'

Each case has to be taken by itself, and care has to be taken to decide whether the reference is to the Jewish law in particular or legalism in general.

LEAVEN: *zumē*. Leaven was a piece of dough kept over from the last baking and in the keeping it fermented; it was fermented dough. The Jews identified fermentation with putrefaction. Therefore leaven stood for that which was rotten, for an evil influence. Twice (1 Corinthians 5.6; Galatians 5.9) we have the proverb: 'A little leaven leavens the whole lump of dough.' The meaning is that a bad influence can begin in a very small way and go on to permeate a whole society, and it is better to translate it so.

In 1 Corinthians 5.7,8 Paul goes on to urge his people to purge out the old leaven. This is a reference to a Jewish custom. Just before the Passover in every Jewish home there was a ceremonial search for leaven, and the last particle of leaven had to be found and thrown away. So the last particle of evil influence has to be banished from the church and the Christian community.

LION OF JUDAH. This is a title of Jesus in Revelation 5.5. A great and heroic figure is often likened to a lion, as, for instance, Hercules and Pericles were in Greece, and as in English Richard was called the Lion Heart. But in regard to Jesus this is a Messianic title, and it takes its origin in Genesis 49.9 where it is said in Jacob's farewell to his sons: 'Judah is a lion's whelp.' The greatest son of Judah is therefore the Lion of Judah.

LOVE: *agapē*. Since love is the very essence of the Christian life, it is necessary to understand what the NT means by *love*.

There are in Greek four main words for love. There is *erōs*, which has always sexual passion in it. It does not occur in the NT. There is *storgē*, which is family love, the love of father for son or daughter, or son for mother or father. It is sexless. There is *philia*, which is warm affectionate love. There is *agapē*. The word *agapē* is so rare that it hardly occurs at all in secular Greek. Trench says of it that it is a word 'born within the bosom of revealed religion', and this is the Christian word for love.

It finds its model in God who 'makes his sun rise on the evil and the good, and sends rain on the just and the unjust' (Matthew 5.45). This is to say that, whether a man is a saint or a sinner, he shares in the gifts and the benevolence of God. *Agapē* is unconquerable benevolence, undefeatable good-will; it is the spirit which will never seek anything but the other person's good, no matter what the other person does.

It is therefore quite different from the love which we bear to our kith and kin. It is not something which we cannot help and which just happens. It is an act of the will. In fact Christian love can love the person it does not like. It is the attitude which, no matter what the other person is like, and no matter how we may feel emotionally towards him, will seek the other person's good, and which will never hate. The opposite of this Christian *agapē* is not hate; the opposite is indifference. This Christian love is undefeatable caring. It is not an emotional outrush of the heart alone; it is a set and disposition of the will. It is not the outgoing of the heart to the other person; it is the outgoing of the whole personality. It is not something we cannot help; it is a victory which the Spirit of Christ enables a man to win. It is an attitude to all men which reproduces the attitude of God.

MANIFOLD: *poikilos*: see DIVERS

MARK: *stigma*. In Galatians 6.17 Paul says that he bears on his body the *stigmata*, the *marks*, of Christ. The reference is to tattooing or branding. In the ancient world such marking was connected with three kinds of people. A slave might be branded with his master's mark of ownership. A temple slave might be branded with the name or emblem of the god or goddess whom he served. A soldier, sometimes voluntarily and as a mark of devotion, branded himself with the name of his general. Paul regarded himself as branded with the mark of Christ, whose slave and soldier he was. The marks in question were the marks and scars his adventures for Jesus had left on his body.

MARK: *charagma*. In the Revelation this word is regularly used of the mark of the beast (13.16; 14.9,11; 16.2; 19.20; 20.4). *Charagma* could be used of a seal or an official mark on a document. It was used of the brand on cattle, so that they could be identified, if they were stolen. The *charagma* was a distinguishing mark as a sign of ownership. There is an interesting papyrus letter in which a son writes to his father. The times are unsettled, and the son fears for his father's safety, and, in particular, he fears that, if anything happens to his father, they may not be able to find his body to give it decent burial. So he writes: 'In view of the unsettled state of things I wanted *to stamp a mark* on you (*egcharassein*).' The *charagma* shows to whom a person or thing belongs.

MEEKNESS: *praütēs*. *Meekness* is the standard and unvarying AV translation of *praütēs* (1 Corinthians 4.21; 2 Corinthians 10.1; Galatians 5.3; 6.1; Ephesians 4.2; Colossians 3.12; 1 Timothy 6.11; 2 Timothy 2.25; Titus 3.2; James 1.21; 3.13; 1 Peter 3.4; 3.15). The RSV varies between *meekness* and *gentleness*. The NEB has *gentle* or *gentleness* in all cases except James 1.21 where it has *quietly*, and in James 3.13 and 1 Peter 3.15 where it has *modesty*.

None of these translations is satisfactory. In Greek *praütēs* is basically connected with anger. In the ethic of Aristotle *praütēs* is the mean between too much and too little anger; it is the quality of the man who is neither angry too much and too often nor ever angry at all. It is the quality of the man who is angry for the right reasons, against the right people, in the right way and for the right length of time. The basic idea of the word is not so much gentleness as strength under control. Plato, for instance, uses it of the sheep-dog who is gentle to the flock but savage to the enemies of the flock. The word indicates a gentleness at the back of which there is courage and strength. This is further illustrated by the fact that the Bible regards this quality of *praütēs* as the distinctive quality both of Moses (Numbers 12.3) and Jesus (2 Corinthians 10.1).

MEDIATOR: *mesitēs*. The word *mesitēs* is used of Moses in Galatians 3.19 and of Jesus in 1 Timothy 2.5; Hebrews 8.6; 9.15; 12.24. *Mesos* means *in the middle*, and a *mesitēs* is one who stands in the middle between two parties, either to unite them when they have disagreed or quarrelled, or to bring them into common action together. Jesus then is the one who stands between man and God. He, as it were, represents God to man and man to God. He is the connecting link between man and God.

THE MIDDLE WALL OF PARTITION: *to mesotoichon tou phragmou*. This phrase occurs in Ephesians 2.14. The AV speaks of Jesus breaking down *the middle wall of partition*. The RSV has *the dividing wall of hostility*. The NEB has *the enmity which stood like a dividing wall between them*. The reference is to the bringing together of Jew and Gentile in Jesus Christ. The picture very probably comes from the Jerusalem Temple. Between the Court of the Gentiles and the Court of the Israelites there was a low wall beyond which no Gentile might go. Inset into the wall there were stone tablets with an inscription which said that any Gentile who passed beyond that wall was liable to instant death.

This indeed was a middle wall of partition; and it was the division which that wall symbolized that Jesus had taken away.

MODERATION: see GENTLENESS

MYSTERY: *mustērion*. In the contemporary Greek of the NT the word *mustērion*, mystery, had a technical significance. It does not mean something which is mysterious and hard to understand. It means something which is secret, and the meaning of which is known only to the initiated. In itself it may be quite simple; but the point is that to the outsider it is meaningless; but to the disciple and the initiate it is meaningful. We might take the Lord's Supper itself as an illustration of this. To the outsider the sight of a group of people taking little cubes of bread and little sips of wine seems a very odd proceeding; to the man inside the faith it is the most sacred moment of his Christian experience.

NAME: *onoma*. There are two uses of the word *name* which require comment.

i. The biblical writers use the word *name* to indicate not so much the name of the person involved, but rather his nature and character in so far as it is revealed and known. So the Psalmist writes: 'Those who know thy name put their trust in thee' (Psalm 9.10). This clearly means not the name by which God is called, but the nature and the character of God as it has been revealed to men. This usage occurs in the NT, as, for instance, in Romans 9.17; 1 Timothy 6.1; Hebrews 2.12; 1 John 3.23; 5.13.

ii. *In the name of* can mean *as the representative of*. For instance, in a papyrus document certain magistrates are said to make sacrifice to the godhead of the Emperor *in the name of* the village, that is, *as the representatives of* the village. This usage may also occur in the NT. When the Christian is urged to act in the name of Christ, it may well be that the meaning is that he is the representative of Christ (e.g. Colossians 3.17; 2 Thessalonians 3.6; James 5.10,14).

NEW: *kainos*. Greek has two words for *new*. There is *neos* which is new in point of time, and there is *kainos* which is new, not only in time, but in character also. In a factory producing pencils the millionth pencil would be *neos*, new in point of time, but it would not be *kainos*, because it would be exactly the same as all the others that went before. *Kainos* is not only new in time; *kainos* describes something which introduces something into the situation which was not there before. *Kainos* is a favourite NT word (e.g. the new covenant, Hebrews 9.15; the new creation, 2 Corinthians 5.17; the new song, Revelation 13.3; the new heaven and earth, Revelation 21.1; the new Jerusalem, Revelation 21.2; all things new, Revelation 21.5).

NOW: *nun* or *nuni de*. In the NT there is a special use of this word *now*. When a sentence begins *but now*, the meaning is often more than merely temporal. It means rather *in the new situation which has emerged*. It means: 'Circumstances have altered and now . . .' (e.g. Romans 6.22; 7.6; 1 Corinthians 12.28; Ephesians 2.23; Colossians 1.21; 3.8).

OFFERED: *spendesthai*. Twice Paul says that he is ready to be offered up· The verb is *spendesthai*. The picture is that at the end of a meal the Greeks took a cup of wine and poured it out as an offering to the gods. So what Paul is saying is that he is quite ready that his life should be taken and poured out as an offering to God.

PALACE: *praitōrion*. This word occurs in Philippians 1.13, and it is clear from the variations in the different translations that there is some uncertainty about its meaning. The AV has it that, through his imprisonment, Paul's bonds became known *in all the palace*. The RSV has it that the gospel became known *throughout the whole praetorian guard*. The NEB has in the text that the gospel became known *to all at headquarters here*, but has two alternative translations in the margin—*to the imperial guard*, or, *to all at the residency here*.
The ambiguity lies in the word itself. The word has two general directions.
(a) It began by meaning, the praetor's, that is, the general's, or the commanding officer's, tent in an army encampment.
(b) It is a small step from there to the meaning headquarters.
(c) The word then widens its meaning to include any governor's residence.
(d) And, of course, if that residence is in Rome, then it is the imperial palace.
(e) The other direction was that the word came to mean the soldiers attached to the residency, and in particular the praetorian guard at Rome who were very specially the emperor's troops.
It can therefore be seen that any or all of the translations may be correct. It is likeliest that the meaning is the praetorian guard. When Paul was in captivity in Rome, he was not in the imperial palace (Acts 28.30), but he would be constantly under the guard of soldiers from the imperial regiment.

PATIENCE: *hupomonē, makrothumia*. There are two great NT words which the AV mainly translates *patience*.
i. There is *hupomonē*. It occurs twenty-nine times in the NT and the consistent AV translation is *patience* (e.g. Romans 5.3,4; 2 Corinthians

6.4; Colossians 1.11; 1 Thessalonians 1.3; 1 Timothy 6.11; Titus 2.2; Hebrews 12.1; James 5.11; Revelation 2.2,3,19).

The RSV sometimes keeps *patience*, and sometimes has *endurance* or *steadfastness*. In Hebrews 12.1 it has *perseverance*. The NEB introduces the translation *fortitude* and in Hebrews 12.1 has *resolution*.

None of the translations is perfect. *Patience* is too passive a translation. Chrysostom called *hupomonē* the Queen of the Virtues. It has been correctly said that *hupomonē* always has a background of courage. It is not the spirit which simply grimly endures or passively accepts or bleakly waits. It transforms even the worst situation with Christian gallantry.

ii. There is *makrothumia*. For it, the AV varies between *long-suffering* and *patience*. The modern translations keep *patience* and sometimes use *forbearance* (e.g. Romans 2.4; 2 Corinthians 6.6; Galatians 5.22; Ephesians 4.2; 2 Peter 3.15). As Trench has pointed out, the basic difference between these two words is that *hupomonē* has to do with circumstances and is the spirit which no circumstance can daunt or defeat; *makrothumia* has to do with people and is the spirit which can always bear with the sins and the follies and the mistakes and the ingratitude of men. It is significant that *makrothumia* is used of God. So these two great words describe gallantry in circumstances and patience with people —which combination is the very essence of the Christian life.

PEACE: *eirēnē*. Some care is needed in the correct understanding of the word *peace* in the biblical writings. Peace has become a very negative word, and so long as no actual war is raging, or so long as two people are not actually disputing with each other, we call it peace. The mere absence of trouble is not peace in the biblical sense of the term.

i. Peace means everything that is to a man's highest good. To wish a man *shalōm*, *eirēnē*, is not simply to wish him freedom from trouble; it is to wish him every blessing which God can give. That is why all Paul's letters begin with the prayer for peace (e.g. Galatians 1.3; 1 Thessalonians 1.1; 2 Thessalonians 1.1; 1 Corinthians 1.3; 2 Corinthians 1.2; Romans 1.7).

ii. Peace means right relationships between man and man. It does not mean an uneasy and a merely negative tolerance; it means that relationship of fellowship in which people find in friendship the completing and the satisfying of their lives (e.g. 2 Corinthians 13.11; 1 Thessalonians 5.13; Colossians 1.20).

PERFECT: *teleios*. The difficulty in the translation of *teleios* arises from the particular idea of *perfection* which is in the word. *Teleios*, *perfect*, is connected with *telos* which means *an end*. And a thing is *teleios*, or a person is *teleios*, if the thing or the person serves the end for which it or he was intended. *Teleios*, at least in the NT, if we may put it so, does not imply philosophical or metaphysical perfection; it implies functional perfection. It describes that which achieves its end and purpose.

So it means full-grown as opposed to the stage of infancy and youth. It describes a student who has passed his degree examinations in contrast with a learner in the elementary stages. It describes an animal which is technically without blemish and which is therefore fit for sacrifice.

It occurs fifteen times in the NT, and the regular AV translation is *perfect* with the exception of Hebrews 5.14 where the AV has *of full age*. The modern translations frequently and correctly retain the translation *perfect* (James 1.4,17,25; 3.2; 1 John 4.18). The alternative translation, which the modern translations rightly use when the word refers to persons, is *mature* (Ephesians 4.13; Philippians 3.15; Colossians 1.28; 4.12).

PREACH: *euaggelizein, kataggellein, kērussein*. The NT has three main words for preaching.

i. *Euaggelizein* is the verb from the noun *euaggelion*, which literally means *the good news*, the gospel (1 Corinthians 15.1,2; Galatians 1.8,11, 16,23; Ephesians 2.17; 3.8; Hebrews 4.2,6; Revelation 14.6). In the English translation the word *gospel* is usually expressed, *to preach the gospel*. This word regards preaching as telling men good news about God.

ii. *Kataggellein* literally means *to pronounce* or *to proclaim*, and the basic idea of the word is authority. It is used, for instance, of the announcement of a festival, of the proclamation of war, of the announcement of an emperor's accession to the throne. It occurs in the NT in 1 Corinthians 9.14; Philippians 1.16,18; Colossians 1.28. The idea in this word is that preaching is the authoritative announcement of the will and purpose of God.

iii. *Kērussein* is the commonest word for preaching (e.g. Romans 2.21; 10.8,15; 1 Corinthians 1.23; 2 Corinthians 1.19; Galatians 5.11; Philippians 1.15; Colossians 1.23; 1 Thessalonians 2.9; 1 Timothy 3.16; 2 Timothy 4.2; 1 Peter 3.19). The word *kērux* means a *herald*, and *kerussein* means to proclaim as a herald. This is a dramatic word. The idea of preaching has acquired a certain dullness. But *kērussein* has the picture of the preacher as the herald of God, announcing God's promises and commands to all whom it may concern—which is to everyone.

PRIDE, PROUD: *huperēphania, huperēphanos, tuphousthai*. These words for *pride* are vivid words.

i. *Huperēphania*, the noun, pride, occurs only in Mark 7.22. *Huperē-*

phanos, the adjective, proud, occurs in Romans 1.30; 2 Timothy 3.2; James 4.6; 1 Peter 5.5. The words are derived from the Greek *huper*, *above*, and *phainesthai*, *to show oneself*. Theophrastus in his *Characters* describes the man who is *huperēphanos*. His great characteristic is disdain for everyone except himself. He will stalk along the street, too proud to notice, far less to recognize, anyone he passes. If he is asked to accept office, he will be too busy. If he entertains, he will not come to the meal himself, but will depute it to some underling to look after his guests. When he writes, his letters contain commands and not requests.

The man who is *huperēphanos* stands on his little eminence and looks down. He will be just as proud alone as he is in company. He may even have the outward appearance of humility, and yet be eaten with pride. This is the sin which is hateful to God (James 4.6; 1 Peter 5.5), for it is the sin of a man who has forgotten that he is a creature, and has usurped the place of the Creator.

ii. *Tuphousthai* means to be swollen up (1 Timothy 3.6; 6.4). It is what modern language calls *puffed up*. It describes the man who is *inflated* with the sense of his own importance.

PRINCIPALITIES AND POWERS. The ancient world believed in spiritual beings which were between God and man. They were formed into a hierarchy, and had different names—principality, power, might, dominion (Ephesians 1.21; cp. 1 Corinthians 15.24; Ephesians 3.10; 6.12; Colossians 1.16; 2.10). They too had to be defeated and subdued by the victory of Christ. A later writer, Ephraem Syrus, gives a full graded list of them in three classes. These are: i. Gods, thrones, lordships. ii. Archangels, principalities, authorities. iii. Angels, powers, cherubim, seraphim. They were all held to be parts of the hierarchy of the spirit and the angelic world.

PURE: *hagnos, eilikrinēs, katharos*. There are three great NT words, which are all translated *pure*.

i. *Hagnos* describes right-living at its most intense, as the Greeks themselves said (Philippians 4.8; 1 Timothy 5.22; James 3.17; 1 John 3.3). The Greeks used it to describe their own divine beings, and the NT can use it to describe God (1 John 3.3). It began by describing ritual purity, the ceremonial purity which entitles a man to enter the presence of God, but it came to be one of the great words for moral purity, especially for chastity, and even for virginity.

ii. *Eilikrinēs*, the adjective, occurs in 2 Peter 3.1, and in Philippians 1.10, where it is translated *sincere*. *Eilikrineia*, the noun, occurs in 1 Corinthians 5.8; 2 Corinthians 1.12; 2.17, in all of which instances it is translated *sincerity*.

Its derivation is uncertain but two vivid pictures have been suggested. It may come from a Greek word *eilein*, which means *to shake in a sieve*, and the meaning of the word may be *sifted* until absolute purity has been achieved. It may come from two Greek words *heilē*, which means *sunlight*, and *krinein*, which means *to judge*, and the idea may be that of something which can be brought out of the trader's dark shop into the sunlight, and which can stand the light of day.

iii. *Katharos* is the greatest word of the three. It is a wide word. It began, in Homer, by simply meaning *clean* as opposed to dirty. It went on to mean unadulterated, and could be used of metal without alloy, of wine without water, of grain that has been winnowed, of white bread. It can mean a man who is free from debt; it can mean of pure blood, and of a book or a saying it can mean genuine or authentic. It can mean ceremonially clean and therefore able to approach the altar of the gods. And, above all, it means innocent and pure from sin. The basic idea is that which has no admixture of anything that is evil.

It is frequent in the NT (e.g. Romans 14.20; 1 Timothy 1.5; 3.9; 2 Timothy 1.3; 2.22; Titus 1.15; Hebrews 10.22; James 1.27; 1 Peter 1.22; Revelation 15.6; 21.18,21; 22.1).

RANSOM, REDEEM, REDEMPTION: *lutron, lutrousthai, apolutrōsis*. There is a group of NT words which have to do with the idea of ransom and redemption, and clearly they are of the first importance theologically.

i. There is the word *lutron*. It is used of Jesus in the saying that Jesus came to give his life a *ransom* for many (Mark 10.45; Matthew 20.28), and there is the closely connected word *antilutron* in 1 Timothy 2.6, which is also used of Jesus giving his life a ransom for many.

The word has certain OT uses. It is used of the penalty a man must pay if he is the owner of an ox, known to be dangerous, which gores and kills another man, if he is himself to escape the death penalty (Exodus 21.30). It is used of the price necessary to ransom prisoners of war (Isaiah 45.3). In Israel the first-born males of man or of any other creature were sacred to God (Numbers 3.13); but the first-born could be *redeemed*, bought back, by their parents for the sum of five shekels, and these five shekels were called the *lutron* (Numbers 3.12,46-51; 18.15,16).

In Greek usage the word was used specially of the price needed to redeem something that was in pawn, and for the price needed to redeem a slave from slavery.

Both in Hebrew and in Greek usage the word *lutron* is the price needed to liberate a man from a situation from which otherwise he could not be released.

ii. There is *lutrousthai*, which means to *ransom* or *redeem*. In OT usage the word is used of redeeming what has been pledged or pawned (Leviticus 25.25,30,33). It is used of buying back the first-born from the service of God (Exodus 13.13; 34.20). It is constantly used of God's rescue and redemption of his people from slavery in Egypt (Exodus 6.6; Deuteronomy 7.8; 13.5). Above all, it is consistently used of God's rescue of his people in every time of trouble. 'Thou hast redeemed me, O God of truth.' It is God who redeems Israel out of all his troubles (Psalm 25.22; 31.5; 26.11; 69.18; 103.4; 130.8). The prophets also use this way of speaking (e.g. Isaiah 43.1; 44.22; Jeremiah 15.21; 50.34). So much so is this the case that the present participle (*ho lutroumenos*) becomes a title of God, 'the redeeming one'. In the NT it occurs in Titus 2.14 and 1 Peter 1.18, in both of which cases it is used of the work of Jesus. Once again, the idea is that of rescuing a man from a situation from which he cannot rescue himself.

iii. There is the word *apolutrōsis*, which is *the act of redeeming*, redemption (Romans 3.24; 8.23; 1 Corinthians 1.30; Ephesians 1.7; 4.30; Colossians 1.14; Hebrews 9.15).

When the idea of ransom is used of the work of Christ, the basic meaning is that man had got himself into a situation from which he was powerless to rescue himself, and that what Jesus did rescued him from it.

READ, READING: *anaginōskein, anagnōsis*. The one point to be noted is that in the ancient world, even when a man was reading to himself, he read aloud. That is how Philip knew what the Ethiopian was reading (Acts 8.28,30). The word is therefore specially used for the public reading of a book or epistle (Revelation 1.3; 1 Timothy 4.13; Colossians 4.16; 1 Thessalonians 5.27). In all these cases it is not private study but public reading which is in question.

RECONCILE, RECONCILIATION: *katallassein, apokatallassein, katallagē*. These are great NT words to express what Jesus Christ has done for man in relation to God.

The basic word is *allassein*, which means to change (Acts 6.14; 1 Corinthians 15.51; Hebrews 1.12).

Katallassein has two technical meanings. It means to change money, and it means—the NT usage—to change enmity into friendship. *Katallagē* is the connected noun which means *reconciliation*. The words can be used of reconciling quarrelling human beings (Acts 7.26; 1 Corinthians 7.11). But the characteristic NT usage is that which describes the reconciliation of man to God. In this case *reconcile* is the word used by all the translations (Romans 5.10; 2 Corinthians 5.18,20; Ephesians 2.16; Colossians 1.21). The noun *katallagē* is regularly translated *reconciliation* (Romans 5.11; 11.15; 2 Corinthians 5.18,19), with in the AV one exception. In Romans 5.11 the AV uses the famous term *atonement*, which is *at-one-ment*, the state of being *at one* instead of being divided and apart.

The basic meaning of the words is the turning of enmity into friendship. And the one fact above all to be noted is that God is never said to be reconciled to man; it is always man who is reconciled to God. The enmity and the breach are never on the part of God, whose attitude to man is always love; they are on the part of man. There is never any need to reconcile God to man; it is man who must be reconciled to God.

REPROBATE: *adokimos, apodokimazein*. The word *reprobate* has a grim sound about it, and it is just as well to see what the picture in the word is. In the AV, *reprobate* is the translation of *adokimos* in six cases (Romans 1.28; 2 Corinthians 13.5,6,7; 2 Timothy 3.8; Titus 1.16). In one case the AV translates it *castaway* (1 Corinthians 9.27); and in another *rejected* (Hebrews 6.8). The RSV and the NEB do not use the translation *reprobate* at all. The RSV has no fewer than six translations, *disqualified* (1 Corinthians 9.27); *worthless* (Hebrews 6.8); *base* (Romans 1.28); *fail to meet the test* (2 Corinthians 13.5,6,7); *counterfeit* (2 Timothy 3.8); *unfit* (Titus 1.16). The NEB has *rejected* in 1 Corinthians 9.27 and Hebrews 6.8. It has *depraved* in Romans 1.28. It uses the idea of *failure to pass the test* in 2 Corinthians 13.5,6,7 and 2 Timothy 3.8, and of *disqualification* in Titus 1.16. The connected verb *apodokimazein* is translated *disallow* by the AV in 1 Peter 2.4,7, where the modern translations have *reject*. In the Gospels *apodokimazein* is the word used for the *rejection* of Jesus by the religious authorities (Mark 8.21; Luke 9.22; 17.25).

The word *adokimos* has two main pictures in it. It is the word used of counterfeit money. It is the word used of a stone which has been rejected as unfit for use by the masons engaged in building. Such a stone was marked by a capital A, the first letter of *adokimos*. That which is *adokimos* is that which is rejected as spurious and counterfeit and unfit for use. In Hebrews 12.17 it is used, for instance, of Esau.

RESPECT OF PERSONS: *prosōpolēmpsia, prosōpolēmptein, prosōpolēmptēs*. These words are respectively the noun for *respect of persons*, the verb for *to show respect of persons*, and the noun for *one who shows respect of persons*. The words are built up from *prosōpon*, which means *the face* and *lambanein*, which means *to receive*. They literally mean *to receive someone's face*. They are not really Greek words; they are Hebrew in their idea. In Hebrew the expression to receive someone's face meant to look with favour on that person. The idea was not necessarily a bad idea, unless the favour was unfair to others. But in the NT these are words for something which is always bad. The AV consistently has *respect of persons*. The RSV just as consistently has *partiality* (Romans 2.11; Ephesians 6.9; Colossians 3.25; James 2.1,9; Acts 10.34). The NEB uses the idea of *favouritism* in Romans 2.11; Ephesians 6.9; Colossians 3.25. In the passages in James 2.1,9, the NEB has *snobbery*. The point that the NT makes is that there is no favouritism with God, and just so there must be no snobbish favouritism with men.

REVEAL, REVELATION: *apokaluptein, apokalupsis*. These two words are common in the NT (e.g. *apokaluptein*, Galatians 1.16; 3.23; Ephesians 3.5; Philippians 3.15; 2 Thessalonians 2.3,6,8; 1 Peter 1.5,12; 5.1: *apokalupsis*, 2 Corinthians 12.1,7; Galatians 1.12; 2.2; Ephesians 1.17; 3.3; 2 Thessalonians 1.7; 1 Peter 1.7,13; Revelation 1.1). They always indicate some direct revelation from God, and in particular the final revelation of Jesus Christ in all his glory.

They are dramatic words. *Kaluptein* is to *hide, cover, veil. Apokaluptein* is to *reveal, uncover, unveil*. It is as if the curtain was drawn and the audience left looking at the unfolding of some dramatic scene.

The word *apokalupsis* has a technical Jewish sense. The Jews thought in terms of this present age and the age to come. This present age is wholly and incurably bad; the age to come is the age of God. The one would turn into the other on the Day of the Lord, when God himself invaded time, when the universe would distintegrate in destruction, when there would be judgment, destruction and death. The works which attempted to describe that indescribable chaos were called Apocalypses. The Revelation in the NT is an example.

The intensely dramatic character of these words now requires some more vivid translation than simply *reveal* and *revelation*. The idea is of some scene or appearance bursting on to the stage of history.

RIGHTEOUSNESS: see JUSTIFICATION

RUDIMENTS: *stoicheia. Stoicheia* is the plural of *stoicheion*, and the word is used in the NT only in the plural.

The word *stoicheia* presents us with a real problem in translation. It occurs in Galatians 4.3,9; 2 Peter 3.10,12; Hebrews 5.12; Colossians 2.8,20.

We shall look first of all at the possible meanings of the word.

i. *Stoicheia* can mean the first principles of anything. It can, for instance, stand for the A B C, the letters of the alphabet.

ii. It can stand for the basic elements of which the world is created —earth, air, fire and water, as the ancients believed.

iii. It can mean the spirits which were supposed to inhabit these elements.

iv. It can mean the heavenly bodies, the signs of the zodiac. The ancient world was steeped in astralism. It believed in the power of the stars. It was haunted by the thought that a man's whole life was fixed and fated by the stars, and therefore the word could also mean the stars regarded as living powers and divinities.

Now let us turn to the NT. In 2 Peter 3.10,12, which speaks of the elements melting with fervent heat, it is clear that the meaning is the elements out of which the world is composed, and on this all the translations agree. In Hebrews 5.12 the meaning is equally clear— the first principles of the Christian faith, or, as the NEB well translates, the A B C of God's oracles.

It is the Galatians and Colossians passages which provide the difficulty. In Galatians 4.3,9 Paul's fear is that his converts will relapse into bondage to *the weak and beggarly elements* under whose sway they had once been. In Colossians 2.8,20 it is Paul's fear that the Colossians will become the victims of *the rudiments of the world*. In both cases the RSV takes it to mean *the elemental spirits of the world*. The NEB has in the text *the elemental spirits*, but has marginal notes with the possible alternative translations *the elementary ideas belonging to this world*, and *rudimentary notions*.

So there are two possibilities. Paul may be saying to his people: 'Before you were converted to Christianity, you lived in terror, haunted by the fear of the spiritual powers, as you believed, in the elements of the world and in the stars. Don't relapse into a fear-haunted world of superstition like that.' Or he may be saying: 'You ought by this time to be mature and intelligent Christians. Don't relapse into the rudimentary notions of religion which were all the world could give before you became Christians.' It may be either a warning against astralism and astrology, or a warning against a relapse into a debased and primitive religion.

I have accepted the second meaning, but the first is perfectly possible.

RULE: *brabeuein*. In Colossians 3.15 the AV has: 'Let the peace of God *rule* in your hearts.' The RSV retains the word *rule*; the NEB has *be arbiter*.

The word *brabeuein* originally meant *to be umpire* or *referee*. It then went on to mean in general *to judge, decide, control*. The translation *rule* is too colourless for the pictorial character of the word.

SAINTS, SANCTIFICATION: see HOLY

SALVATION, SAVE, SAVIOUR: *sōtēria, sōzein, sōtēr*. These are such universal NT words that it is unnecessary to cite any individual examples of them. But it is important to establish their meaning.

These words have now a highly religious and theological sound and flavour about them, but it is important to remember that in NT times they were part of the ordinary, everyday vocabulary of the people.

Sōtēria has what may be called a negative and a positive direction. First, on the negative side, it means *rescue, deliverance, preservation* in any dangerous situation, such, for instance, as a storm at sea or an illness. And the verb *sōzein* means *to bring safely through* such a situation. Second, on the positive side, in the papyrus letters of the ordinary people by far the commonest use of *sōtēria* is in the meaning of *health.* 'Write me a note about your *sōtēria*,' is to say: 'Let me know how you are.' So salvation has the double idea of rescue for the past, and welfare for the present and the future.

Sōtēr, saviour, was also commonly used. It was a very common title for the gods—Zeus, Apollo, Hermes, and very naturally for Asclepius, the god of healing. It further became a quite common title for an emperor, king or governor who had ruled well and gained the gratitude of his people. The world of the NT was well acquainted with so-called saviours.

SATAN. The word Satan did not begin by being a proper name, nor did it begin by being a bad word at all. Originally the word *Satan* simply meant an *adversary* (1 Samuel 29.4; 2 Samuel 19.22; 1 Kings 5.4; 11.14,23,25). It could even be applied to an angel of the Lord (Numbers 22.22). In Job, Satan is one of the sons of God (Job 1.6). At this stage Satan was an angel whose duty it was to say all that could be said against a man. Satan was, so to speak, the prosecutor, when a man was on trial before God. But in the NT Satan has become the personification of all that is against God (Romans 16.20; 1 Corinthians 5.5; 7.5; 1 Thessalonians 2.18; 2 Thessalonians 2.9; 1 Timothy 1.20; 5.15; Revelation 2.9,13,24; 3.9; 12.9; 20.2,7). Satan stands for everything which tries to separate man from God.

SCHOOLMASTER: *paidagōgos. Paidagōgos* occurs in two passages in the NT. It occurs in 1 Corinthians 4.15, where Paul speaking of his own relationship to the Corinthians, says that they may have ten thousand *paidagōgoi,* but they do not have many fathers, and in Galatians 3.24,25, where Paul says that the law is our *paidagōgos* to lead us to Christ. The AV translates *schoolmaster.* The RSV has it that the law is our *custodian;* the NEB has it that the law is *a kind of tutor.* Moffatt has it that the law *held us as wards in discipline.*

None of these translations is really satisfactory, because the difficulty is that there is no modern person who corresponds to the ancient *paidagōgos.* The *paidagōgos* was not the schoolmaster. He was a slave whose duty it was to take the boy to school, and there to hand him over to the teacher. He was responsible for the boy's manners and deportment and morals on the street, but he was not the school-master. At the door of the school he handed over the boy to the school-teacher.

What Paul is saying is that life under the law was designed to lead men to the school of Christ. To put it a little more fully, the law with its impossible demands drove men to realize their own utter inade-quacy, and thus brought them to Christ for the peace and the power which it itself could never give. Thus the law acted as the *paidagōgos* to bring men to Christ and to leave them with him.

SEAL: *sphragizein* (verb), *sphragis* (noun). Sealing had certain standard usages in the ancient world.

i. It was used for *security*. In the Greek world a will was sealed with seven seals by seven different people; and the will could only be opened when the seven people or their legal descendants or represen-tatives were present. This is the picture of the roll with the seven seals in Revelation 5.1.

ii. It was used to denote *ownership*. The seal was the sign and the proof of ownership. This is the usage in 1 Corinthians 1.22; 9.2; 2 Timothy 2.19; Revelation 7.3-8.

iii. It was used as a sign and guarantee of *quality*. Thus the possession of the Holy Spirit is the sign and guarantee that a man really belongs to God. God seals the Christian with his Spirit (Ephesians 1.13; 4.30).

SELF-WILLED: *authadēs*. The word *authadēs* occurs twice in the NT. It occurs in Titus 1.7 and in 2 Peter 2.10. In both cases the AV translates it *self-willed*. In Titus the RSV translates it *arrogant* and the NEB *over-bearing*. In 2 Peter the RSV translates it *wilful* and the NEB *headstrong*. The word comes from two Greek words which mean *to please oneself*. The man who is *authadēs* (the adjective) is obstinate and stubborn. As R. C. Trench puts it, he regulates his life with no regard for others. Aristotle, with his usual way of defining a virtue as the mean between an extreme of excess and an extreme of defect, places in the middle the man who is *semnos*, dignified. On the one side of him there is the *areskos*, who is out to please and to be agreeable at all costs. On the other side of him there is the man who is *authadēs*, who is boorish and discourteous, and who has no regard for the feelings or the opinions of others.

SENSUAL: *psuchikos*. *Psuchē* is commonly translated *soul*, and it at first surprises us when we find *psuchikos* translated *sensual*. It occurs in James

5.15 where the AV has *sensual*, the RSV and the NEB *unspiritual*. It occurs in Jude 19, where the NEB has *unspiritual*, and the RSV *worldly*, *devoid of the Spirit*. In 1 Corinthians 2.15 the AV has *natural*, and the RSV and the NEB *unspiritual*. In 1 Corinthians 15.44,46 Paul is contrasting the body we have and the body we shall have. The word *psuchikos* is used to describe our present body. The AV has *natural*, the RSV has *physical*, and the NEB has *animal*.

The point at issue is this. According to the Greek psychology that Paul is using, everything that has life, animal or man, has a *psuchē*, for *psuchē* is simply the life principle, and has none of the high sense that the word *soul* has in English. It is simply, as it were, the breath of life. *Natural* or *physical* well translates it. In modern English *sensual* has become a bad word, and is not a good translation. In Greek psychology the word that is used as soul is in English is *pneuma*, *spirit*. It is the possession of *pneuma*, *spirit*, which differentiates man from the creatures which have only *psuchē*, *physical life*.

SERVANT, SERVE. There are a number of words for serving in the NT, each with its own picture and its own implications.

i. There is *doulos*. Paul calls himself the *doulos* of Jesus Christ (Romans 1.1; 2 Corinthians 4.5; Philippians 1.1). So do Peter (2 Peter 1.1), James (James 1.1) and Jude (Jude 1). Epaphras is called the *doulos* of Christ (Colossians 4.12).

The duties of the *doulos*, *the servant*, in the ordinary human sense of the term are more than once set out in the NT (Ephesians 6.5; Colossians 3.22-4.1; 1 Timothy 6.1; Titus 2.9).

In the Old Testament the proudest title that a man can have is that he is the *doulos* of God, as Moses was called (e.g. Joshua 1.1).

The strictly correct translation of *doulos* is not *servant* but *slave*. In the ancient world the slave was the absolute possession of his master. Legally, the slave was not a person, he was a thing. He was defined as a living tool. His master could beat him, maim him, and even kill him, if he chose to do so. The flavour of this word is absolute possession. To say that a Christian is the *doulos* of Christ is to say that he is the absolute possession of Christ, that he claims no rights of his own, that he is ready for Jesus Christ to do with him as he wills.

ii. There are the words *leitourgos* (noun) and *leitourgein* (verb), from which the English word *liturgy* comes.

These words have a great history. In Greece a *leitourgia*, a *liturgy*, was originally a great service which a man rendered the state because he loved his country. There were four of these great services. There was *chorēgia*, which was the undertaking of the expenses of the training of a chorus for one of the great Greek dramatic performances. There was *gumnasarchia*, which was the paying of the expenses of the training of a team for the Olympic games. There was *architheōria*, which was the paying of the expenses of an embassy sent out by the state. There was *triērarchia*, which was the undertaking of the expense of fitting out and maintaining a trireme or warship in the service of the state. So these words have the background of a great love for the state, expressed in service freely given. They went on to mean the giving of any kind of public service, not only freely, but on compulsion. They went on to mean the rendering of any service, and in later Greek could be used of flute-players, dancing-girls, musicians, workmen and even of a prostitute serving a client. But in NT times these words had acquired one almost technical sense—the service that a priest or other servant rendered in the temples of the gods. They are the words of priestly service.

In the NT they are used of the service rendered by the collection taken for the poor Christians at Jerusalem (Romans 15.27; 2 Corinthians 9.12). They are used of the service that magistrates render to the state and to God (Romans 13.6). They are used of Paul's work for the Gentiles (Romans 15.16). They are used of religious service (Hebrews 8.2,6). There are two implications here in the history of these words. The one is that any service given to men or God should be the outcome of love and loyalty, like that of the ancient Greeks who gave to their state, and that any service is a priestly service. Not only as a priest in a temple, but as a servant of the state or of his fellowmen just as much, a man is the priest of God.

iii. There is the verb *latreuein*. In contrast with the situation of the *doulos*, *latreuein* began by always describing service for pay or for hire. That meant that it does not describe service like that of the slave, given by compulsion, but service freely and voluntarily chosen and given. The third step that this word took was that it began to mean the service of the gods or of God, and in the Greek OT it never means anything else than that. But it has this difference from *leitourgein*. *Leitourgein* is the technical word for the service of the priest; *latreuein* is the word for the service of any Christian, layman or priest (e.g. Romans 9.4; Hebrews 12.28; Romans 15.16; Philippians 2.17). *Latreuein* looks on the layman as the servant of God just as much as the priest.

iv. There is the word *therapeuein*. This word is used of the service of Moses (Hebrews 3.5). It can be used in Greek for the service of the gods, but it is commonly used for the service of a doctor. It is a word of very personal, cherishing service.

v. There is the word *diakonos* (2 Corinthians 3.6; Colossians 1.23). Not always, but very often, this word speaks rather of the service of a work than of a person.

vi, There is *oiketēs*. *Oikos* is a house, and this word implies rather domestic service (Romans 14.4; 1 Peter 2.18).

vii. There is the unusual word *hupēretēs*. Paul uses this of himself in 1 Corinthians 4.1, and it is the word which is used of Mark in Acts 13.5. Originally it meant the rower in the lower bank of rowers in one of the great galleys, and indicates rather subordinate service.

The wealth of the NT's service vocabulary is plain to see.

SOBER, SOBRIETY: *sōphrōn, sōphronein, sōphrosunē*. *Sōphrosunē* (the noun), *sōphronein* (the verb), and *sōphrōn* (the adjective), are among the great Greek ethical words, long before they were used in the NT.

Sōphrosunē occurs twice in the NT, in 1 Timothy 2.9 and 1 Timothy 2.15. The AV translates it *sobriety* or *soberness*. The RSV has *sensibly* and *modestly*. The NEB has *soberly* and *with a sober mind*. The verb *sōphronein* is the word used of the Gerasene demoniac being *in his right mind*, and it is also used as the opposite of madness in 2 Corinthians 5.13. In 1 Peter 4.7 the AV translates it *to be sober*; the RSV, *to be sane*; the NEB, *to live an ordered life*. In Titus 2.6 the AV translates it *to be sober-minded*; the RSV, *to control themselves*; the NEB, *to be temperate*. *Sōphrōn* occurs four times. In all the cases the NEB has *temperate*. In Titus 2.5 the AV has *discreet*, and the RSV, *sensible*. In 1 Timothy 3.2 the AV has *sober*, and the RSV, *sensible*. In Titus 1.8 the AV has *sober*, and the RSV, *master of himself*. In Titus 2.2 the AV has *temperate*, and the RSV, *sensible*.

None of these translations really does justice to these words. The Greeks themselves derived them from two words which mean *to keep the mind safe*. Plato defined *sōphrosunē* as the ability to control pleasures and desires *(Republic* 430 E). Aristotle defined it as the attitude by which men have to the pleasures of the body the attitude the law commands *(Rhetoric* 1.9.9). It is an attitude in which men remove wrong and excessive desires, and use necessary desires when and how they should be used. Euripides called *sōphrosunē* the fairest gift of God. The Greeks defined it as the mean, the happy medium, between the excess of debauchery *(asōtia)* and the defect of stinginess and meanness *(pheidōlia)*. R. C. Trench defines *sōphrosunē* as the state of an entire command over the passions and desires, so that they receive no further allowance than that which the law and right reason admit and approve.

Aristotle *(Nicomachean Ethics* 3.15) defines the man who is *sōphrōn* as the man who desires the things he ought to desire, and in the way and at the times he ought to desire them.

It would be right to say that these words describe the man who is a master of the art of living.

SOUND, TO BE: *hugiainein*. *Hugiainein* literally means *to be in good health*, and is so used in 3 John 2. But the main use of the word is in the Pastoral Epistles where it is translated *sound* consistently by the AV and the RSV. In 1 Timothy 1.10; 2 Timothy 4.3; Titus 2.1 there is the phrase *sound* doctrine. In each of these cases the NEB has *wholesome*. In 2 Timothy 1.13 we have *sound* words in all three translations. In 1 Timothy 6.13 we have *sound* words in the RSV and *wholesome* in the AV and NEB. In Titus 1.9 the AV has *true* doctrine. In Titus 1.13 and 2.2 we have the phrase *sound* in faith. In Titus 1.13 the NEB speaks of *sane* belief.

So the changes are rung on *sound, wholesome, true, sane*. These words describe teaching and faith which are at one and the same time healthy and health-giving.

STRANGER and PILGRIM: *paroikos, parepidēmos*. These words occur either together or separately in Hebrews 11.13; 1 Peter 1.1; 1.17; 2.11 to describe the Christian in his relationship to this world. *Parepidēmos* means a stranger living in a strange place, away from home. *Paroikos* means a resident alien. *Metoikos* is the more usual word. It means a person living in a country of which he is not a citizen, and of which he has no intention of becoming a citizen.

They describe the Christian as a person who is living on earth, but whose true home is in heaven.

TEACH: *katēchein*. *Katēchein* is an important word because it came to be the standard word for Christian teaching. *Catechumen* is the technical word for a person under Christian instruction, and it is from this verb *katēchein* that *catechumen* comes. It is translated *instruct* in Romans 2.18, and *teach* in 1 Corinthians 14.19 and Galatians 6.6.

It literally means *to sound through*. It implies oral instruction and it almost means *to din into someone's ears*.

TEMPERANCE, TEMPERATE: *egkrateia, egkratēs*. It is better, as the modern translations do, to translate these words *self-control*, and *self-controlled*. *Egkrateia* occurs in Galatians 5.23 and 2 Peter 1.6, and *egkratēs* in Titus 1.8. The verb *egkrateuomai* occurs in 1 Corinthians 7.9 in connection with sexual self-control, and in 1 Corinthians 9.25 in connection with the self-discipline of the athlete. The root of the words is *kratein*, which means to *hold, grip, control*. And they describe the man who has control of himself. Plato describes *egkrateia* as the mastery of pleasures and desires (*Republic* 430 E). Aristotle (*Virtues and Vices* 5.1) says that *egkrateia* has 'the ability to restrain desire by reason, when it is set on base enjoyments and pleasures, and to be resolute and ever in readiness to endure natural want and pain.' They are the words which describe a man who is master of himself.

TEMPT, TEMPTATION: *peirazein, peirasmos*. A certain care is needed in the translation of these words. The normal AV translation of them is *tempt* and *temptation* (1 Corinthians 7.5; 10.13; Galatians 6.1; 1 Thessalonians 3.5; Hebrews 2.18; 3.9; 4.15; 11.37; James 1.13,14; 1 Corinthians 10.13; 1 Timothy 6.9; Hebrews 3.8; James 1.2,12; 1 Peter 1.6; 2 Peter 2.9; Revelation 3.10). On certain occasions the AV translates *peirazein to try* (Hebrews 11.17; Revelation 2.2; 2.10; 3.10). In very many cases the better modern translation is *test* or *trial*. Genesis 22.1 pinpoints the AV usage. There the AV has: 'God did *tempt* Abraham.' It is obviously impossible to think of God trying to seduce Abraham into sin, and the modern translation is not *tempt*, but *test*; and this is the case in many of the instances of these words.

TEST, TRY: *dokimazein, dokimē, dokimos, dokimios.* There is a group of words in the NT all of which have got to do with testing and trying, proving and approving. The AV uses so many translations of them that it is worthwhile looking at them and their background.

Dokimazein means *to assay, to put to the test, to prove by testing,* and therefore *to approve as genuine and tested.* The main AV translation is *to prove* (Romans 12.2; 2 Corinthians 8.8; 8.22; 13.5; Galatians 6.4; Ephesians 5.10; 1 Thessalonians 5.21; 1 Timothy 3.10; Hebrews 3.9). Closely connected with this is the translation *to try* (1 Corinthians 3.13; 1 Thessalonians 2.4; 1 Peter 1.7; 1 John 4.1). Other AV translations are *to allow* (Romans 14.22; 1 Thessalonians 2.4), *to approve* (Romans 2.18; 1 Corinthians 16.3; Philippians 1.10). The modern translations have *to prove, to test, to examine, to accredit, to approve.* It is the classical background which is interesting and significant. *Dokimazein* in secular Greek can mean to prove a candidate fit for service after scrutiny, and to prove a person to be suitable for entry to a society.

Dokimē is a *test* or *ordeal.* It is then the quality which emerges after the test and the ordeal. It is that which has been tested. It is the word which is used in Romans 5.4 and which the AV translates *experience.* The RSV better translates *character,* and the NEB in terms of *standing the test.* In 2 Corinthians 9.13 the AV has *experiment,* which is Elizabethan English for *test* (RSV) or *proof* (NEB). In 2 Corinthians 2.9 and 13.2 the translation is *proof.* In Philippians 2.22, when Paul is speaking of Epaphroditus, the AV has: 'You know the *proof* of him.' The RSV has *his worth* and the NEB *his record.* In 2 Corinthians 8.2 the AV translation is *trial,* which is rather *test.* The basic idea is that the word means, first, a test, and, second, that which emerges triumphantly from the test.

Dokimos is nearly always translated *approved* by the AV (Romans 14.18; 16.10; 1 Corinthians 11.19; 2 Corinthians 10.18; 13.7; 2 Timothy 2.15). The modern translations have *genuine, accepted, sound, vindicated, well proved, passed the test.* The most illuminating thing about the word is that in regard to money it is the word for *genuine* as opposed to *counterfeit*. It therefore can well be translated *sterling*.

Dokimion is either *a means* of *testing, a touchstone*, or else something which has emerged triumphantly from such a test, and is therefore *genuine*. It occurs in 1 Peter 1.7 where the meaning is *genuineness*, and in James 1.3 where the meaning is *testing*. It can either be the touchstone, or that which has been proved by the touchstone to be without alloy.

THORN: *skolops*. This is the word which is used for Paul's *thorn* in the flesh (2 Corinthians 12.7). The word is used in the Greek OT in Numbers 33.55—'pricks in your eyes.' The doubt about this word is whether *thorn* is a strong enough translation. The word originally meant a *stake*, as used in a palisade. It was also used for the stake on which a man was impaled, and heathen writers sometimes use it of the cross of Jesus. It may be that the pricking of a thorn is too weak a picture and it should rather be the twisting of a stake.

TIME, TIMES AND HALF A TIME. There is in the Revelation a group of phrases which all mean the same period of time. There is the phrase *a time, times and half a time* (Revelation 12.14). The parallel phrases are *forty-two months* (Revelation 11.2; 12.6; 13.5), and *one thousand two hundred and sixty days* (Revelation 11.3). All stand for three and a half years. Three and a half years was in fact the length of time that the Temple in Jerusalem was occupied and desecrated by Antiochus Epiphanes in the second century B.C. And in the apocalyptic literature this became the standard symbolic figure for a period, but a limited period, of deep distress.

TRIUMPH: *thriambeuein*. The rather unusual word *thriambeuein* is used in 2 Corinthians 2.14 and Colossians 2.15. When a Roman general had won a really notable campaign he was given a triumph. He was allowed to lead his army through the streets of Rome with his trophies and captives on show. The word is used of the triumph of Jesus.

TROUBLE: *anastatoun*. The word is used in Galatians 5.12. As the modern translations show, it means *to upset* or *to unsettle*. It is the word used in Acts 17.6 for *turning the world upside down*. In a papyrus letter, written by a small boy, the boy tells us that his mother said: 'Take him away! He upsets me!' (*anastatoun*). It is the word used for a disruptive influence.

UNBELIEF, UNBELIEVING: *apistia, apistos, apistein, apeitheia, apeithēs, apeithein*.

There are two sets of words which the AV at least sometimes translates in terms of *unbelief*.

The words *unbelief* and *unbelieving* have a religious flavour, but it is well to begin by noting that they have a secular background. Theophrastus has a character study on *Apistia*, which A. D. Knox translates *Distrustfulness*. There *apistia* is defined as 'a presumption of dishonesty against all mankind.' To take but one instance from Theophrastus, the distrustful man sends one servant to the market, and then sends another after him to check that the first servant actually paid for the goods purchased. *Apistia* was to the Greek the quality of the man who believed no one about anything.

The second thing to note is that the adjective *pistos*, which is the positive word of which these words are the negatives, has two meanings. First, as for instance in 1 Corinthians 4.2; 2 Timothy 2.2; Hebrews 3.5, *pistos* means *trustworthy, reliable*. In inscriptions it became almost a technical adjective of praise for a good official—as we say in English 'our trusty servant'. Second, as for instance in Galatians 3.9 (of Abraham) it means *believing, trusting, full of faith*. So much so is this the case that *hoi pistoi* (the plural) comes to mean practically Christians, the *believers* (2 Corinthians 6.15; 1 Timothy 4.10; Titus 1.6).

These two different meanings of *pistos* explain a good many of the differences in translation.

Apistein, the verb, occurs in Romans 3.3 and 2 Timothy 2.13. In both cases the AV translates it *not believe*, whereas the RSV and the NEB translate it *to be unfaithful* and *to be faithless*. It is the second translation which is correct, for the verb *apistein* can be used of a soldier who defects from his loyalty.

The AV always translates the noun *apistia* by *unbelief* (Romans 3.3; 4.20; 11.20; 11.23; 1 Timothy 1.13; Hebrews 3.12; 3.19). The RSV has *faithlessness* in Romans 3.3 and *distrust* in Romans 4.20. The NEB has *faithless* in Romans 11.23 and in Hebrews 3.12, where it uses the word *deserter* in close association. *Apistia* thus also has the two directions. It can describe either *unbelief* or *faithlessness*.

The negative adjective *apistos* is regularly translated *unbelieving* by the AV and the RSV (1 Corinthians 6.6; 7.14,15; 14.23; 2 Corinthians 6.14; Titus 1.15). The word practically means a *non-Christian*. So much so is this the case that in 1 Corinthians 7.14,15 the NEB translates it *heathen*.

The second group of words are all connected with the verb *peithesthai* which means *to obey* and which in the negative means to *disobey*. The translations vary between *disobedience* and *unbelief*.

The AV translates the noun *apeitheia* by *disobedience* in Ephesians 2.2; 5.6; in Colossians 3.6 by *disobedience*, and in Romans 11.30,32; in Hebrews 4.6,11 by *unbelief*. The RSV consistently translates by *disobedience*.

In the Ephesians passages the NEB has *rebel*, and in the Hebrews passages *unbelief*.

There is the same variation in the translation of the verb *apeithein*. The AV with one exception (Romans 10.21: *disobedient*) translates *apeithein* by *not believe* (Romans 11.30,31; 15.31; Hebrews 3.18; 11.31). The RSV regularly translates in terms of *disobedience*, except in Romans 15.31 where it has *unbelievers*. The RSV translates in terms of *disobedience*, except in the two Hebrews passages where it has *unbelief*.

It can be seen that none of the translations is consistent. What is to be said is that the *apistia* group describes a lack of faith which comes from lack of trust, or a character which is not trustworthy, while the *apeitheia* group describes a lack of faith which issues in disobedience.

UNCLEANNESS, UNCLEAN: *akatharsia, akathartos*. These words have three areas of meaning.

i. They can describe physical dirt. For instance, in the papyri a seller who is handing over a house guarantees to hand it over free of all *akatharsia*, free of all dirt, and clean.

ii. They can describe ritual impurity. They describe that which because it is ritually unclean cannot enter the temple of God.

iii. They end by describing that which is morally unclean and morally repulsive.

The AV never varies from the translation *uncleanness*. The RSV retains *uncleanness* in Ephesians 4.19 and in 1 Thessalonians 2.3; 4.7. Elsewhere its translation is regularly *impurity* (Romans 1.24; 6.19; 2 Corinthians 12.21; Galatians 5.19; Ephesians 5.3; Colossians 3.5). The NEB uses a wide variety of translations—*vileness* (Romans 1.24); *impurity* (Romans 6.19; Galatians 5.19; 1 Thessalonians 4.7); *unclean lives* (2 Corinthians 12.21); *foul desires* (Ephesians 4.19); *indecency* (Ephesians 5.3; Colossians 3.5); *base motives* (1 Thessalonians 2.3).

The corresponding adjective is *akathartos*. It is commonest in the Gospels in the phrase 'an unclean spirit'. In the letters it occurs in 1 Corinthians 7.14; 2 Corinthians 6.17; Ephesians 5.5. The AV translates it *unclean* in all cases. The RSV has *impure* in Ephesians 5.5, and *unclean* in the other cases. The NEB has *unclean* in 2 Corinthians 6.17, and *given to indecency* in Ephesians 5.5. The NEB has an interesting translation in 1 Corinthians 7.14. The AV is: 'The unbelieving husband is consecrated through his wife, and the unbelieving wife is consecrated through her husband. Otherwise your children would be unclean, but as it is they are holy.' The NEB rightly has: 'The heathen husband now belongs to God through his Christian wife, and the heathen wife through her Christian husband. Otherwise your children would not belong to God, whereas in fact they do.' Here the translation is basically contrasting *hagios* and *akathartos* in their ritual sense. That which is *hagios* is *holy* and is consecrated and dedicated to God; that which is *akathartos* is *unclean* and barred from the presence of God.

UNGODLY, UNGODLINESS, UNRIGHTEOUS, UNRIGHTEOUSNESS: *asebēs, asebeia, adikos, adikia*. The two words *asebeia* and *adikia* occur together in Romans 1.18, where the AV translates *ungodliness* and *unrighteousness*. In secular classical Greek the two words were clearly distinguished. *Asebeia* was sin against God; *adikia* was sin against men. *Asebeia* was therefore *impiety*; *adikia* was *injustice*. In the NT the distinction often, though not always, still holds true.

Asebeia occurs in Romans 1.18; 11.26; 2 Timothy 2.16; Titus 2.12; Jude 15, 18. All the translations use the idea of *ungodliness* or *godlessness*. The only departures from that are in the RSV in Titus 2.12 where the translation is *irreligion*, and in the NEB in Romans 11.26 where the translation is *wickedness*.

The adjective *asebēs* occurs in Romans 4.5; 5.6; 1 Timothy 1.9; 1 Peter 4.18; 2 Peter 2.5; 3.7; Jude 4, 15. The AV consistently translates it *ungodly*. The RSV has *ungodly* except in 1 Peter 4.18, where it has *impious*. The NEB has many translations—*guilty* (Romans 4.5); *wicked* (Romans 5.6); *impious* (1 Timothy 1.9; 1 Peter 4.18); *godless* (2 Peter 2.5; 3.7; Jude 15); *enemies of religion* (Jude 4).

In the case of *asebēs* and *asebeia* there is no doubt that the sin is against God.

In the case of *adikos*, which, as we have noted, was connected with sin against man, the AV has two translations—*unjust* (1 Corinthians 6.1; 1 Peter 3.18; 2 Peter 2.9) and *unrighteous* (Romans 3.5; 1 Corinthians 6.9; Hebrews 6.10). The modern translations also vary between *unjust* and *unrighteous*. The only unusual usage is in the NEB in 1 Corinthians 6.1 where *adikos*, as describing the heathen law-courts, is translated *pagan*.

In the case of the noun *adikia* the AV has two main translations—*iniquity* (1 Corinthians 13.6; 2 Timothy 2.19; James 3.6), and *unrighteousness* (e.g. Romans 1.18,29; 2.8; 3.5; 6.13; 9.14; 2 Thessalonians 2.10,12; Hebrews 8.12; 2 Peter 2.13,15; 1 John 1.9; 5.17). The modern translations use other words—*wickedness* (NEB, 2 Timothy 2.19; James 3.6: RSV, Romans 1.18; 1.29; 2.8; 3.5; 6.13); *injustice* (NEB, Romans 1.29; 3.5; NEB and RSV, Romans 9.14); *sinfulness* (NEB, 2 Thessalonians 2.10,12); *wrong doing* or *doing wrong* (RSV, 2 Peter 2.13,15; 1 John 5.17; NEB, Romans 6.13; 2 Peter 2.15).

It cannot be said that in the NT *adikia* and *adikos* are consistently used for sins against men.

UNLEARNED: *amathēs, apaideutos, idiōtēs*. In the letters the NT uses three words which the AV translates *unlearned*.

i. There is the word *amathēs* (2 Peter 3.16). Both the RSV and the NEB translate it *ignorant*. It is connected with the word *manthanein*, which means *to learn*. It describes the person who has never learned. Of animals it can mean *untrainable*, and of people *inhuman*. It is used of the people who in their ignorance twist scripture to suit themselves, and the word has a certain derogatory flavour about it.

ii. There is the word *apaideutos* (2 Timothy 2.23), which the RSV translates *senseless*, and the NEB *ignorant*. Its meaning is uneducated, sometimes with an overtone of boorish rudeness.

iii. There is the word *idiōtēs* (1 Corinthians 14.16,23,24). The RSV translates it *outsider*, and the NEB *the plain man* and the *uninstructed person*. Originally an *idiōtēs* was a private person as opposed to someone holding an official position. It then came to mean a person with no special skill and no professional training. It then came to mean the *common* or *average* man, which is the sense in which Paul uses it. It still later came to mean an ignorant person. Paul uses it in the passage when he is thinking of the effects of a service where people were speaking with tongues on the average man who chanced to come in.

VAIN, VANITY, IN VAIN: *mataios, mataiotēs, eikē, kenos. Mataios, eikē* and *kenos* are all used very nearly interchangeably for *vain* and *in vain*. This comes out very clearly in the AV in 1 Corinthians 15. 1 Corinthians 15.7 reads :'If Christ be not raised your faith is *vain*,' and the word is *mataios*. 1 Corinthians 15.2 reads: 'Unless you believed *in vain*,' and the word is *eikē*. 1 Corinthians 15.10 reads: 'His grace toward me was not *in vain*,' and the word is *kenos*, as it is also in verses 14 and 58.

But each of the words has its own flavour, and it is worthwhile looking at them.

The adjective *mataios* occurs in 1 Corinthians 3.20; 15.17; Titus 3.9; James 1.26; 1 Peter 1.18. The AV regularly translates it *vain*. With the one exception of James 1.26, where it retains *vain*, the RSV consistently translates it *futile*. The NEB is more varied. In 1 Corinthians 3.20 and James 1.26 it has *futile*; in 1 Corinthians 15.7, *nothing in it*; in Titus 3.9, *pointless*; in 1 Peter 1.18, *empty folly*.

The essence of the word is futility, purposelessness, transitoriness and therefore frustration. It is the word which describes the pointless life of the Christless world.

The AV translation of the noun *mataiotēs* is much more likely to mislead, although it was perfectly correct in 1611. The AV always translates it *vanity*, and in modern language *vanity* means *self-approval* and *conceit*. But the original meaning of *vanity* was *futility, emptiness, purposelessness.* In Romans 8.20 the AV has: 'The creature was made subject to vanity.' The RSV has: 'The creation was subjected to futility.' The NEB has it that the created universe was 'made the victim of frustration.' In Ephesians 4.17 the AV has it that the Gentiles walk 'in the vanity of their mind.' The RSV has 'in the futility of their minds.' The NEB has 'with their good-for-nothing notions.' In 2 Peter 2.18 the AV has 'great swelling words of vanity.' The RSV has 'loud boasts of folly.' The NEB has 'big empty words.' In these three passages the word *vanity* is liable to be misunderstood.

The word *eikē* means *without cause, to no purpose, in vain.* In *mataios* the basic idea was futility; here in *eikē* the basic idea is random purposelessness. It occurs in Romans 13.4; 1 Corinthians 15.2; Galatians 3.4; 4.11; Colossians 2.18. The AV always has *in vain.* The RSV retains *in vain* except in Colossians 2.18, where it has *without reason.* The NEB is more varied. In Romans 13.4 it has *for nothing,* i.e. *to no purpose;* in 1 Corinthians 15.2 and Galatians 3.4, *in vain;* in Galatians 4.11, *labour lost;* and in Colossians 2.18, *futile.*

Kenos is the commonest of the words. It means *empty* in every sense of the word. It can mean literally *empty;* it can describe *empty* words, an *empty-headed* person, a course of action which has been *empty* of result. It occurs in 1 Corinthians 15.10,14,58; 2 Corinthians 6.1; Galatians 2.2; Ephesians 5.6; Philippians 2.16; Colossians 2.8; 1 Thessalonians 2.1; 3.5; James 2.20. The AV always has *in vain.* The RSV keeps *in vain* except in Ephesians 5.6 and Colossians 2.8 where it has *empty,* and in James 2.20 where it has *foolish.* The NEB uses more translations. It keeps *in vain* in 1 Corinthians 15.10; Galatians 2.2; Philippians 2.16. This word is specially used of work and effort which come to nothing, and the NEB rings the changes on this idea—*null and void* (1 Corinthians 15.14); *labour lost* (1 Corinthians 15.58; 1 Thessalonians 3.5); *fruitless* (1 Thessalonians 2.1); of words or persons, *shallow* (Ephesians 5.6); *hollow* (Colossians 2.8); *quibbler* (James 2.20).

Mataios has futility in it, *eikē* has random purposelessness, *kenos* has emptiness.

VISIT, VISITATION: *episkeptesthai, episkopē.* The translation of these words by the English word *visit* is now an archaism. *Episkeptesthai* is to come to look at a person either for that person's weal or woe. James 1.27 speaks of true religion being *to visit* the fatherless and widows. The RSV keeps this; but the word means far more than *to visit.* The NEB rightly has *to go to the help of.*

1 Peter 2.12 speaks of the day of *episkopē,* the day of *visitation.* Again, there is more to it than that. The NEB rightly has, 'on the day when he comes to hold assize.' The idea of God visiting his people in

love or in wrath is a common OT idea (e.g. Psalm 106.4; Numbers 14.18).

WALK: *peripatein*. One of the most characteristic usages of the Greek NT is the use of the word *peripatein, to walk,* to describe a man's life and conduct. So in the NT we hear of walking in newness of life (Romans 6.4); walking after, in, or according to the flesh (Romans 8.4; 2 Corinthians 10.2,3); walking honestly (Romans 13.13); walking not charitably (Romans 14.15); walking in craftiness (2 Corinthians 4.2); walking by faith (2 Corinthians 5.7); walking in the Spirit (Galatians 5.16); walking in love (Ephesians 5.2); walking in wisdom (Colossians 4.5); walking circumspectly (Ephesians 5.15).

There is nowadays an un-English and archaic flavour about this way of speaking and the modern versions have largely abandoned the word *walk* for such expressions as *behave* (NEB, Romans 13.13; Colossians 4.5); *practise* (RSV and NEB, 2 Corinthians 4.2); *conduct oneself* (RSV, Romans 13.13; NEB, Ephesians 5.15); *live* (RSV, Ephesians 5.15; NEB, Ephesians 4.17; 5.2); *act* (2 Corinthians 10.2,3).

The one thing that the word *walk* did was to tie up the Christian life with the first title of Christianity, which was the Way (Acts 9.2; 19.9,23; 24.22). The very word *walk* did show that life for the Christian is an active pilgrimage rather than a meditative retiral.

Notes on Passages

I said in the introduction to the first volume of this translation that one of its aims was to enable the person who is not a technical New Testament scholar to read the New Testament without the aid of a commentary. I am well aware that this is not fully possible, but if it is to be even partly possible, expanded translation has sometimes to be used. It has to be used in two kinds of passages.

First, there are times when Paul can write very elliptically, and when what he writes reads almost like notes rather than, as it were, a completed sermon. This is the case, for instance, in Romans 4.16. In the early part of that verse there are no verbs at all. Literally translated it reads:

> 'Therefore in consequence of faith, in order that according to grace, to the being sure of the promise.'

This is the kind of sermon note that a preacher might make in preparation, and to make sense it has to be expanded:

> 'This is why the whole matter is based on faith. It was so based that it might move in the realms of grace. This had to be so in order to confirm the promise.'

Second, there are times when the point being made depends on some ancient Jewish or Roman or Greek custom. The notes in a commentary would make this clear enough. But I think that sometimes the passage should be clarified by, so to speak, incorporating the explanation into the text.

I am well aware that all this becomes interpretation rather than translation, but I think that it has to be done to aid the non-technical reader who possesses only the New Testament, and who is a stranger to commentaries.

In what follows I have noted the main passages in translating which I have allowed myself to use expansion. In each case I have begun by setting down the passage in its AV version.

Galatians 3.20

'Now a mediator is not a mediator of one, but God is one.'

This is a notoriously difficult passage because of its extreme brevity.

J. B. Lightfoot says in his commentary that there are between two hundred and fifty and three hundred different interpretations of it! The point is the contrast between the law and the promise. In a double sense the law came through a mediator. It came through Moses. And by NT times the Jews so stressed the transcendence of God that they taught that God could not have given the law to Moses directly, but that he gave the law to angels who gave it to Moses. In the case of the law there was more than one person concerned, and to that extent its connection with God is indirect. But in the case of the promise it was made direct. There is no mediator. There is only one person involved and that person is God. The translation has therefore to be expanded to become clear:

'This is to say that the validity of the law depends on two parties, one to give it, and one to keep it, and on a mediator to bring it from one to the other. But a promise depends on only one person, the person who makes it, and when there is only one person involved there is no necessity for a mediator. And in this case God is the one person, and on him alone the promise depends.'

Galatians 5.9

'A little leaven leaveneth the whole lump.'

To the reader with a biblical background this proverb is quite clear. Leaven was fermented dough kept over from the baking. The Jews identified fermentation with putrefaction. And therefore leaven stood for an evil and defiling influence. It is better to make the meaning unmistakably clear:

'Once even the slightest infection gets into a society, it spreads until the whole society becomes infected.'

1 Corinthians 4.9

'For I think that God hath set forth us the apostles last, as it were appointed to death; for we are made a spectacle unto the world, and to angels and to men.'

The picture behind this is a Roman general's triumph. If a general won a spectacular and important campaign, he was granted a triumph. He was allowed to lead his victorious armies through the streets of Rome, with all the spoils he had won carried in front of him. At the end of the procession there came a group of selected captives. They were led through the streets to be jeered at, and for them the end of the journey was the arena, where they would be butchered as gladiators or thrown to the lions. Paul likens the apostles with all their sufferings and with the martyrdom which threatened them to that little group of doomed captives bringing up the rear of the general's procession. We have incorporated the picture into the translation:

'For I think that God has brought us apostles on to the scene like the little company of captives who bring up the rear of a victorious general's pageant of triumph and who are doomed to die in the arena. We have become a public spectacle to the world, both to angels and to men.'

1 Corinthians 5.6-8

'Your glorying is not good. Know ye not that a little leaven leaveneth the whole lump? Purge out therefore the old leaven, that ye may be a new lump, as ye are unleavened. For even Christ our passover is sacrificed for us: therefore let us keep the feast not with old leaven, neither with the leaven of malice and wickedness; but with the unleavened bread of sincerity and truth.'

As in Galatians 5.9 the leaven is here again the symbol for an evil influence and infection. But the picture here comes from Jewish Passover customs. First of all, Christ is likened to the Passover lamb. The blood of the Passover lamb kept the houses of the Israelites safe, when the angel of death walked abroad in Egypt (Exodus 12.21-24). So the sacrifice of Christ rescues and saves the Christian. But there is another Jewish Passover custom involved. Before the Passover Feast every particle of leaven had to be sought out in every house and had to be completely destroyed. There was a ceremonial search for leaven, and by midday not the smallest scrap of leaven must remain in the house. So Paul says that, just as the leaven was purged out of the house before the Passover, every evil influence and infection must be cleansed out of the life of the Christians, and from now on they must live a life from which every evil influence has been banished. So the Jewish background picture has been integrated into the translation:

'Your proud pretensions have an ugly look about them. Are you not aware that an evil influence can from the smallest beginnings spread like an infection through a whole community? Get rid of the last remnants of the tainted life that once you lived, so that not a suggestion of evil infection may be left. That is the way you ought to be in any event, for the last evil taint ought to have been eradicated from your life, just as before the Passover sacrifice the last particle of leaven is removed from every house. For Christ is for us the Passover lamb, sacrificed for our deliverance. Let us then live life as if it were a continual festival, with not a taint of evil or wickedness left, but in the purity of sincerity and truth.'

1 Corinthians 8.10

'For if any man see thee which hast knowledge sit at meat in the idol's temple, shall not the conscience of him which is weak be emboldened to eat those things which are offered to idols?'

As was explained in the note at the head of 1 Corinthians 8, much of the social life of the ancient world centred in the heathen temples. Normally only a very small token part of a sacrificial animal was burned on the altar. Part of the meat went to the priests as their perquisite, and part went to the worshipper. With his share the worshipper frequently gave a party in the temple precincts, and the question at issue was whether or not a Christian could attend such a party. This background custom has been integrated into the translation:

'It is in the heathen temples that people hold their social occasions, and the meat for the meal is their share of the meat that was offered to the idol. Well then, if someone whose conscience is weak and over-sensitive sees you with your superior knowledge sitting as a guest at a party in the shrine of a heathen idol, will he not be encouraged by your action to eat meat which has formed part of a sacrifice offered to an idol?'

1 Corinthians 9.9

'For it is written in the law of Moses, Thou shalt not muzzle the mouth of the ox that treadeth out the corn. Doth God care for oxen?'

The point of the passage is that the workman always gets a share of that which he produces. I have therefore added to make the point clear:

'That is, the ox must be free to eat what it is threshing.'

1 Corinthians 10.28,29

'But if any man say unto you, This is offered in sacrifice unto idols, eat not for his sake that shewed it, and for conscience sake: for the earth is the Lord's and the fullness thereof: conscience, I say, not thine own, but of the other: for why is my liberty judged of another man's conscience?'

The contrast in this passage is between the man whose conscience is strong and the man whose conscience is over-sensitive and weak. Here Paul has written very summarily, and I have expanded it to bring out the meaning:

'But if anyone present says to you in warning: "This meat was part of a sacrifice offered to an idol," then don't eat it. Don't eat it for the sake of the man who warned you and for the sake of his conscience. I am not talking about your conscience. (Your conscience is clear.) It is the other man's conscience I am talking about. (His conscience is over-sensitive.) "But," you say, "why should my liberty have to submit to the judgment of another man's conscience?"'

1 Corinthians 11.29

'For he that eateth and drinketh unworthily, eateth and drinketh damnation to himself, not discerning the Lord's body.'

Two points arise here. The word translated *damnation* is simply *krima*, which means *judgment*, and *damnation* is far too strong a translation.

The more important point is that in the best Greek text there is no word for *Lord's*. *Kuriou, Lord's*, is omitted by the following manuscripts —Chester Beatty, Sinaiticus, Alexandrinus, Vaticanus and Ephraemi Rescriptus. Almost, if not quite, certainly it is not part of the text.

The ordinary interpretation of the verse is that the sin of the man in question consists in his failure to see that the elements of bread and wine are in fact the body and blood of the Lord. This must be rethought. It must be rethought in the light of two things. First, it must be rethought in light of the fact that *Lord's* is not part of the original text. Second, it must be rethought in light of the whole context of the passage. Paul's account of the institution of the Lord's Supper arises out of the situation of disunity in the church at Corinth. 1 Corinthians 11.17-22, the immediately preceding verses, describes the situation in which the Corinthian congregation is split into cliques and sects and parties and class divisions. Paul's account of the sacrament arises out of a situation in which there was disunity, a situation which was proving fatal for the church (1 Corinthians 11.30). When, therefore, Paul speaks of not discerning the body, he is speaking of the tragic fact that even at the Lord's Table the Corinthian congregation did not realize that the congregation was part of the body of Christ and therefore an indivisible unity, a fact which he goes on to stress still more in 1 Corinthians 12. I therefore believe that the translation should be:

'For a man's eating and drinking become a judgment on himself, if in eating and drinking he does not realize that the church is the body of Christ, and therefore a unity.'

It seems to me that both text and context demand this translation.

2 Corinthians 2.14-16

'Now thanks be unto God, which always causeth us to triumph in Christ, and maketh manifest the savour of his knowledge by us in every place, for we are unto God a sweet savour of Christ, in them that are saved and them that perish. To the one we are the savour of death unto death; and to the other the savour of life unto life.'

It may not unfairly be said that this is a very un-English passage. Its background, as in 1 Corinthians 4.9, is a general's triumph. But this time the picture is the picture of the apostles sharing the triumph of Christ, walking in his triumphal procession. During the triumphal procession incense was burned, producing a perfume, a sweet savour. And, of course, to the victors in the procession the incense was a beautiful perfume, which they were glad and happy to savour. But to the vanquished the smell of the incense was the smell of death. So the apostles march with Christ in his victory march, and the message they bring is a sweet perfume to those who accept Christ as Lord, but the stench of death to those who do not. With this picture integrated into it the translation runs:

'Thanks be to God, for he always gives us a place as sharers in the victory procession of Christ, and, just as at such an earthly triumph, the perfume of incense fills the streets, so God through us has displayed in every place the fragrance of the knowledge of himself. You might call us in our work for God the means whereby the fragrance of Christ comes to those who are on the way to salvation and to those who are on the road to ruin. For those who are on the way to ruin it is a deadly and poisonous stench; for those who are on the way to salvation it is a living and life-giving perfume.'

Romans 7.24,25

'O wretched man that I am! Who shall deliver me from the body of this death? I thank God through Jesus Christ our Lord. So then with my mind I serve the law of God; but with the flesh the law of sin.'

In the literal translation of the AV the sentence: 'I thank God through Jesus Christ' comes in very awkwardly, and I have expanded it into:

'I am a wretched creature. Who will rescue me from the body which turns life into death? God alone can through Jesus Christ our Lord! Thanks be to him! So then, I am in a situation in which with the spiritual part of my nature I serve God's law, and with the lower part of my nature I serve sin's law.'

Romans 8.2,3

'For the law of the Spirit of life in Christ Jesus hath made me free from the law of sin and death. For what the law could not do, in that it was weak through the flesh, God sending his own Son in the likeness of sinful flesh, and for sin, condemned sin in the flesh.'

In this passage the AV is obscure because the Greek is awkward. For clarity's sake I have expanded:

'For, when through union with Christ Jesus I came under the law of the life-giving Spirit, I was emancipated from the law of death-bringing sin. For what the law was unable to do—that is to say, to effect this emancipation from sin—because human nature rendered it impotent and ineffective, God did. He did it by sending his son with a human nature like our human nature.'

Colossians 2.14

'Blotting out the handwriting of ordinances that was against us, which was contrary to us, and took it out of the way, nailing it to his cross.'

What is said to be blotted out is a *cheirographon*, which is a note of hand, admitting and accepting personal liability, a kind of IOU. The idea is that men by accepting the law with all its rules and regulations had voluntarily put themselves into a position in which they had accepted a liability which they could never pay. This liability Jesus Christ in his grace wipes out on his cross. The note of hand is cancelled, and the liability is gone. I therefore translate:

'He cancelled the bond by which we were self-committed to the decrees of the law, and by which we stood condemned. He completely removed it and nailed it to the cross.'

Colossians 2.20-22

'Wherefore if ye be dead with Christ from the rudiments of the world, why as though living in the world, are ye subject to ordinances (Touch not; taste not; handle not; which are all to perish with the using) after the commandments and doctrines of men?'

'Touch not; taste not; handle not' might well have a claim to be considered one of the most misused texts in the NT, for it has often been used as Christian advice to abstain from certain things. In point of fact it is the reverse. In this passage Paul is pleading with the Colossians not to revert to that kind of life which sees religion in terms of rules and regulations to observe this or that food law. Paul is not urging abstention from anything; he is forbidding a legalistic asceticism. To make this clear I have translated as follows:

'Your death with Christ means that the world's rudimentary teaching has nothing more to do with you. Why then go on living as if your life was dominated by the world? Why pay any more attention to those whose slogans are: "Don't handle this! Don't taste that! Don't touch the next thing!" All these regulations refer to things which are bound to perish in the course of being used. They move in the sphere of human regulations and human teaching.'

Philippians 2.17

'Yes, and if I be offered upon the sacrifice and service of your faith, I joy, and rejoice with you all.'

This AV translation sounds strange in English. Behind Paul's words there is a picture. Often in the ancient world sacrifice was concluded by pouring out a cup of wine as a libation to the gods. Very often a meal finished like that. The poured-out cup of wine was a thank-offering to the gods. It is that of which Paul is thinking, and he is thinking of his life being poured out in sacrificial loyalty to God, just as that cup of wine was. He also thinks of the faith and the loyalty of the Philippians as their sacrifice to God. To make this clear I have integrated the picture into the translation:

'When men make their sacrifices to the gods, they pour out upon them a sacrificial cup of wine. Your faith and your service are a sacrifice to God, and it may be that my life, like that cup of wine, must be poured out to crown and complete your sacrifice. If it must be so, I am glad and I share my joy with you; and in the same way you must be glad and share your joy with me.'

The same picture is to be found in 2 Timothy 4.6.

Hebrews 1.3

'The brightness of his glory and the express image of his person.'

The word for *brightness* is *apaugasma*, which means *effulgence*. It means the light which the sun shines forth. The word for *express image* is *charaktēr*, which means the *impress* that a seal leaves on wax. It is best to amplify the translation a little to make the point of the close connection between the ray and the sun, and the impress and the seal, for it is the indissoluble connection between the Father and the Son which is being stressed.

'This Son is the radiance of his glory, just as the ray is the light of the sun. He is the exact impression of his being, just as the mark is the exact impression of the seal.'

Hebrews 1.8

'Thy throne, O god, is for ever and ever.'

An alternative translation of the Greek is:

'God is thy throne for ever and ever.'

Hebrews 9.5

'And over it the cherubims of glory shadowing the mercy-seat.'

The preceding verse has just spoken of the ark of the covenant. The mercy-seat was the top, the lid of the ark. The ark and the mercy-seat are described in Exodus 25.10-22. This has been brought out in the translation:

> 'Above were the cherubim of the glory of God, with their wings over-arching the mercy-seat, as the lid of the chest was called.'

Hebrews 10.9

'Then said he, Lo, I have come to do thy will. He abolishes the first in order to establish the second.'

The contrast in the context of this passage is between the ancient system of animal sacrifice and the perfect sacrifice of perfect obedience which Jesus brought to God. It is better to bring this out:

> 'Then he said: "Here I am. I have come to do your will." Thus he cancels the first, that is, animal sacrifice, to establish the second, that is, perfect obedience.'

James 1.9

'Let the brother of low degree rejoice that he is exalted.'

This is a very concentrated way of saying:

> 'The brother who is nobody in the eyes of the world must take pride in the way that the hard experiences of life, rightly accepted, raise him to new heights of character.'

James 1.17

'Every good gift and every perfect gift is from above, and cometh down from the Father of lights, with whom is no variableness, neither shadow of turning.'

The Greek phrase which the AV translates 'no variableness, neither shadow of turning' is notoriously difficult. The Greek text itself is not quite certain.

The word translated *variableness* is *parallagē* which does mean *variety, variation, alteration of position*. It was, for instance, used of the sun's apparent change of position. The word translated *shadow* is *aposkiasma*, and of the meaning of this word there is no doubt. The word for *turning* is *tropē*. It does mean *turning* or *change*. It was used of the place on the horizon where the sun sets and vanishes. It was used for the solstices, when the year, as it were, turns. The RSV has: 'no variation or shadow due to change'. The NEB has in the text: 'no variation, no play of passing shadows'. In the margin, as alternative translation, the NEB has: 'no variation, or shadow caused by change.'

It will have been noted that both *parallagē* and *tropē* can be astronomical terms. I have translated it: 'In him there is no change, nor does he turn away from us and leave us in the shadows.' What the exact picture is is hard to say. It might be possible that in the mind of James there was the thought or the memory of an eclipse, and he may be saying that God is not like the heavenly bodies with their variation, nor even like the sun which can be eclipsed, and leave the world in the shadow.

James 2.18

'Yea, a man may say, Thou hast faith and I have works. Shew me thy faith without thy works, and I will shew thee my faith by my works.'

This verse comes in very awkwardly, and it is not clear what it means. I have expanded it to fit the context:

'But someone will say: "You get different kinds of people. One man may well claim to be a man of faith, while another man may equally claim to be a man of action." I challenge you to prove to me that you have faith in any other way than by actions. For my part, I am perfectly willing to prove my faith to you by my actions.'

1 John 5.6

'This is he that came by water and blood.'

This is a very difficult saying. I think that the *water* is the water of Jesus' baptism, when the Spirit came so fully upon him (Matthew 4.16; Luke 3.22), thus, as it were, equipping him for life. I think that the *blood* is the blood of the cross. It is better to make this clear:

'This is he who came through the water of his baptism and the blood of his cross.'